D1195362

BACKDROP TO TRAGEDY

William R. Polk, who was born in Texas, studied at Harvard and Oxford universities. He is the author of the Foreign Policy Association booklet *What the Arabs Think* and was the editor of the *Atlantic Monthly* supplement "Perspective of the Arab World." A Fellow of the Rockefeller Foundation from 1951 to 1955, he is now on the staff of the Center for Middle Eastern Studies at Harvard.

David M. Stamler was born in London. He studied Hebrew and Arabic at Oxford University, and specialized in modern Hebrew literature. In 1955 he came to Brandeis University on an English-Speaking Union and Fulbright Fellowship. He is at present Vice-Principal of Carmel College in England. Mr. Stamler, a student of the history of Zionism and a Zionist himself, is nevertheless not tied to the support of any party ideology. He holds that the real test of the true quality of Zionists and of Israel lies in their ability to view themselves critically and with historical objectivity.

Edmund Asfour was born in Palestine, graduated from Oxford University, and did graduate work there. He served on the staff of the Economic Division of UNRWA as Senior Economic Analyst from 1951 until 1955, in which year he became a Research Fellow at the Center for Middle Eastern Studies at Harvard. Since writing Part IV of this book, Mr. Asfour has joined the United Nations Secretariat as Economic Affairs Officer, dealing with Middle Eastern Affairs. (The views expressed in Part IV are Mr. Asfour's and do not in any way reflect those of the United Nations.)

BACKDROP TO TRAGEDY

THE STRUGGLE FOR PALESTINE

By William R. Polk, David M. Stamler, and Edmund Asfour

BEACON PRESS BEACON HILL BOSTON

© 1957 by the Beacon Press
Library of Congress catalog card number: 57-12743
Printed in the United States of America

To the memory of

George Polk

who wanted to know

CONTENTS

INTRODUCTION

Part I. THE HISTORICAL BACKGROUND

1. Out of the Past 3
2. The Coming of Islam 8
3. The Crusades 22
4. The Ottoman Empire 29
5. The Great Powers in the Middle East 34
6. The Sick Man of Europe 47
7. The First World War and Its Spore 55
8. Emir Feisal and Dr. Weizmann 64
9. Establishment of the Mandate 70
10. Material Growth and the Gathering Storm 82
11. The Wisdom of Solomon 94
12. From War to War 106
13. Inquiries, Reports, and Plans 110
14. The Mandate's Last Bitter Days 126

Part II. JEWISH INTERESTS IN PALESTINE (by David M. Stamler)

1. The Age-Old Longing 133
2. The European Background 139
3. The Birth of Political Zionism 148
4. The Land of Promises 159
5. Internal Conflicts 170
6. The Seeds of Conflict 175
7. The War and the Biltmore Program 179
8. Anglo-American Reactions 185
9. Postwar and Economic Plans 187
10. A United Nations Solution: The State Is Born 194
11. East and West: The Problem of Absorption 197
12. Politics in Israel 205
13. Religion and the State 219

Part III. THE ARABS AND PALESTINE (by William R. Polk)

1. "The Existing Non-Jewish Communities" 225
2. The Arab Gentry 241
3. The Arab Element in Arabism 247
4. Modern Arab Nationalism 254
5. The Reaction to Zionism 265
6. Pan-Arabism 273
7. War, Refugees, and Humiliation 286

Part IV. THE ECONOMIC FRAMEWORK OF THE PALESTINE PROBLEM (by Edmund Asfour)

1. Introduction 307
2. The Mandate Period 309
3. The Land and Its People 312
4. Immigration and Land 324
5. Land and Capital 329
6. Economics of the Refugee Problem 336
7. The Economy of Israel 342
8. Economic Relations Between Israel and the Arabs 352

Part V. CONCLUSION 365

SELECT BIBLIOGRAPHY 375

INDEX 387

MAPS

Kingdoms of Israel and Judah 4
Ottoman Empire Administrative Units 53
Sykes-Picot Agreement (1916) 59
Land Claimed at Peace Conference by Zionists 72
Mandate of Palestine 78
1936 Royal Commission Proposal 96
Partition Commission: Plan A 101
Partition Commission: Plan B 102
Partition Commission: Plan C 103
1946 Provincial Autonomy Plan 113
UNSCOP Majority Proposal 119
UNSCOP Minority Proposal 121
UN Resolution, November 1947 125
The Arab World 285
Armistice Agreements 1949 288
Registered Palestine Refugees 297
Land Classification in Palestine 313
Rainfall Yearly 314
Section of Palestine from West to East 315
Jewish Land Holdings (1947) 327

TABLES

Important Dates in the History of Palestine xiii
Immigration to Israel According to Countries of Origin 198
Election Results, 1949-55 206
Population Growth, 1922-46 319
Estimated Number Engaged in Each Branch of Production, 1945 321
Estimated Number Engaged in Each Branch of Production, 1936 322
Population, Output, and Income of Jews and Arabs in 1936 and 1945 323
Jewish Land Holdings in Palestine in 1946 330
Investment in the Jewish Sector, 1921-40 335
Arab Population of Palestine, 1956 337
Population of Area Occupied by Israel, 1947-56 343
Jewish Immigrants by Country of Birth and Emigrants by Country of Destination 344
Employed Jews by Occupation 345
Gross Investment, 1949-55 346
Available Resources and Their Use, 1954-55 348
National Income of Israel, 1950-55 349
Israel: Net Imports of Capital and Capital Servicing, 1949-55 351

TABLES

xiii Important Dates in the History of Palestine

198 Immigration to Israel according to Countries of Origin

306 Election Results, 1919-55

319 Population Growth, 1922-46

321 Estimated Number Engaged in Each Branch of Production, 1945

322 Estimated Number Engaged in Each Branch of Production, 1936

328 Population, Output, and Income of Jews and Arabs in 1936 and 1945

330 Jewish Land Holdings in Palestine in 1946

335 Investment in the Jewish Sector, 1921-40

337 Arab Population of Palestine, 1946

343 Population of Area Occupied by Israel, 1947-58

344 Jewish Immigrants by Country of Birth and Emigrants by Country of Destination

345 Employed Jews by Occupation

346 Gross Investment, 1949-55

348 Available Resources and Their Use, 1954-55

349 National Income of Israel, 1950-55

351 Israel: Net Imports of Capital and Capital Servicing, 1949-55

INTRODUCTION

The Tragedy of Palestine involves a clash of ideals, desires, and acts which individually and in other circumstances might well be praised as conducive of the "good life" desired by all its actors. The tragedy is essentially the fact that the several and differing ideals, desires, and acts have, in our time at least, proved to be incompatible. As a result Palestine has become the stage on which has been played one of the most heart-rending dramas of our time.

In our generation Palestine has had two devoted populations sustained in large part by that vast mystical resource which is Palestine's major gift to Jews, Muslims, and Christians. In comparison with this resource, its rocky, stingy hills and narrow valleys offer little. The outsider is apt to find this mystical resource elusive: one can feel it in certain situations but it is difficult to define. It is, moreover, compounded by the experiences, the hopes and the fears, of Arabs and Jews outside of Palestine itself. The story of Palestine cannot be told apart from European enlightenment—and persecution. Nor may we ignore the social ethics of the two populations, even when these are different from or even contrary to our own. The attempt to understand Palestine in purely "rational" terms is not unlike trying to gain a perspective of a needle from head on. Behind the tiny point of fact looms a shaft of emotion.

It is the purpose of this study to present that perspective. This is what we have called the "backdrop" to the day-to-day events upon which attention is usually focused.

We have divided our problem into four parts.

First we give the historical background of Palestine. Modern political events do not happen *in vacuo,* and this is perhaps nowhere so striking as in Palestine.

Part II discusses the Jewish interests in Palestine: the reaction of Jews to European persecution, the powerful emotional force of Zionism, the problems and prospects of Israel.

In Part III we turn to the Arab involvement in Palestine:

the source of the Islamic ties to Palestine, the notion of Arabism, the inarticulated but deep attachments of the peasantry to the soil, and the profound disruption of Arabdom as a result of the humiliating defeats of 1948-49 and 1956.

Part IV presents the economic "framework" into which the psychological aspects of the problem of Palestine must fit. What are the prospects for the Arab refugees? Can Jordan and Israel work together? Will economics make for peace or for continued hostility? And, indeed, can economics provide us with a key to understand the present situation?

It has been the sincere resolve of the authors to treat their subjects as "objectively" as possible. We take this to mean that we should be conscious of, and point out, our different backgrounds and that we should by juxtaposing our interpretations of the flow of events show those events as we find them and as they have been interpreted by Arabs and Zionists. This necessarily involves us in occasional duplications of material, presented from differing perspectives. This has seemed necessary here because the events and situations have meaning in our story —"effective reality"—only as they have been interpreted by the actors. Thus while Part I attempts to give the objective background, Parts II and III will show the emotional reaction to this background and the way in which it was digested into the lives of the communities.

We would like to express our gratitude for help, suggestions, and criticisms to the following: Eliahu Elath, "Dani," H. A. R. Gibb, A. Hourani, Charles Issawi, Adib el Jader, Saeb Jaroudi, Matthias Landau, Ludwig Lewisohn, Miss M. K. Lim, Moshe Perlman, Mrs. Joan C. Polk, Fayez Sayegh, H. Schmidt, Mrs. Susie Sherman, Israel M. Sieff.

While expressing these thanks, however, we must stress that the views expressed in *Backdrop to Tragedy* are our own and are not to be taken as necessarily having the agreement of the abovementioned, to whom we are in debt for giving us a deeper understanding of the problem.

Important Dates in the History of Palestine

ca. 1700 B.C.	Abraham's journey from Ur to Canaan
ca. 1240	Exodus from Egypt
ca. 1200	Israelites enter Palestine
ca. 1000	Height of David's reign
722	Destruction of northern kingdom of Israel by Assyria
586	Destruction of First Temple and southern kingdom of Judah by Babylon
ca. 440	Nehemiah begins rebuilding Jerusalem
331	Alexander takes the Levant
165	Maccabean Revolt against Greeks and Hellenism
64-63	Roman Conquest
70 A.D.	Destruction of Second Temple by Romans
135 A.D.	Revolt of Bar-Cochba against Romans
ca. 390	Beginning of Christian intolerance in Roman Empire
614	Persian (Sassanian) invasion of Palestine
629	Reestablishment of Roman (Byzantine) Empire
636	Arab invasion
638	Conquest of Jerusalem
661-750	Umayyad dynasty
1099	Crusaders capture Jerusalem
1187	Saladin reconquers Jerusalem
1290	Expulsion of Jews from England
1492	Expulsion of Jews from Spain
1517	Ottoman conquest of Palestine
1897	First Zionist Congress at Basle
1916	Arab Revolt
1917	Balfour Declaration
1917-18	British military government of Palestine (OETA) established
1920	First Arab outbreak of violence
1920	Civil Government of Palestine
1921	Second Arab outbreak of violence
1923	Mandate comes into effect
1929	Third Arab outbreak
1930	Hope-Simpson Report
1936	Arab Revolt and Royal Commission
1938	Partition Commission
1939-44	Relative calm in Palestine
1946	Anglo-U. S. Commission of Inquiry
1947	UNSCOP Report. Partition plan
1948	End of Mandate, establishment of Israel, Arab-Israeli War
1956	Anglo-French and Israeli attack on Egypt
1957	Continued instability in Arab lands

BACKDROP TO TRAGEDY

Part I. THE HISTORICAL BACKGROUND

1. OUT OF THE PAST

Throughout its long and tortured history, the land of Palestine has been a station on the natural highway between Asia and Africa. Its domestic political history has been influenced more by its neighbors than by the many and rich facets of the legacy it has bequeathed to the rest of the world. Were we to trace this in detail in the millennia before the establishment of the Roman Empire, we should find that it was a buffer state, almost a plaything, between Egypt, Assyria, Babylon, and the Persian Empire. Only rarely did its own inhabitants—themselves layer upon layer of invaders—enjoy periods of autonomy.

Around 1200 B.C., possibly at about the same time the Israelites were arriving from Egypt, the Philistines settled along the coast and gradually extended their rather tenuous control over most of the land. From the Book of Joshua and from the Tel el-Amarna tablets discovered at Ugarit in 1929, we can infer that the Canaanites—the then "existing communities"—were divided into numerous, often hostile petty kingdoms which lived largely on the exploitation of a semi-slave class. Thus, social dissatisfaction and internal weakness allowed Joshua to subdue the country by stages. It was not, however, until the reign of David (*ca.* 1000 B.C.) that the Israelites conquered Jerusalem and most of what we would today call "Palestine." [1]

With both the empires of Egypt and Assyria in temporary decline, David's son Solomon was able to consolidate and expand the miniature empire built by his father. Making alliances by marriage and entering into trade relations with the Phoenician cities to the north and Arabian towns to the south, Solomon raised Israel to the apex of its political and cultural history; however, his lack of regard for tribal autonomy, his heavy taxation, and the tensions resulting from the division of the kingdom after his death led to a rapid decline of his legacy.

In the eighth century B.C., Assyria recovered its initiative and

[1] We shall use this name henceforth, although at many periods such a political territorial unit did not exist.

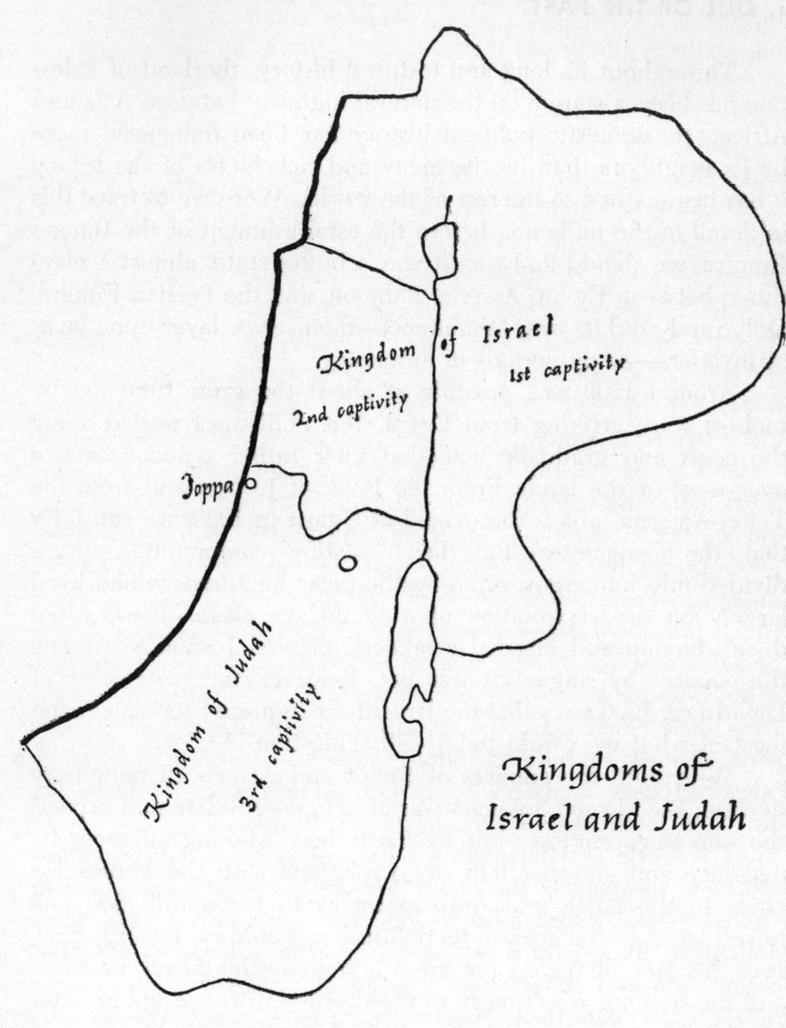
Kingdom of Israel
1st captivity
2nd captivity
Joppa
Kingdom of Judah
3rd captivity
Kingdoms of Israel and Judah

advanced into the Mediterranean hinterland. The Assyrians took Galilee and then Samaria. Judah tried to save itself by an alliance with Egypt, hoping that the Great Powers—Assyria, Babylon, and Egypt—would destroy one another. The prophets had warned against relying on an alliance with Egypt, and Egypt proved to be a broken reed; when it was defeated in 586 B.C., Jerusalem was taken, the Temple destroyed, and most of the upper class and even the artisans led off into captivity in Babylon.

The Babylonian Captivity was short-lived—Babylon was itself captured by the Persians and in 538 B.C. the Jews were permitted to return to their homes—but the captivity was long enough to change the nature of political expectations in Judaism. Palestine tempted back only a portion of what, in the exile, had become a well-organized expatriate community. In effect if not in thought, Judaism ceased to be a state and became a cultural and religious community; under Ezra (*ca.* 400 B.C.) the Second Jewish Commonwealth developed into a theocratic, largely apolitical hierarchy controlled by an aristocracy of priests, scholars, and scribes. Partly by necessity and partly by desire, these hierarchs created a new sort of Judaism which became, in some senses, meta-historical. Judaism became something different from a Jewish state and something abstract from Palestine. Even the later collapse of the Maccabean state and the destruction of the Second Temple by the Romans in 70 A.D. had comparatively little effect upon the stream of Jewish life. Palestine became an ideal in Judaism, while the actual land and people of Palestine came increasingly under the influence of Hellenism and were incorporated into the Greek Empire.

The world of Hellenism was cosmopolitan, rich, and stimulating. Consequently the newly developing Rabbinical Judaism reacted violently and tried to hold its congregation aloof from Hellenism. As in later times, a split separated those who favored assimilation and those who opposed; it is possible, indeed, to interpret the Maccabean struggle as being as much against Jewish defaulters as against the occupying military forces. But even the sternest opponents of Hellenism could not deny its attractions. Stoic systems of argumentation found their ways into the schools of the rabbis, and by the middle of the third century

B.C. Greek had so thoroughly displaced Hebrew as the language of the Alexandrian Jewish community as to require a Greek translation of the Old Testament.

Rome further extended the frontiers of the world of Hellenism; by 100 B.C. her dominion was complete in Palestine and Palestine was pulled into the great imperial community. The earliest Jewish associations with Rome were friendly. In fact, as a result of civil strife in Judea, the remnants of the priestly family of Maccabees had vied with one another in trying to induce Rome to take over control of Palestine. Many Jews were already living in parts of the Roman Empire, even in Rome itself, by the time of Pompey's invasion, and these Roman Jews are thought to have wielded considerable influence over Roman policies. But, as one might expect, it was the upper classes that were most converted to support of the empire. In the lower classes there was a ferment of dissatisfaction and Messianic yearnings. This is mirrored in the teachings of John the Baptist, the Essenes, as we know of them in the Dead Sea Scrolls,[2] and above all in the teachings of Jesus.

Pagan Rome was a tolerant master of its subjects' minds. However, by the time of Hadrian, the Roman administration realized that the Judaic scholars were the source of national strength and a fount of dissatisfaction with Roman rule. Partly in response to this came the rebellion of Bar-Cochba (135 A.D.), which many Jewish scholars regard as being primarily a secular and nationalist movement rather than one devoted to the preservation of Judaism. Indeed, it may be doubted that the religion of Judaism was itself under severe attack. Certainly the Roman administration usually was, within the limitations of a military government, fair and just and the Roman pantheon was quite prepared to accept Judaism as a provincial religion. But for Bar-Cochba and his followers, toleration ceased to be satisfactory: alien rule in any form, just or unjust, was hateful.

During the centuries after the life of Jesus, the Christian element in the population of Palestine grew rapidly, especially in the south of the land. The north which had been almost en-

[2] Though the Essene connection with the Dead Sea Sect is disputable.

tirely Jewish began to lose its Jewish population and to show an increase in the Christian community. The main influence of Christianity, however, was not the result of domestic changes but was rather the effect of the conversion of the Roman emperors to Christianity. This led to a rapid deterioration in the relationship of the Jews to the empire. Jews lost their civil rights, were banned from military service, and were popularly judged as a nation to be guilty of the death of Jesus and as such beyond all hope of toleration and social betterment. For the Jewish community, the transition of the western Roman Empire to eastern Byzantium was of little import except that this transition seemed to coincide with an increased influence over the state by the church. Interfaith marriage and conversion to Judaism became punishable by death. In the economic sphere, Jews were forbidden to own even pagan slaves—upon whose labor the whole economy was based. And by the second half of the fifth century the term "Jew" had become an expression of loathing. Within Palestine the Jewish community was a shadow of its former self, and in many of the imperial cities something not unlike the ghetto system was rapidly evolving.

In the Persian Empire, Jews were encouraged to settle and were granted the sort of religious autonomy they had enjoyed in pagan Rome. Those parts of the old Roman Empire which were now separated from Byzantium—Italy, Spain, the Balkans —received numbers of immigrants and throughout the Arabian peninsula there were Jewish communities; indeed, the ruling dynasty of Yemen in the far south of Arabia was converted to Judaism about a century before the preaching of Islam. In effect, by the end of the fifth century the major outlines of the Jewish community—fractured, scattered, precarious, ever shifting—were established as they were to remain for the next fourteen centuries.

As a result of its internal weakness and the fact that even in Palestine it was a small minority, the Jewish community was able to do little on its own behalf. In 611 A.D. the Persian army invaded Palestine and in 614 captured Jerusalem, thus removing the Christian-Byzantine rule and providing a rule which was happy to find a friendly local community; but even then the Jews were unable to evolve any policy. This last flicker of hope was used only to exact a bloody revenge on the hated symbols of Christian rule and on the local Christian community. Persians and Jews burned churches and massacred Christians. Jews hoped for a rebuilding of the Temple and for the rebuilding of the community in a fashion parallel to the Persian liberation of the Jews from the Babylonian Captivity eleven centuries before. Such was not to be. Within fifteen years the Byzantine emperor Heraclius had retaken Jerusalem. The land was famine-stricken, burned, and ravaged and the Christian population thirsting for revenge. Mob violence took its course and Heraclius established the empire's policy as extermination of the Jewish community by forcible conversion and by the exclusion for all time of Jews from Jerusalem. This was in 634 A.D.—one of those historical dates in which, retrospectively, we can see the world on a precipice.

2. THE COMING OF ISLAM

While the Sassanian and Byzantine empires were locked in their mutually exhausting struggle for mastery of the Fertile Crescent, unknown to them a new system of political power was being forged and a new religion unfolded in the desert lands of Arabia to the south. This was Islam, the monotheistic faith revealed to Mohammed, whose adherents were shortly to engulf the one empire and to take the lion's share of the other. Of such crucial importance is an understanding of Islam to our study and yet still so little known to non-Muslims is it that a certain deviation both in point of time and place is necessary to gain some perspective on the subsequent history of Palestine.

In the year 570 A.D., in Mecca, Mohammed was born. The Mecca of his youth was a great entrepôt, situated at the juncture of the Yemen-to-Syria and Africa-to-Persia trade routes, a cosmopolitan and rich community. Enveloped in legend, its religious center, the Kaaba, was a center of pilgrimages as the "House" of the most widely recognized of the pagan gods of

Arabia. Shrine and market merged. The merchant oligarchy depended upon the religious sanction of "forbidden [to warfare] months" for a yearly period of peace to ply their far-ranging caravans and upon the attractions of a center of pilgrimage to gather in their customers. Meccans—that is, those who were citizens in the sense Plato would have understood—had much for which to be grateful. They had waxed rich from trade, and in religion and commerce had woven a social fabric of considerable—for the time and place, of remarkable—strength.

To some within the patrician class and presumably to most below it, however, this life was not satisfying. If some became very rich, others remained or became very poor; and if the social fabric of Mecca was strengthened by religion, the culture of Mecca was little enriched by it. Yet so intricately intertwined with the existing social order was the cult as to make understandable the fact that both intellectual ferment and social discontent should be expressed in a religious idiom.

A "Hero," to borrow Carlyle's term, Mohammed was unquestionably a man of genius and great sensitivity. Although in middle age he was a successful merchant in his own right (albeit with his wife's capital), Mohammed belonged to a branch of the patrician tribe which seems to have been losing its political and economic footing in the community. Perhaps partly because of this he was acutely aware of Mecca's social problems. And although his personal motivations were surely complex, it is striking that both Mohammed's acts and words exhibit a considerable desire for a new social order in which men could assay to attain that brotherhood which he understood to have been the goal of "the prophets who went before." The problem of how Mohammed received his knowledge of Biblical tales and his new messages may be bypassed. (Muslims of course believe God directly inspired him.) Whatever may have been Mohammed's source, we can infer from the Koran and the chronicles that his audience also had a general familiarity with Judaism and Christianity. Meccans, after all, had direct or indirect trade relations with Monophysite Christian Abyssinia, Zorastrian Iran, Hindu India, and Orthodox Christian Byzantium. In the market centers of Yemen and Palestine they met men of many creeds and, even closer to Mecca, had relations with tribes of Christian Arabs as well as communities of Jews or Judaized Arabs. Wandering Nestorian monks carried their own versions of Biblical tales from camp to camp over the Arabian steppe as their successors did centuries later in Central Asia. Even in the technical religious language of the Koran one finds evidence, in the form of borrowed non-Arabic words, of extensive intellectual contacts with neighboring countries using other Semitic languages.

Non-Muslims are apt to believe that Mohammed is to Islam what Jesus is to Christianity, but Mohammed made no such claim to divinity, he simply saw himself as but one in a sequence of prophets, and conceived of his role as the bringing of God's message in Arabic to the Arabs. The message was the essential unity of God and it was formally identical with Judaism and Christianity:

> Say [O Muslims]: We believe in Allah and that which is revealed unto us and that which was revealed unto Abraham, and Ismael, and Isaac, and Jacob, and the Tribes, and that which Moses and Jesus received, and that which the Prophets received from their Lord. We make no distinction between any of them, and unto Him we have surrendered.[1]

Thus, Islam took into itself, took for its own, the sum total of the religious heritage *as it understood this* from Judaism and Christianity. It falls outside the scope of this work to analyze this in detail but the point must be noted that along with a veneration of the prophets there existed in Islam already in Mohammed's lifetime an emotional attachment to Jerusalem.

Other factors in Mohammed's experience shaped the relationship of Islam and the other two religions. Two of these factors may be singled out as of sufficient importance to events in Palestine to require some notice here. Both may be said to have resulted from contact with Jews. The first is the growing awareness that Islam was a distinct religion in which, as it was more fully elaborated, Jews in the first instance and then Christians and others would not and could not participate. The second is

[1] Koran, ii/136. Koranic passages will be given as translated by M. Pickthall, *The Glorious Koran* (London: 1930).

a realization that Islamic-Judaic-Christian differences are, so to speak, within the family of those who accept God.

As mentioned, above, Mohammed early in his career saw Islam as but the Arabic version of the Word of God which had earlier been given in other languages to other peoples. It was the same Word from the same God. Therefore, Mohammed had reason to believe that his message would be accepted by those who already believed in God. There was a time of despair when this may have seemed the only hope. In Mecca the vested patrician class rightly saw the pagan cult to be the source of its well-being. To them Mohammed's attack upon that cult was the most dangerous sort of subversion. By 620 A.D., Mohammed's own clan would no longer protect him from the hostility of the community, and his own small band of believers was as yet unable to do so. As public hostility mounted he was forced to leave Mecca and tried to spread the Word of God in neighboring Taif, but there he was promptly stoned out of town. Taif, like Mecca, was prosperous, well organized, and happily pagan. In failure, Mohammed returned to a hostile Mecca to spend months of anxiety and soul-searching. At the next trade fair, however, he was out preaching to any who would listen, and among those who would was a small band from the northern Arabian town of Yathrib (which subsequently was called Madinah). These Arab pilgrims, pagans though they were, were impressed by Mohammed's message and by his sincerity. Moreover, their community, unlike those of Mecca and Taif, was neither prosperous nor well organized. In fact, Yathrib had for some years been ravaged by a civil war and its rival faction desperately needed the services of the traditional Arabian arbitrator to bring them peace. For his part, Mohammed identified his audience as men from two tribes famous as "the protectors of the Jews." [2] At the least, he could expect them to be sympathetic to monotheism. And since in Mohammed's view Islam was but the "religion of Abraham," there was reason to hope that if he moved to Yathrib

[2] Ferdinand Wüstenfeld (ed.), *Das Leben Muhammed's nach Muhammed Ibn Ishak bearbeitet von Abd el-Malik Ibn Hischam* (Göttingen: 1858—in Arabic), p. 286.

he could immediately gain a sizeable and prosperous group of ready converts.

Negotiations with Yathrib lasted nearly two years, for Mohammed was hardly the wild-eyed fanatic he has often been pictured as being, and the example of rashness at Taif must have been painfully fresh in his mind. He was a practical, shrewd merchant and man of affairs.[3] And he wanted his exact station in the new community to be clear from the beginning. A significant aspect of his agreement with Yathrib Arabs stipulated that Mohammed's core of Meccan followers should precede him to Yathrib, where they would become the nucleus of his new community. This was the essence of the Hijra (or Hegira) of 622 A.D., from which the Islamic calendar is dated.

Once in Yathrib and secure in his position Mohammed made a pact, the so-called Constitution of Madinah, in which tribe by tribe the Arab adherents of Islam and the resident Jews are listed as "together . . . a single community."[4] Of lasting significance to the subsequent history of Islam was the fact that Mohammed could visualize a community in which all members of *the* religion of God—the "People of the Book"—could participate. Both the fact that when Muslims were politically weak, as a group, they had to live alongside of non-Muslims in a community desperately anxious for peace and the fact that Arabic society was traditionally organized by tribes or corporations which were not only politically autonomous but each governed by its own social code (*sunna*) provided the situation in which Mohammed was able to formulate one of the most characteristic and praiseworthy features of Islamic society, organized toleration, which we will subsequently meet in Palestine as it comes to be called the *millet* or community system.

Very early in the Madinah period, however, Mohammed was disappointed by the Jews. Of first importance, naturally, was the refusal of the Orthodox Jewish community to accept his Mission. We know from the Koran itself that Jews openly ridiculed the Islamic version of Old Testament episodes. Thus, Mohammed came to realize that Orthodox Judaism differed

[3] L. Caetani, *Studi di Storia Orientale* III (Milan: 1914), 29.
[4] Wüstenfeld, pp. 341-44.

from Islam; and this, to Mohammed, convinced as he certainly was of the direct divine inspiration of his information, could only mean that the Jews had corrupted their God-given texts. Christians, he felt, had done likewise in ascribing divinity to Jesus. Theoretically, then, the religions remained one—the worship of The One God. Differences there were, but beside this central fact they were minor. Islam must tolerate them. This order is clearly stated in the Koran:

> Lo! those who believe (in that which is revealed unto thee, Muhammad), and those who are Jews, and Christians, and Sabaeans [variously interpreted in different places]—whoever believeth in Allah and the Last Day and doeth right—surely their reward is with their Lord, and there shall no fear come upon them neither shall they grieve. [Koran II/62] . . . Then bear with them (O Muhammad) and say: Peace. But they will come to know. [XLIII/89]

The price for this toleration was acceptance of the civil authority of Islam. It was this unwillingness of the Jews of Yathrib, not religion as such, which led to a rupture between Mohammed and the Jewish community and to the final expulsion from Madinah of the Jews. We shall see later in our narrative that it was a similar unwillingness by Arabs, Greeks, Armenians, and others to pay the same price which was to be the reef on which the great multinational, multireligious Ottoman Empire was to crash in the nineteenth and twentieth centuries.

By his death in 632, Mohammed had conquered Mecca and most of the Arabian peninsula; but he must have realized that he held an ephemeral if huge empire. To preserve it beyond his own life he spent his last years in the careful development of the new *sunna* or social ethic of the young Islamic community. The framework he managed to complete before his death and its elaboration became the central task of medieval Islamic civilization. The initial triumph of his statesmanship was the fact that his community was able to survive the tribal revolts which followed his death. Islam was able to incorporate its internal enemies by hurling them onto the world as a conquering army.

The spread of Islam to the known world seems to have been a natural goal to Mohammed. In Syria, as the present states of

Jordan, Syria, Lebanon, and Israel were known to the Arabs, lived a population which was mainly Semitic and partly Arabic-speaking. In his youth Mohammed may have accompanied one of Mecca's caravans to the north, but even if he did not, the image of Jerusalem was impressed upon his thought from the earliest days of his Mission. It was to Jerusalem, not to Mecca, that Muslim prayers were directed in the early years of Islam and it was from Jerusalem (according to the Muslim tradition) that Mohammed was conveyed to Heaven. Moreover, Islam, as we have noted, incorporates both the Old and New Testaments just as Christianity incorporated the Old. And acquisition of Holy Places seems to be a common goal of most religious groups. So it is not surprising that Mohammed had, before his death, organized campaigns to probe the frontiers of Byzantine Syria and to try to win over the Christian Arab tribes who guarded its southern marches. His successors Abu Bakr and Omar took the task begun by the Prophet to be a sacred duty. Thus in the year 12 A.H. (634 A.D.), the caliph Abu Bakr sent proclamations to the main towns of Arabia to announce a Holy War; in response, 24,000 men volunteered and went forth to wrest Syria from the mightiest empire then known.

Byzantium was exhausted by its long war with the Sassanian Persian Empire, and the chronicler Theophanes reported that, as a measure of economy, the empire had stopped the subsidy paid to the "inner barbarians." This may have had a good deal to do with the success of Islam. Certain it is that these Christian Arab tribes went over to the side of the Muslim Arabs. They were not alone. Even the population of the settled areas was restless, for Byzantium had proved a hard master. Taxes were high. State-imposed religious Melkite Orthodoxy was intolerant of Syrian popular Monophysitism. Many, including the Jews, had welcomed the Persian invaders, and for this treason Byzantium charged them heavily when the Persians were driven out. Lastly, as Semites, speakers of one or another of the Semitic languages and heirs to the general body of Semitic culture, the native population of Christians—the population was then overwhelmingly Christian—and Jews was bound to feel more akin to the invading fellow-Semite Arabs than to the Persians or to the eastern Romans.

The first Arab campaign was little more than a raid on Gaza, but the Byzantine governor either misjudged it or was caught off guard by it. Perhaps a stern defeat would have discouraged what had not yet the confidence of numbers or success, but the governor with only a small force was caught and killed. Returning with booty and a whetted appetite, the new Muslim army attracted large numbers of the young bloods of Arabia. If tribal warfare had been the zest of Arabian life, *here* was a feast of glory. On the steppe south of Damascus, Islam met the host of Byzantium and utterly defeated it. Only remnants of the Byzantine forces managed to find shelter in Jerusalem, whose walls were proof against light cavalry (and whose citizens were Orthodox and so less likely to go over to the Arabs), and in Cesarea, then the capital of Palestine, where the Byzantine fleet could supply them. A counterattack was launched—this much Byzantium could do. But at the battle of Yarmuk in modern Jordan, Byzantine Syria found its political grave. The mass of chained infantry was no match for the bedouin light cavalry.

Jerusalem—the center of Orthodox Christian Palestine—was then faced with the problem of surrendering. It could bargain from the strength of its superb military location while Islam was constrained, by its veneration for the city and its toleration of the People of the Book, to deal kindly. Jerusalem demanded and Islam agreed that the Caliph himself should come to accept the surrender and to restrain the wild bedouin army which faced the city. At the town of Jabia, Omar concluded a treaty which set forth the position of Jerusalem in Islamic imperial administration.

> In the name of God, the merciful, the compassionate: Here is the pledge which the servant of God, Omar, the prince of the faithful, has given to the inhabitants of Alia [Jerusalem]. To all, without distinction . . . security of their persons, their goods, their churches, their crosses and all that concerns their cult is guaranteed. Their churches will not be transformed into houses nor will they be destroyed . . . They shall not be forced to change their religion nor will anyone have aught to fear. The Jews shall not inhabit Alia to-

gether with the Christians. [Heraculus, reconquering Palestine from the Persians, excluded all Jews from a three-mile radius around Jerusalem so that there were no Jews living in Jerusalem at this time—i.e., Omar just guaranteed the status quo.] The inhabitants of Alia will be obliged to pay the same tax as those of other towns. The Romans and the bandits must leave the city but they will be given safe conduct for their persons and their goods; those who wish to remain must pay the same tax as the other inhabitants while those inhabitants who wish to depart with the Romans, abandoning their churches and their crosses, are given the same safe-conduct as the Romans. Country people now in the city may remain provided they pay the tax or they may return to their families or leave with the Romans . . .[5]

Arabic tradition tells us that Omar, riding on his camel, clad in worn and desert-stained robes, aloof in a simple rustic dignity, scandalized the Arab troops who already in the first flush of victory had developed a taste for the pomp that had characterized the rule of defeated Byzantium. When he alighted to pray at the site of the Temple of Solomon, the patriarch Sophronius was heard to remark through his tears, "behold the abomination of desolation, spoken of by Daniel the prophet, now occupies the Holy Place." [6]

Better had the Patriarch and his flock rejoiced that day, for as Sir William Fitzgerald wrote:

> Never in the sorry story of conquest up to that time, and rarely since, were such noble sentiments displayed by a victor as those extended by Omar to the conquered. The lives, churches, and property of the Christians were spared. Freedom of religious worship was guaranteed. Muslim and Christian lived in amity.[7]

It has seemed worth stressing this point because the popular notion of Islam being spread by the sword dies hard. Paradoxically the fact is that for reasons of state economy the Islamic government did not even encourage conversion to Islam. The government had no need of converts, in effect it was swamped with Arab converts (*Muslimun*) who were not yet in the fullest

[5] M. J. de Goeje, *Mémoire sur la Conquête de la Syrie* (Leiden: 1900), pp. 152-53.

[6] *Ibid.*, pp. 157-58.

[7] "The Holy Places of Palestine in History and in Politics," *International Affairs*, XXVI (1950), 4.

sense Believers (*Mu'minun*); but it required revenue, and from the early date in Madinah of the so-called Constitution the principle had been established that non-Muslims would pay an extra tax in lieu of military service. So religiously Islam proved a lenient master. It was unconcerned with minor or even with major deviations from religious orthodoxy—after all, even *Orthodox* Christianity and *Orthodox* Judaism were corruptions in the terms of Islam so why worry about deviation from corruption. Islam only required that its civil authority be accepted. As a result it was only after centuries of Islamic occupation had passed that the majority of the population became Muslim.

As a religious symbol and as a place of pilgrimage, Jerusalem remained the capital of Palestine although it was not the political capital even of its own district.[8] Muslims made the pilgrimage to Jerusalem; but, since about the same time as Mohammed's split with the Jews of Madinah, Mecca had replaced Jerusalem as the target of Muslim prayers and the main goal of pilgrimage. Then, a generation after the conquest, the Islamic Empire was split by civil war. One caliph ruled from Damascus and another from Mecca. The Omayyad house of Damascus held the vast majority of the empire but was seriously weakened by the inability of its caliph to perform the caliphal duty of leading the faithful on pilgrimage. Until Mecca could be retaken, Jerusalem was the only possible substitute. Consequently, in the time of the caliph Abd al-Malik (685-705 A.D.), Jerusalem experienced a sort of renaissance[9] and gained that magnificent structure, the Dome of the Rock, which remains today one of its most impressive sites. What might have been the position of Jerusalem in the subsequent development of Islam we do not know, since the Omayyads were able to recoup their position in Mecca. But even this brief period of Omayyad particularism probably did considerably popularize the Muslim feeling for the city of the prophets. There is a tradition which sets forth this sentiment, as it were this competition in sanctity with Islam's other Holy Cities:

[8] Guy Le Strange, *Palestine Under the Moslems* (Boston: 1890), p. 84.

[9] J. Wellhausen, *The Arab Kingdom and Its Fall* (Calcutta: 1927), pp. 212-14.

On the authority of Anas Ibn Malak [the source of many of the traditions relating to the Prophet] it is related: The Apostle of Allah said, Who makes pilgrimage to Jerusalem, counting upon merit, Allah will give him the reward of a thousand martyrs.[10]

Christian pilgrimage to the Holy Land was obviously impeded by the sporadic warfare which embittered Byzantine-Islamic relations in the centuries after the conquest. For a short period Jerusalem was isolated from the Western world, yet by 700 A.D. Bishop Arculf was able to make the pilgrimage, visit the Omayyad capital at Damascus, and then to travel to the capital of the arch-enemy, Byzantium. Wrote the Bishop:

On the 15th of September, annually, an immense multitude of people of different nations are used to meet in Jerusalem for the purpose of commerce, and the streets are so clogged with the dung of camels, horses, mules, and oxen, that they become almost impassable, and the smell would be a nuisance to the whole town. But, by a miraculous providence, which exhibits God's peculiar attachment to this place, no sooner has the multitude left Jerusalem than a heavy fall of rain begins on the night following, and ceases only when the city has been perfectly cleansed.[11]

Contacts with the West, however, dwindled, partly as a result of piracy in the Mediterranean but largely as a result of factors which form a part of western history and lie outside the scope of this work. In the "dark ages," most of Europe ceased to be able to afford the luxury of pilgrimage. The Italian merchant cities were first to restore this contact. For those who could afford it in the tenth century—and an increasing number could—passage was available direct to the Holy Land from Venice and Genoa. Then in the eleventh century, when the Hungarians were converted to Christianity and Emperor Basil II had conquered the Balkan peninsula, a pilgrim could travel by land from western Europe through Byzantium and on to Palestine. For the foot-strong, at least, pilgrimage became possible for men of any means.

[10] Translation from C. D. Matthews, *Palestine—Mohammedan Holy Land* (New Haven: 1949), p. 5.

[11] Thomas Wright (ed.), *Early Travels in Palestine* (London: 1848), p. 1.

Meanwhile, during these centuries of "darkness" and the rebirth of commerce in the West, Palestine remained a province of the Islamic Empire. Until 750 A.D., that empire was ruled by the Omayyad successors of Abd al-Malik, who, as mentioned above, found it expedient to encourage a certain Syrian particularism from which Jerusalem had profited. In 750 A.D., however, the Omayyads succumbed to a social revolution in which a new ruling dynasty, the Abbasids, emerged. The Abbasids, who had lived in Palestine since the conquest, were forced by the nature of their political support to move eastward to Iraq where they founded Baghdad.

Both because it was able to control its internal routes to Mecca and because it was established largely with the support of non-Orthodox Muslim groups, the Abbasid caliphate found expedient a parade of orthodoxy and piety. Such caliphs as Harun ar-Rashid encouraged and led the yearly pilgrimages to Mecca. Jerusalem, tainted with Omayyad patronage, is hardly mentioned in the state chronicles of the period.

In its turn, however, the Abbasid caliphate was sapped by ambitious provincial governors, Turkish mercenaries, and tribal disaffection; by the late ninth century, Abbasid dominance over Syria had become tenuous in the extreme. Arab tribal dynasties controlled the steppe as their predecessors had, except for brief intervals, time out of mind of man. And, lured as they were by the adventure, glory, and—not least—booty of the Byzantine frontier, these tribal dynasties became masters of all of northern Syria.

In the tenth-century writer, al-Muqaddasi ("the dweller in the Holy City"), we find a statement of the traditional Muslim attachment to the city and the sort of panegyric we will subsequently hear from Muslim, Christian, and Jew alike. Hallowed ground must be productively and worldly so:

> Neither the cold nor the heat is excessive here, and snow falls but rarely . . . 'Just as is that [climate] of Paradise.' The buildings of the Holy City are of stone, and you will find nowhere finer or more solid construction. In no place will you meet with people more chaste. Provisions are most excellent here; the markets are clean, the Mosque is of the largest. The grapes are enormous, and there are no quinces to equal those of the Holy City. In Jerusalem are all

manner of learned men and doctors, and for this reason the heart of every man of intelligence yearns toward her. All the year round, never are her streets empty of strangers. As to the saying that Jerusalem is the most illustrious, of cities—is it not the one that unites the advantages of this World with those of the Next? He who is of the sons of this World and yet is ardent in the matters of the Next, may find there a market for his wares; while those who would be the men of the Next World, though his soul clings to the good things of This, he, too, may find them there! . . . And as for the Holy City being the most productive of all places in good things, why, Allah—may He be exalted!—has gathered together here all the fruits of the lowlands, and of the plains, and of the hill country, even those of the most opposite kinds: such as the orange and the almond, the date and the nut, the fig and the banana, besides milk in plenty, and honey and sugar. And as to the excellence of the City! why, is not this to be the place of marshalling on the Day of Judgment; where gathering together and the appointment will take place? Verily Makkah [Mecca] and Al Madinah have their superiority by reason of the Ka'abah and the Prophet—the blessing of Allah be upon him and his family!—but in truth, on the Day of Judgment both cities will come to Jerusalem, and the excellencies of them all will then be united.[12]

Of one condition al-Muqaddasi was forced to complain. In his time, he wrote, a good Muslim found life difficult in Jerusalem because the Christians and Jews had the upper hand in all affairs.

Also contending for mastery of Syria in this period of Abbasid weakness was the Shi'ite Muslim dynasty of Fatimid Caliphs which had invaded Egypt from North Africa. By 969 A.D., armies of the Fatimids had conquered southern Syria and Palestine, to the great benefit of these regions. By their careful cultivation of international trade between India and Europe the Fatimids enriched the caliphate, made Cairo one of the greatest of medieval cities, and played no small part in the development of European urban life. To Fatimid policy is owed much of the new flood of European pilgrimage. Curiously it was not to their policy itself that the attention of Europe was attracted, but rather to a breach of Islam's general policy. Between 996 and

[12] Le Strange, pp. 85-86. (The book gives no errata but one mistake has been corrected in the text as given here.)

1021, the Fatimid Empire was ruled by an eccentric caliph known as al-Hakim. It must be stressed that we know of him only through the reports of his enemies, and they were many, so it is often difficult to achieve a balanced perspective of his reign. It has been suggested that the picture we get, in all of its grotesqueness, might well be simulated by those we would have of Atatürk or Peter the Great if we knew only what the enemies thought of their often eccentric policies.

For reasons which remain obscure, al-Hakim (whom the Druzes of the Levant regard as God incarnate) in 1008 A.D. opened a seven-year persecution of Christians and Jews which he later followed by an attack on Muslims as well. In 1009, on his orders, the Holy Sepulcher was demolished, to the delight of the native Syrian population which was then suffering from a half century of Byzantine raids.[13] Al-Hakim's policies promoted an Arab tribal revolt in Palestine, and the leader of this revolt began in 1011 to rebuild the Holy Sepulcher; but a short time later the Fatimids regained their initiative and routed the bedouin tribesmen in a battle near Tiberias. Finally, in a peace treaty with Byzantium in 1038, it was agreed that the Emperor should be allowed to rebuild the Holy Sepulcher.

The rival Islamic caliphates of Baghdad and Cairo were exhausted, partly from their wars with one another and with the reinvigorated Byzantine Empire and partly from the breakdown of the spirit which had sustained them. Both Islamic empires had come to rely upon Turkish mercenaries, and these exacted a heavy toll for their military support. The first Turks to appear in the Middle East were imported slaves, and these caused enough havoc, but after 1064 Turks began to enter in tribes, on their own, owing and giving allegiance to no man. In 1070 a Turkish band conquered Palestine and sacked Jerusalem. In the following year, a thousand miles away in Anatolia at Manzikert, the Seljuq Turks met and shattered the military power of Byzantium. Quickly they overran Anatolia and thus

[13] Sir Hamilton A. R. Gibb, "The Caliphate and the Arab States," in M. W. Baldwin (ed.), *A History of the Crusades* (Philadelphia: 1955), I, 90-91.

cut the land route from Europe to Palestine. If Yarmuk had been the grave of Byzantine Syria so Manzikert was the end of the empire in Anatolia.

Byzantium, heir to the Roman Empire and the great eastern bulwark of Christianity, was in peril; pilgrimage, so popular and so important an expiation, was again denied to all but the rich; and Jerusalem had fallen into the hands of a group of rougher, less civilized, recent converts to Islam who had all of the intolerance implied in these attributes. Events in Palestine, Anatolia, and in western Europe gradually prepared the way for the Council of Clermont in 1095, when Pope Urban II preached the First Crusade.

3. THE CRUSADES

The Crusades are far too complex a topic to receive more than a brief mention here. It is important to note, however, that the Council of Clermont did not inaugurate the Crusade. Religiously inspired warfare—to Christians the Crusade and to Muslims the Jihad—had been a feature of the marches of the Islamic Domain since the era of Mohammed. In the West the Muslims had pushed into Spain and then into France, where they were stopped by the Battle of Tours in 732; and in the East they twice threatened Constantinople during the same period. Raids and counterraids were a distinctive feature of frontier life; and between these two points of the Muslim advance, the sea was compassed by nests of pirates and privateers. In 846 a group of these raiders sacked St. Peter's Basilica in Rome. Retaliation, raid, and reconquest occupied a good many Christian and Muslim warriors before 1095, but the combination of the Crusade with pilgrimage provided a new and explosive element in Christian endeavor.

The motives of the crusaders were, like the motives of any large group of men, complex. Some certainly were inspired by a pure religious feeling while others seem to have been spurred on by naked greed for an easier and richer life than the already overpopulated Normandy could provide. Stephen Runciman has well written:

> Apocalyptic teachings added to the economic inducement. It was an age of visions; Medieval man was convinced that the Second Coming was at hand. He must repent while yet there was time and must go out to do good. The Church taught that sin could be expiated by pilgrimage and prophecies declared that the Holy Land must be recovered for the faith before Christ could come again. Further, to ignorant minds the distinction between Jerusalem and the New Jerusalem was not very clearly defined. Many of Peter's [the Hermit who had popularized the Crusade] hearers believed that he was promising to lead them out of their present miseries to the land flowing with milk and honey of which the scriptures spoke. The journey would be hard; there were the legions of Anti-Christ to be overcome. But the goal was Jerusalem the golden.[1]

After the long march through the Balkans and across Anatolia, the crusaders were able, because of the motley array of mutually hostile petty dynasties into which Islam was divided in 1096, one by one to defeat and seize the towns they passed. Antioch's superb Byzantine walls, then manned by Muslims, blocked their progress for so long that even Peter the Hermit tried to desert the army. In the end the city was taken with the aid of an Armenian convert to Islam who, for a price, "sold the city." Eastern Christians then learned to their horror that in the estimate of the crusaders spoils were spoils, of whatever source, as with fine impartiality the crusaders looted the houses of Muslims and Christians alike. Thus, when finally on the evening of June 7, 1099, the crusaders encamped before the Holy City, it may be imagined that its native Christian population (then a majority) might have had misgivings as to the nature of this intended liberation. The Fatimid governor spared them this problem, however, by expelling them from the city. The small Jewish population which had returned under Muslim rule was allowed to remain, perhaps in the knowledge that the Crusade had begun in Europe by a series of vicious attacks on the Jews of Germany and France.

The walls of Jerusalem had withstood other sieges, and reinforcements were thought to be on the way from Egypt. It is

[1] *The Crusades* (Cambridge: 1951), I, 115.

interesting that Jerusalem's environs could not even at that date provide enough wood with which to make siege engines. The Crusade commanders were in a quandary. Past experience had shown how frail was the morale of greedy piety. All, it was judged, must be risked on one great effort, and that quickly; so recourse was had to psychological warfare—to the popular preachers, to a barefoot walk around the Holy City walls (amid much jeering from those walls), to a three-day fast. The result was a sort of mob ecstasy which ended in a furious all-night assault. The horror of that night is graphically portrayed by Runciman:

> The Crusaders, maddened by so great a victory after such suffering, rushed through the streets and into the houses and mosques killing all they met, men, women and children alike. All that afternoon and all through the night the massacre continued . . . When Raymond of Aguilers later that morning went to visit the Temple area [where a group of Muslims were supposed to be safe after surrendering] he had to pick his way through corpses and blood that reached up to his knees.
>
> The Jews of Jerusalem fled in a body to their chief Synagogue. But they were held to have aided the Moslems; and no mercy was shown to them. The building was set on fire and they were all burnt within.
>
> The massacre at Jerusalem profoundly impressed all the world. No one can say how many victims it involved; but it emptied Jerusalem of its Moslem and Jewish inhabitants.[2]

By 1163 when Rabbi Benjamin of Tudela visited Jerusalem some of the old aspects of the city had been restored. The population he found to be numerous and composed of "Jacobites, Armenians, Greeks, Georgians, Franks, and indeed people of all tongues."[3] Some two hundred Jews had returned to the city where they purchased the dyeing monopoly; these two hundred and the fifty in Tiberias contrast with the more than three thousand Jews who then lived in Muslim Damascus.

The Crusade is important to our narrative mainly in that contact with the East established in the West a sort of idealized

[2] *Ibid.*, 286-87.

[3] Thomas Wright (ed.), *Early Travels in Palestine* (London: 1848), pp. 83 ff.

image which is again and again evoked by western rulers in the coming centuries. In the East, the Crusades when remembered at all were thought of with a shudder of horror. Modern Arab scholars are fond of quoting incidents to show the relative crudity, brutality, and ignorance of the crusaders.[4] But this is too simple to be true. If the Latin kingdom was founded upon force and was rarely far from war, it was also able to evolve a legal system, a military architecture, and a commercial life which compared well with those of contemporary Europe. The roughness and intolerance of the early crusaders was mitigated both by the softer life of the East and by the contacts with Muslims which became possible in the frequent periods of peace.

Because modern Arabs and others are wont to think of the state of Israel in Crusader terms, it is well to establish the essential differences. The most important of these is that the crusaders were always a small minority in their kingdom. They lived as a military aristocracy on the basis of native peasant labor. In this they differ strikingly from modern Zionists, who, as we shall see below, created a self-contained Jewish nation even before they became a state.

Not less important is the fact that the crusaders came into Palestine on their own, with the sword as the only justification they worried about, and without promises or pledges to anyone. The Zionists, to the contrary, came into Palestine in small batches as a tolerated minority in the first (pre-1918) phase and then as the protégés of another world power which in its foreign policy had committed itself to a series of restricting agreements with others. Thus, whereas the crusaders were able with no qualms to massacre and dispossess the infidel, the British were in no mood to permit Zionists to so do even had they so wished. Thus perhaps the greatest contrast is to be found in the minds of men. Conquest was its own justification in the day when men's consciences at least were "made of tougher, sterner stuff." We shall see that it was the very lack of sureness, the inability to see problems in simple and stark contrasts, and the

[4] See P. K. Hitti (trans.), *An Arab-Syrian Gentleman and Warrior in the Period of the Crusades* (New York: 1929). This is the source of many quotations to this effect.

preoccupation with justice which became ingredients of the increasing political tension in the Mandate of Palestine. Hamlet could not play Richard III.

The Crusades had been successful, so to speak, in the fissures of the Islamic world; to reunify at least the central portions to the point that they would prove "just strong enough to meet the challenge from the West" was to be the triumph of Saladin, whose reign

> is more than an episode in the history of the Crusades. It is one of those rare and dramatic moments in human history when cynicism and disillusion, born of long experience of the selfish ambitions of princes, are for a brief period dislodged by moral determination and unity of purpose.[5]

The Islamic world proved "just strong enough." Acre fell and the Latin Kingdom was ended, but under Saladin's successors Islam again shattered into hostile fragments. It was small consolation to Islam that the Latin crusaders were seemingly happier to make war on their Byzantine coreligionists than upon Islam. But as an ironic afterglow to the Crusades, a quarter of a century after the Franks captured Constantinople, the cultured, cosmopolitan, and excommunicated Emperor Frederick II, who knew Arabic and encouraged Islamic studies at his capital, obtained Jerusalem, as it were, on loan. This was a feat his more warlike fellows were unable to do by arms. It was a gentlemen's agreement with the equally cosmopolitan ruler of Egypt, and it so outraged both Christendom and Islam as to come within an ace of leading to the deposition and lynching of both gentlemen.

In 1244 Jerusalem was again sacked, this time by the Khwarizmi Turks who had fled before the onslaught of the terrible Mongols. The Mongols themselves, after having destroyed scores of important cities in China, Russia, central Asia, and the Middle East followed the Khwarizmis. Saladin's successors, the Mamluks of Egypt, however, recovered from the Eighth Crusade (Saint Louis's attack on Egypt) in time to retake and hold Palestine against them. These were grim, uncertain years in which the traveler had either to be very brave or very foolish.

[5] Sir Hamilton A. R. Gibb, "The Rise of Saladin, 1169-1189," in M. W. Baldwin (ed.), *A History of the Crusades* (Philadelphia: 1955), I, 563.

His possession of either of these qualities was matched only by his rarity. One of the few descriptions of Jerusalem at this period is a 1267 letter from Moses Nahmanides, who wrote:

> . . . Great is the solitude and great is the devastation, and, to put it briefly, the more sacred the places, the greater their desolation . . . [the city] has about 2,000 inhabitants: about 300 Christians live there who escaped the sword of the Sultan. There are no Jews. For, after the arrival of the Tartars, some fled while others died by the sword.[6]

For western Europeans, Jerusalem was all but inaccessible both because the policy of the Christian states was to encourage the Mongols and because the Arab memory of the Crusades was still vivid and painful.

One of the after-effects of the Crusades was a second surge of Muslim interest in the religious merit of Palestine. This is not surprising. Islam had been challenged in the heart of its empire by a group acting in the name of a rival universal religion. We may well question the religious motives of the individual crusaders, but it would appear that as a group they communicated at least certain aspects of their view of the Holiness of Palestine to their Muslim rivals. This, as we have seen, is not the beginning of Muslim veneration but certainly was a new exemplar. And in response we find such works as that of the thirteenth-century Syrian writer al-Fazari, *The Arousing of Souls to Visits to Jerusalem the Guarded.*[7] The work is mainly a series of quotations from the sayings and writings of prominent Muslims and Biblical prophets and from the *Hadith* (tradition) of Islam urging the benefits to be derived from visits to Jerusalem. Pilgrimage to Jerusalem was thought to have assured the pilgrim's entry into Heaven and Jerusalem itself was presented as a sort of earthly representative of Paradise in spite of the destruction of the recent centuries. Muslims and Christians could agree that it was the "Navel" of the earth.

Some Christians, at least, had not given up the idea of reconquest and Bertrandon de la Brocquière was one of these. In

[6] Quoted in F. Kobler, *Letters of the Jews Through the Ages* (London: 1952), p. 225.

[7] See C. D. Matthews: *Palestine—Mohammedan Holy Land* (New Haven: 1949).

maintenance of its internal order and for the payment of taxes. The Jews of Spain, many of whom were highly cultured, came in large numbers eastward. It was thus that various cities of the empire, particularly Salonika, developed flourishing Jewish communities.[2]

Under the Ottoman conditions of freedom and security many Jews achieved prominence but none rivaled Joseph Nasi. Having won the heart of the crown prince Selim, son of Sulaiman the Magnificent, Nasi profited by becoming Duke of the Isle of Naxos in 1566 when the crown prince became Sultan Selim II ("the Sot").[3] With his extensive connections in Europe, where his family was prominent before the expulsion, and with his great wealth, Joseph Nasi was able to play something of the part later to be taken in Austria by the Rothschilds. Like refugee Jews of our own age, miserable in their sense of having lost home, many of Nasi's contemporaries felt a special intensity of longing for the "Land of Milk and Honey." The Duke felt sufficiently akin to this sentiment to secure the grant from the Ottoman government of certain privileges, the exact nature of which is unknown, allowing him to rebuild the town of Tiberias. It is easy, retrospectively with the recent history of Zionism begging a parallel, to read too much into this story, but this is how it was interpreted at the time.

> The French Ambassador reported to his king that the Nasis have received permission from the Grand Signior, confirmed by Sultan Selim and his son Sultan Murad, to build a city on the shore of the Lake of Tiberias, beneath Safed, wherein Jews only are to live. In fact, he proposes to begin his achievement here by this renewal, having the intention so far as one can judge of proclaiming himself King

[2] See W. J. Fischel, *Jews in the Economic and Political Life of Medieval Islam* (London: 1937); A. S. Tritton, *The Caliphs and their non-Muslim Subjects* (London: 1930); and, on the Ottoman period in particular, J. Nehama, *Histoire des Israélites de Salonique* (Paris and Salonika: 1935-36); M. S. Goodblatt, *Jewish Life in Turkey in the XVI Century* (New York: 1952).

[3] Nasi's most recent biographer, Cecil Roth, remarks that it "was through the palate—or perhaps it is more correct to say the gullet—that he had first commended himself to his gourmandizing master, long before he came to the throne. Naturally, he did not forget this now. Every Friday, a gift of choice wines and delicacies was borne by his servants to the imperial seraglio" (*The House of Nasi* [Philadelphia: 1948], p. 43).

of the Jews. This is why he is demanding money from France so insistently.[4]

Meanwhile contacts between the western states and the Ottoman Empire were growing; in a sense this contact tended to shift diplomatic concern away from Palestine toward Constantinople, and the Levant came increasingly to figure in the literature and thought of Europe in the new Ottoman guise. To the already established Venetian and Genoese ambassadors were added those of various other European powers. English and French commercial factories were established at key points all over the empire. In the accounts of the period, the merchant joins the pilgrim; indeed, in the person of Henry Maundrell, sometime fellow of Magdalen College, Oxford, we find the combination of the two: Maundrell was chaplain of the Levant Company factory at Aleppo. In 1697 at Christmas he made a rapid horseback pilgrimage to Jerusalem, and in his account there is a charming blend of this dual personality:

> The country discovered a quite different face from what it had before, presenting nothing to the view, in most places, but naked rocks, mountains, and precipices; at sight of which pilgrims are apt to be much astonished and baulked in their expectations, finding that country in such an inhospitable condition, concerning whose pleasantness and plenty they had before formed in their minds such high ideas from the description given of it in the Word of God, insomuch that it almost startles their faith, when they reflect how it could be possible for a land like this to supply food for so prodigious a number of inhabitants as are said to have been polled in the twelve tribes at one time, the number given in by Joab [2 Sam. 24] amounting to no less than thirteen hundred thousand fighting men, besides women and children.[5]

The good reverend, fortunately, found solace for his doubting heart in a way strikingly like that of some modern writers. He reflected that "such a mountainous and uneven surface affords a larger space of ground for cultivation than this country would amount to if it were all reduced to a perfect level."

As he rode out of the country, Maundrell briefly witnessed

[4] Roth, p. 10; also see fn. 6, p. 241.

[5] *A Journey from Aleppo to Jerusalem* (Oxford: 1714) pp. 64-65 (put into modern spellings).

the abiding sin of the Ottoman Empire in its long decline. The administration was unable to provide dependable public security in the provinces. Thus, roving bands of nomads cut the roads, swept over such fertile and cultivated areas as the Vale of Esdraelon, and posed a constant threat to pilgrims and peasants alike. Throughout the seventeenth and eighteenth centuries the empire was largely content to exercise a loose suzerainty over its hinterland. In Egypt the Mamluks again rose to virtual independence and a similar dynasty was established in Iraq. In the mountainous areas of the Balkans, Anatolia, and Syria, local governors, adventurers, and tribal chiefs managed to set up as "lords of the valleys" not unlike the "robber barons" along the Rhine of the early Middle Ages. Each lord recognized no law save his own capricious edict—unless the sword of his overlord be near; all took what they could from the weak and gave what they must to the mighty.

The results of this situation were many and varied. Not all of them were wholly bad. Trade, for example, became so expensive as to be virtually impractical. This forced small areas to achieve a sort of independence since local handicraft industry had to supply local wants. In Palestine, as elsewhere, the limited natural resources became economic in default of other sources of supply. Besides cotton and silk, which were the staple of trade with Europe and which were made into cloth for local use, the Levant hinterland produced some iron, manufactured gunpowder, pottery, and agricultural equipment. All in all, the area developed a certain local and small-scale prosperity and stability which it was to lose as the nineteenth century brought increased contacts with Europe's booming industry.

The produce of the Levant, in the eighteenth century, was gathered into the port of Saida (ancient Sidon), which was the seat of a pasha of the Ottoman empire. In the middle of that century as so often before a local strong man, in this case a bedouin shaikh named Dahir, seized a portion of north Palestine and Saida. From the Ottoman point of view he was but one in a long sequence of vassals who while a rebel today might be a useful ally tomorrow. As the contemporary French traveler, Volney, observed:

> the strategy of Turkish politics involves not holding vassals to strict obedience. Long ago, they realized that if they made war on all rebels, that would be a ceaseless task, and a great expenditure of men and money . . . So they have taken the way of patience: they temporize, they play off neighbors, relatives, and children. And sooner or later, the rebels follow the same course, submit and end by enriching the sultan with their spoils.[6]

Shaikh Dahir, however, was something more than just another rebel; he appears to have been a man of foresight and temperance—rare qualities in his age. Relying upon the military prowess of his sons and their warriors, Dahir set to work to encourage trade. He established his capital at Acre, which he rebuilt from a mass of Crusades rubble, and attracted to it most of the merchants and sailors of Saida. With success came greater ambition. Clashes with the Ottoman government grew violent, and, in his need, Dahir called for aid upon the ruler of Egypt and upon the Russian fleet.[7] The former failed him but the latter somewhat over performed by pillaging Beirut and then agreeing to withdraw upon payment of a large ransom. The Ottoman government roused itself and by careful intrigue laid its plans. In the time-honored way, this involved instigating Dahir's cannibal colleagues to pounce upon him.

As always the government won, but the expectations of the Sultan were not completely met, in that the man who took his place was an equally ambitious and perhaps even stronger man known as Jazzar ("the Butcher"). Unlike Dahir, who was a native of Palestine, Jazzar was a Bosnian Turk, but during his thirty-year rule he continued most of the policies of his predecessor. So able a ruler was he that he was in a position to hold Acre not only from the Ottoman tax collectors but even from the newly arrived conqueror of Egypt, Napoleon.

[6] *Travels* (London: 1788), II, 95-96. For the history of this period see H. Lammens, *La Syrie* (Beyrouth: 1921), II, 104 ff.

[7] Russian ships under the command of Alexis Orlov, brother of the leman of Catherine the Great, were sent around Europe from the Baltic to attack Turkey in the rear.

5. THE GREAT POWERS IN THE MIDDLE EAST

Napoleon landed in Egypt in 1798 with the first modern army to be seen in the Middle East. With stunning ease he defeated the famed Mamluk cavalry—it had changed but little since its defeat by Sultan Selim the Grim—and seized all of lower Egypt. Then, in 1798, like so many of his predecessors in the thousands of years of recorded Egyptian history, Napoleon decided that he must add Syria to his domain as the shield of Egypt. But Napoleon was a wise enough general to rely as little as possible on military might. He sent ahead rumors, published proclamations, gathered intelligence. Acre was to be his first target as it was the seat of the pasha Jazzar and the key to the hinterland. If his advisors had read the most recent French account, Volney's *Travels,* they would have found:

> . . . The fortifications [of Acre], though more frequently repaired than any other in all Syria, are of no importance; there are only a few wretched low towers, near the port, on which cannon are mounted, but these rusty iron pieces are so bad, that some of them burst every time they are fired. Its defence on the land side, is only a mere garden wall without any ditch.[1]

In February 1799, Napoleon sent his forces into south Palestine, seizing the important coastal towns. Meanwhile the English fleet sailed along the coast which it had patrolled since the battle of Abuqir, where it had destroyed most of Napoleon's transports. Napoleon issued proclamations posing as a Muslim (to the Muslims) and made vague promises to the Jews to restore to them the Holy Land, meanwhile unintentionally terrifying the whole population by the severity of his military acts. In Jerusalem, in an almost unique moment of agreement, the Jews, Christians, and Muslims joined to fortify the city against him, but his goal was not Jerusalem. It was the port of Acre, and what a shock it must have been to the French army to find Acre to be a well-equipped fortress backed by English naval cannon. Appeals to

[1] II (London: 1758), 226-27.

local Christians and Druze were coolly received or at best answered by promises of support *after* victory. Victory never came. Acre held for two wearisome months while disease and the fear of the loss of Egypt took their toll of French life and morale. Finally, from his ramparts, Jazzar could see Napoleon's troops begin their retreat into Egypt. Ottoman laxity, as Volney had described it, here found its justification; the great rebel had in an hour of need become the great ally. As Napoleon later remarked, Acre was the rock on which his dreams of eastern empire had crashed.

Meanwhile life in Syria and Palestine continued much as it had in the previous two centuries except that improved transportation and new methods of warfare gave to would-be tyrants more efficient means of despoiling the countryside. By 1804, the English-sponsored traveler John Burckhardt, one of the most acute observers ever to travel in the East, noted that commerce of the Levant ports showed signs of a recent decline and that the interior was becoming rapidly depopulated. In the town of Tiberias, whose population Burckhardt estimated at 4,000, he found a Jewish community of some two hundred families. Of these, forty or fifty families were Polish and the rest from various parts of the Ottoman Empire. Virtually nothing remained of the vague plans of Joseph Nasi; Burckhardt does not even record any local mention of the Nasis or their patronage. This is how he describes the Jewish part of the town community of his day:

The great part of the Jews . . . do not engage in mercantile pursuits; but are a society of religious persons occupied solely with their sacred duties. There are among them only one or two who are merchants, and men of property, and these are styled Kafers or unbelievers by the others, who do nothing but read and pray . . . But the offering up of prayers by these devotees is rendered indispensable by a dogma contained in the Talmud, that the world will return to its primitive chaos, if prayers are not addressed to the God of Israel at least twice a week in these four cities [Saffad, Jerusalem, Hebron, and Tiberias]; this belief produces considerable pecuniary advantage to the supplicants, as the missionaries sent abroad to collect alms for the support of these religious fraternities plead the danger of the threatened chaos, to induce the rich Jews to send supplies of money, in order that the prayers may be constantly offered up . . . Great jealousy seems to prevail between the Syrian and Polish Jews. The former being in possession of the place, oblige the foreigners to pay excessively high for their lodgings . . . They all write Hebrew; but . . . their learning seems to be on the same level as that of the Turks . . . The Jews enjoy here perfect religious freedom, more particularly since Soleiman, whose principal minister, Haym Farkhy, is a Jew, has succeeded to the Pashalik of Akka [Acre].[2]

In other parts of Palestine and Syria, Burckhardt found the Christians engaged in that fierce fraternal strife which has been a distinguishing mark of Eastern Christian life since the earliest days of the faith.

fanatism (sic) . . . is not directed so much against the Mohammedans, as against their Christian brethren, whose creed at all differs from their own. It need hardly be mentioned here, that many of those sects which tore Europe to pieces in the earlier ages of Christianity, still exist in these countries. Greeks, Catholics, Maronites, Syriacs, Chaldeans, and Jacobites, all have their respective parishes and churches. Unable to affect anything against the religion of their haughty rulers the Turks,[3] they turn the only weapons they possess, scandal and intrigue, with fury against each other, and each sect is made enough to believe that its church would flourish on the ruins of those of their heretic brethren . . . The intrigues carried on at Jerusalem between the Greek and Latin monks contribute to increase these disputes, which would have long ago led to a Christian civil war in these countries, did not the iron rod of the Turkish government repress their religious fury.[4]

The first half of the nineteenth century is still, in many ways, the "darkest" of Islamic history. We know far less of this period than of the early centuries of Islam; this to a certain extent is true because much of our information on the previous century comes from local chronicles. And the small societies which had produced these records were themselves in the nineteenth century gradually broken down and reabsorbed by the reviving empire. Paradoxically the resurgence of the central government came coevally with a rise of provincial particularism. This is

[2] *Travels in Syria and the Holy Land* (London: 1822), pp. 332-36.

[3] Elsewhere in his account, Burckhardt notes, "I have heard only of one instance during the last century . . . of the conversion [to Christianity] of Mohammedans . . ." (p. 586).

[4] pp. 28-29.

evident in the Balkans, in Anatolia, Iraq, and other areas, but is perhaps nowhere more striking than in Egypt.

In Egypt the Albanian adventurer Mehmet Ali, who had originally gone to Egypt in an Ottoman contingent of troops to help oust the French, had by skillfully playing off his various rivals for power managed to seize power. As a witness to the French military superiority over all Middle Eastern forces, Mehmet Ali realized that in the new world of the nineteenth century he would have either to copy the new order or lose out to those who would. If the French could defeat those who were to be his rivals, to defeat those same forces he must copy the French. The genius of Mehmet Ali lay in his ability to realize that military power, in the new order, was not merely a question of having quantities of rifles, powder, uniforms, and men but also involved having the economic base to support men and to supply arms. Therefore, early in his career as lord of Egypt, Mehmet Ali began to send promising young men of all classes to Europe to be trained as technicians for the industry and army he was building.

Since Jazzar Pasha's death in 1804, Acre and its hinterland of Palestine and Lebanon had been ruled by the pashas Sulaiman (or Soleiman) and Abdullah. The former was the ruler mentioned by Burckhardt as having a Jewish minister; he was more pacific, less ambitious, but far more greedy than Jazzar. Corancez wrote in 1810 that his levies on Jerusalem had "brought desolation even to the Catholic establishments [to such a degree that] the religious authorities [came] to the point of abandoning them."[5] But if Sulaiman made the country suffer from his avarice, at least he gave it in return some stability. His successor was the young and frivolous Abdullah Pasha who extorted and gave nothing in return. Abdullah seems to have given himself over to pederasty after entrusting his finances to the Jewish banking house of Haim. If he had a policy, it was simply the old tradition of divide and despoil, but even at this he was not successful. His lack of rule served as a lure to all ambitious

[5] *Histoire des Wahabis* (Paris: 1810), p. 108; quoted in Lammens, *La Syrie* (Beyrouth: 1921), II, 133.

powers: the bedouin were more out of control than ever before, the Druzes and Maronites were disturbed and disturbing, and Mehmet Ali was tempted.

Mehmet Ali, at that point (1822) was well on his way toward creating a Middle Eastern equivalent of later-day Japan. Alone among the Middle Eastern powers, he had a powerful, modern army supplied by domestic Egyptian industry and a fleet built in Egyptian yards. Like other pashas of dubious loyalty, he was needed by the Sultan. In wars against the Greeks and against the Wahabis of Arabia, he deserved well of the empire, but also in them Mehmet Ali waxed mighty and ambitious. Like Napoleon he gradually felt himself drawn into Syrian affairs to safeguard Egypt.

In 1831 the Egyptian army was well trained, partly by French officers, hardened by years of warfare, and ably led by Mehmet Ali's son Ibrahim Pasha with the aid of Colonel Sèves (a French convert to Islam). It had one big initial advantage over Napoleon, in his previous attempt, in having supply problems solved by the Egyptian fleet. Speedily the Egyptians thrust into Palestine and with little difficulty took Acre; beyond Acre Syria lay open. The battle of Homs in 1832 severed it from the Ottoman and welded it to the new Egyptian empire. For a decade all Syria (including what is now divided between Lebanon, Syria, Jordan, and Israel) was administered by Egypt and naturally was affected by Egypt's policy of encouraging Westernization. In particular, Mehmet Ali allowed French Catholics and American Protestants to open mission schools; in line with traditional Islamic policy he paid little attention to religion provided the due of Caesar was promptly paid—and the new definition of Caesar's due was a literate and trained society.

Of course, Mehmet Ali was a despot. This surprised no one. Every pasha in the memory of men had been such. Democracy and freedom were of the heritage of the Desert, not of the Sown. But there was a difference. Mehmet Ali was a more efficient despot than any in memory. He had been accustomed to dealing with the populace of the Nile Delta, which perhaps for lack of any place to hide is traditionally submissive. In Palestine and Lebanon, he met a very different folk. The mountains of the Levant had been a sort of shield against tyranny and their inhabitants had a tradition of independence and a tenacity in freedom more like the nomads than that of the Egyptian peasant.

Unable to crush them by direct military means, the Egyptians had recourse to the usual techniques; they armed the Maronite Christians and incited them against the Druzes. This was successful as always because if there is one tradition stronger than intragroup independence in Middle Eastern society it is intergroup hostility. However, when the Egyptians came to reap the harvest of their policy, in the form of new taxes and military conscription, they wisely judged it advisable to disarm their new allies. At this the Maronites, as they rarely before or since have done, joined forces with the Druze. The two groups then induced a visiting French viscount, who might be expected to interest Europe in their fate, to be their titular leader. Such encouragement was hardly needed, since Europe had been looking for just such an opportunity to clip Mehmet Ali's wings. The British and French fleets played along the coast, bombarded Beirut, landed troops, and raised Mount Lebanon's population against the Egyptians. Further south they rained 60,000 shells on Acre in less than three hours, exploding the powder magazine and turning the fortress into a cauldron of fire.

The Ottoman Empire was able to recoup its position in Syria and Palestine. In Great Britain it had a powerful new ally. Britain's position may be summarized as the desire to uphold the Ottoman Empire as a barrier to Russia in the north and yet to keep the empire sufficiently weak in the south to pose no threat to British interests. The essence of the British interests of this period of course was communication with India. For years the route of communication went through Syria—Alexandretta to Aleppo and by the Euphrates to Basra on the Persian Gulf. In Aleppo was the major factory of the Levant Company (which was abolished in 1825). Then, in 1837, the French opened steamer service between Alexandria and France. A short overland ride in the relatively safe countryside of Egypt brought the traveler or the mail pouch to the steamer of the

East India Company at Suez. Bombay was suddenly only half as far (in traveling time) as it had been on the new route to India.[6]

This fact coincided with two situations which had developed over the preceding years. The first was a growing fear of Russia. When Britain had seemed unable or unwilling to stop Mehmet Ali in his first attack on Syria, the Turks had been thrown into the willing arms of Tsar Nicholas. By the terms of the treaty of Unkiar Skelessi (1833), any threat to the Sultan by Mehmet Ali could be used as an excuse for a Russian intervention. This the British wished to avoid at all costs.

The second was a curious surge of fascination among the English ruling class with the Old Testament and so with Judaism; one need not dig in English history to find examples of previous interest—this exists throughout the Protestant period—but it becomes significant for our purposes only when it comes to be felt in the government. This it does in the late 1830s when Lord Ashley, son-in-law of Lady Palmerston whose husband was then Foreign Secretary, began "crusading for the return of the Jews to Palestine under some Great Power protection." This began the curious union of empire policy with a sort of paternalistic Christian Zionism which is evident in British policy in succeeding generations. As Sir Charles Webster has written, there was "a mystical idea, never altogether lost in the nineteenth century, that Britain was to be the chosen instrument of God to bring back the Jews to the Holy Land." [7]

Effectively to bolster the Ottoman Empire against Russia, it was necessary not only to restrain Mehmet Ali, under the pretext of whose aggression Russia might enter Turkey, but to foster a growth of internal strength and to win for the Ottoman government the good will of Englishmen. In effect the British Government had to find a means of creating the atmosphere of domestic public opinion in which it could carry the nation with its policy of support for the empire. To this end, England

[6] This led to the British taking of Aden just as Mehmet Ali was about to do so; see H. W. V. Temperley, *The Crimea* (London: 1936), p. 95.

[7] Sir Charles Webster, *The Foreign Policy of Palmerston* (London: 1951), p. 761.

constantly urged reforms of various sorts and also urged the Sultan to invite European Jews to settle in Palestine under British protection. In a private letter to the British ambassador in Constantinople, Lord Palmerston wrote:

> Pray don't lose sight of my recommendation to the Porte to invite the Jews to return to Palestine. You can have no idea how much such a measure would tend to interest in the Sultan's cause all of the religious party in this country, and their influence is great and their connexion extensive. The measure moreover in itself would be highly advantageous to the Sultan, by bringing into his dominions a great number of wealthy capitalists who would employ the people and enrich the Empire.[8]

Realistically permission could hardly be expected from an empire beset, as was the Ottoman, on all sides with would-be protectors and already smarting from the nascent nationalism of its many religious and ethnic communities. Britain did, however, in 1838 establish a vice-consulate in Jerusalem with express instructions to protect the 9,690 Jews found to be settled thereabouts. And, for its part, the Ottoman government did allow Jews to settle within the empire—indeed, in fairness, it deserves to be emphasized that few contemporary states equal the Ottoman record of tolerance—but the empire could hardly be blamed for not wishing to add to its centrifugal tendencies.[9]

It is arguable that Great Britain's foreign policy was concerned with the Jews in Palmerston's days largely because Britain had no traditional partisan group in the area. Such was certainly not the case for the French.

[8] *Ibid.*, p. 762. Palmerston in 1840 "listened with sympathy to Lord Shaftesbury, who exhorted him to repatriate Jews into Palestine, and helped a little in that direction. Palmerston next proposed (and it was a daring suggestion) that England should take charge of Jewish interests in Palestine. His proposal was approved by the Queen." (Temperley, pp. 443-44). See A. M. Hyamson, *The British Consulate in Jerusalem in relation to the Jews of Palestine, 1838-1914* (London: 1939); and "British Projects for the Restoration of the Jews to Palestine," American Jewish Historical Society, XXVI.

[9] See Paul Goodman, *Moses Montefiore* (Philadelphia: 1925), pp. 70-71; and Noël Verney and George Dambmann, *Les Puissances étrangères dans le Levant* (Paris: 1900), p. 145. Verney and Dambmann felt that it was because the Sultan feared the European connections of the Jews that he refused permission for them to settle in Palestine as such.

Fancifully as it now appears, France was wont to attribute to her interest in the Middle East a historical depth to the Crusades or even to the era of Charlemagne. The image of the Crusades, in which the French played an important role, deeply impressed itself upon French emotional aspirations. And since the days of Francis I and Sulaiman the Magnificent, France maintained diplomatic contact with the Ottoman Empire. In 1535 France and the Ottoman Empire were in alliance against the Hapsburgs and in 1581 France received the privilege of acting as consular representative for all European merchants and pilgrims.

In the East, France was able to act in concert with the powerful and widely scattered Franciscan Order which was made responsible for all western pilgrims. In 1555 the Franciscans, this time with Spanish help, had managed to secure control of the Holy Sepulcher, and they used their position to keep out or restrict members of other churches. The reaction of their colleagues and rivals was immediate, bitter, and fertile. From this emotional soil was to come a several-century-long harvest of reproach, hate, and bloodshed. The Ottoman government was unconcerned except when the balance of domestic order was upset; it intervened only when the Orthodox and the Catholics or the myriad of lesser churches were at one another's throats or when moved by bribes or diplomatic pressure. Actually, through it all, as a British governor was later to find,[10] the Muslims made rather better guardians of the Holy Places than any *one* Christian power could have, for they alone were acceptable to all.

French statesmen kept in their minds' eye a sort of neo-Crusades, French-supported Christian enclave in Palestine. In 1840, just about the same time England was becoming concerned with Palestine and with the Suez route to India, the French minister Guizot formulated a plan—if indeed it ever amounted to that much—of making Jerusalem a Christian city separate from the pashalik of Syria (of which it was then a part) in much the same way as planned by the partitioners a century later in 1936, 1938, and 1947. The idea grew in the telling, and the

[10] Sir Ronald Storrs, *Orientations* (London: 1945), p. 299.

King of Naples suggested that his brother, the Prince of Capua, be made ruler of "the new Christian state of Palestine which the Four Powers intended to set up."[11] The plan, in even its more modest form, came to naught because England was hardly interested in assisting or allowing a French puppet state to be established in the Middle East. France had to take what satisfaction she could by setting up a consulate in Jerusalem in 1843. The consulate, of course, acted closely with several of the Catholic Holy Orders, and it was also able to maintain almost sovereign relations with the Uniate Christians and the Catholics who, according to the *millet* system were quasi-autonomous.

In 1847 Pope Pius IX moved the Latin patriarchate of Jerusalem back to the Holy Land from Rome, where since the reconquest of Acre by Saladin it had remained merely a title without a function. The various Catholic Orders, notably the Jesuits, maintained schools in many parts of the Levant and ministered to a large native population. France took upon herself a vague duty, which as the Ottoman government grew weaker was so encroached upon as to become accepted as a right, to protect these Catholics and Uniates. On their behalf she attempted to secure control of Holy Places, to ease taxes, to secure the release of criminals or suspects from Ottoman jails, and even to remove altogether from Ottoman law an ever widening circle of clients.

The third great power interested in the Middle East was imperial Russia. Like France, she had a ready-made native client community inherited from the dim past. Indeed, Russia's client, the Orthodox *millet*, may be regarded as a part of the Byzantine heritage of the tsars. Under Byzantium, Jerusalem like the majority of urban Syria was primarily Orthodox, and it was from the Orthodox patriarch that the caliph Omar had accepted the surrender of the city. Omar granted freedom of worship and property to the Orthodox community, and his successors in the following centuries found the patriarchs to be useful adjuncts to government. It was a good deal more economical to rule the non-Muslims through someone acceptable

[11] Webster, p. 760.

to them, and this mediating function the patriarchs were well suited to perform. Ottoman sultans in their turn strengthened the hand of the prelates, and so contributed to the cohesion of their flock still further, by handing over to them control over virtually all internal affairs. Ordinarily members were not allowed to leave the *millet* into which they were born, and the *millet,* in the person of the government-appointed patriarch, controlled their marriages, inheritances, etc., and kept the peace with state support. Thus, the Orthodox *millet,* like the other protected and tolerated non-Muslim communities, became an autonomous corporation within the empire.

For a considerable time after the fall of Constantinople in 1453, the Orthodox community had little or no contact with Russia; Russia had not yet a patriarch and her church ritual differed in certain respects from that of the Byzantine church. Gradually, however, the upper clergy and the tsars became captivated by the vision of Byzantium. Ivan III in 1472 married the niece of the last Byzantine emperor, and somewhat later the Russian patriarch Nikon undertook to purge the faulty ritual of his church and to bring it into closer intellectual contact with the corpus of church literature as preserved in other, partly Ottoman, centers of learning.

In 1690 the Orthodox community lost control of some of the Holy Places to the French-aided Catholics. The Orthodox within the Ottoman Empire were able to appeal only to one power to counter the coalition of Catholics and France. On their behalf Russia made a half-hearted gesture to restore the *status quo ante*. In the treaty of Karlowitz of 1699, she almost casually, perhaps merely for the purpose of bargaining, acquired a vague and for long unclaimed right to protect the Orthodox subjects of the Ottoman Empire.[12] Peter the Great was the first tsar to evoke the chimera of Orthodox union, and so badly did he judge both his enemies and his supposed friends during his invasion of the Balkans that he had to ransom himself from an encircling Ottoman army. Although Peter took his own revenge, it was not until the time of Catherine the Great that the Rus-

[12] B. H. Sumner, *Peter the Great and the Ottoman Empire* (Oxford: 1949), pp. 30-34.

sians again took up their claim to protect the Orthodox in the treaty of Kuchuk Kainardji in 1774. Even in Catherine's time, however, the Russians were little concerned with Palestine but rather concentrated on the Balkans and areas fronting on the Black Sea. Catherine's grandson, Alexander I, likewise dealt with Balkan affairs as a part of his European policy. It is only toward the end of Alexander's reign, in one of those curious "might have been" notes to history, that Palestine merits our attention in Russsian affairs.

Colonel Pavel Pestel, one of the leaders of the secret revolutionary society which has become known as the Decembrists, worked out a sort of paternal Zionist plan not unlike that which appealed to English statesmen. In his work, *Russian Justice,* which outlined the state he hoped to establish after overthrowing the monarchy, Pestel mentioned that he would deport all Russian Jews to Asia Minor where he would help them to establish their own state. Like some later plans of paternal Zionism, this was certainly motivated by a sort of anti-Semitism, but it all came to nothing when Nicholas I crushed the revolt and hanged Pestel.

Nicholas I came to the throne and ruled Russia during the formative years of British foreign policy in the Middle East; he stood at the end of a two-centuries-old process of Russian aggrandizement at the expense of the Ottoman Empire in the areas around the Black Sea. The next logical step for Russia was the dismemberment of the empire. The empire was "rotten," it was the "sick man of Europe," it needed only an agreement between the powers to bring about a healthy new order in which the ambitions of the powers could be fulfilled at the expense only of a derelict. Nicholas, as Temperley has written, was obsessed with the "sickliness" of Turkey during his whole reign.[13] Britain tended to agree that the empire was sick but hoped that it could be kept sufficiently alive, at least in its more northern parts, to block Russian advances toward the areas of British interest. The real danger to the empire was Egypt's ambitious ruler Mehmet Ali Pasha. In his attacks on his suzerain Mehmet forced the Ottoman Empire into an alliance with

[13] p. 272.

Russia which allowed Russian troops to enter the empire in case of need. Thus the big-power line-up fell into a logical if complex pattern: Britain tried to shore up the empire internally in the north while keeping Mehmet Ali from subverting it in the south; France vacillated between favoring partition and following Britain; and Russia, while openly offering to defend the sultan against all comers, privately sought an understanding on his political death.

In the area itself, this international rivalry was translated into a religious idiom. On one side were the French-supported Catholic missions and their flocks and on the other the Russian-supported Orthodox and their flocks. The focal point of conflict was the prime symbol of them all, the Church of Bethlehem. Louis Napoleon, grasping at this symbol, instructed his ambassador in Constantinople to demand from the Sultan permission for the Catholic monks to guard it.

> Stated in bare terms [wrote Kinglake] the question [which culminated in the Crimean War] was whether for the purpose of passing through the building into their Grotto, the Latin monks should have the key of the chief door of the Church of Bethlehem, and also one of the keys of each of the two doors of the sacred manger, and whether they should be at liberty to place in the sanctuary of the Nativity a silver star adorned with the arms of France.[14]

Tsar Nicholas was equally intent upon preservation of the Orthodox position and made conflicting demands upon the Sultan who vainly tried to acquiesce to both. In Jerusalem, the rivalry was not less intense and often found expression in drosses and candlesticks in the hands of angry monks. As tempers mounted, Nicholas finally, to precipitate the death of the "sick man," sent Prince Menshikov to Constantinople with instructions to get the *status quo ante* for the Orthodox of Jerusalem, to get permission to repair the dome of the Jerusalem church (which by local usage meant future control of the building), and to obtain for Russia a clear mandate to protect the Orthodox Christian

[14] *Invasion of the Crimea* (London, 1936), I, 46; as quoted in J. A. R. Marriott, *The Eastern Question* (Oxford: 1940), p. 252. Also see *Cambridge History of British Foreign Relations*, II, 348; Great Britain Foreign Office, *Correspondence Respecting the Rights and Privileges of the Latin and Greek Churches in Turkey* (London: 1854).

subjects of the Ottoman Empire. Russia's demands were so stated as to be incapable of satisfaction, and in 1853 Nicholas invaded the Danubian principalities. The Crimean War had begun.

6. THE SICK MAN OF EUROPE

The Crimean War, whose course falls far outside our narrative, sobered the powers to a limited extent and solved the problem of Jerusalem in that Russia was temporarily removed from the scene.[1] This situation, together with certain factors of internal development, allowed the Ottoman government to re-establish its rule over several precariously held provinces. One by one the "Lords of the Valleys" were overcome. Turkey's able administrator Midhat Pasha, in his government of the Danubian provinces and of the Baghdad *vilayet* or provinces, set examples of the empire at its best. In particular his policy toward the bedouin tribes was important and if more actively followed by his successors might have been crucial.

For centuries the bedouin tribes, around the shores of the "waterless sea" of the Syrian desert, had been in every practical sense outside the Ottoman Empire. Indeed, not since the early centuries of the Islamic Empire had the bedouin really been a part of the urban Islamic society. In the time of Harun ar-

[1] Yet Russian pilgrimage took a sharp upward swing after the war. In 1859 Grand Duke Constantine Nicholaivich made the pilgrimage, and the Russian government donated 500,000 rubles to which popular subscription added 600,000 to purchase ten acres outside Jerusalem to build Trinity Cathedral and several hostelries. By 1880 some 2,000 Russians were visiting Palestine each year. In 1881 Grand Duke Sergai Alexandrovich organized the Imperial Orthodox Palestine Society and had new accommodations built during his visit. In 1889 about 9,000 pilgrims were arriving yearly. The English traveler Stephen Graham found that the trip cost on the average only £1/5/0, whereas a century earlier (C. F. Volney, *Travels through Syria and Egypt* [London: 1788], II, 309) had found it to be £166 (*With the Russian Pilgrims to Jerusalem* [London: 1890?], p. 87. For the Russian government use of the Church for its foreign policy see Sir A. Bertram and J. W. A. Young, *The Orthodox Patriarchate of Jerusalem* (London: 1926), pp. 25-26.

Rashid the bedouin were known as "bad neighbors" to the central government whose laws they recognized only when caught by a punitive expedition. One could recall that even the Prophet had his problems with them. Islamic society has ever been conscious of the fundamental antagonism between Abel and Cain. And this antagonism is nowhere and at no time more clear than in the early years of the nineteenth century in the Ottoman Empire. Looking at any standard historical map, one is apt to get the impression that the empire was indeed the huge solid block painted on the map. This is true in the sense that no comparable power exercised jurisdiction over that area but it is profoundly untrue in the sense that the Ottoman Empire *ruled* it. The Arab areas consisted rather of a scattered collection of fortified towns between which communication was possible only under armed escort. The task of policing this vast area was beyond the resources of the central government and so public security was virtually nonexistent except in areas controlled by such powerful local lords as Dahir and Jazzar in north Palestine and south Lebanon. These men, like city bosses, had a price, but it was a price worth paying if the peasants gained the security to till their land and reap a crop. All too frequently, however, the local lord was strong only in relation to the peasants. After all manner of taxes and extortions were exacted, the peasant was left to satisfy the "brotherly" demand of the fast moving, far ranging, and ever hungry bedouin with the little that remained. As H. B. Tristram wrote in the middle of the nineteenth century, "Dreary and desolate looked the plain [of Esdraelon] though of exuberant fertility." The reason, the author explains, is that the bedouin carry off in raids everything the peasants produce:

> Only a few weeks ago, the Sakk'r Bedouin, the strongest tribe on the western side of the Jordan, made a raid, and swept off the whole of the cattle on the plain. The villagers naturally live in perpetual terror of these freebooters, and every man guides the plough with one hand, and holds his weapon in the other. (Neh. iv. 17) The protection of the Government has proved worse than none. The Turkish troops, who took care not to arrive till after the retirement of the Bedouin, taught the unhappy fellahin to pray, "Save me from my friends," judiciously selecting the finest plots of standing corn for

their camping-ground, in order to save themselves the trouble of having to forage from a distance; which they followed up in many instances by levying heavy fines on the luckless villagers for the crime of non-resistance to the Sakk'r . . . Finally . . . the Turkish locusts had eaten everything the Arabian hail-storm had left . . .[2]

The bedouin always kept the "inland sea" as a safe retreat from the heavily armed, slow, and thirsty troops of the government; and thus, before the day of the airplane and armored car, they were able to elude tax collector and policeman alike. However, the bedouin have an economic value and this is today often forgotten. Only the bedouin can use the resources of the desert which although scant in the particular are considerable in the whole. From them they supplied the towns with wool, meat, and butter. It was the merit of Midhat Pasha that he recognized both the utility of the bedouin and the futility of war without the means of war. The way to control the bedouin, he argued, was to give them a stake in the settled society. Land he rightfully saw to be the key to public security. Once a man invests in the land, he can be caught. Arabic has a verb which sums up this sentiment rather neatly—*qantara* means both to "possess a hundred weight" and to "settle down." Thus by giving to nomads some permanent reason to expect benefit from peace, the government could induce them to cooperate in its achievement. This was the essence of the Turkish policy as it was evolving when the First World War interrupted; and in a sense all the western techniques and gadgets, roads, railroads, telegraph, and a modern army, which Turkey was acquiring, were aspects of this policy.

The process of change was necessarily slow. Therefore, at points as distant as Palestine, the Ottoman government was forced to operate through men who were as much its partners as its agents. Great tax farmers such as the Beirut family of Sursuk, whose fortunes will be discussed below, were virtually independent princes within the empire. They had the persistent interest, capital, and capacity to control the countryside and to control it more efficiently than the government through its distant, ill-trained, and often corrupt provincial officialdom.

[2] *The Land of Israel* (London: 1865), pp. 125-26.

At the same time the Ottoman government was engaged in plans to settle the bedouin, stimulate its agriculture, and rationalize its administration, others were becoming interested in the land of Palestine. Settlements of both Jews and Protestants began to be founded in the country.

English Jews had long been interested in Jewish religious communities in Palestine and had helped to support such groups as that in Tiberias which Burckhardt described. During the second quarter of the nineteenth century, as they were relieved of civil handicaps in England, it was therefore not surprising that they attempted to communicate this concern to their fellow countrymen. The leader of this movement was Sir Moses Montefiore who was the London agent for the Rothschilds and one of the twelve Jews allowed to trade on the London Exchange. He visited the East in 1827 and 1840 and in the latter visit encountered one of those curious signs of nineteenth-century popular superstition which excited world comment. The disappearance of a child in Damascus led to the charge that Jews had engaged in ritual murder, which in turn produced anti-Jewish riots.[3] Montefiore became involved in the case but could do little to remove what he took to be a prominent cause.[4] However, partly because of this he became interested in ways to uplift the eastern Jewish community. With his great wealth he was able to make significant personal contributions by opening a girls' school and dispensary. The English Jewish community raised £20,000 and an American Jew from New Orleans left a bequest of £10,000, so that in 1855 Montefiore was able to open a small agricultural settlement at Tiberias and another at Safed. His school in Jerusalem closed in 1857 for lack of support and this convinced Montefiore that such projects could only succeed if sponsored by some sort of organization. Then in 1860 the

[3] Achille Laurent, *La Procédure Complète dirigée en 1840 contre les Juifs de Damas* (Paris: 1846).

[4] A plaque in the Capuchin church charging the Jews with having murdered a monk for ritual purposes. The Jewish communities of the Levant in this time were in mixed fortune: some were poor but others lived in regal opulence. See John Bowring, "Report on Commercial Statistics of Syria," *Parliamentary Papers* (London: 1840), XXI, 7; and later in the century see Louis Lortet, *La Syrie d'aujourd'hui* (Paris: 1884), p. 574.

French Jewish community created the Alliance Israélite Universelle, which was the most important Jewish organization in Palestine for the coming decades.

After the murder of Tsar Alexander II in 1881 a vicious pogrom greatly stimulated Jewish emigration from Russia. Most of these Jews went to western Europe and America but the Jewish population in Palestine almost doubled within a decade. By 1893 it was estimated at 100,000. In these years Baron Edmond de Rothschild, both on his own and through the Alliance Israélite Universelle, sponsored a number of agricultural experiments in Palestine. They were not successful, however, until Rothschild insisted that they could no longer be treated as pious charities but must make a profit. To this purpose he hired western (Christian) agronomists, and the agronomists in turn found that the Jews knew nothing about agriculture and began the practice of hiring Arab workers. So the settlements became perhaps the best examples in the history of Palestine of interfaith relations. We shall subsequently see that the change in this policy of using Arab labor had a good deal to do with embittering Arab-Jewish relations after the First World War.

The last European power to enter upon the scene before the First World War was Germany. Germany was opposed to partition of the empire,[5] and in her competition with France, and eventually with Russia, was a most attractive ally for Turkey. Emperor William made a pilgrimage to Jerusalem in 1898 and had a good deal to do with the stimulation of German investment in the empire. The Germans of course played a large part in the creation of the "Berlin-to-Baghdad" Railway and sent training missions to reform the Ottoman army (which had been trained on the patterns of each of her successive European patrons in turn). Germans also began to settle in the empire. Insofar as this affected Palestine it involved a relatively small group of members of the Temple Society. Like the Jewish groups, so the Templers of the late nineteenth century were inspired by religious considerations. Their society was founded by the Lutheran Christophe Hoffman of Würtemberg,

[5] W. L. Langer, *The Diplomacy of Imperialism* (2d ed.; New York: 1951), pp. 637 ff.

who had the notion of settling Christian permanent pilgrims in the Holy Land. Also like the Jews they were primarily committed to agricultural settlements, but unlike the Jews they were excellent farmers. The sons and grandsons of the original settlers were still in Palestine at the beginning of the Second World War.[6]

After the 1906 Franco-British alliance led to the formation of the Entente, a revolution in British policy toward the Middle East and in Ottoman relations with the West was inevitable. Russia remained the natural and main enemy of the Ottoman Empire and now she was the ally of Great Britain. In Turkish terms, this meant that a new counterweight to Russia or to Anglo-Russia must be found. That role could only be played by Germany.[7]

In the distressing years of the Young Turk revolution and the Balkan wars, Germany came to seem the only reliable foreign friend. Turkey was having trouble finding friends. Most of Europe sympathized with the nations in the Balkans which were struggling to throw off their Ottoman allegiance. One by one as they were inflamed by nationalism the Greeks, Bulgars, Serbs, and Armenians had revolted. Nationalism was slower in reaching Turkey itself and to Turks these movements were mere subversion. With justification the Turks could point out that they had tolerated these *millets* within the empire in the terms evolved from the practice of Mohammed. They had not only permitted Christianity of various sorts but had enforced the rule of Christian prelates. Indeed, antagonism and discontent was often the result of the tyranny of these prelates themselves, but in general terms we can see that the Balkan nations were simply unwilling to pay the price demanded by the government for toleration—obedience to the laws of the Ottoman Empire. It was this disavowal of "Ottomanism" which eventually led the

[6] Laurence Oliphant, *Haifa* (London: 1887). On their descendants see H. D. Schmidt, "The Nazi Party in Palestine and the Levant, 1932-39," *International Affairs,* XXVIII (1952).

[7] See Sidney B. Fay, *The Origins of the World War* (New York: 1928), I, 214, 498 ff; Elie Kedourie, *England and the Middle East* (London: 1956), pp. 22 ff.

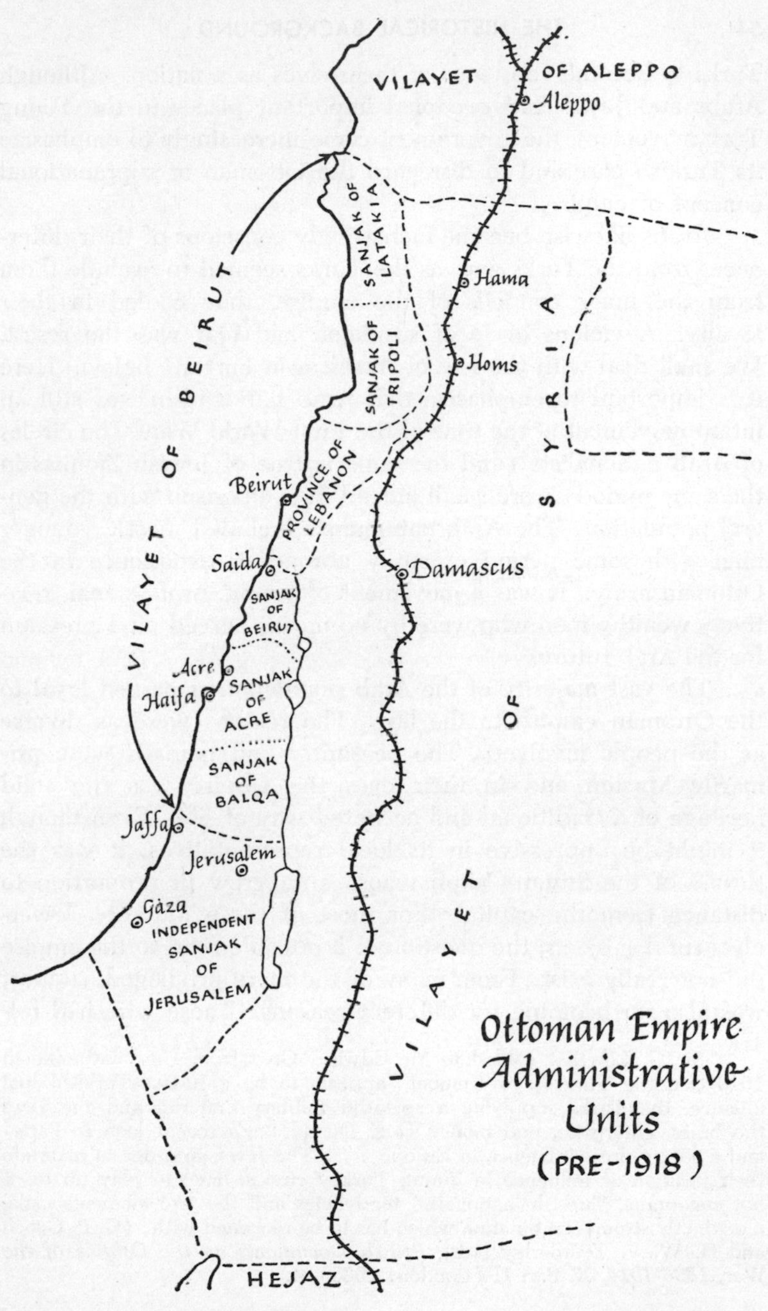
VILAYET OF ALEPPO
Aleppo
SANJAK OF LATAKIA
Hama
SANJAK OF TRIPOLI
Homs
VILAYET OF BEIRUT
SYRIA
Beirut
PROVINCE OF LEBANON
Saida
Damascus
SANJAK OF BEIRUT
Acre
Haifa
SANJAK OF ACRE
OF
SANJAK OF BALQA
Jaffa
Jerusalem
Gaza
INDEPENDENT SANJAK OF JERUSALEM
VILAYET
HEJAZ
Ottoman Empire Administrative Units (PRE-1918)

Turks to become conscious of themselves as a nation. Although Arabs and Jews[8] had occupied important places in the Young Turk movement, the government came increasingly to emphasize its Turkish core and to disregard the Ottoman or supranational concept of empire.

Arabs likewise became increasingly conscious of their differences from the Turks and, as the Turks seemed to exclude them from the inner councils of the empire, they cooled in their loyalty. A vicious cycle of suspicion and fear was the result. We shall deal with the rise of Arabism in Part III below. Here it is important to emphasize that Arab nationalism was still an infant movement at the time of the First World War. The circles of Arab nationalists (and the same is true of Jewish Zionists in the same period) were small indeed in comparison with the general population. The Arab nationalists included mostly younger men with some period of study abroad or experience in the Ottoman army. It was a movement of young, professional, relatively wealthy men who were by no means agreed on a program for the Arab future.

The vast majority of the Arab population remained loyal to the Ottoman empire to the last. The reasons were as diverse as the people involved. The peasantry and nomads were primarily Muslim and in their eyes the empire was the solid heritage of a traditional and accepted way of life. Even though it might be oppressive in its local representatives, it was the throne of the Sultan-Caliph whose aura grew in proportion to distance from the capital. For most of these illiterate, lower-class rural subjects, the question of a possible rival to the empire did not really exist. From many of the more privileged, support was also forthcoming for different reasons. Those who had fol-

[8] Sir G. Lowther cabled to Sir Edward Grey from Constantinople in 1910 that the Turkish government "appears to be a Judaeo-Turkish dual alliance, the Turks supplying a splendid military material and the Jews the brain, enterprise, and money (e.g. Djavid Bey's recent loan in Paris) and a strong press influence in Europe . . . The Jews, in order to maintain their position of influence in Young Turkey circles, have to play up to, if not encourage, Turkish 'nationalist' tendencies and the two elements make a distinctly strong combination which has to be reckoned with" (G. P. Gooch and H. W. V. Temperley [ed.], *British Documents on the Origins of the War, 1898-1914,* X, Part II (London: 1938), 4.

lowed the events of the history of Ottoman-European relations for a generation were well aware of the realities of European imperialism. Italy's attack on Libya in 1911 made a profound impression on the whole literate population of the empire, and tended to coalesce support behind the Ottoman government in spite of its Turkification.

In the empire, however, were the traditional rebel groups. If the Jazzars had been partially tamed by the telegraph and the railway, the Dahirs had not. In the tribes of the Great Syrian desert, the Euphrates valley, and the Arabian steppe were many virtually independent rulers. They were little concerned with the question of nationalism, although they maintained a pride in Arabic culture, but they were interested in the subsidies, the arms, and the protection offered them by the Government of India and subsequently by the British administration in Egypt.

Lastly, the Arab population had its own religious minorities who were as afraid of an Arab-Muslim hegemony as the Arabs were of a Turkish tyranny. Particularly the Maronite Christians of the Lebanon were anxious to expand their autonomy into an independence from the empire under French guarantee.

7. THE FIRST WORLD WAR AND ITS SPORE

As in Europe so in the Middle East, the First World War was a great *rite de passage.* In its course was celebrated the death, after a century of "sickness," of the Ottoman Empire and the creation of a tangle of international agreements and political arrangements which set the course of events down to our own day.

Those who had accepted the description of the Ottoman Empire as the "sick man of Europe" could only explain the Turkish war effort as a remarkable *tour de force.* It is truly difficult to explain in any other way. Its ill-equipped and ill-supported armies were forced to cover, and until late in the war did successfully cover, a longer potential front than any other power. In effect the whole frontier was a target for British, French, Russian, and other armies; and within the empire were several ethnic groups which were emotionally—some even were formally—committed to the Allied side.

We have pointed out above that the Arabs, although more intimately linked to the Turks by religion and culture than any of the other ethnic groups had been, came to feel that they had no future in the empire. Those who were non-Muslim tended to look for succor to their traditional European protectors, now Turkey's opponents; others conspired to create an Arab national state; and still others bided their time in uncertain neutrality. In alarm, the Turkish military governor of Syria found himself obliged to break up and scatter most of the Arab regiments in the Ottoman army.[1] This did not prevent many Arabs from fighting on the Ottoman side in the war, which some of them did with distinction,[2] but it did remove from contact with the Arab general population those young men of daring and ability who had conspired to create the Arab revolt. The effect was just what the Turks expected. Out of long habit, the population acquiesced.[3] When the population grew restive, the Turks were prepared to take whatever security measures were required, as they showed by hanging a number of Arab young men suspected of nationalist agitation.[4] As a result, the role played by most of the Arabs in the war "was one of passive suffering rather than active participation."[5] The coast was blockaded, the Turkish forces had to live off the land, and typhus and other diseases took a heavy toll.[6]

[1] See below, Part III.

[2] For example, the 27th (Palestine) Arab Division. See Cyril Falls, *Military Operations: Egypt and Palestine* (London: 1930), pp. 34-35, 42; Sir Ronald Storrs, *Orientations* (London: 1945), p. 351.

[3] See Mohammed Kurd Ali, *Memoirs* (Washington, D. C.: 1954—a partial English translation of the original), p. 38, for the fear of collective responsibility. Families thus became hostages for their adventurous younger sons.

[4] George Haddad, *Fifty Years of Modern Syria and Lebanon* (Beirut: 1950), p. 48; George Antonius, *The Arab Awakening* (New York: 1939), p. 186. The Mufti of Gaza was among those hanged (Storrs, p. 351).

[5] Albert Hourani, *Syria and Lebanon* (London: 1946), p. 48.

[6] Sir Ronald Storrs, who was first military governor of Jerusalem, describes the condition of that city when the British troops arrived (pp.

The war was, as we have said, a tour de force, but few who encountered the Ottoman armies failed to admire their martial qualities. Ottoman troops captured a whole British task force (as we should today call it) of 10,000 men in south Iraq and managed both to cut the Iranian oil supply for a short period and to hold off a large British army until 1918; in Palestine the fighting was heavy and balanced—the Turks even briefly cut the Suez canal early in the war—until Allenby's strategy began to pay off late in the war; and Gallipoli has come down to us as a synonym for dogged determination as the British effort to break through a sea route to Russia failed. Britain was acutely aware of the importance of the Middle East, partly for those reasons we know so well today: oil and the transport route to Asia. Added to these were reasons of great import in that era—the desire to control what was taken to be the nexus of the Islamic world. Britain as the ruler of India, France as the ruler of North Africa, and Russia as the ruler of Central Asia had scores of millions of Muslim subjects and could not neglect this fact. Perhaps even more immediate was the desperate need in the hungry and decaying Russian Empire for the sinews of war if she was to divert German forces from the embattled western front.

As a result of these factors—Turkish might, Muslim restiveness, and Russian needs, the Allies, and especially Britain, entered into a series of agreements of a "tactical" nature to accomplish various aspects of this policy. Within two years Britain had made three conflicting statements, to one of which the Arab allies were to rally as the fount of their rights in the Middle East. To another, Zionists pinned their hopes; and on yet a third, the French based their claims to culminate their traditional desires of a French enclave in the Levant.

First in point of time came the letters exchanged between the Arab Sharif Hussein of Mecca, who was then an official in the Ottoman administration, and the British High Commissioner

---

294-96); and the Arabic novel, *ar-Raghif* (The Loaf), by Tawfiq Yusif Awwad, captures the atmosphere of desperation. Also see Cmd 1499, p. 3; and Government of Palestine, *Report on Palestine Administration* (London: 1922), p. 9.

of Egypt, Sir Henry McMahon. This is the Hussein-McMahon correspondence, which contains the terms upon which the Arabs revolted and entered the war on the Allied side.

The first letter in the series may be dated, by an accompanying letter, as of July 14, 1915. In it the Arabs set out their terms. These demands were answered in a letter from Sir Henry McMahon of October 24, 1915. The correspondence was not officially published until 1939,[7] when a special Anglo-Arab committee was set up to evaluate its importance to Palestine. The existence of the exchange was of course known and the terms had been printed in part in 1919, in the Paris newspaper *Le Temps*;[8] but in spite of the urging of Earl Grey, who was Foreign Minister during this period,[9] the British government refused for twenty years to publish the full text.

Nowhere in the text (which was in Arabic) of the letters is Palestine specifically mentioned. In the first letter, the Arabs had claimed the whole area now divided between Syria, Lebanon, Israel, Jordan, Iraq and Saudi Arabia. In reply the British excluded from the area promised to the Arabs the land to the west of the "districts" (*wilayat*) (the Arabic plural) of Aleppo, Hama, Homs, and Damascus. The later British contention was that *wilayat* meant here both "town" in the cases of Aleppo, Hama, and Homs and the Turkish administrative district known as a *vilayet* in the case of Damascus (see map, p. 53). But if the word means the same in all four instances, then it must mean only town or township, since the towns of Hama and Homs were in the same *vilayet* and only the sea is to the west of the *vilayet* of Aleppo. West of the district of Damascus is Mount Lebanon, which had long been subject to strong separatist feelings and

[7] The Emir Feisal received two sets of the correspondence. The one he got from King Hussein contained (so Feisal was told) an extra letter promising more than that granted in the set which he received from the British government. This led to considerable embarrassment for Feisal in his meetings with the British Cabinet and to a clash with his father. See E. L. Woodward and R. Butler, *Documents on British Foreign Policy, 1919-1939,* First Series, IV (1919) (London: 1952), Nos. 283, 289, 290, 291, 293, 374.

[8] See *Le Temps,* September 18, 1919.

[9] In a speech in the House of Lords on March 27, 1923, partly reprinted in Cmd 5974, pp. 18-19.

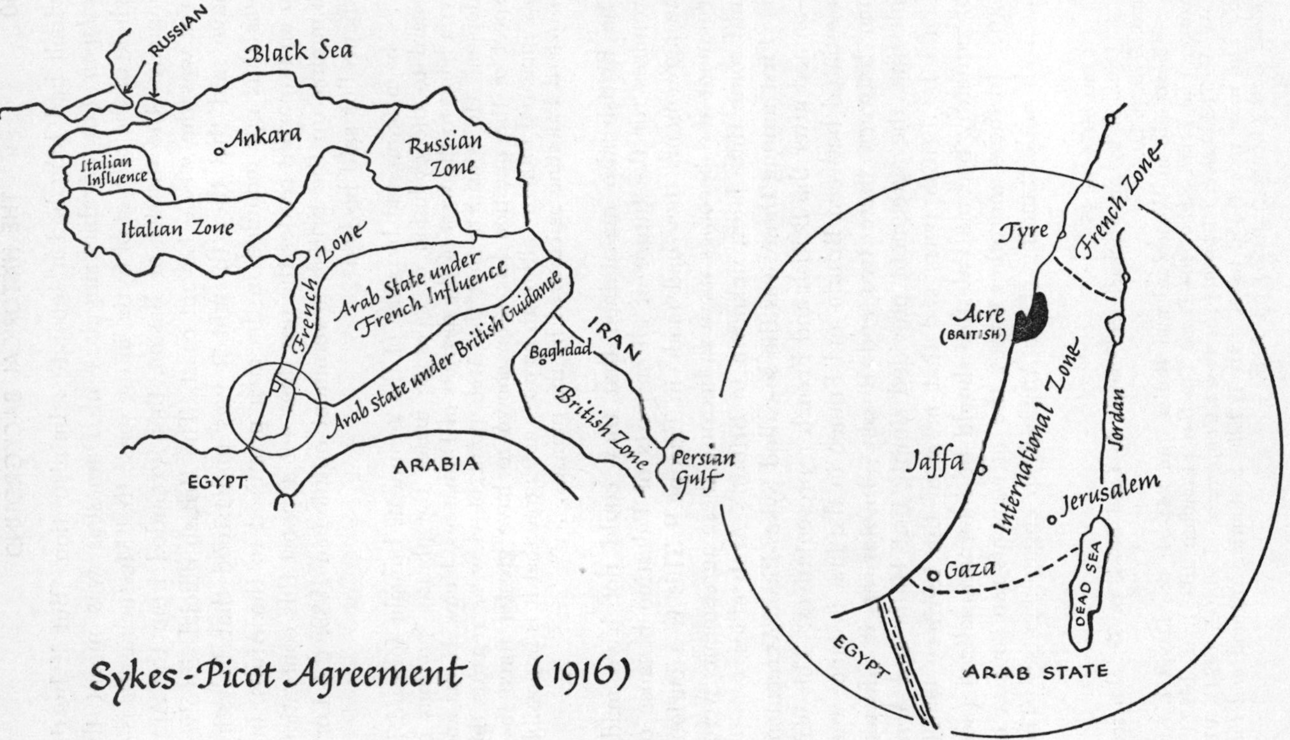
RUSSIAN
Black Sea
Ankara
Russian Zone
Italian Influence
Italian Zone
French Zone
Arab State under French Influence
Arab State under British Guidance
IRAN
Baghdad
British Zone
Persian Gulf
EGYPT
ARABIA
Tyre
French Zone
Acre (BRITISH)
International Zone
Jordan
Jaffa
Jerusalem
Gaza
DEAD SEA
EGYPT
ARAB STATE

Sykes-Picot Agreement (1916)

which had long had a separate administration. But if by the *wilayah* (the Arabic singular) of Damascus was meant the whole of the *vilayet* of Syria, in the sense that Massachusetts is—vaguely—the district of Boston, then excluded from the Arab area was the whole Levant coast. The British officials involved have said that they thought it was understood that Palestine was thus not included in the area promised to the Arabs, but to an impartial reader the text does not support this contention. Summing up the British government opinion in 1939, the Lord Chancellor said he had

> . . . been impressed by some of the arguments brought forward in regard to the exclusion of Palestine under the phrase "portions of Syria lying to the west of the districts of Damascus, Homs, Hama and Aleppo." He considers that the Arab point of view as regards this aspect of the question has been shown to have greater force than has appeared hitherto, although he does not agree that it is impossible to regard Palestine as covered by the phrase . . .[10]

The British also maintained that they could not have made promises for the future of all or parts of Palestine because of the agreements they had made in Europe.[11] This is a curious argument and becomes more so because these agreements were, until some time later, unknown to Britain's Arab allies.

First among these was the so-called Sykes-Picot Agreement —named after the British and French representatives. This was negotiated between Britain and France in the first instance and then between these two and Russia. Insofar as it affected Palestine, the agreement provided simply that Haifa and Acre should be British ports and that most of the territory which subsequently became Palestine should be internationalized (see map). In these and other senses, the agreements ran counter to the Arab understanding of the Anglo-Arab engagements.[12] The

[10] Cmd 5974, p. 45.

[11] Opinion by Sir Michael McDonnell, in Cmd 5974, p. 38; also see Cmd 5479, p. 20.

[12] Texts are in Woodward and Butler, pp. 241-54; see David Lloyd George, *The Truth About the Peace Treaties* (London: 1938), II, 1022 ff; H. W. V. Temperley, *History of the Peace Conference* (London: 1924), VI, 1 ff. The most recent and novel study is Elie Kedourie, *England and the Middle East* (London: 1956) pp. 29 ff.

Arabs had heard of the agreement, by way of diplomatic hints before, but it was not until the Bolshevik government published the Russian Foreign Office Archives late in 1917 [13] that the Arabs knew the full extent of the agreements. This information was obligingly passed along by the German General Staff to the Turks, who relayed it, with an offer of a separate peace, to Hussein.[14] To his credit it must be said that Hussein simply turned the message over to his British ally with a request for an explanation. In reply, the British informed him that the Sykes-Picot Agreement was merely a series of exchanges of views which in any case no longer represented the situation created by the Russian withdrawal from the war.[15]

The second, and much more important, European agreement was the Balfour Declaration of November 2, 1917.[16] During the next thirty years this was to the Zionists what the Hussein-McMahon correspondence was to the Arabs: the final rallying point in the struggle for supremacy over British policy on Palestine. The declaration is disarmingly simple, is so balanced in phraseology as to be virtually meaningless, is described only as an "expression of sympathy," and is only sixty-eight words long. Yet it was the result of months of discussion in the British Cabinet and was carefully and deliberately constructed to tread the finest rail on the fence of political indecision. Before we deal with the text itself, it is necessary to set forth the circumstances in which it was framed.

The key figure among the group of supporters of the idea of Zionism in England was Dr. Chaim Weizmann. He was particularly fortunate in having the support of the secretary of the War Cabinet on Middle Eastern Affairs, Mark Sykes, and the influential editor of the *Manchester Guardian*, C. P. Scott, and his lead writer, Herbert Sidebotham. These men made a con-

[13] *Izvestia*, November 24, 1917. See F. S. Cocks, *The Secret Treaties and Understandings* (London: 1918).

[14] The text of the Turkish message is given in Antonius, pp. 255-56.

[15] Woodward and Butler, No. 286, p. 407; and Antonius, p. 257.

[16] Sir Mark Sykes, who was instrumental in the negotiations leading to the Balfour Declaration, realized before it was framed that it ran counter at least to the Sykes-Picot Agreement (Christopher Sykes, "The Prosperity of His Servant," *Two Studies in Virtue* [London: 1953], p. 182).

certed effort to convince the government of the value to Britain of a pro-Zionist declaration.[17]

Their efforts could not have come at a more favorable moment. In the first place, European Jewry was naturally suspicious of the Entente, for the same reason that the Turks were hostile to the Entente: Russia was a member. To the Turks, Russia was the aggressor par excellence; and to the Jews, she was the home of the pogrom. Russian oppression had displaced many eastern European Jews—including Weizmann himself—and sent them into the West, where some had reached positions of influence. Thus, to a considerable extent, Great Britain and France labored under the bad reputation of their ally. Germany, on the contrary, had perhaps the best record in Europe of something better than mere toleration; there Jews had been accepted into the national life of the country. Many Jews had achieved national prominence and the Jewish community as a whole was more assimilated than in almost any other European country. Germany had not yet had her pogroms or even her Dreyfus case. When World War I broke out, the Zionist Organization declared itself neutral but retained an office in Germany.

The Russian Revolution somewhat reversed the situation in Russia by bringing a number of Jews into key government and public-opinion-forming positions. The strong sentiment in Russia for leaving the war was an important element in the Revolution, and both the British Foreign Office and the German General Staff thought that Jews in Russia were leaders of this move. To encourage this feeling and to win over those who wavered, the Germans put pressure on their Turkish ally to grant concessions to Jews to colonize Palestine.[18] Turkey delayed, perhaps fearing to antagonize the Arabs who had remained on her side in the war,[19] until the moment had passed, but eventually, as

[17] The "British Palestine Committee," as this group was called, was founded in 1916. See Nevill Barbour, *Nisi Dominus* (London: 1946), pp. 57-58; Temperley, VI, 172; and the work noted in previous footnote.

[18] Temperley, VI, 173; and Lloyd George, II, 1121.

[19] See M. Perlmann, "Chapters of Arab-Jewish Diplomacy 1918-1922," *Jewish Social Studies* (New York), VI (1944), 128.

her armies were being pushed out of Palestine, granted the Zionists a concession there similar to the Balfour Declaration.[20]

At the time the Germans were making a determined effort to win Jewish support, Britain was worried both about keeping Russia in the war and about American nonintervention in the war. In both cases, she seemed (for the documents are not yet completely available) to feel that Jewish support could greatly aid her policy.[21] It thus would appear likely that the Balfour Declaration is rightly to be regarded as a declaration *through* rather than *to* English Jews, of whom a good many were opposed to Zionism. The real audiences were in Russia, Germany, and America. To inform them of the Balfour Declaration millions of leaflets were dropped by air, circulated by hand, and printed in the press.[22] In the Middle East, however, the declaration was withheld by military censorship for over a year, until May 1, 1919, when it was read in Nablus, Palestine, by Allenby's successor, General Bols.[23]

The declaration reads as follows:

I [Balfour] have much pleasure in conveying to you [Lord Rothschild] on behalf of His Majesty's Government the following declaration of

[20] The Turkish concession was provisionally announced December 31, 1917, but was not granted until July 1918.

[21] Temperley, VI, 172-74; Mark Sykes, in particular, was alarmed by the American position and thought pro-German Jews to be the cause. (C. Sykes, p. 181); Lloyd George noted that "their [the Jews'] aid in this respect [financial affairs] would have a special value when the Allies had almost exhausted the gold and marketable securities available for American purchases" (II, 1122).

[22] Cmd 5479, pp. 22-23.

[23] M. F. Abcarius, *Palestine Through the Fog of Propaganda* (London: 1946?), p. 67; the chief political officer, Col. Meinertzhagen (whose appointment had been urged by Weizmann as one who had "the full confidence of the Zionist Organisation" and who was a Zionist himself), reported on September 26, 1919, that "the people of Palestine are not at present in a fit state to be told openly that the establishment of Zionism in Palestine is the policy to which H.M.G., America and France are committed. They certainly do not realise this fact" (Woodward and Butler, p. 427). For this reason he had not, he continued, circulated Lord Curzon's message of August 4 saying that the Mandate of Palestine would go to Britain and would contain the Balfour Declaration, that "the matter is a 'chose jugée' and continued agitation would be useless and detrimental" (p. 329).

sympathy with Jewish Zionist aspirations, which has been submitted to and approved by the Cabinet:

"His Majesty's Government view with favour the establishment in Palestine of a National Home for the Jewish people, and will use their best endeavours to facilitate the achievement of this object, it being clearly understood that nothing shall be done which may prejudice the civil and religious rights of existing non-Jewish communities in Palestine, or the rights and political status enjoyed by Jews in any other country."

I should be grateful if you would bring this declaration to the knowledge of the Zionist Federation.[24]

In this form the declaration was approved, before issue, by President Wilson and subsequently was endorsed by the French and Italian governments. It was reaffirmed at the San Remo Conference in 1920, was written into the Mandate instrument for Palestine and so passed by the Council of the League of Nations, was unanimously passed by both Houses of Congress, and approved by the Vatican. In 1922 the Colonial Office declared it to be the basis of policy in Palestine and as such "not susceptible to change."

But what did it mean?

8. EMIR FEISAL AND DR. WEIZMANN

At the Peace Conference in 1919 neither the Arab representative Emir Feisal nor the Zionist representative Dr. Weizmann could, of course, be sure that the fate of Palestine was sealed. Neither had access to the information which has subsequently become available, and both must have realized that all of the Powers were feeling their way into a new world in which many courses could be set.

Before the Peace Conference, King Hussein had been informed by Mark Sykes and Georges Picot that Arab aspirations for independence in Syria and Iraq would be limited in certain respects. It is not clear how Hussein understood this, but he

[24] Cmd 5479, p. 22.

seems to have thought his government would have to accept political advisors from the Powers unless—as very nearly happened—they quarreled over policy in the Middle East. Hussein was probably aware of the hostility which a number of British statesmen and local officials felt toward France, and he may have been banking on winning more at the Peace Conference than he had so far gained in his exchanges with the Foreign Office through Sir Henry McMahon. Then, two months after the Anglo-Turkish armistice was signed, the British Government representative, Commander Hogarth of the Arab Bureau in Cairo, informed Hussein that British policy for Palestine foresaw some sort of control over the Holy Places and intended to allow Jewish immigration "in so far as is compatible with the freedom of the existing population, both economic and political . . ." [1] Hussein must have felt that this statement clashed with a somewhat vague Anglo-French announcement known as the "Declaration to the Seven" [2] which seemed to promise real independence and was, moreover, by British order widely circulated in the Arab press.[3] In effect, in this period, as during most of the Mandate, the Arabs were never sure what British policy was, and consequently they were never able to decide between trying to work within the framework of what the policy seemed to be or trying to upset the situation and so reverse the policy. We can see this indecision most clearly in the complicated relations between the Arabs and the Zionists.

In regard to both Hussein and his son Feisal, at this period, it must be remembered that their careers had given them only a limited contact with the settled populations of the Levant coast. They had made contact with the Syrian Arab nationalist groups only in the middle of the war, and of course during the war had little chance to gauge the development of opinion in those areas. Moreover, as claimants, bargaining from the virtuous weakness of promises and past services, they could not afford

[1] Cmd 5964, p. 3; message dated January 4, 1918.
[2] *Ibid.*, pp. 5-6.
[3] David Lloyd George, *The Truth About the Peace Treaties* (London: 1938), II, 1036-37.

to lose all by trying to gain a part of what they claimed. It is these factors which form a background to Feisal's negotiations with Weizmann.

Weizmann, partly as a result of urging by Sir Mark Sykes, went to the Middle East in the spring of 1918 to make contact with the Arabs. He stopped in Cairo long enough to win Dr. Nimr Faris, editor of the influential newspaper *al-Muqattam* and an early member of an Arab secret society, over to support of Arab-Jewish understanding and cooperation.[4] Then he went to Jerusalem. There the military governor, Ronald Storrs, in spite of his personal misgivings, assembled the notables of the town so that Weizmann might explain his mission.[5] Weizmann denied the allegation that Zionists sought political power, and he stressed cooperation between brother Semites. The local Arabs do not seem to have been much impressed, but Weizmann was to achieve more success on his next visit. At the suggestion of Allenby, he went to Aqaba to meet Feisal.[6] We have Weizmann's version of the visit[7] and can infer Feisal's understanding of the visit by his subsequent public statements.

We know that Feisal felt terribly isolated and ignorant of the ways of the European powers. Later in the year, he and a staff including Nuri Said (later Prime Minister of Iraq) met with Zionist leaders in London. At a banquet given in his honor by Lord Rothschild, he is reported to have said:

> I have been told by people who regard themselves as civilized that the Jews want our Mosque in Jerusalem as a temple, and to grind down and stamp out the peasantry of Palestine. For my part, I know that no true Jew holds these views. These insinuations have no effect on any of us. We are demanding Arab freedom, and we would show ourselves unworthy of it, if we did not now, as I do, say to the Jews —welcome back home—and cooperate with them to the limit of the ability of the Arab State.
>
> Dr. Weizmann's ideals are ours, and we will expect you, without our asking to help us in return. No state can be built up in the

[4] George Antonius, *The Arab Awakening* (New York: 1939) p. 270.
[5] Sir Ronald Storrs, *Orientations* (London: 1945), pp. 340-41.
[6] M. Perlmann, "Chapters of Arab-Jewish Diplomacy 1918-1922," *Jewish Social Studies* (New York), VI (1944), 132.
[7] *Royal Commission Minutes of Evidence* (London: 1936), p. 37.

Near East without the goodwill of the Great Powers, but it requires more than that. It requires the borrowing from Europe of ideals and materials and knowledge and experience. To make these fit for us, we must translate them from European shape into Arab shape—and what intermediary could we find in the world more suitable than you? For you have all the knowledge of Europe, and are cousins by blood . . .[8]

It is clear that at this period Feisal was far more worried about French intervention in the Levant than he was about any possible future clash with Zionism. France had meanwhile laid claim to most of the Levant coast; and even if she chose not to push into the interior, Feisal realized before he left the Middle East that her position would give France a strangle hold on the Arab state. The British Foreign Office *seemed* prepared to agree to the setting aside of the Sykes-Picot Agreement, on which France's claims rested, but seemed equally firm on insisting that the Balfour Declaration must stand. In these circumstances Feisal must have realized as few Arabs have since that politics is indeed the science of the possible and so came to a provisional agreement with Dr. Weizmann.[9] The agreement was written up as a formal document in eleven articles. In brief they recognized the need to work together to achieve their mutual aims, to give effect to the Balfour Declaration, to facilitate Jewish immigration provided the rights of the Arab peasant and tenant farmers be protected, to ensure freedom of worship and protection of Holy Places, to provide Jewish economic help to the Arabs, and to constitute the British government as their

[8] *Jewish Chronicle,* January 3, 1919; quoted in Perlmann, p. 134.

[9] During Feisal's visit to London in the fall, Colonel Cornwallis reported that "I understand that Dr. Weizmann, in return for the Emir's help in Palestine towards realization of Zionist aspirations, proposes to give money and advisers, if required, to the Arab Government and claims that the Zionists can persuade the French Government to waive their claims of influence in the interior. The Emir is strongly inclined to come to an agreement but matters are at present at a deadlock since the Emir asks the Zionists to throw in their lot definitely with the Arabs against the French while Dr. Weizmann is in favour of allowing the French to occupy the coastal districts saying that they can be squeezed out later" (E. L. Woodward and R. Butler, *Documents on British Foreign Policy, 1919-1939,* First Series IV (1919) (London: 1952), pp. 421-22).

arbitrator. To this agreement Feisal appended in Arabic above his signature the following condition:

> Provided the Arabs obtain their independence as demanded in my Memorandum dated the 4th of January, 1919, to the Foreign Office of the Government of Great Britain, I shall concur in the above articles. But if the slightest modification or departure were to be made I shall not then be bound by a single word of the present Agreement which shall be deemed void and of no account or validity, and I shall not be answerable in any way whatsoever.[10]

Feisal realized, it would appear from a statement made in March, that the local population of Palestine strongly opposed the creation of a Jewish state.[11] But Feisal seemed to think he could act on his own, to lose what he must in order to save his state from the French. However, like some other figures at the Peace Conference, Feisal lost sight of the intensity of feeling at home. In Palestine itself, the coming of the Zionist commission had roused the strongest feelings and fears in the local population. The Assistant Political Officer in Jerusalem wrote in August, 1919,

> . . . if we mean to carry out any sort of Zionist policy we must do so with military force . . . In my opinion, Dr. Weizmann's agreement with Emir Feisal is not worth the paper it is written on or the energy wasted in the conversation to make it. On the other hand, if it becomes sufficiently known among the Arabs, it will be somewhat in the nature of a noose about Feisal's neck, for he will be regarded by the Arab population as a traitor. No greater mistake could be made than to regard Feisal as a representative of Palestinian Arabs (Moslem and Christian natives of Palestine who speak Arabic); he is in favour with them so long as he embodies Arab nationalism and represents their views, but would no longer have any power over them if they thought he had made any sort of agreement with Zionists and meant to abide by it.[12]

When he returned to Syria in the spring, Feisal found feeling much more roused than when he had left, and consequently found himself less a free agent than he had assumed when in

[10] Antonius, pp. 437-39; also see pp. 284 ff.
[11] Perlmann, p. 139.
[12] Woodward and Butler, pp. 364-65.

Europe. In spite of Feisal, the Arab Congress at Damascus repudiated the essence of his agreement with Weizmann, saying:

> We reject the claims of the Zionists for the establishment of a Jewish commonwealth in that part of southern Syria which is known as Palestine, and we are opposed to Jewish immigration into any part of the country. We do not acknowledge that they have a title, and we regard their claims as a grave menace to our national, political and economic life. Our Jewish fellow-citizens shall continue to enjoy the rights and to bear the responsibilities which are ours in common.[13]

When he returned to London in September, Feisal informed the Zionists that he could agree only to limited immigration and that he had intended that the Jewish homeland should be thought of as a province of the larger Arab state. "I quite understand," he said, "the desire of Jews to acquire a country, a homeland. But so far as Palestine is concerned . . . it must be subject to the right and aspirations of the sentiments of the present possessors of the land." Jewish rights he brushed aside as the sort which would give the Arabs a right to take over Spain, which they had ruled for as long as the Jews had Palestine.[14]

Feisal's Syrian days were numbered. In March 1920, Feisal was named king of Syria and Palestine by an Arab congress at Damascus and accepted. The governments of Britain and France repudiated the move and in San Remo, on April 24, 1920, the Powers decided to establish mandates over Syria, Palestine, and Iraq. There followed an outburst of popular resentment in the Levant. The French had in the meantime been almost totally pushed out of the districts of Turkey they had tried to seize, and had partly because of this managed to concentrate some 90,000 troops in the Levant. On July 14, 1920, the French general officer commanding the troops, Gouraud, sent Feisal an ultimatum demanding that he accept the mandate. Feisal accepted, but the French decided that since a minor attack had been made by Arab horsemen on a French outpost, they were entitled to

[13] See Antonius, pp. 440 ff, for text.

[14] *Jewish Chronicle,* October 3, 1919; quoted in Perlmann, p. 143.

disregard the terms they had set and so advanced, routed the small Arab force opposing them, seized Damascus, and overthrew the Arab government.[15]

Never again were the Arabs of Palestine to find a spokesman of the international stature of Feisal and not for years were they to be represented by an Arab state with even the shadowy prestige enjoyed by Feisal's Syrian government.

9. ESTABLISHMENT OF THE MANDATE

Between October 1917 and September 1918 the whole of the area which was subsequently split off from "geographical Syria" and made into the Mandate of Palestine was occupied by British forces. It was placed under a military government known by the initials of its title as OETA and this administration was to govern the land until July 1920.

OETA felt itself obliged by the rules of war to make no major changes in the social or economic structure of the country and to try to maintain, insofar as was possible, the *status quo ante*.[1] General Allenby issued a proclamation to this effect and informed the Emir Feisal on October 17, 1918, that

> whatever measures might be taken during the period of military administration . . . were purely provisional and could not be allowed to prejudice the final settlement by the peace conference . . . I added that the instructions to the military governors would preclude their mixing in political affairs, and that I should remove them if I found any of them contravening these orders.[2]

Immediately after OETA was established, it was found that the land system of Palestine was in a state of chaos. Not only had the retreating Turks taken along with them most of the key

[15] H. W. V. Temperley, *History of the Peace Conference* (London: 1924), VI, 156-59; Arnold Toynbee, *The Islamic World Since the Peace Settlement, Survey of International Affairs* (1925), I, 388-89.

[1] *Manual of Military Law*, Ch. 14 (quoted in Cmd 5479, pp. 153-54).

[2] Cmd 5974, p. 54. The circumstances surrounding the proclamation, which was written by Sir Mark Sykes, are recounted in Sir Ronald Storrs, *Orientations* (London: 1945), p. 301. Text of the proclamation is in H. Luke and E. Keith Roach, *Handbook of Palestine and Trans-Jordan* (London: 1934), p. 28.

administrative personnel of the district, but they had also taken the official registers of land holdings. Moreover, it was soon discovered that even if these official registers were available, they could give only a partial account of actual ownership. The reason was that a dual set of land records, one open and official and the other secret and private, had been kept since the late-nineteenth-century Turkish ban on foreigners owning property in Palestine.[3] For half a century, the many foreigners who had bought land had registered it in the name of some citizen of the empire. And because the land might have been sold or inherited several times during the half century, it was often difficult to decide just who held title. Moreover, since the Ottoman land-tenure system was superimposed on local usage, rights of various sorts were often exercised by different parties in any given piece of land. (On some of these cases the courts were to spend a good part of their energies for the next thirty years.) Lastly, it was found by OETA that in the privation of war, a number of small holders had been forced to mortgage their lands at ruinous rates and that they would be dispossessed if forced to meet their obligations immediately. For these reasons, in November 1918 OETA declared the land registry closed, voided all transactions since the occupation,[4] and arranged to lend sums of money to farmers to buy animals and seed.

During the tenure of OETA upwards of 5,000 Jewish immigrants were allowed to enter the country,[5] Hebrew was adopted as one of the official languages of the country, and a Zionist delegation was allowed to tour the country to survey development possibilities. In these ways, OETA has been accused of falling short of the terms of military government. But taken as a whole, it made the best of a very difficult situation.

Meanwhile, the future status of Palestine was being dis-

[3] Col. 5, p. 41; E. L. Woodward and R. Butler, *Documents on British Foreign Policy 1919-1939,* First Series (London: 1952), IV (1919), pp. 338-39.

[4] Government of Palestine, *Report* (London: 1922), p. 110.

[5] No exact figure has been seen by the author. Churchill (Cmd 1700, p. 19) gives the figure 25,000 in June 1922 for the total to that date and the reports of the civil administration account for *ca.* 20,000 of this (*Report* [July 1920–December 1921], pp. 126-27; *Report* [1922], pp. 52-55).

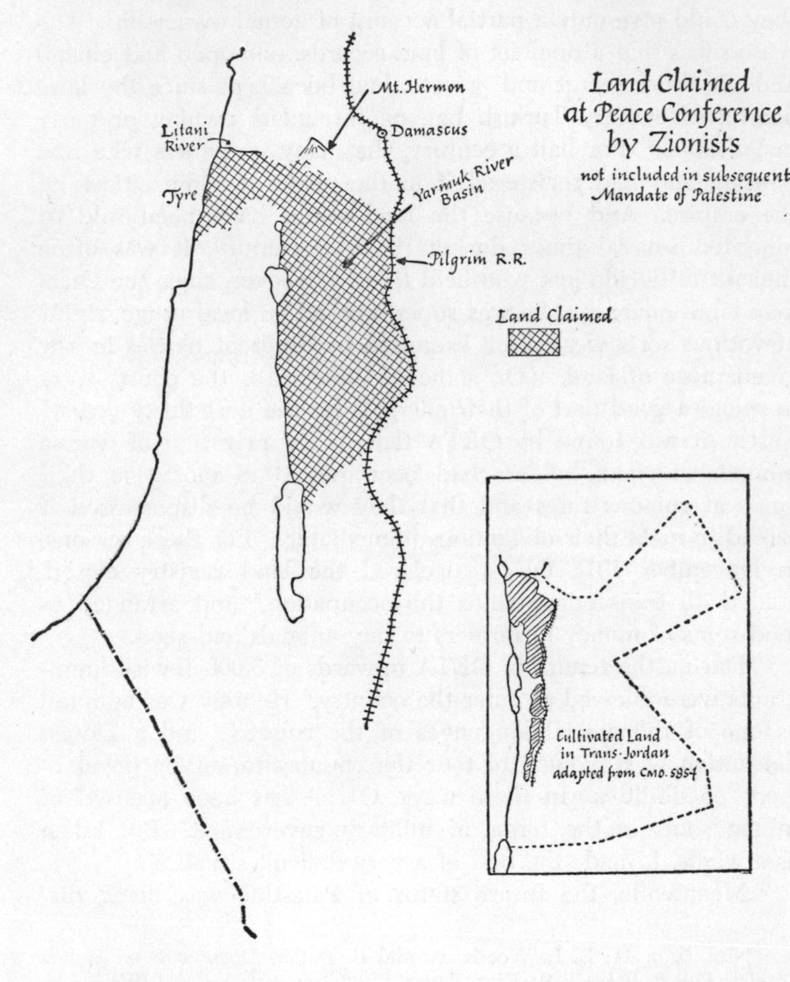
Land Claimed
at Peace Conference
by Zionists
not included in subsequent
Mandate of Palestine
Mt. Hermon
Damascus
Litani
River
Tyre
Yarmuk River
Basin
Pilgrim R.R.
Land Claimed
Cultivated Land
in Trans-Jordan
adapted from CMD. 5854

cussed in Europe and in Damascus. The National Syrian Congress at Damascus declared that Syria, including Palestine, should be recognized as an independent Arab state or at the least should be entrusted as an Arab state under mandate to the United States. In Paris, the complicated series of arrangements made by the British government in the stress of the war began to cause the utmost confusion at the Peace Conference.

We have summarized above in Chapter 7 the conditions in which these arrangements were made. The Zionists had gone to the Peace Conference with the Balfour Declaration as their foundation; their representatives Weizmann and Sokolow wanted the Conference members to "recognize the historic title of the Jewish people to Palestine and the right of the Jews to reconstitute in Palestine their National Home" (see map). In reply to a question from Secretary of State Lansing, Weizmann defined "National Home" as a situation created by governmental arrangements, not necessarily administered by Jews at first, which would allow them to "build up gradually a nationality, and so make Palestine as Jewish as America is American or England English. Later on, when the Jews formed the large majority, they would be ripe to establish such a Government as would answer to the state of development of the country and to their ideals." [6]

This was more or less the interpretation placed upon the declaration by the Arabs. And to this interpretation most were hostile. The Arabs living in Palestine pointed out that the Jewish population of Palestine was only 10 per cent of the total. They also felt that this was a direct denial of the privilege afforded them in President Wilson's Twelfth Point, which stated that

> the other [non-Turkish] nationalities which are now under Turkish rule should be assured an undoubted security of life and an absolutely unmolested opportunity of autonomous development.

They gave British political officers on the spot to understand that they would never peacefully allow the imposition of a Jew-

[6] David Lloyd George, *The Truth About the Peace Treaties* (London: 1938), II, 1156-58.

ish majority in Palestine. General Bols, the chief administrator of Palestine, urged that the Zionist program be dropped as inimical to public security in Palestine, and the King-Crane Commission, which President Wilson sent to the Middle East to ascertain the wishes of the population, reported an overwhelming rejection by the population of Zionist aspirations.[7]

The British government definition of the key phrases in the Balfour Declaration is somewhat more complex. In 1936 the Palestine Royal Commission, which was allowed to examine records not yet available to the public, noted that some of the phrasing in the statement was the result of a compromise between factions within the Cabinet. The phrase "a National Home," for example, was thought to meet the demands of those who wanted to establish some sort of Jewish state and those who, at most, would agree only to a "Home" in Palestine for the Jews. The article "a" is supposed to have replaced "the" when non-Zionist English Jews objected to the notion of Palestine being *the* Jewish homeland and pointed out that they felt themselves to be, and intended to remain, English.[8] They also realized that such a strong statement could be used to weaken their position in European society.

The word "Home" is equated to *Heimstätte,* something less than state. (The Arabic translation, incidentally, fails to catch the subtlety of the distinction, making it if anything stronger than a more abstract notion of government.)[9] To the British

[7] Their report was probably never read by President Wilson. The conclusions were reported to the British government on July 19, 1919 (Woodward and Butler, pp. 315-16). The report was published in the December 2, 1922, issue of *Editor and Publisher* Magazine. Insofar as it relates to Zionism, the essence of the report is contained in prior dispatches from British intelligence officers, e.g., Woodward and Butler, pp. 272-74, 281-82.

[8] The Secretary of State for India, Mr. Edwin Montagu, strongly opposed Zionism (Lloyd George, pp. 1132-34). He "accepted the [Balfour] declaration as a military expedient." Also see Blanche Dugdale, *Arthur James Balfour, 1906-1930* (London: 1936), pp. 214 ff.

[9] The Arabic contains three of the strongest modern words which deal with the concepts of nationalism: *watan, qawm,* and *sha'b.* See Najib Sadqa, *Qadiyat Filastin* (Beirut: 1946), pp. 19, 31; and see below, Part III. The term *Heimstätte* was invented by Max Nordau as a subterfuge, "to deceive by its mildness" until such time as "there was no reason to

statesmen who framed the declaration, it seemed to involve an element of gradualness; the home was the seed of a state, but none doubted the eventual growth of the state. Balfour, after the war, cautioned a Zionist audience on the dangers of speed,[10] and Lloyd George subsequently informed the Royal Commission:

> The idea was, and this was the interpretation put upon it at the time, that a Jewish State was not to be set up immediately by the Peace Treaty without reference to the wishes of the majority of the inhabitants. On the other hand, it was contemplated that when the time arrived for according representative institutions to Palestine, if the Jews had meanwhile responded to the opportunity afforded them by the idea of a national home and had become a definite majority of the inhabitants, then Palestine would thus become a Jewish Commonwealth.[11]

We shall see, as the Mandate period progresses, that the net effect of the guarded and gradual emphasis put upon the Balfour Declaration focused attention of both Jews and Arabs upon the twin issues of land purchase and immigration. Both groups clearly saw that only in the purchase of large blocks of land lay any hope of supporting the thousands of immigrants available—not to mention the fantastic figure of several millions mentioned by some—in the 1920s and 1930s. Thus, the essence of the politics of the Mandate period is the struggle on the part of the Arabs to slow down or stop immigration and land sales; the Jewish struggle centered likewise on increasing both available land and density of population.[12] This is the thread which runs through the twenty-eight years from 1920 to 1948.

Meanwhile, on July 1, 1920, in Palestine OETA had handed over authority to Sir Herbert Samuel as first High Commissioner of a civil government. This was a step of questionable legality as the Treaty of Sèvres did not take effect and the Treaty of

---

dissimulate our real aim" (C. Sykes, on the basis of Nordau's manuscript, "The Prosperity of His Servant," in *Two Studies in Virtue* [London: 1953], p. 160, fn. 1.)

[10] Dugdale, p. 221.

[11] Cmd 5479, pp. 24-25.

[12] To facilitate Jewish land purchase, General Clayton reported on June 19, 1919, that the "land registry is controlled by the Acting Senior Judicial Officer Colonel Bentwich who is himself a prominent Zionist" (Woodward and Butler, pp. 280-81).

Lausanne, in which Turkey gave up all claim to Arab Asia, was not in effect until July 24, 1923. Although the Peace Conference had decided in 1919 the future of Palestine, it was thus not until 1923 that it legally ceased to be a part of the Ottoman Empire and became a mandate of the League of Nations.

One of the first acts of the new civil government was the issuance of the September 1920 Land Transfer Ordinance. This reopened the registry so that lands could once more be bought and sold. The law required that the government be informed of, and give consent to, the transfer of large parcels of land,[13] and in the first year of operation the government approved twenty-three transactions of estates each valued at more than £3,000. One of these was the first major purchase by the Jewish National Fund and the Palestine Land Development Company Ltd. of seven Arab villages in Galilee. During the year, the government decided to amend the ordinance to include some restrictions on sale of lands in which others held tenant rights, but this was a restriction most difficult to define or defend. The largest case of land purchase of these years and the subsequent Arab attitude toward land purchase is discussed in Part III, below.

Jewish immigration into Palestine began during the days of OETA, and had already occasioned an outburst of Arab violence before the establishment of the civil government. The official investigation of this "disturbance" was never published, but it clearly was a result of the interpretation Arabs had put upon the Balfour Declaration.[14] Everyone even among the moderates was bound to put as a minimum interpretation the notion that sooner or later a Zionist state would be created if a sufficiently large number of Jews had moved to Palestine. Just after the riots, in September 1920, the first immigration ordinance was enacted and Sir Herbert Samuel set the quota for the first year at 16,500.[15] The ordinance set no definite quota for each

[13] Government of Palestine, *Report* (July 1, 1920–December 31, 1921), pp. 110-12.

[14] Government of Palestine, *Survey Prepared for the Anglo-American Committee of Inquiry* (Jerusalem: 1946), I, 17.

[15] Government of Palestine, *Report* (July 1, 1920–December 31, 1921), pp. 126 ff.

year but stipulated that the quota depended upon the "economic needs of the country." During the first year only about two thirds of the quota was filled, and in May 1921 immigration was suspended after a second series of attacks on Jews and Jewish settlements. But, in spite of the findings of the investigating commission that Arab unrest was due to fear of Zionism, immigration was again allowed the next month with fewer restrictions than prior to the outbreak.

The Arab unrest of May 1921 was really just a continuation of the mounting hostility to Zionism witnessed already in 1919. But now it was compounded by the great disappointment with the results of the peace settlement. This is dealt with in detail in Part III when the growth of Arabism is discussed; here we need only remark that the Mandate government set two precedents in 1921 which were to be of some importance in the following years. On the one hand, it *did* suspend immigration in response to acts of violence. And the idea never died during the whole of the Mandate period that violence could force the hand of the government. On the other hand, after the situation had been brought under control and a commission had studied the underlying causes of the trouble, no account was taken of these in the subsequent policy of the government. The warning signs were clear, but the government chose to make no concession which could be locally regarded as such.

In 1922, after two Arab outbursts against Zionism, Sir Herbert Samuel, who was one of the main English Jewish supporters of Zionism during the war,[16] was moved to request that the Colonial Office define exactly what it was prepared to support by way of a "National Home."[17] To this purpose, Winston Churchill, who was then Colonial Secretary, published a statement of policy in which he reaffirmed that "there can be no

[16] The Earl of Oxford and Asquith wrote that Samuel's wartime memorandum, "The Future of Palestine," which advocated British annexing of Palestine and the settling of three to four million European Jews there was an "almost lyrical outburst proceeding from the well ordered and methodological brain of H.S." (*Memories and Reflections* [Boston: 1928], pp. 70-71). In retrospect Samuel's vision seems to have bordered on the prophetic.

[17] Col. 15, p. 27.

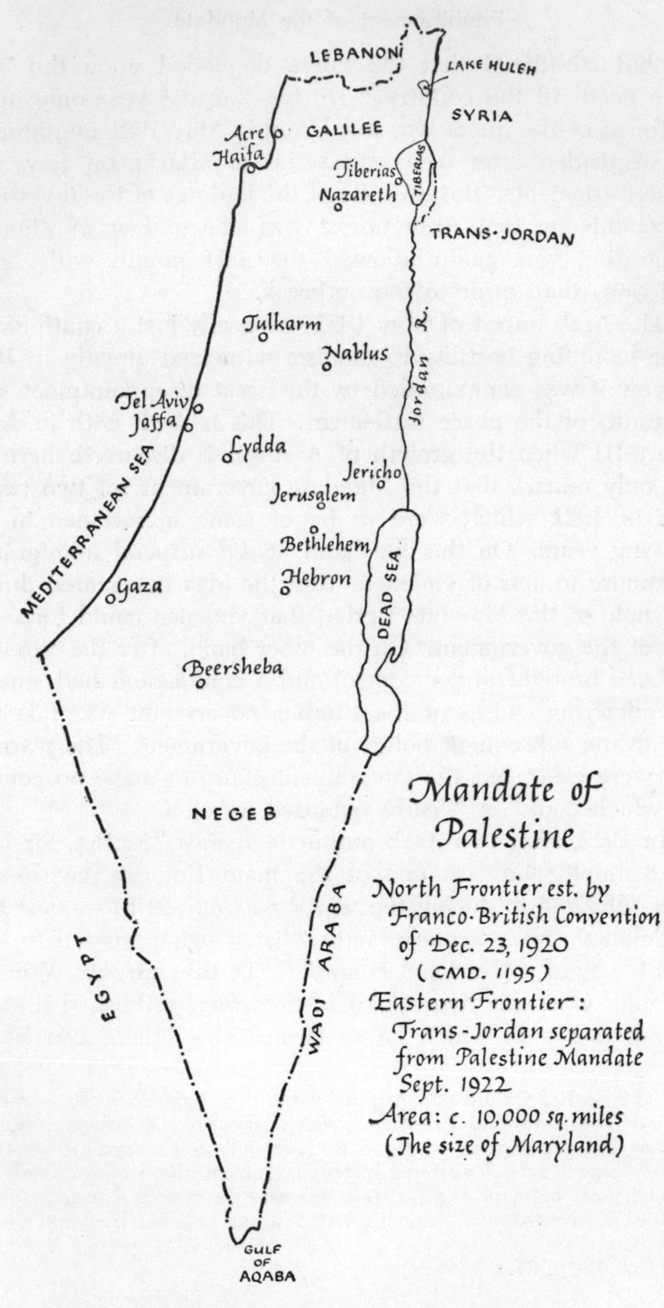

LEBANON
LAKE HULEH
SYRIA
Acre
GALILEE
Haifa
Tiberias
TIBERIAS
Nazareth
TRANS-JORDAN
Tulkarm
Nablus
Jordan R.
Tel Aviv
Jaffa
Lydda
Jericho
Jerusalem
Bethlehem
Hebron
Gaza
MEDITERRANEAN SEA
DEAD SEA
Beersheba
NEGEB
EGYPT
WADI ARABA
GULF OF AQABA
Mandate of Palestine
North Frontier est. by Franco-British Convention of Dec. 23, 1920 (CMD. 1195)
Eastern Frontier: Trans-Jordan separated from Palestine Mandate Sept. 1922
Area: c. 10,000 sq. miles (The size of Maryland)

question of rescinding the Balfour Declaration" but sharply rebuked Weizmann's definition of what it meant.

Unauthorised statements have been made to the effect that the purpose in view is to create a wholly Jewish Palestine. Phrases have been used such as that Palestine is to become "as Jewish as England is English." His Majesty's Government regard any such expectation as impracticable and have no such aim in view . . . They would draw attention to the fact that the terms of the Declaration referred to do not contemplate that Palestine as a whole should be converted into a Jewish National Home, but that such a Home should be founded *in Palestine*.[18]

The modern wisdom of Solomon involved telling both "mothers" that the baby would be cared for as a state ward until such time as it could be decided which mother was the more worthy or the stronger—or how best to cut up the baby.

The initial cut into Palestine was proposed, and approved, in September 1922 when Great Britain divided Trans-Jordan off from the Palestine Mandate (see map). The British government in this way felt that they had honored both the Sykes-Picot Agreement, which made Trans-Jordan a part of the Arab state under British influence, and the provisions of the Hussein-McMahon correspondence in which the hinterland had been promised to the Arabs as a part of their state. Until 1922 Britain had taken little interest in Trans-Jordan, being content to make her influence felt by the presence of a small group of political officers scattered among the tribes. But after September of that year it was officially stated that Trans-Jordan was not subject to the Balfour Declaration, which had been incorporated into the Mandate instrument, and Jews were forbidden to buy land there.[19] As can be imagined, no one was satisfied by the move. The Zionists felt that if their historical claim was justified in principle it was just in its particulars; so they argued now as they had at the Peace Conference that the land across the Jordan was necessary to their national development. They further pointed out that since the exclusion was couched in religious terms—no *Jew*

[18] Cmd 1700, p. 18.

[19] Royal Institute of International Affairs, *Great Britain and Palestine, 1915-45* (London: 1946), p. 15.

could buy land—it was a violation of the Mandate.[20] On their part, the Arabs felt that Britain's act tended to weaken the position of those on the west bank of the Jordan and salved the conscience of Britain at a time when the Arabs were trying to invoke that conscience. They were not less annoyed by the fact that this tended to give a greater degree of independence and self-government to Arabs far less "advanced" than those settled in Palestine and thus mocked the idea of tutelage in statecraft inherent in the Mandate idea.[21]

For the fact that they had no real voice in the government of Palestine, the Arabs are not altogether devoid of responsibility. In August 1922, Sir Herbert Samuel had tried to establish a government agency in which Arabs would have a voice.[22] This was little more than an elected version of the nominated Advisory Council which had been established in 1920. In the Advisory Council, the ten places were divided between Arabs and Jews as follows: 4 Muslims, 3 Christians, and 3 Jews. (Major policy, of course, was still to be set by the British government.) Under the system proposed by Samuel, there would be 23 members including the High Commissioner. Of the other 22, 10 would be official appointments, and the remaining 12 would be elected. Of these, 2 were to be Christian, 2 Jews, and 8 Muslims. On the face of it, this seemed to promise the Arabs proportional representation in the government.[23] However, as the Arabs pointed out, the line of division in their terms was pro-Balfour Declaration 13 and anti-Balfour Declaration 10. This meant that they would be a permanent minority when it came to deciding on such matters as land policy, immigration, and Zionism. Samuel was attacked as an "ardent Zionist"[24] and accused, among other things, of having used his position to undermine the economic

[20] Chaim Weizmann, "The Palestine White Paper," *Week End Review* (November 1, 1930); quoted in *ibid.*

[21] Executive Committee, Palestine Arab Congress, *Two Memoranda submitted to the Council and Permanent Mandates Commission of the League of Nations* (Jerusalem: 1925), pp. 3-4.

[22] Government of Palestine, *Report on Palestine Administration* (London: 1922), p. 3.

[23] Col. 15, p. 44.

[24] Executive Committee *Memoranda,* pp. 11-12.

position of the country.[25] The Arabs indicated that they felt their taxes to be too high, that the government was much too large, and that it compared badly with the Ottoman administration.[26] Moreover, they pointed out that in Ottoman times the government had allowed much more municipal autonomy and

> when the Colonial Office flung to Palestine that sham Constitution in 1922, in which the people had no say and which was fit for a very backward colony rather than for a mandated territory which "has reached a stage of development where its existence as independent can be provisionally recognized," all their confidence was wiped out and they determined to adopt a totally negative attitude.[27]

As a result, Samuel dropped the plan for a legislative council and decided simply to reconstitute the old advisory council but to do so on the same lines as the proposed legislative council. The invited Arabs accepted; but in the face of great hostility on the part of the general Arab population, seven of the ten invited Arabs immediately withdrew. As a result, the High Commissioner dropped the whole project.[28]

In 1923 the High Commissioner tried again. This time, with commendable fairness in spite of what his Arab critics thought and said of him, he reported that

> His Majesty's Government were still desirous of giving the fullest opportunity to the leaders of the Arab people to share in the administration of public affairs, without inconsistency with the principles that had been laid down. They examined the question afresh in July 1923; they recognised that the fourth article of the Mandate, under which a special position is accorded to a Jewish Agency in Palestine was resented by the Arabs, as involving preferential treatment for the Jews. I was, therefore, instructed to convey to them an offer of equal

[25] Both by grossly favoring the Zionists in the letting of concessions (pp. 13-21) and by "his Zionist coup d'état in prohibiting exportation of local products" in 1920 when farmers were short of cash and the crop had been plentiful. See Executive Committee, *Report on the State of Palestine submitted to His Excellency the High Commissioner for Palestine* (Jerusalem: 1925), p. 13. He was similarly attacked by the Zionists for being pro-Arab! (See Part II below.)

[26] Executive Committee *Report,* pp. 5-6.

[27] Page 4.

[28] Col. 15, pp. 45-46.

representation by means of an Arab Agency, which should be established with analogous functions. A meeting of the leaders of all sections was accordingly summoned and this proposal laid before them. It received no favour, and it also was not proceeded with.[29]

The reasons for this Arab refusal, which many have subsequently felt was a serious tactical mistake, were analogous to those behind the legislative commission failure. The Arabs felt that if they joined in any such group, they were acquiescing in the policy of the administration, and this formal acknowledgment they regarded as a snare in which the morality of their claim would be caught and taken from them. We see again and again in the following years the Arabs' desperate concentration on lack of public involvement and their adamant refusal to regard themselves as but *one part* of the population of Palestine.

10. MATERIAL GROWTH AND THE GATHERING STORM

The middle years of the 1920's saw a number of noteworthy developments in education, public works, health facilities, and rationalization of the land-tenure maze inherited from the Ottoman government. In these years the administration picked the country up by its bootstraps and was able to effect a balanced budget while carrying on a vigorous program of modernizing the land. To this period the Jewish and the Arab communities owed a good deal more than either has often been prepared to admit. Yet little was done to solve the political problems of the country. In the excitement of nonpolitical activity and perhaps from the exhaustion of the first troubled years of the administration, these questions seem to have been shelved.

To a certain extent this is true because the worst fears of the Arabs had not been realized. The country had not been swamped by Jews, a Jewish state seemed no nearer to establishment than in 1922, and as long as times were good, everyone

[29] *Ibid.*

was prepared to deal in the present and leave the future worries for bad times. Then, somewhat curiously, the arrival of a sharp economic depression, which resulted partly from a collapse of the Polish currency,[1] instead of increasing Arab discontent tended to lessen Arab fears. From 1925 to 1928 no meetings of the Palestine Arab Congress were held and no protests were voiced over Jewish immigration. As might be expected the immigration figures themselves provide us with an index.

In 1925 a series of Arab representations of discontent were made to the mandate authority and that was the largest immigration year to that date with a net Jewish immigration increase of 31,650. The next year, however, only about one sixth as large a net immigration was recorded. The Arabs could thus feel that with their high birth rate they were not in danger of losing their majority of the population. Then, in 1927, the Jewish community had 2,358 more emigrants than immigrants. By the Arabs this was taken as a sign that the National Home had failed and that they could relax in victory. In the following year, however, the trend was reversed; a very slight net gain was made and in 1929 the net gain was 3,503. The optimism of the Arabs was shattered.[2] They could see also that the Zionist crisis had tended to heal the breach between the Zionist and non-Zionist Jews and even led to an enlarging of the Jewish Agency.

These developments occurred just at a time when Arabs in surrounding areas again took major steps towards independence. In Trans-Jordan, in February 1928, a representative government was established under a provisional constitution. Egypt entered into treaty relations with Great Britain, which, although subsequently rescinded, seemed at the moment to be a considerable concession by Britain. Iraq was promised that Britain would promote her entry into the League of Nations shortly; and even in Syria, which had witnessed a major rebellion in 1925, reforms were promised and a constituent assembly set up to draft a constitution. As the Royal Commission subsequently pointed out, "among all that group of kindred countries it was

[1] RIIA, *Great Britain and Palestine, 1915-1945* (London: 1946), p. 43.
[2] Cmd 5479, pp. 63-64.

only in Palestine that no advance whatever had been made towards popular government or national independence." [3]

These are the factors which form the background to the outbreak of violence, the first since 1921, of August 1929. The immediate causes of the disturbances were, as is so frequently the case, trivial.

In Jerusalem, as elsewhere in Palestine, are numerous shrines which are sacred to one or more of the three major religions, but none compare in Jewish eyes with the Wailing Wall. However, the wall is also the western wall of the most sacred Muslim shrine in Palestine, Aqsa Mosque in the Haram ash-Sharif. It is regarded by Muslims as the place from which Mohammed ascended to Heaven on his Night Journey. Moreover, the land in front of the wall is a *waqf* or pious foundation of Muslims. The wall itself was regarded by the Mandate government as the property of Islam,[4] and yet rights in usage were conferred upon Jews by long custom. Twice before 1929 minor incidents had occurred and these had led the government to define carefully the rights of all parties and to formalize the procedure to be followed in exercising those rights. Then in 1928 began a series of controversies over minor repairs and questions of ritual involving both Jews and Muslims. The Muslims, ever ready to take any Jewish move as a sinister attack on their traditional rights, announced that the Jews intended to take over the entire Muslim shrine.[5] Tempers increased and finally:

> On the 15th August, 1929, some hundreds of young Jews organised a demonstration at the Wailing Wall, in the course of which the Zionist flag was raised and the Zionist anthem sung. Incensed by this, the Moslems held a counter-demonstration at the same spot on the following day, when written prayers placed in the crevices of the wall by Jewish worshippers were taken out and burned.

This was followed by riots and attacks in Jerusalem and in various other parts of the country. British troops were rushed

[3] *Ibid.*, p. 65.

[4] Col. 75, p. 197.

[5] *Memorandum from the Mufti of Jerusalem to the Government of Palestine,* October 8, 1928; quoted in Cmd 3530, pp. 31-32. For events in detail see Cmd 3530, pp. 26 ff; Cmd 5479, pp. 64 ff; and RIIA, pp. 44-46.

to Palestine. And by August 29 the casualties numbered 472 Jews and at least 268 Arabs.

The Shaw commission, which investigated the disturbances, noted:

> In less than ten years three serious attacks have been made by Arabs on Jews. For eighty years before the first of these there is no recorded instance of any similar incidents . . . representatives of all parties told us that before the [First World] War the Jews and Arabs lived side by side if not in amity, at least with tolerance, a quality which today is almost unknown in Palestine.[6]

The underlying causes were found by the Commission to be Arab resentment and disappointment at the course of events since the end of the war, fear for the future under even the mildest Zionist program:

> . . . the Arabs have come to see in the Jewish immigrant not only a menace to their livelihood but a possible overlord of the future . . . and the results of Jewish enterprise and penetration have been such as to confirm that they will be excluded from the soil.

The Commission pointed out that Palestine had the highest rate of immigration of any country in the world, even in the "slow" years 1925 to 1927,[7] and that while Zionism had benefited the country as a whole in economic terms, it had not appreciably benefited the individual peasant. Indeed, in such instances as the sale of lands in the Vale of Esdraelon,[8] the peasantry saw their eventual displacement from the soil.

It will be recalled that the findings of the Shaw Commission in this incident were almost exactly the same as those of the 1921 investigating commission; the fundamental opposition of the Arabs to Zionism in any form.

The government was able to remove the problem of the Wailing Wall by establishing a definitive set of rules; moreover, to prevent similar attacks on unarmed, isolated communities of Jews, the government placed sealed arms stores in the colonies. Yet, when it came to deal with the underlying causes of dis-

[6] Cmd 3530, p. 150.

[7] International Labour Office, *Migration Movements 1925-1927;* Cmd 3530, p. 152.

[8] See below, Part III.

content, the British government initially did little more than reaffirm the principles contained in the Mandate documents.[9] The government then came under severe attack from the League of Nations Permanent Mandates Commission and decided in May 1930 to appoint a special commission to study the underlying causes of the disturbance. Once again immigration into Palestine was suspended.

Sir John Hope-Simpson, of the League Refugee Settlement Commission for Greece and formerly of the Indian Civil Service, was appointed to inquire into the background situation. In his report, he emphasized the smallness of Palestine, the limited extent of its resources, and the necessity for large-scale economic developments if further immigration was to be allowed. The area of Palestine, he pointed out, was only 10,000 square miles, of which more than three quarters was "uncultivable" by normal economic standards. Over 16 per cent of the "cultivable" land was owned by Jews or Jewish groups, and it was his opinion that if the land not occupied by Jews were divided among the Arabs, there would not be land enough to satisfy their needs. The report recommended an immediate halt to immigration but suggested that immigration might again become possible on a limited scale in future years.

The government accepted the report and on the basis of it made a statement of policy, the so-called Passfield White Paper, which went further toward granting Arab desires than did the report.[10] It did, however, indicate that the British Government was annoyed at the lack of cooperation from both Jewish and Arab communities in the months following the August 1929 outbreak. On its part, the government was willing to try once more to facilitate the creation of a legislature which "should be of special benefit to the Arab section of the population, who do not at present possess any constitutional means for putting their views on social and economic matters before the Government." The government policy henceforth would be to set aside government lands for the use of landless Arabs, rather than for Jews, and in determining the absorptive capacity of Palestine

[9] Hansard, April 3, 1930, Col. 1466-67; RIIA, p. 48.
[10] Cmd 3692.

at any time it would take account of the Arab as well as the Jewish unemployment.

Jewish reaction was immediate and effective. The Zionist leaders protested to the Colonial Office. Weizmann, who was more closely identified with Britain than any other Zionist leader, resigned in protest from the presidency of the Jewish Agency, and other prominent public figures including Lord Melchett and Baron Edmond de Rothschild made representations. Dr. Stephen Wise described the government policy as a "great betrayal," and the Vaad Leumi or National Council of the Jews of Palestine informed the High Commissioner that it would boycott the proposed legislature. General Smuts telegraphed the Prime Minister urging a repudiation of the policy.[11] The leaders of the Conservative Party, Baldwin, Chamberlain, and Amery wrote a letter to *The Times* on October 23 in which they denounced the government policy as a violation of the terms of the Mandate and an arbitrary act without the chance being given to Parliament or to the people of Palestine to discuss its merits. Immediately the government began to retreat. In a letter to Smuts, published in *The Times* on October 27, Prime Minister MacDonald denied that the government intended to stop the development of the National Home at the stage it had then achieved. Subsequent remarks in Parliament and in the press still further modified the intent of the Passfield White Paper. The Jewish Agency issued a memorandum in November which severely criticized the statistics on which the Hope-Simpson report and the White Paper were based. Weizmann was then called to a series of meetings with the Cabinet committee charged with Palestine affairs. In December and January, the Jewish Agency and the government finally evolved a new policy acceptable to the Zionists. The government refused to rescind the White Paper or to issue another in its place, but Prime Minister MacDonald agreed to embody the new agreement in a public letter to Dr. Weizmann, published in *The Times* on February 14, 1931. The letter, which was written "In order to remove certain misconceptions and misunderstandings which have arisen as to the policy of His Majesty's Government with

[11] ESCO, II, 644 ff.

regard to Palestine," virtually explained away the entire White Paper. It decided that immigration "can be fulfilled without prejudice to the rights and position of other sections of the population of Palestine," and it defined "landless Arabs" as meaning only those who had lost their lands to Jews, not landless Arabs in general.

Coming as this letter did only as the result of protests by one group in Palestine and their supporters, without reference to another government study or commission, it was naturally taken by the Arabs as a concession to political pressures. They called it, in bitter jest, the "Black Letter," redefining the White Paper. For the first time, Arab hostility began to be directed at the government rather than toward the incoming Jews.

The immediate result was an Arab boycott of some phases of government activity and a refusal to work together with the Jewish community on various civic matters. Yet the Arab community could only continue its negative attitude. Lacking a constituted representative, as the Jews possessed in the Jewish Agency, the Arabs tended to be divided into a number of mutually hostile groups and to be ineffective in expressing their desires to the government. Moreover, their minimum program was independence, end of immigration, and restriction of land sales. On these terms the government had shown itself unwilling, if not unable, to negotiate. As a result, moderate Arabs could have no concrete and positive program to urge upon the government.

The Zionist Organization, to the contrary, had shown itself flexible in case of need and determined when there seemed to be a chance of molding government policy. It could swing between Weizmann's position at the Peace Conference, or indeed his even more extreme position in the Twelfth (1921) Zionist Congress,[12] and his acceptance of the watered-down definition of the National Home given in 1922 by Mr. Churchill. In the last years of the 1920s, however, his position had been greatly strengthened by the adhesion of many American and European Jews who had heretofore been hostile to Zionism. Then, with the rise to power of the Nazis in 1932, a new sense of urgency

[12] Nevill Barbour, *Nisi Dominus* (London: 1946), p. 104, fn. 1.

and desperation caused by the increasing scale of emigration from Germany stiffened the Zionist Movement. The number of immigrants tripled between 1932 and 1933, and in 1933 Dr. Arlosoroff of the Jewish Agency, who was known as a moderate, was killed, it was thought by Jewish terrorists.

The government was able to carry out a limited project in self-rule, which had been planned for 1930, to create municipalities. This had been one of the complaints of the Arab executive in the early 1920s; they had pointed out that since these groups existed under the Ottoman administration, they should have been reconstituted by the British administration. However, the government could and did point out that it had attempted to create even more important forms of self-government which first the Arabs and then the Zionists had rejected.

Sporadic outbreaks occurred of Jews and Arabs in 1930, 1933, and 1935.

> As the National Home expanded from 1933 onwards, so the Arab hate and fear of it increased . . . the attitude of the Arab leaders became more hostile to the Government, and the tone of the Arab Press more bitter. In the autumn of 1934 the Arab Executive submitted to the High Commissioner a formal expression of their view that the safeguards for Arab interests embodied in the Mandate had broken down. A campaign, in which the Supreme Moslem Council took an active part, was set on foot to prevent more Arab land passing into Jewish hands. Small landowners were persuaded to register their lands as family *awqaf* [pious foundations] to preclude alienation. One particular contract for the sale of 5,000 dunums [1,250 acres] to Jews was cancelled at the direct instance of the Supreme Moslem Council. Arabs accused of facilitating the sale of land to Jews were denounced in the Mosques, at public meetings and in the Press as traitors to the nation. An Arab bank was started with a capital of £60,000 for the development of Arab land or its exclusion from alien purchase. Attempts were made, moreover, by organized trespass and fictitious litigation, to prevent the settlement of Jews on land they had already bought.[13]

Yet in December 1935 the Governor General decided that the municipal councils had proved that the country could handle more of its own problems by representative government. So he circulated among the Arab and Jewish recognized leaders copies

[13] Cmd 5479 pp. 86-87.

of a proposed constitution.[14] This time the nongovernment representation would predominate although the government retained control by selecting some of the nongovernment members. The proposal called for 28 members, of whom only 5 were officials. The rest consisted of 2 commercial members; 11 Muslims, of whom 8 were to be elected; 7 Jews, of whom 3 were to be elected; and 3 Christians, of whom 1 was to be elected. It was hardly to be an independent chamber, but it can be regarded as a step toward the creation of a forum which could at least air problems in more peaceful and constructive ways than those afforded by the press and crowds on street corners. It is not the least factor in the breach between the Jewish and Arab communities that there was no such forum in which the leaders could exchange views and develop those personal ties of respect, if not sympathy, which are so vital to the functioning of any nation.[15]

The government also, in February 1936, announced to the Arabs that it intended to prohibit future Arab sales of land which did not leave to the Arab cultivators a "viable minimum" of land and that it intended more carefully to adjust the rate of immigration to the economic capacity of the country.

As might be expected, this proposal raised more protest than it quieted. Some Arabs were in favor of accepting the offer, thinking that this was about as much as could be hoped for. They also pointed out that point-blank refusals in the past had not resulted in greater concessions but often led to a policy less favorable to the Arabs. Of course this group, like moderates in all countries, could not prevail in a period of rising fears, tensions, and hostility. The contrast with the already independent governments in the other Arab states, especially in Iraq and Egypt, could not but make the Palestine Arabs bitterly aware that the constitution was not "democratic" nor did it give the Arabs with their nine elected members in a council of twenty-eight any chance of putting an end to Zionism. Indeed the legis-

[14] Cmd 5119.

[15] As late as 1948 Robert Graves, then governor of Jerusalem, felt this to be an important failing (*Experiment in Anarchy* [London: 1949], pp. 10-11).

lature would be forbidden to discuss the Mandate terms, which incorporated the Balfour Declaration.

And on their part the Jews, who by this time were fairly united in support of Zionism, were strong in protesting that the government was now doing in *sotto voce* what the Passfield White Paper had attempted and what the government had specifically renounced in the MacDonald letter to Dr. Weizmann. The ensuing events were similar to those which followed the Passfield White Paper; protests were sounded in London, the Jewish Agency charged that the land restriction was a definite violation of the terms of the Mandate which enjoined the facilitation of Jewish settlement on the land, and the government came under strong criticism in both Houses of Parliament. In the League of Nations, the Permanent Mandates Commission discussed the general proposal by the Palestine government and was critical of it.

The Arab community watched the developing situation through the perspective of the Passfield episode and concluded that their chances of winning control of the country by peaceful means were almost nil. The immigration statistics again provide us with an index of Arab fears. Jews fleeing from Nazi persecution were coming to Palestine in increasing numbers, and the Arabs while sympathizing in the abstract could not but look upon these refugees as a potential majority in the numbers then coming. In 1935, the biggest year, as many (61,854) arrived as in the first five years of the Mandate; and in the four years 1933 to 1936, the Jewish population quadrupled, almost as many people arriving in the one year 1934 alone as the entire Jewish population of Palestine in 1931. It had been pointed out by the Shaw Commission that if the Jewish immigration ran at a rate of 25,000 per year, Jews would become the majority by 1948 and would be larger than the Muslim population by 1944.[16] And the capital investment of the Jewish community doubled between 1932 and 1933. This meant that land could be purchased more readily.[17]

Moreover, the Arabs had observed that in Egypt, as a seem-

[16] Graph # 1, p. 203; Cmd 3530.
[17] Cmd 5479, p. 82.

ing result of student rioting in Cairo, the British government had accepted an Egyptian request to negotiate a new treaty and in January 1936 a strike in Syria forced the French government to announce that they had decided to begin negotiations to end the mandate over Syria. To the Arabs, the moral seemed clear.[18]

In the debates in the English Parliament in February and March it seemed extremely unlikely that the government program would survive. The Jewish press hailed this as a "great Jewish victory." The Arabs agreed. The Arab and Jewish reactions and actions in this period are discussed below in Parts II and III. Here it is necessary only to sketch the events of the following tense and bloody months.

On April 15, 1936, Arab highwaymen held up a number of cars on the road between Tulkarm and Nablus and shot three Jewish passengers.[19] The following night two Arabs were murdered, probably as a reprisal.[20] The funeral of one of the murdered Jews in Tel-Aviv led to a series of mob demonstrations and attacks on the Arabs of neighboring Jaffa. Rumors spread that Arabs had been killed and this in turn led to Arab mob attacks on Jews. On April 20 an Arab National Committee was formed in Nablus. This seems to have been quite spontaneous and was not directly connected with the previous Arab leadership. The Nablus group called for a general strike to continue until the government accepted the Arab demands of the previous November—establishment of a democratic government, prohibition of sale of land to the Jews, and end of Jewish immigration until "economic absorptive capacity" could be determined. By the end of the month similar committees had been constituted all over Palestine. And on the day after the Nablus group was formed, all five Arab political parties dropped their mutual antagonism to form a united front. This latter group came subsequently to be called the Arab Higher Committee. On May 8 the various National Committees met together in Jerusalem and decided to urge their members to stop paying taxes and to adopt a sort of Palestine version of Indian passive resistance. The

[18] Arnold Toynbee (ed.), *Survey of International Affairs, 1936* (London: 1937), pp. 726-27.

[19] *Ibid.;* and Col. 129 p. 37; Cmd 5479 Ch. 4.

[20] C. 330. M 222, pp. 144-45; and Col. 129, p. 7.

strike proved to be far more effective than any, including the Arab leaders, had thought likely, and although the Committees declared that they did not favor "civil disobedience" in its more violent forms, attacks on Jews and Jewish property continued. The Arab Higher Committee offered to use its influence to call off the outbursts if the government would halt Jewish immigration. The government refused and on May 18 issued an immigration schedule which was somewhat higher than in previous years. The general strike developed into a state of siege. Two trains were derailed, a bridge blown up, and armed bands which included volunteers from Syria and Iraq began to operate in the hill country. On May 23 mass arrests of Arab leaders were made and in June some of the members of the Arab Higher Committee were interned in a concentration camp. Toward the end of June, 137 Arab senior officials and judges in the Palestine government presented a memorandum to the government in which they said that the disturbances were caused by the fact that

> . . . the Arab population of all classes, creeds and occupations is animated by a profound sense of injustice done to them. They feel that insufficient regard has been paid in the past to their legitimate grievances, even though those grievances had been inquired into by qualified and impartial official investigators, and to a large extent vindicated by those inquiries. As a result, the Arabs have been driven into a state verging on despair; and the present unrest is no more than an expression of that despair.
>
> The fact must be faced that that feeling of despair is largely to be traced to loss of faith on the part of the Arabs in the value of official pledges and assurances for the future, and to the fact that they are genuinely alarmed at the extent to which His Majesty's Government have from time to time given way to Zionist pressure. Their confidence was severely shaken as far back as 1931, when the Prime Minister's letter to Dr. Weizmann was issued as an interpretation of the White Paper of 1930. But more recently, when the projects regarding the Legislative Council and the restriction on sales of land were hotly challenged in Parliament, their loss of confidence turned to despair.[21]

This memorandum was followed by a second from 1,200 lower-rank Arab officials. Coming as they both did from the more

[21] Cmd 5479, pp. 401-3.

moderate and responsible—and personally committed—members of the Arab community, the memoranda made a considerable impression on both the government and the Royal Commission which was sent to investigate.

Meanwhile, Emir (later King) Abdullah of Trans-Jordan intervened and tried to calm the passions of the Arab leaders. They informed him that under the circumstances they could not control the Arab populace. The Prime Minister of Iraq then offered to mediate, but his attempt failed when the government could not agree to discuss the general issue of the terms of the Mandate and the National Home.

11. THE WISDOM OF SOLOMON

By September 1936 the Colonial Office, deciding to put down the "disturbances" by force, had moved a division of troops into the country. The scattered Arab bands then found themselves facing upwards of 20,000 regular troops. The activity of the bands was further diminished when much of the country was placed under martial law and severe punishment, including destruction of villages and the quartering of troops, was meted out to villages accused of harboring rebels. Arab casualties mounted to over 1,000.[1] In this situation, and exhausted by their long general strike, with the failure at this gamble of force without the means of force, the Arab committees found a face-saving formula by accepting the advice of the Arab kings and princes to "rely on the good intentions of our friend Great Britain, who has declared that she will do justice." By October 12 the strike had ended and the Arab bands melted away.

In November the Royal Commission arrived in Palestine. The government announced that, unlike its action in the previous occasions of investigations, it would not suspend immigration; as a result the Arab Higher Committee decided to boycott the commission. Thus throughout most of its hearings the Royal Commission had no official access to the opinions of the Arab community.

[1] RIIA, *Great Britain and Palestine, 1915-1945* (London: 1946), p. 95.

It was not until January 6, 1937, again at the request of the non-Palestinian Arab rulers, that the Arab Higher Committee decided to participate.

After careful study of the current situation and its underlying causes the Royal Commission decided that the Mandate was unworkable in its existing form. Their conclusions are still worthy of attention:

An irrepressible conflict has arisen between two national communities within the narrow bounds of one small country. About 1,000,000 Arabs are in strife, open or latent, with some 400,000 Jews. There is no common ground between them. The Arab community is predominantly Asiatic in character, the Jewish community predominantly European. They differ in religion and in language. Their cultural and social life, their ways of thought and conduct, are as incompatible as their national aspirations. These last are the greatest bar to peace . . . The War and its sequel have inspired all Arabs with the hope of reviving in a free and united Arab world the traditions of the Arab golden age. The Jews similarly are inspired by their historic past. . . . In the Arab picture the Jews could only occupy the place they occupied in Arab Egypt or Arab Spain. The Arabs would be as much outside the Jewish picture as the Canaanites in the old land of Israel. The National Home . . . cannot be half-national . . . This conflict was inherent in the situation from the outset. The terms of the Mandate tended to confirm it [and] the conflict has grown steadily more bitter . . . In the earlier period hostility to the Jews was not widespread among the fellaheen. It is now general . . . The intensification of the conflict will continue . . . it seems probable that the situation, bad as it now is, will grow worse. The conflict will go on, the gulf between Arabs and Jews will widen.[2]

The Royal Commission felt that it might be possible to rule by repression, but that besides being abhorrent to the English mind,[3] "the worst of it is that such a policy leads nowhere." This being the situation, it adopted the sensible (to the English mind) notion that "half a loaf is better than no bread" and suggested the first of many subsequent plans of partition (see map).

[2] Cmd 5479, pp. 370-72.

[3] Sir John Chancellor said in a talk in London in 1937, "As High Commissioner, in trying to do justice to both parties I used to feel what I have felt in no position that I have occupied under the Crown—namely, that my every act and every decision was based upon an equivocal moral foundation" (quoted in Arnold Toynbee [ed.], *Survey of International Affairs* [London: 1936], p. 743, fn. 1).

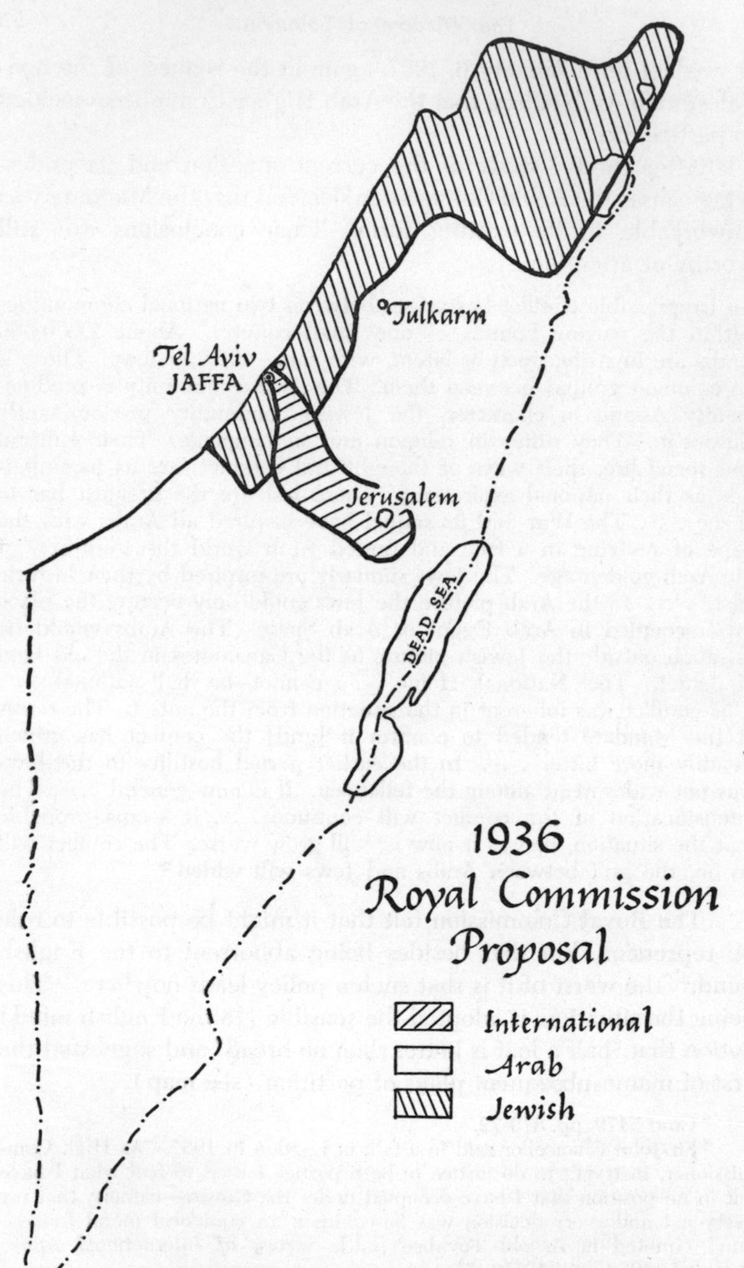
Tulkarm
Tel Aviv
JAFFA
Jerusalem
DEAD SEA
1936
Royal Commission
Proposal
International
Arab
Jewish

The British government accepted the report and issued a White Paper[4] announcing that they accepted the notion of partition. However, in the debate in the House of Lords, Lord Samuel pointed out that the Jewish state, as small as it would be, would contain a population of Arabs (225,000) almost equal to that of the Jews (258,000). Later he wrote that

> The Commission seemed to have picked out all the most awkward provisions of the Peace Treaties of Versailles, and to have put a Saar, a Polish Corridor and a half a dozen Danzigs and Mamels into a country the size of Wales.[5]

Such a monstrosity would patently be impossible either to administer or to defend.

The reaction of both Arabs and Jews was guarded and mildly unfavorable. The question was debated at the Twentieth Zionist Congress in Zürich in August 1937. Opinions divided. The Jewish Agency land expert, Dr. Ruppin, pointed out that he thought the partition ought to be accepted since "there are 2,000,000 donums [500,000 acres] of land in Palestine upon which as many people could live as in the whole of the remainder of the country [and] . . . this area of high fertility would, according to the Commission's map, lie almost entirely within the Jewish state . . ."[6] Earlier in the year, the leader of the Militant Revisionist wing of the Zionist Movement, Vladimir Jabotinsky, had warned the Royal Commission in London, that "we cannot accept cantonisation, because it will be suggested by many, even among you, that even the whole of Palestine may prove too small for that humanitarian purpose we need. A corner of Palestine, a 'canton,' how can we promise to be satisfied with it. We cannot. We never can. Should we swear to you we should be satisfied, it would be a lie."[7] The Zionist Congress also refused the Royal Commission plan.[8]

[4] Cmd 5513.
[5] *Foreign Affairs Quarterly,* XVI (1937), p. 152.
[6] Quoted in Toynbee (ed.), *Survey of International Affairs* (London: 1937), I, 545.
[7] *New Zionist Publications # 3* (London: 1937).
[8] The resolution is quoted in Cmd 5854, pp. 18-19.

The initial reaction of the League of Nations was unfavorable but the League, in the final analysis, could do little but accept the advice of the British government.

Meanwhile the Arabs had come to realize that partition would probably involve the transfer of populations from important districts and would create for them, as well as for the Jews, an undefensible jigsaw puzzle of a country. Pressure was of course brought to bear by residents of those districts which would be lost to the Arab state. The Arab National Defense party issued a suggestion that without partition, the whole country now come under treaty relations with Great Britain on the understanding that the then existing ratio of Arabs to Jews be maintained. It, like the Jewish Agency, wanted to avoid partition if possible. The Royal Commission had pointed out that the phrase, "one loaf is better than no bread," is a peculiarly English one and neither side saw the issue in these terms. Neither considered the possibility that it would get no bread. But the world situation was getting increasingly serious. Thus, Dr. Weizmann and others urged that any haven, even a small one, must be secured for the refugees from Europe. In these conditions, the British government decided to send to Palestine a technical commission to study in more detail the problems of partition.

The Palestine Partition (Woodhead) Commission unfortunately was not able to make its study in any sort of comfortable atmosphere. In September 1937 the Acting District Commissioner of Galilee, which under the Royal Commission proposal would have been given to the Jewish state, was murdered by Arab terrorists. It seemed likely that this was not an isolated act, and the government moved swiftly to stamp out the last sparks of the rebellion. On October 1, a week after the assassination of its Commissioner, the government outlawed the Arab Higher Committee and all the National Committees, ordered the arrest and deportation of six leading Arab figures, and severed the connection between the Mufti, Hajj Amin al-Husseini, and the source of his funds, the *Waqf* (Pious Foundation) Committee. The Arab leaders the government found must be "morally responsible for the campaign of terrorism and murder." One of the six Arab leaders evaded arrest and fled to Syria. He was followed a few days later by the Mufti. General security regulations were tightened and the carrying of arms was made punishable by death. The government statistics showed that during the year 438 attacks had been made with bombs and firearms, divided almost equally between attacks on the police and military forces, Jewish settlements, and Arab houses. Almost one thousand people were interned.

When the Partition Commission arrived in Palestine in April 1938, the leaders of the Arab community were mainly under detention, but the community itself was united in what had by now assumed the proportions of a civil war, and not one Arab collaborated with the Commission.

The Jewish community, meanwhile, had been drawn closer to the government by the Arab hostility to both. Moreover, in the Royal Commission partition scheme it could see the possibility of the immediate creation of a Jewish state, which although small could consummate the Zionist ideal. As an outward sign of cooperation, the government armed nearly 5,000 Jews as active and reserve police.

Outside encouragement to the Arabs was not lacking. For several years the Italian government had been interested in embarrassing Great Britain in her Mediterranean policy. To this end, the Italian radio station in Bari had broadcast in Arabic programs calculated to encourage hostility to Britain. Finally in 1938 Radio Berlin also took up this task. After the Anglo-Italian agreement of April 16, 1938, Germany predominated in this field and on April 24, 1938, began to broadcast on British "atrocities." [9]

The period of Jewish cooperation with the government was broken in June by the hanging of a Revisionist terrorist who had been convicted of firing on an Arab bus. This led to Jewish demonstrations, attacks on government buildings, and bombings of Arab markets. In one such attack in Haifa 74 Arabs were killed and 129 others wounded. However, the continuation of the Arab civil war necessarily forced Jews and the government to cooperate.

[9] *The Times,* April 29, 1939; Vernier, *La Politique Islamique de l'Allemagne* (Paris: 1939); and Viton, "Hitler Goes to the Arabs," *Asia,* July 1939.

By midsummer, the Arab revolt had become organized and its supporters had even set up a postal system, courts martial, and a sort of loose general staff. Another senior British official was murdered and government property was raided systematically to seize arms and supplies. During 1938 the incidence of violence increased to the point where it could no longer be considered "peace." The government reported 5,708 "incidents of violence," including over a thousand attacks on troops or government facilities. Two thousand five hundred people, almost all Arabs, were interned and it was estimated that at least one thousand rebels were killed by the police and army.

In November 1938 the Partition Commission published its recommendations. After noting that the "Arabs remain inflexibly hostile to partition" and pointing out that "it is impossible to divide a country of its size and configuration into areas the frontiers of which, having regard to the conditions of modern warfare, will have any real military significance," the Commission devised three plans for partition. It urged caution in the optimism for economic development of the country, but pointed out that the "present desperate needs" of the European Jews weighed heavily on the Palestine issue. Thus it attempted to create two states which would be viable and yet in which the Jewish would not have an Arab majority. They were not hopeful of success but put forward as their best effort Plan "C" (see maps for all three plans). Plan "C" would still leave an Arab minority of 54,000 (one fifth of the total) who owned most of the land in the Jewish state. That state, small as it would be, would have the advantages of being compact, and of containing most of the good land in Palestine (see land map in Part IV). The Commission pointed out that the plan of giving Galilee to the Jews involved dispossessing (at least in the political sense) 96 per cent of the population which owned 97 per cent of the land. It will be recalled that Galilee was awarded to the Jewish state by the Royal Commission and that this had led to the murder of the senior British official there. They also rejected Jewish claims to areas in which the entire population was Arab. Emphasizing the Arab feeling for the land, which is discussed in Part III below, the Commission doubted that the Arabs would peacefully accept

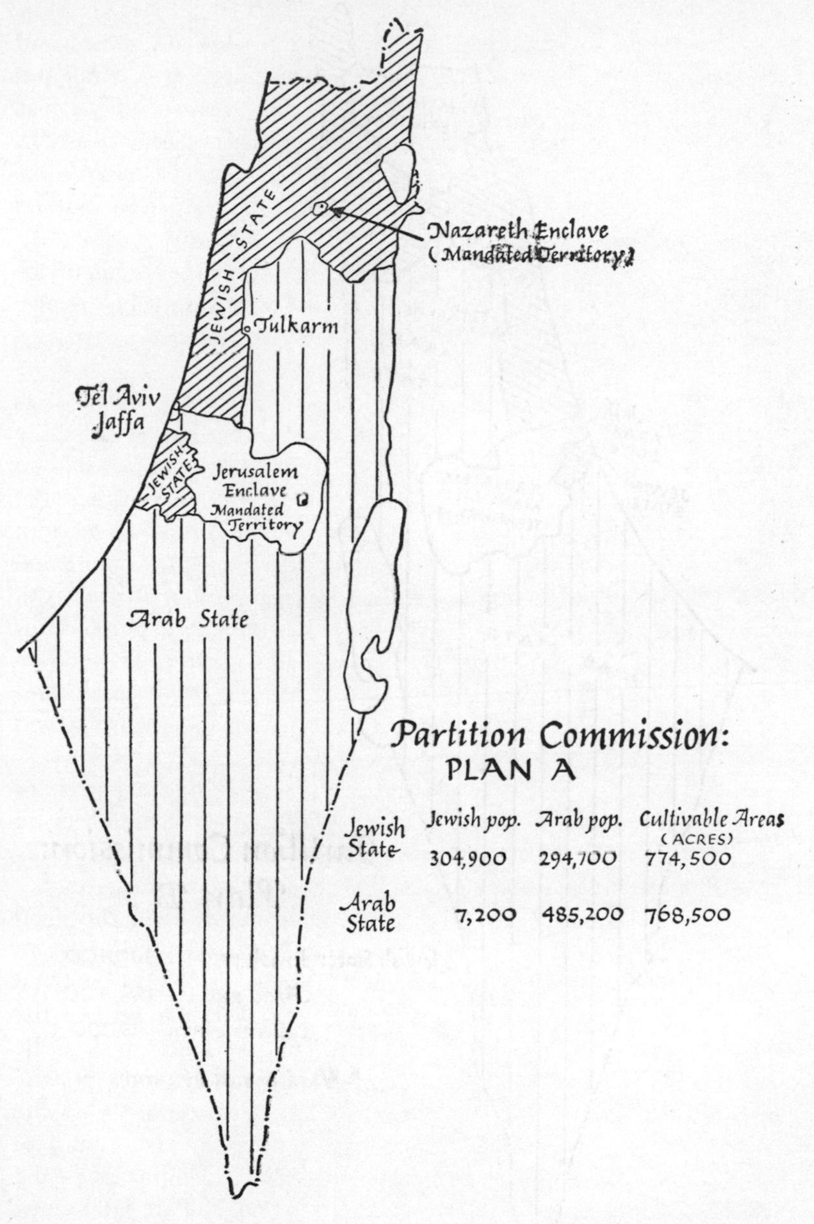

JEWISH STATE
Nazareth Enclave
(Mandated Territory)
Tulkarm
JEWISH STATE
Tel Aviv
Jaffa
JEWISH STATE
Jerusalem
Enclave
Mandated
Territory
Arab State
Partition Commission:
PLAN A
Jewish pop.
Arab pop.
Cultivable Areas
(ACRES)
Jewish State
304,900
294,700
774,500
Arab State
7,200
485,200
768,500

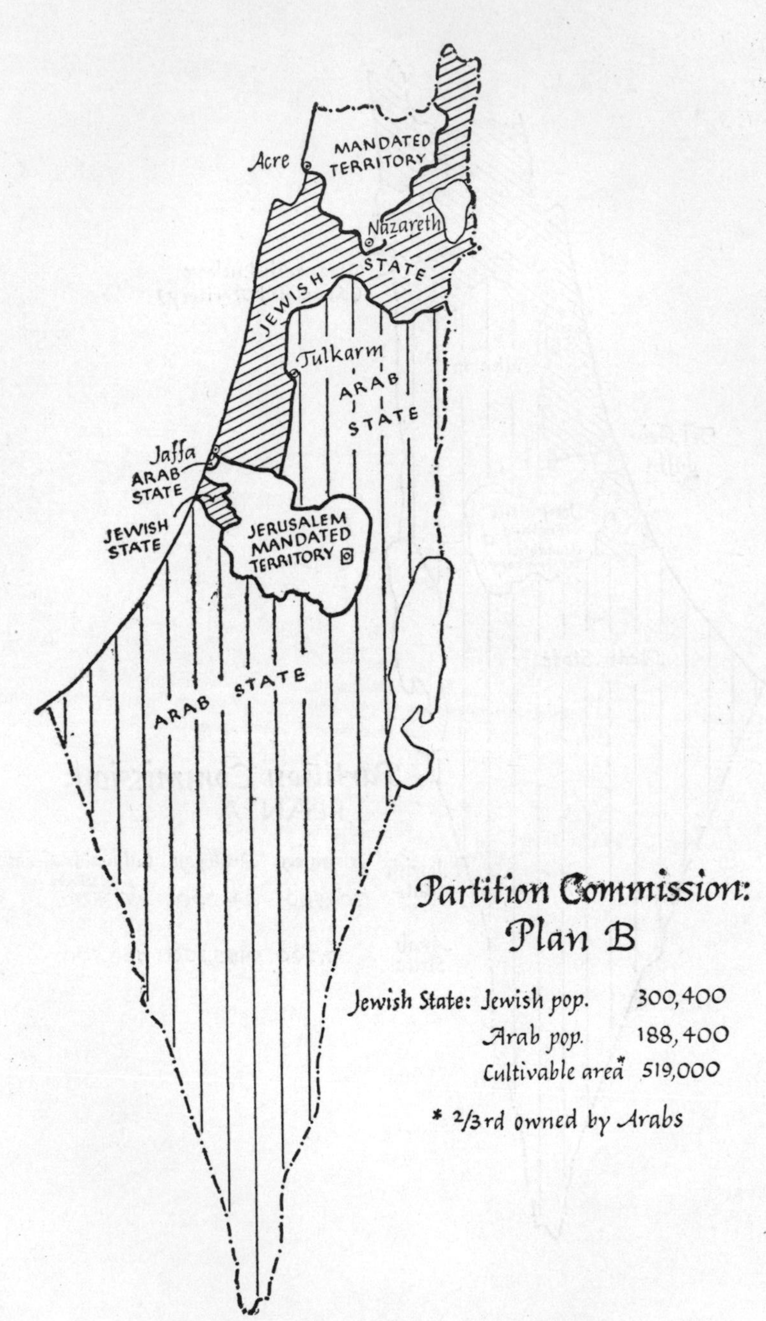
MANDATED TERRITORY
Acre
Nazareth
JEWISH STATE
Tulkarm
ARAB STATE
Jaffa
ARAB STATE
JEWISH STATE
JERUSALEM MANDATED TERRITORY
ARAB STATE
Partition Commission:
Plan B
Jewish State: Jewish pop. 300,400
Arab pop. 188,400
Cultivable area* 519,000
* 2/3rd owned by Arabs

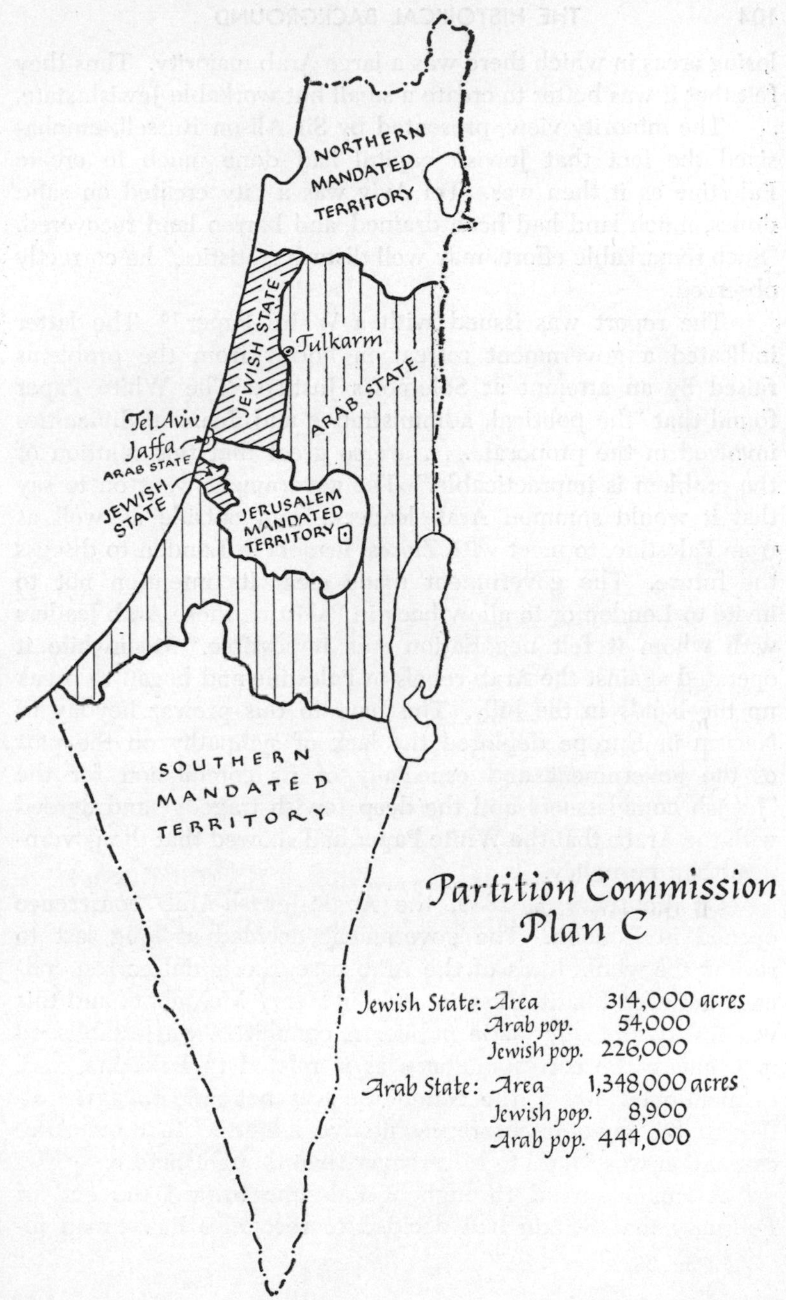
NORTHERN
MANDATED
TERRITORY
JEWISH STATE
Tulkarm
ARAB STATE
Tel Aviv
Jaffa
ARAB STATE
JEWISH
STATE
JERUSALEM
MANDATED
TERRITORY
SOUTHERN
MANDATED
TERRITORY
Partition Commission
Plan C
Jewish State: Area 314,000 acres
Arab pop. 54,000
Jewish pop. 226,000
Arab State: Area 1,348,000 acres
Jewish pop. 8,900
Arab pop. 444,000

losing areas in which there was a large Arab majority. Thus they felt that it was better to create a small but workable Jewish state.

The minority view, presented by Sir Alison Russell, emphasized the fact that Jewish capital had done much to create Palestine as it then was. Tel Aviv was a city created on sand dunes, much land had been drained, and barren land recovered. "Such remarkable efforts may well disturb statistics," he correctly observed.

The report was issued with a White Paper.[10] The latter indicated a government retreat in horror from the problems raised by an attempt at Solomon's Justice. The White Paper found that "the political, administrative and financial difficulties involved in the proposal . . . are so great that this solution of the problem is impracticable." The government went on to say that it would summon Arab leaders, from outside as well as from Palestine, to meet with Zionist leaders in London to discuss the future. The government made clear its intention not to invite to London or to allow back in Palestine those Arab leaders with whom it felt negotiation was impossible. Meanwhile it operated against the Arab rebels in Palestine and began to break up the bands in the hills. The Jews in this prewar heyday of Nazism in Europe deplored the lack of sympathy on the part of the government and especially of its commission for the "Jewish homelessness and the deep Jewish tragedy" and agreed with the Arabs that the White Paper had showed that the government had no policy.

On February 7, 1939, the Anglo-Jewish-Arab conference opened in London. The government decided at long last to review the whole basis of the Arab case, the initial correspondence between Sharif Hussein and Sir Henry McMahon, and this was finally officially made public. A committee was established to evaluate the correspondence as it related to Palestine, and, as mentioned above, the committee was not able to agree although the government representative admitted that the Arab contention was found to be stronger than thought before.

A rumor spread throughout Palestine toward the end of February that Britain had decided to recognize Palestinian in-

[10] Cmd 5893.

dependence, and this gave rise to Arab demonstrations of joy and to Jewish bombings of Arab areas in which 38 Arabs were killed. Neither party had cause for its feelings, however, as the conference failed to reach any agreement. The meetings adjourned on March 27. Both Jews and Arabs resolved to resist any limitation on their rights. From exile in Lebanon, the Mufti issued a manifesto calling on Arabs to support the rebellion which was being slowly worn down, and in Palestine the Histadrut issued a counter-manifesto calling upon Jews to resist any limitation on the National Home. To this end, and because of the situation in Europe, Jewish illegal immigration was greatly accelerated.

In the deadlock, the British government issued a new statement of policy[11] in which it decided to adhere to the proposals which *it* had submitted to the London Conference. It declared that Palestine would not be considered by the British government as a part of the territory promised to the Arabs by Sir Henry McMahon but also stated that it could not believe that the framers of the Balfour Declaration had intended to convert Palestine into a Jewish state against the will of the Arab population. It offered a plan whereby Palestine would if possible within ten years be given representative institutions and a constitution. After five years Jewish immigration would cease and Arab land sales would be permitted only in selected areas. The White Paper ended with a plea that both Jews and Arabs take note of the reverence of "many millions of Moslems, Jews and Christians throughout the world who pray for peace in Palestine and for the happiness of her people."

In Palestine, Jewish reaction was unanimous and furious. The transmission lines of the broadcasting station were cut so that announcement of the White Paper was delayed. Government offices were burned or sacked, police were stoned, and shops were looted. The government thus found itself under attack by both the Arab and the Jewish communities. Jewish hostility, however, began to convert the more moderate Arab leaders to support of the government. The policy was approved by Parliament on May 23. But the Permanent Mandates Com-

[11] Cmd 6019.

mission questioned the validity of the policy, and in Palestine Jewish attacks on the government increased in intensity and violence. On August 26 two British police inspectors were killed in Jerusalem.

Five days later the German army and Death Head units invaded Poland in "Operation White." The Second World War had begun.

12. FROM WAR TO WAR

The outbreak of world war came as a shock to everyone in Palestine. War, under whatever legal definition, had been endemic there since 1936, but suddenly the local conflict seemed petty. This reaction was unfortunately short-lived. Among both the Arab and the Jewish communities, there were some who either refused to let the world struggle hinder their own struggle or who used it as a lever against the British. The "Stern Gang," as the most extreme members of the Zionists came to be called, under the leadership of Abraham Stern, never let the war hinder their activities and even murdered a British Minister of State in the midst of the war. Some of the Arab leaders, notably the Mufti Hajj Amin al-Husseini, threw in their lot publicly with the Axis. However, the initial reaction of both communities was to pause in their own struggles and to volunteer to fight for Britain. The Jewish Agency issued an appeal to all Jews to assist in the war effort against Nazi Germany and obviously the Jewish response to fight against Hitler's dark forces ran flood tide. Over 134,000 Jews volunteered for service provided they were allowed to serve as a separate, national unit. The British felt that as badly as they needed men, they could not accept this condition and in the end 21,000 Jews and 8,000 Arabs agreed to serve and were accepted by the British in all branches of the British armed forces.

Within Palestine itself most of the Arab community also joined in support of the Allies. The Arab rebellion did not

(NOTE: See below, Part II, for more details on this period.)

cease immediately but it did lose its national basis. A number of Jews, including some Revisionists, were arrested in October and November and sentenced to long prison terms for carrying bombs and arms, and this led to some Jewish demonstrations. The government issuance of land-sales restrictions likewise led to Jewish demonstrations, and David Ben-Gurion on behalf of the Jewish Agency announced that he would not attempt to end the disorder.

The major cause of friction came with the rapid increase of Jewish illegal immigration. Feeling as it did acutely the hostility of Arabs to its prewar policy, the British government decided to do what it could to stop this illegal immigration and did deport several shiploads of illegal immigrants to Mauritius. The *Patria* was blown up in Haifa harbor to prevent the reshipment of its refugee passengers. An extreme wing of the terrorist Irgun, which had decided to cooperate with the British at the beginning of the war, continued its policy of terror. In 1942 Abraham Stern was killed by the police and many of his "Stern Gang" were imprisoned. We shall hear more of this group.

The immediate German threat to the Middle East was ended in the winter of 1942 with the British victory at el-Alamein, and this is seen in retrospect by the British government and most students of this period as the turning point in Anglo-Zionist relations. From November 1942 onward, the activist aspects of the Zionist program are again predominant. American politics had not a little to do with this, for the statements of Wendell Willkie, Senator Wagner, and those who supported the "Biltmore Program," (on which see below) indicated than even in the midst of a global war the Palestine issue could engage the attention of a Great Power far from Palestine. If this was the case so far from the scene, how much more might those in Palestine who were parties to the dispute be agitated.

Worried by the rising Jewish demonstrations and expressions that Palestine alone could be considered the haven for persecuted European Jewry, the Arab community was at a great disadvantage. Its only recognized and experienced leaders were in exile (and some had sided with Germany) and were not allowed to return even after the crisis seemed to be at least under control. Leadership of the Arab community in fact came increasingly to devolve upon non-Palestinian Arabs, and this factor led initially to Arab governments' protests to the American government over American support of Zionism and eventually to Arab military involvement in the 1948 war.

During the last stages of the Second World War, the Jewish paramilitary groups grew rapidly in size and equipment. Thefts on a large scale from military dumps became an undeclared policy of the Haganah and the terrorist groups. Regular training camps were established at the Jewish settlements. Bombings and shootings increased, and the number of British police casualties mounted steadily. On August 8, 1944, a Jewish attempt was made to assassinate the High Commissioner. Government installations were raided and looted, and the commander-in-chief of British forces in the Middle East was moved to issue a communiqué pointing out that the "active and passive sympathisers [of the Terrorists] are directly impeding the war effort of Great Britian . . . [and] assisting the enemy." Finally, on November 6, 1944, the British Minister of State, Lord Moyne, was murdered in Cairo by two members of the Stern Gang. This came as a shock to Prime Minister Churchill and led him to announce in Commons:

> If our dreams for Zionism are to end in the smoke of assassins' pistols and our labours for its future are to produce a new set of gangsters worthy of Nazi Germany, many like myself will have to reconsider the position we have maintained so consistently and so long in the past. If there is to be any hope of a peaceful and successful future for Zionism these wicked activities must cease and those responsible for them must be destroyed, root and branch.[1]

The Jewish Agency appealed to the Jewish community to "cast out the members of this destructive band, to deprive them of all refuge and shelter, to resist their threats and to render all necessary assistance to the authorities in prevention of terrorist acts and in the eradication of the terrorist organization." [2]

Security improved slightly in 1945, but during January a

[1] Reprinted in *Survey of Palestine,* I, 73.
[2] *Ibid.*

member of Haganah, which was an open secret though its existence was denied by the Jewish Agency,[3] was caught carrying a hand grenade while participating in a mock attack on an Arab village. His imprisonment led to a press attack on the government for this "provocative act." In the late spring of 1945 the incidence of attacks on the government and on British army units greatly increased. Raids were made with great precision on arms dumps, banks, and communication facilities. Once again, as Europe emerged from the war, Palestine took up war in earnest.

As the full horror of the war in Europe and the massive murder of Jews came to the public attention, it inevitably further inflamed the already critical situation. The British government was blamed, because of the restrictions on immigration which followed the 1939 White Paper, for the death of hundreds of thousands of European Jews who failed to escape from Europe. It is certainly true that more might have been done, but this is as true of America as of any other country. Indeed the enormity of the Nazi crime and the desperate plight of the survivors completely obscured the fact that Palestine had absorbed almost half a million Jews during the first twenty-four years of the Mandate—a six fold increase in the Jewish community. In the United States, which was the center of the protests made on Britain's handling of the Mandate, President Truman announced in December 1945 that the United States would facilitate the immigration of European refugees, but a year later he said that only 4,767 refugees had been admitted under these regulations.[4] In the same period, Palestine took in 7,851 registered immigrants and an unknown number of illegal immigrants.

With an unbroken record of failures in its attempt to settle the Palestine problem, the British government asked the United States to participate in one further inquiry. This time the Committee of Inquiry had, as a key part of its terms of reference, instructions to inquire into the European Jewish community's needs. None of the previous commissions had dealt with prob-

[3] See Kirk, *The Middle East 1945-1950* (London: 1954), pp. 211-12.
[4] *Ibid.*, pp. 188-89.

lems outside of Palestine, although the Royal Commission of 1936 had noted the European background of Zionism and the Partition Commission of 1938 had indicated that the problem it found was accentuated by the plight of the European Jewish communities. However, the Anglo-American Committee of Inquiry was to pay equal attention to European Jewry and to the Palestine problem. Foreign Secretary Ernest Bevin, in explaining the Commission to the House of Commons, pointed out that Palestine itself would be unable to cope with the general problem of Jewry at the end of the war, that Britain must continue to honor her obligations to Arabs, and that she must not lose sight of the interest of others in her empire, notably the 90 million Muslims of India, in the Palestine problem.

President Truman had suggested in August 1945 that Palestine should immediately admit 100,000 European Jews, and this the British government refused to do, but the figure was a convenient one and stuck.

13. INQUIRIES, REPORTS, AND PLANS

The Anglo-American Committee of Inquiry began its short life by a soul-rending tour of the assembly points for the survivors of Nazi bestiality. The emotional impact of this tour—a sort of gauntlet of nightmare horror—is eloquently described in the report:

In the cold print of a report it is not possible accurately to portray our feelings with regard to the suffering deliberately inflicted by the Germans on those Jews who fell into their hands. The visit of our Sub-Committee to the Ghetto in Warsaw has left on their minds an impression which will forever remain. Areas of that city on which formerly stood large buildings are now a mass of brick rubble, covering the bodies of numberless unknown Jews. Adjoining the Ghetto there still stands an old barracks used as a place for killing Jews. Viewing this in the cold grey light of a February day one could imagine the depths of human suffering there endured. In the courtyards of the barracks were pits containing human ash and human bones. The effect of that place on Jews who came searching, so often in vain, for any trace of their dear ones, can be left to the imagination.[1]

In Palestine, the Committee found the observations of the Royal Commission to be valid, as valid in 1946 as in 1936. Hostility of the Arabs to Zionism was unanimous. The major difference between the two dates was the new and increasing power of the Jewish Agency with its unofficial army estimated at 60,000. The description of Palestine will be recognized by all who saw it in these violent days.

Army tents, tanks, a grim fort and barracks overlook the waters of the Sea of Galilee. Blockhouses, road barriers manned by soldiers, barbed wire entanglements, tanks in the streets, preemptory searches, seizures and arrests on suspicion, bombings by gangsters and shots in the night are now characteristic . . .[2]

While awaiting the report of the Anglo-American Committee, the government of Palestine had set the immigration legal quota at 1,500 monthly, and had tightened up on penalties for armed attack, possession of firearms, and membership in terrorist groups. These attempts did little to calm the situation. Indeed it may now be doubted that the government of Palestine really knew the extent to which forces were being organized and equipped. In the matter of illegal immigration, which occupied much of the energies of the underground, General Morgan (then head of UNRRA in Germany) reported that he believed some "unknown Jewish organization" was conducting a "well organized, positive" program of getting Jews out of Europe.[3] This led to a storm of protests in America, to charges that Morgan was an anti-Semite; his remarks were compared to those made by the Nazis and his disclosure to the "Protocols of the Elders of Zion." In London it was charged that Morgan made his statements to attempt to influence the Anglo-American Committee. However, now that the story has been told by those who were on the inside, it comes clear that Morgan erred only in not realizing the full extent of the underground. Representatives

[1] Cmd 6808, pp. 12-13.
[2] *Ibid.*, p. 18.
[3] George Kirk, *The Middle East 1945-1950* (London: 1954), p. 204.

of the Jewish Agency or its various offshoots took over by the most incredible examples of bravery, bluff, and bribes the Red Cross organization in Rumania. They established a working relationship with the Czechoslovak government, which was persuaded either to turn a blind eye or to facilitate the passage of Jewish emigrants out of Poland and Russia. Greek passports were provided for thousands of Polish Jews, and the British Army Jewish Brigade in Italy served as a far ranging supplier, transporter, and troubleshooter for the whole network.[4] War experience—both positive in the sense of training and negative in the sense of desperation—had made of the Jewish paramilitary groups organizations of a degree of effectiveness unknown before in the Middle East.

The Anglo-American Committee's report was published April 20, 1946, and contained as its most publicized recommendation the immediate admission of 100,000 Jewish refugees into Palestine. This was supported by President Truman, but the State Department informed the Arab heads of state that the Committee recommendations were not binding and that the American government would make no moves on Palestine without consulting the Arabs.[5] The British government pointed out that the question of immigration was but one of many in the Committee proposals and sought to deal with the entire problem including the bloody and expensive item of public security. It pointed out with some logic that failing a general settlement, the admission of an additional 100,000 Jews would probably force the government to dispatch at least another division of troops to the already huge military establishment in Palestine.

On June 16 the tempo of military activity in Palestine quickened. The commando group of Haganah, the Palmach, destroyed nine bridges in different parts of the country in one night. The next night the Stern Gang attacked railway installations in Haifa, and on the 18th the Irgun kidnaped six British army officers and held them as hostages. In July the government published a series of intercepted telegrams which showed that

[4] Jon and David Kimche, *The Secret Roads* (London: 1954), passim.

[5] See *A Decade of American Foreign Policy* (Washington, D. C.: 1950), pp. 810-11; and Kirk, p. 204.

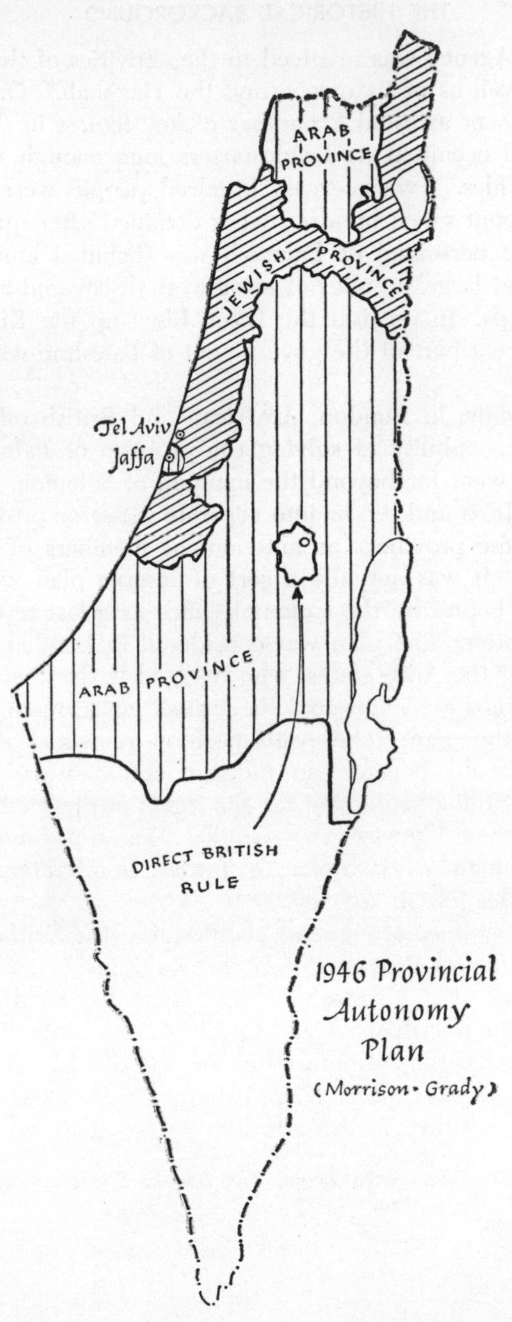

1946 Provincial Autonomy Plan (Morrison-Grady)

the Jewish Agency was involved in the activities of the terrorist groups as well as of its own army, the Haganah.[6] On June 29 the government arrested a number of key figures in the Jewish Agency and occupied its headquarters long enough to seize a part of its files. Twenty-seven hundred people were arrested, of whom about seven hundred were detained after questioning. Most of the personnel of Palmach was included among those arrested, and large supplies of arms were discovered and seized by the troops. In reprisal the Irgun blew up the King David Hotel, where a part of the government of Palestine was housed, on July 22.

Meanwhile, in London, American and British officials discussed the possibility of solving the problem of Palestine in a way which went far beyond the cunning of Solomon. It was to divide the Jews and Arabs into separate zones or provinces but to leave these provinces as autonomous members of one state (see map). It was actually a sort of reserve plan worked out some years before by the Colonial Office as a last resort failing anything better. The plan was considered in London by representatives of the Arab states, who rejected it. Neither Palestine Jews nor Arabs even accepted the British government invitation to discuss the plan. The Arab position remained as it had: Palestine should become an independent state ruled by its majority with due protection for the rights of the minority. The Zionist position likewise was familiar: Palestine should be a Jewish commonwealth, open to Jewish immigration as controlled by the Jewish Agency.

As yet another attempt at compromise, the British government suggested in February 1947 that Palestine be administered for five years as a trusteeship with substantial local autonomy in areas with Jewish or Arab majorities, the protection of the minority being the responsibility of the British High Commissioner, and provision be made to allow nearly 100,000 refugees to enter the country in the first two years.[7] This proposal was

[6] Cmd 6873; Menachem Begin, *The Revolt: The Story of the Irgun* (New York: 1951), passim.

[7] Cmd 7044.

rejected both by the Arabs (including the Arab Higher Committee) and the Jewish Agency.

Just prior to this last attempt at compromise with the main interested parties, and in the midst of the civil war in Palestine, America had taken the issue of Palestine deeply into domestic politics. This was not a new development. The American Congress had approved the Balfour Declaration and the State Department had recognized the Mandate in 1923. Then, during the war, petitions urging the creation of a Jewish state in Palestine had grown as Americans became more aware of the Nazi program in Europe. Political leaders from Taft to Wallace all supported Zionism. It may be doubted that the motives of the politicians were always combined with a full knowledge of the difficult position in which Britain was placed or even of the scope of the problem in Palestine, but the propaganda efforts of the Zionists were alone enough to swing even the uninterested into line. In 1946 both the Democratic and Republican parties determined to make gestures for the electorial support of Jews of New York by declarations favoring mass immigration into Palestine. This was of course at a delicate point in the diplomatic negotiations—which *might* have prevented the war—but scant attention was paid to this fact. First President Truman and then Mr. Dewey called for immediate admission of large numbers of immigrants. Since Mr. Truman had come first with his call, Mr. Dewey upped the ante—from 100,000 in the Democratic appeal to the Republican "several hundreds of thousands." [8]

In these circumstances—failure, heavy expenditure of men and money, and what the British regarded as American irresponsibility[9]—Britain decided to turn the problem over to the United Nations. Speaking in the House of Commons, on February 18, 1947, Mr. Bevin said the government had

> been faced with an irreconcilable conflict of principles. There are in Palestine about 1,200,000 Arabs and 600,000 Jews. For the Jews, the essential point of principle is the creation of a sovereign Jewish

[8] Kermit Roosevelt, "The Partition of Palestine, a Lesson in Pressure Politics," *Middle East Journal,* II (1948), 5 ff.

[9] This opinion was shared by the opposition as well as the government. Churchill made a speech to this effect in Commons, August 1, 1946.

State. For the Arabs, the essential point of principle is to resist to the last the establishment of Jewish sovereignty in any part of Palestine. The discussions of the last month have quite clearly shown that there is no prospect of resolving this conflict by any settlement negotiated between the parties. . . . We have, therefore, reached the conclusion that the only course now open to us is to submit the problem to the judgment of the United Nations . . . We shall then ask the United Nations . . . to recommend a settlement of the problem. We do not intend ourselves to recommend any particular solution . . .[10]

The United Nations had previously taken official recognition of the problem of Palestine, in the Security Council and General Assembly, but it had not itself investigated the situation. On April 2, the British delegate to the United Nations requested that the Secretary General call a special session of the General Assembly so that this session might create an agency to report on Palestine at the regular fall session. The Soviet Union wanted the five permanent members of the Security Council to assume the responsibility for finding a solution, but the British and American governments, anxious that Russia not get involved in the problem, countered by urging that all the Big Powers be excluded from membership. On May 15, 1947, the General Assembly voted to create a Special Committee on Palestine (UNSCOP), to submit not later than September 1, 1947, "such proposals as it may consider appropriate for the solution of the problem of Palestine." [11] Members of the Committee were representatives of Australia, Canada, Czechoslovakia, Guatemala, India (then undivided), Iran, Netherlands, Peru, Sweden, Uruguay, and Yugoslavia.

UNSCOP members arrived in Jerusalem on June 14 and first met on June 16. They had decided not to follow the course of the Anglo-American Committee in discussing the refugee problem before they had made a study of the situation in Palestine; so mid-June may be taken as the date of their effective beginning. The government of Palestine issued a supplement to the survey it had prepared for the Anglo-American Committee,

[10] Quoted in, *The Political History of Palestine Under British Administration* [Memo for UNSCOP] (Jerusalem: 1947).

[11] Resolution 106 (S-1); quoted in UNSCOP, *Report,* I, 2-3.

but when one reads the documentation of this period, he cannot but be struck by the fact that there was little material change in the situation or the information on that situation from the previous year. Once again the Arab Higher Committee showed itself inflexible by refusing to participate in the meetings of the Special Committee.[12] The Arab states, however, did make their views known by repeating arguments they had previously advanced.

The Jewish Agency, to the contrary, cooperated in full with the UNSCOP and provided its members with extensive documentation and appeals. Even the Irgun, then engaged in a game of hide-and-seek with the whole of the British forces in Palestine and not always on friendly terms with the Haganah, managed to hold a lengthy meeting with the chairman of the Committee.

The Committee found little that was different from what its predecessors had reported. It pointed out that Palestine was a small country and of its limited extent somewhat over 10,000 square miles, only about half was inhabitable by settled people. Although the country was principally agricultural—65 per cent of the population gained a living directly from agriculture—some 50 per cent of the cereals used by the population had to be imported. Its major geographical feature involved "the ill-matched gifts of political strife and economic advantage" in being on the "cross-roads" of Europe, North-Africa, and Asia. Palestine, it noted, "is exceedingly poor" in all of the resources needed for modern industry. The population was then 1,203,000 Arabs to 608,000 Jews—*i.e.*, 2 to 1—but since the Arab birth rate was much higher than the Jewish, these figures would probably, if immigration were stopped, by 1960 be 1,533,000 to 664,000—or almost 5 to 2. Lastly, to complicate the problem of any sort of partition, the UNSCOP found that there "is no clear territorial separation of Jews and Arabs by large contiguous areas."

> Jews are more than 40 per cent of the total population in the districts of Jaffa (which includes Tel-Aviv), Haifa and Jerusalem. In the northern inland areas of Tiberias and Beisan, they are between 25 and 34 per cent of the total population. In the inland northern dis-

[12] UNSCOP, *Report*, II, Annex 8.

tricts of Safad and Nazareth and the coastal districts of Tulkarm and Ramle, Jews form between 10 and 25 per cent of the total population, while in the central districts and the districts south of Jerusalem they constitute not more than 5 per cent of the total.[13]

Unquestionably the problems involved in partition were great, yet the urgency of the problem was even greater than in the previous year. Some 17,873 illegal immigrants were under detention and 820 Palestinians were under arrest for security reasons. And the general situation reported by the Anglo-American Committee prevailed:

The atmosphere in Palestine today is one of profound tension. In many respects the country is living under a semi-military regime. In the streets of Jerusalem and other key areas barbed wire defenses, road blocks, machine gun posts and constant armoured car patrols are routine measures. In areas of doubtful security, Administration officials and the military forces live within strictly policed security zones and work within fortified and closely-guarded buildings. Freedom of personal movement is liable to severe restriction and the curfew and martial law have become a not uncommon experience. . . .[14]

The administration found that virtually its whole energies had to be devoted to public security and eventually, in all truth, to self-security. The government stated:

The right of any community to use force as a means of gaining its political ends is not admitted in the British Commonwealth. Since the beginning of 1945 the Jews have implicitly claimed this right and have supported by an organized campaign of lawlessness, murder and sabotage their contention that, whatever other interests might be concerned, nothing should be allowed to stand in the way of a Jewish State and free Jewish immigration into Palestine . . . the Jewish community still publicly refuses its help to the Administration in suppressing terrorism, on the ground that the Administration's policy is opposed to Jewish interests.[15]

This being the situation, UNSCOP recommended that the Mandate be terminated "at the earliest practicable date"; that "Independence shall be granted in Palestine at the earliest

[13] *Ibid.*, p. 13.

[14] *Ibid.*, p. 28.

[15] Government of Palestine, *Supplementary Memorandum*, p. 56; as quoted in *ibid.*

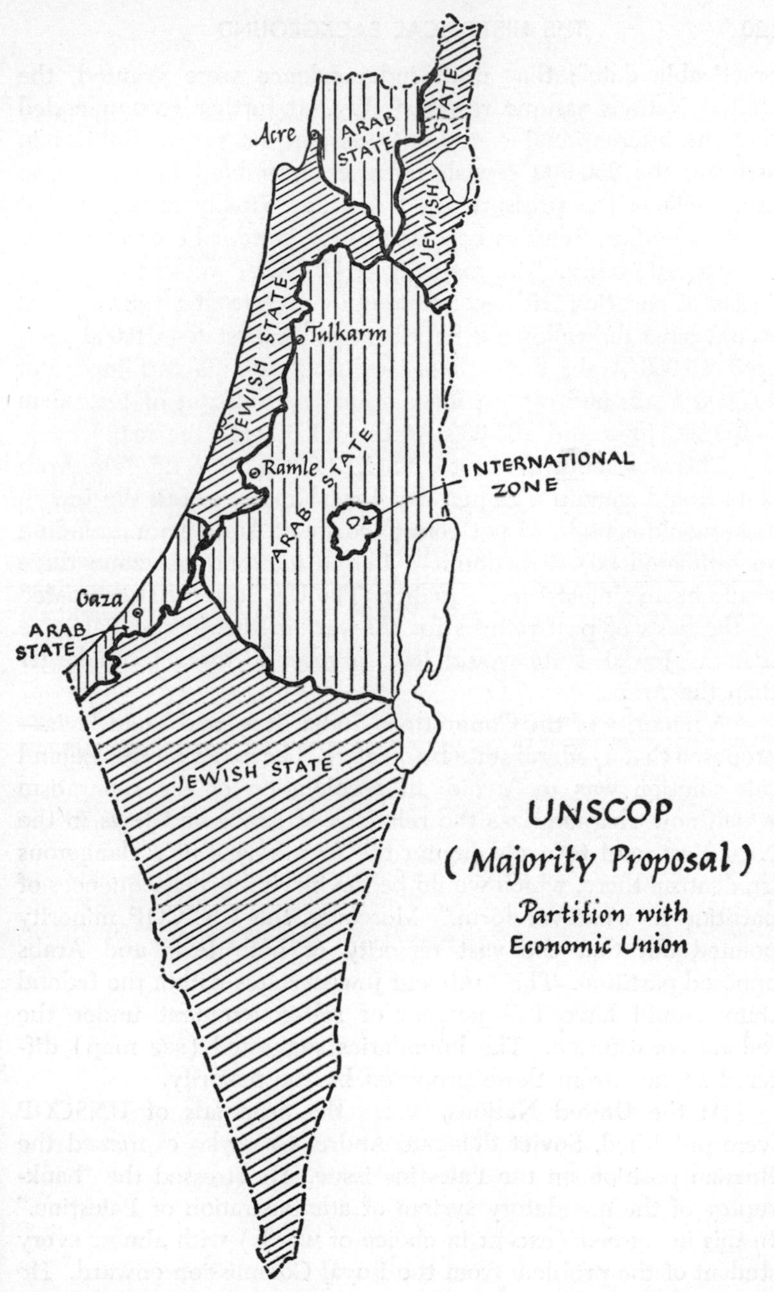
Acre
ARAB STATE
JEWISH STATE
JEWISH STATE
Tulkarm
Ramle
ARAB STATE
INTERNATIONAL ZONE
Gaza
ARAB STATE
JEWISH STATE
UNSCOP
(Majority Proposal)
Partition with
Economic Union

practicable date"; that until independence were granted, the United Nations assume responsibility. It further recommended that the international community assume *its* responsibilities in assisting the 250,000 Jewish refugees assembled in Europe so as to relieve the pressure on Palestine. Finally it urged that whatever other divisions be made in Palestine it be preserved as an economic unity. The majority of UNSCOP voted to approve a plan of partition with economic union. The states thus created would have the following populations: Arab state—10,000 Jews and 725,000 Arabs and others; Jewish state—498,000 Jews and 407,000 Arabs and others; internationalized district of Jerusalem —100,000 Jews and 105,000 Arabs and others (see map).

This was about the best UNSCOP felt it could do. The Arab state would contain a 1½ per cent Jewish minority but the Jewish state would contain 45 per cent minority of Arabs (not including an estimated 90,000 bedouin). In the international zone there would be an almost 1 to 1 equality. The UN Secretariat estimated on the basis of past returns for the various districts of Palestine that the Jewish state would have a revenue three times larger than the Arab.

A minority of the Committee—India, Iran, and Yugoslavia—proposed that a federal state be created. The major motive behind this solution was to "avoid an acceleration of the separatism which now characterizes the relations of Arabs and Jews in the Near East, and to avoid laying the foundations of a dangerous irredentism there, which would be the inevitable consequences of partition in whatever form." Moreover, the UNSCOP minority pointed out that the vast majority of both Jews and Arabs opposed partition. The Arab and Jewish states within the federal state should have full powers of self-government under the federal constitution. The boundaries suggested (see map) differed slightly from those proposed by the majority.

At the United Nations *before* the proposals of UNSCOP were published, Soviet delegate Andrei Gromyko expressed the Russian position on the Palestine issue. He stressed the "bankruptcy of the mandatory system of administration of Palestine." In this he agreed (except in choice of words) with almost every student of the problem from the Royal Commission onward. He

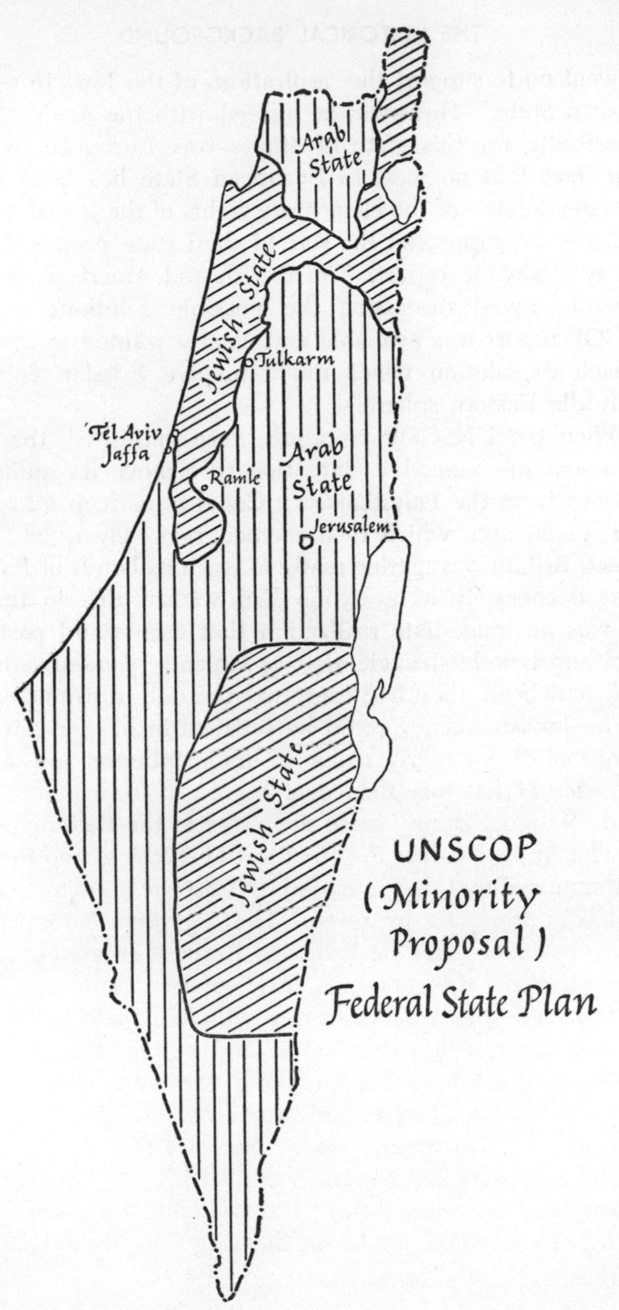

UNSCOP (Minority Proposal) Federal State Plan

then went on to support the "aspirations of the Jews to establish their own State." However, he agreed with the Arabs that the responsibility for this state of affairs was European, was due to the "fact that no western European State has been able to ensure the defense of the elementary rights of the Jewish people," and finally he supported the sort of dual state proposed in the minority UNSCOP report. The British and American delegates wanted to avoid discussing the possible solutions until the UNSCOP report was available and clearly wanted to avoid any approach to solution which might involve Russian entry into the Middle Eastern sphere.

When the UNSCOP proposals were published, the British government announced its intention to remove its military installations from the Palestine-Suez Canal area deep into central Africa, to an area which then seemed relatively quiet, Kenya. In effect, Britain was getting ready to wash its hands of Palestine, and as desperately as everyone had wished this in the past, there was an immediate realization that this would participate a grim and bloody struggle, that as violently condemned as the British had been, they had exercised the only restraint existing.

The Jewish Agency could be satisfied in having gained the recognition of her early claim to independence and a much larger slice of territory than ever before offered, except in the limited "National Home" sense suggested in the Balfour Declaration. The Arabs felt that they had lost everything, and they publicly announced that they intended to resist the implementation of UNSCOP's proposals by force. The Egyptian newspaper *al-Ahram* predicted that "the Palestine Arabs will launch a relentless war to repel this attack on their country, especially as they know that all the Arab countries will back and assist them, supplying them with men, money, and ammunition." [16]

The rival communities prepared for war. The Arabs in two—rival—paramilitary organizations neither of which proved to amount to much when tested. The Jews of course had large cadres of men who had served in the British army or the American army and air force during the war, and they already had standing, if concealed, armies in the Haganah, its Palmach elite

[16] Quoted in Kirk, p. 247.

corps, the Irgun, and the smaller Stern Gang. Quantities of equipment and ammunition were being seized from British stores and soon the Jewish purchasing agents were able to begin to send into Palestine considerable American and Czech equipment.

At the United Nations, both the U. S. and U.S.S.R. supported partition, and by agreement, arrived at on November 10, decided that the British Mandate should end May 1 and that the two states would be established by July 1. The British delegate announced that the British army would have evacuated the country by August 1, 1948, and that Britain would thereafter not participate in whatever efforts were made to police the area.

When the General Assembly met on November 26, Sir Alexander Cadogan announced that Britain wanted to make quite certain that the General Assembly realized it could not count upon British forces to impose its decisions on either Jews or Arabs.

As one rereads the speeches of these meetings, he cannot but be struck by the unwillingness of the responsible public officials to take note of the countless warnings of investigators of the intensity of feeling on all sides in the Palestine conflict. The American delegate, for example, felt that a partition of the country need not create an emotional frontier, even though it be forced upon the people, and fondly suggested that it could be thought of in terms parallel to that which separates America from Canada. Hindsight is of course the great advantage of the historian, but by the winter of 1947 it might well have been included in the arsenal of the statesman. Warning after warning had been sounded on the probable consequences of an imposed settlement. Yet we shall see that the United Nations continued to act on the highly unrealistic assumption that everyone concerned would accept its moral authority and acquiesce.

In the Middle East, outside of Palestine itself the growth of anti-Zionism among the Arabs had reached a fever pitch. Ugly demonstrations broke out in many points all over the Middle East in which not only American and Soviet property but Jews and Jewish property were attacked. In points as widely scattered as Aden, Libya, and Baghdad attacks were made on

Jews. The reasons for these are not complex. They are the result of a growing feeling of anger over Palestine which could not be expressed against the distant Palestine Jewish community and so was vented locally upon Jews who in most cases had little or no contact with Zionism. Local conditions certainly had much to do with the nature of the attacks, but the fact that the Zionist movement had from its earliest days proclaimed itself the representative of the entirety of world Jewry had not a little to do with the growth of Arab hostility. A number of younger Arab men interviewed by the authors indicated that during this period they had decided in regard to Jews—just as the Turks had decided about the fathers of these young Arabs in the period just before the First World War—that they could no longer be trusted, that their emotional ties were sundered, and that they had "gone over" to the enemy. The Jewish communities in their turn reacted as the Arabs had done in that earlier case by recoiling in fear from the nations in which many of them had participated, often at the highest levels of government. This ugly situation slowly developed in the ensuing months until it led to a large-scale migration from Iraq and Yemen, and so increased the immigration pressure upon Palestine.

It should not be forgotten, in condemning these attacks upon Jews, as they should certainly be condemned, that even in England during the same period tempers ran high. Particularly after the Irgun kidnaped and executed two British army sergeants in reprisal for the hanging of Irgun terrorists, compounded as this act was by the attempt to murder British public figures with letter bombs, anti-Jewish feeling assumed proportions unknown in Britain in modern times.

At the United Nations, after study by various subcommittees and after lengthy debates on the floor, a proposal was made to partition Palestine. It was suggested to accept in general UNSCOP's recommendations with minor frontier changes (the main feature being to include Jaffa within the Arab state—see map). Considerable lobbying took place behind the scenes for the votes of several smaller states which had either been opposed

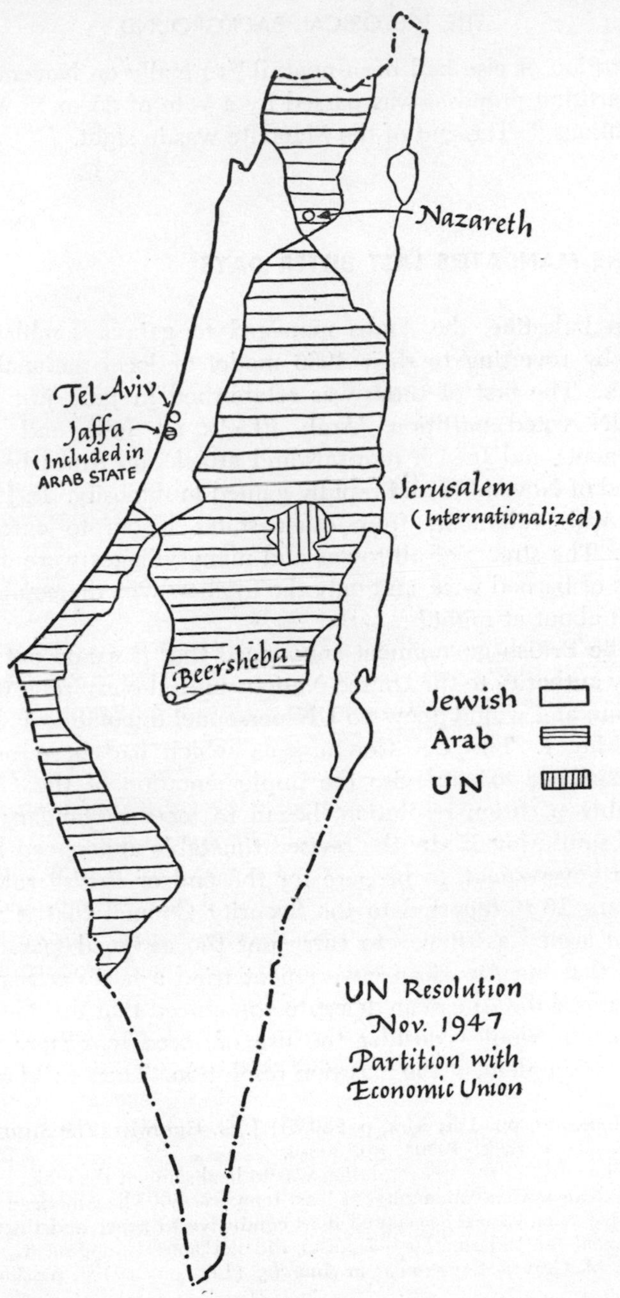
Nazareth
Tel Aviv
Jaffa
(Included in
ARAB STATE
Jerusalem
(Internationalized)
Beersheba
Jewish
Arab
UN
UN Resolution
Nov. 1947
Partition with
Economic Union

to partition or else had been neutral.[17] Finally on November 29 the partition proposal was passed by a vote of 33 to 13 with 10 abstentions.[18] The end of the Mandate was in sight.

14. THE MANDATE'S LAST BITTER DAYS

In Palestine, the Arabs managed to gain a semblance of unity by reverting to their 1936 model of local national committees. The first of these was established in Jaffa just before the UN voted partition. Arab attacks on Jews and Jewish settlements and Jewish reprisals and attacks on Arabs began at the end of November and rapidly gained in intensity. In January 1948 Arab volunteers from other states began to enter Palestine. The streets of all towns and many villages were already forests of barbed wire, and only the foolhardy or the combatants moved about at night.[1]

The British government announced that it would not transfer any authority to the United Nations until the expiration of the Mandate and would allow no UN personnel to come to Palestine until May 1. The UN Commission, which had been ordered into existence to supervise the implementation of the General Assembly partition resolution, began to meet in January 1948. It had until May 15, by the revised timetable announced by the British government, to prepare for the end of British rule. On February 16 it reported to the Security Council that it would require armed assistance to carry out the assigned task. Then it was that the American government tried a hasty retreat. On February 24 the American delegate announced that the American government would consider the use of force to restore peace but not to implement the partition resolution. Then on March 19

[17] Roosevelt, pp. 1 ff; Kirk, p. 250-51; J. C. Hurewitz, *The Struggle for Palestine* (New York: 1950), pp. 308-9.

[18] The effect of the UN resolution was to heal some of the major splits in the American Jewish community, at least temporarily. The American Jewish Committee (non-Zionist) accepted it as conducive to peace and the American Council for Judaism (anti-Zionist) did not actively oppose it.

[1] R. M. Graves, *Experiment in Anarchy* (London: 1949), passim.

he suggested that action on partition be suspended and a trusteeship over all Palestine be established to delay final settlement. Britain refused to extend the Mandate, and the U.S.S.R. insisted that the original decision be carried out. Thus, as the remaining days were used in debate, the UN was never able to decide to create any means of implementing the policy it had, which was a policy no one really wanted.

The situation in Palestine was rapidly coming to a head. The Arab leader of the 1936 revolt was again in Palestine with about 5,000 volunteers in scattered and uncoordinated bands. As the British troops exposed themselves less and less and began to withdraw from remote positions, these bands raided settlements and even managed to cut the road from Tel-Aviv to Jerusalem, but they soon showed that they were no match for the Jewish military units. Both Jews and Arabs set up shadow governments by drawing on the personnel of the Mandate government and their respective organizations. In the Jewish Agency, of course, the Jewish community had a ready-made government. The Arabs were more restricted in their experience—in never having a comparable organization to the Jewish Agency, and in having their leaders absent for a decade from the local scene.

The day-to-day events in Palestine from December 1947 to May 1948 belie the arbitrary classifications of peace and war. There were 5,000 casualties[2] during this period and the damage to property may be estimated in the millions of dollars. In some days as many as 50 "incidents" were reported all over Palestine. Trains were blown up, banks robbed, government offices attacked, convoys ambushed, and mobs and gangs looted, burned, and clashed with troops or rival mobs.

The surrounding Arab states prepared for war and their presses proclaimed in lurid and strident tones that they would resist to the death the UN decision. However, on March 21, the Political Committee of the Arab League unexpectedly made a bid for a compromise peace. It decided to insist that the original British proposal, which the American government was also considering, be enforced. This would have put Palestine

[2] *Ibid.*, pp. 171-72.

under a temporary trusteeship. The committee further urged that the Jews then on Cyprus be accepted into the several Arab states as immigrants and that those in Palestine be assured their rights as a minority in an Arab state. If the proposal was in earnest, it was certainly too little and too late. Psychologically no one could retreat, least of all the Arab governments.

As this period draws to its close, it is worth pausing for a moment to survey the relative positions of the parties to the struggle.

The Jews, as mentioned above, could draw and did draw effectively upon their skills and resources as a highly educated, efficient, and determined community. Although their army was theoretically "underground,"[3] they were able to create out of existing or imported personnel a good air force, albeit with very few planes, with considerable battle experience in the RAF and American air force. Their army, the Haganah, which had been created in the 1930's by the British officer Orde Wingate, was stiffened by veterans of several European armies and had a grasp of modern warfare foreign to their opponents. Agents abroad did a remarkable job of assembling the arsenal of these forces.[4] Lastly, the Jewish community felt, with considerable justification according to the Arab press, that this was a war to the knife and that whatever pious resolutions might be made at Lake Success the future would be made in Palestine.

On the surface, the Arabs appeared infinitely stronger. After all, the whole Arab world was publicly pledged to intervene in the war. Egypt, Iraq, Syria, Lebanon, and Trans-Jordan all had standing armies and were receiving surplus British or French equipment. Public enthusiasm, especially among students and the middle class, was high. Yet it was

[3] It was not, however, really "underground" since it was able to maintain recruiting centers in December 1947 and began a registration of Jewish youth (including foreign nationals) on December 8.

[4] The full story of arms procurement has yet to be told. Much was obtained in Italy, where Zionist agents were active in the summer of 1947; some came from America in spite of a legal ban. For example, a shipment of "used machinery" was found in New York harbor to contain 65,000 lbs. of TNT, and a number of B-17 bombers were ferried across the Atlantic which eventually got to Palestine. Much materiel was subsequently purchased from Czechoslovakia.

little realized at the time how weak the Arab governments were. None of the governments was "popular" in its own home, and subsequent events proved that corruption was not only prevalent but existed to such an extent as to all but incapacitate most of the Arab forces. The army commands proved inefficient particularly in logistics but lacked initiative in tactics as well. The troops were poorly trained and often poorly led. And finally, even in dire need, the Arab governments proved that their jealousies and personal quarrels were of much more importance to them than their declared interest in Palestine. None of the Arabs, Palestinian or other, except the Arab Legion of Trans-Jordan, could begin to match the level of personal technical competence of the Jewish forces. Finally, in the Arabs of Palestine they found little support. These had been virtually leaderless since 1938 and had never really recovered from their great rebellion of 1936-38.[5] As we shall see, by the end of the Mandate, they had become a series of terrorized, psychologically defeated mobs, fleeing in all directions.

Early in April the pattern of events began to assume some shape. British forces had been steadily pulling out of the country. The March 20 statement by the Secretary General of the Arab League that the Arabs would accept a truce and limited trusteeship for Palestine if the Jewish Agency would agree, was rejected out of hand by David Ben-Gurion "for even the shortest time." Fighting raged over most of Palestine. On March 27 Jewish aircraft had begun to participate in the fighting for the first time. Then on April 8 the most active and popular Arab leader, Abd el-Qadir Huseini (who was then chief of the Arab national guard) was killed. On April 10 the Irgun with the help of Haganah attacked and took the village of Deir Yasin. After Haganah had left, the Irgun, in a deliberate attempt to promote terror among the general Arab population, massacred all the village inhabitants and widely publicized its action. Arab attacks on settlements and Jewish areas began

[5] Robert Graves wrote in his diary on April 25: "It seems to me that the Arabs have a definite leaning towards anarchy, and that their lawlessness, disorderliness and lack of organisation may enable the Jews to perform a miracle and achieve a state of their own in Palestine" (p. 187).

to be beaten off and on April 15 Haganah launched a major counterattack against the main Arab army under Fawzi el-Qawaqchi. From then on the Arab forces began to fail in their attempts and to assume the defensive. On April 19 Haganah took Tiberias as the British evacuated its Arab population. April 21 saw the Irgun and Haganah offensive on Haifa, which surrendered and was evacuated by the Arab population. (On April 22 President Truman announced that the U. S. would be willing to furnish its share of troops to a UN force for Palestine.) April 27 the Stern Gang seized $1 million from Barclay's Bank in Tel-Aviv. On May 2 the British ordered a 48-hour cease fire in part of Jerusalem and announced that they were returning some troops to Palestine to attempt to restore some order. Shortly thereafter Jaffa was declared an open city under Haganah control and on May 14 Haganah captured Acre. Staggering from these defeats, Arabs were pouring out of the country by every road. On May 14 in the afternoon at Tel-Aviv, David Ben-Gurion proclaimed the establishment of the State of Israel.

The Mandate had ended.[6]

[6] On the last days of the Mandate, see Sir Alan Cunningham [the last High Commissioner], "Palestine; the last days of the Mandate," *International Affairs,* XXIV (1948), 481 ff; and Harry Sacher, *Israel: The Establishment of a State* (London: 1952). Cunningham probably summed up the British unofficial attitude when he wrote, " . . . every Jew brought to Palestine during the last twelve years, up to the termination of the Mandate, was brought in under the protection of British bayonets, and was protected against Hitler through the same agency. I wonder if many Jews in Palestine ask themselves what would have happened in that country had we not barred the way to Palestine in the face of the German southward drive of 1941?" (p. 482).

Part II. JEWISH INTERESTS IN PALESTINE

by David M. Stamler

1. THE AGE-OLD LONGING

The roots of few modern problems are to be found so deeply embedded in the past as are those of the Palestine problem, and no true understanding of Zionism can be obtained by examining only those aspects of the movement which might be labeled "political Zionism." For while Zionism as a political movement is but a recent growth, a product of the closing years of the nineteenth century, Zionism as an emotional force—and few movements have been as dependent upon emotional drive as has this one—is clearly discernible within Jewish history for over two thousand years. Moreover, this almost mystical yearning for the restoration of national independence was no vague nostalgia. In a religion which has turned even ethical principles into carefully regulated legislation in order to ensure their observance, the settlement of the soil of Palestine became a holy act even though in the nineteenth century the trends of Messianic thought of the Orthodox and the lack of religious practice on the part of many of the early Zionists turned many of the most Orthodox elements against the movement.[1] When military action was possible it was resorted to, as in the case of the revolt of Bar-Cochba against the Romans in 135 A.D. and in the uprisings such as that against the Byzantine powers in 614 when the Jews took sides with the Sassanian Persians who had promised them independence. When independent action was denied them, the land of Israel was absorbed into the corpus of Jewish law, into the prayer book, into the very hearts and minds of the people.

[1] An interesting development at the same time, however, was the emigration to Palestine of small numbers of the most strictly Orthodox who, like the German Templars and the American Colony awaited the final divine redemption and spent their lives in study and prayer. Among the modern descendants of these Jews are the *"neturei Karta,"* the ultra-Orthodox sect in Jerusalem which refuses to acknowledge the authority of the Jewish state, maintaining that only the Messiah can bring about the third Jewish Commonwealth.

It would be a grave mistake to underestimate the force of this passionate longing. To dismiss it as a yearning wholly relegated to a Messianic age would be incorrect; even the hope for a Messianic age was considered a practical ideal realizable at any time. The majority of the Jews of Europe lived in the midst of poverty, hatred, and physical restrictions. But the eyes of the Jew rested not only on the ghetto walls but also on the walls of Jerusalem. His thrice daily prayers were directed there; when he built a house he left a portion unpainted to remind him that Jerusalem was as yet unbuilt. At the circumcision mention was made of God's promise to Abraham to give him the land of Israel; at weddings a glass was crushed to remind those present that as long as the Temple was destroyed unrestrained pleasure was out of place; and in death a bag of earth from the Holy Land was placed in the grave so that the final resting place might be on sacred soil.

This age-old desire for a return to Palestine was characterized too by the small but steady trickle of Jews from Europe and North America who emigrated there throughout the years: some to live and settle, others merely to spend their remaining years. For the majority of these Jews—and their number was always small—the spur was not always one of physical danger in their homeland. The peril of the journey and the difficulties of life in the Holy Land were often as great. They were motivated almost entirely by a purely religious impulse, an impulse similar to that which urges the Muslim to make his Meccan pilgrimage. There was little to attract them either in the physical or legal welcome which awaited them. By 1839 when the Committee of the General Assembly of the Church of Scotland for the Conversion of the Jews sent two of its members to report on the condition of the Jews in the Holy Land, they estimated their numbers, apart from some five thousand in Damascus, as only 13,000. With the Turkish rulers in no way concerned with the welfare of the Jewish population, disease, extreme poverty, heavy taxation and the lack of public security had reduced the Jews to a state of despair.

The mainstay of their support was provided by the system of *"Chalukah"*—the organized collection of money throughout the Diaspora for the support of the many Talmudical colleges and students in Palestine. With the extension of this system to include not only the students themselves but also their families and even distant relatives, the danger of the scheme became very real. Even apart from misuse of funds by the accredited collectors, the Chalukah turned the whole Yishuv (the Jewish Community in Palestine) into a charitable organization. Their total reliance on it for aid removed all thought and desire for self-help. The scheme—begun with the best intentions—became the perpetuator of poverty in the Holy Land.

It might well be asked why it was, if the love for Zion was primarily a religiously motivated love, that not until the last quarter of the nineteenth century did the movement assume any appreciable proportions, particularly since this period saw a decline in Jewish religious practice among many of the younger generation. However, even spiritual aims are rarely free from more mundane influences, and economics can play a part in the development of even religious trends.

With the advent of the industrial revolution in the countries of eastern Europe, the structure of Jewish economic life began to crumble. Admittedly the more enterprising few and those with the greater opportunities gained from this large-scale capitalist expansion. But the majority of the Jews who had occupied positions as small shopkeepers, peddlers, coachmen, carters, and craftsmen suffered severely from the change. The village lost much of its importance and income with the flow of the population to the towns. The government-controlled railways, in whose service Jews could rarely find employment, destroyed the business of the carter and coach driver, while the machine removed much of the income of the artisan. Thus the driving impulses of anti-Semitism (which will be discussed in more detail in the following chapter), and that of economic need, were to combine with the age-old longing to produce a political movement whose existence was to hold the attention of the world.

Zionism has never been a movement wholly within the control of those Jews who were its main supporters. Like almost every aspect of Jewish life it has been receptive to the slightest tremor of the outside world; the course along which it has moved has ever been sensitive to other factors with which it had no direct connection. The fate of the Jew has rarely been decided by him alone. Thus the desire to aid and strengthen the Jewish community in Palestine was by no means restricted to Jews alone; moreover the range and vision of the non-Jewish supporters of a Jewish revival was, at first, broader and more far reaching in scope.

Since the French Revolution the whole problem of Jewish rights had been growing more important and pressing. The proposal of Napoleon[2] made during his Near Eastern campaign that he would help resettle the Jews in Palestine if they would aid his forces produced but little effect. However, during the nineteenth century (and long before Pinsker and Herzl made of Zionism a political movement) a succession of men added their efforts to the fight for a Jewish restoration. Particularly in Britain there arose such a group. Nurtured on a powerful Old Testament tradition and motivated partly through humanitarian motives, though not blind to the advantages which might accrue to Great Britain through such a scheme, men like Colonel Henry Churchill (in a letter to Sir Moses Montefiore) proposed the "regeneration of Syria and Palestine" by the Jewish people.

The notorious blood-libel murder case in Damascus and the loosing of the grip of Mehmet Ali over Palestine had served to highlight the events of the region; and Britain, concerned for her interests and trade routes in the area, saw in a revived Jewish community a stabilizing factor. Throughout the 1840's Colonel George Gawler, one-time Governor of South Australia, pressed the claims for Jewish resettlement in Palestine in order that Britain might ensure her unbroken lines of communication; while in 1840 the Earl of Shaftesbury had petitioned Lord Palmerston,

[2] Published in the *Moniteur Universel* (Paris), April 20, 1799; see also *The New Judaea* (London), September 1940–February 1941.

the British Foreign Secretary, on the same subject. Some thirty-six years later Shaftesbury—a man whose philanthropy and humanitarian interests were deeply moved by the political and social restrictions upon the Jews—was still to speak of "the crowning bond of union" between the Jewish people and the Land of Israel.

In 1879 Sir Laurence Oliphant, one of the most active of all British advocates of Jewish resettlement in Palestine, visited that country and attempted to obtain a concession from the Ottoman government. Oliphant, who "shared much of the facile anti-Semitism of his time,"[3] was motivated by a curious mixture of sentimental, political, and economic motives, though there is little doubt that the economic motive predominated. Admittedly Oliphant was interested in the fulfilling of a Biblical prophecy; certainly too he was concerned for the "oppressed Jews from Roumania and the South of Russia" who would compose "the bulk of the immigrants."[4] However, his main idea was that his scheme would ensure "the political and economic penetration of Palestine by Britain." Though verbal support for his scheme was plentiful, Oliphant found the Ottoman government slow to act. More possibly the Sultan was delaying in order to ascertain British motives; for when the British fleet demonstrated in the Dardanelles,[5] the Sultan, realizing the full implications of the British plan, turned to Russia and refused to countenance any further British suggestions. Ruefully Oliphant adds, "Either we should have made no demonstrations or we should have carried it out sharp . . ."

While France's ambition in the Middle East continued to serve as an obstacle to the British advance, it was Russia's ever present desire for a southern penetration to the sea that presented the greatest threat. That Britain might at some stage come to an

[3] P. Henderson, *Life of Laurence Oliphant* (London: 1956), p. 203.
[4] *Ibid.*, p. 204.
[5] On February 8, 1878, in pursuance of its policy of keeping Russia out of the Mediterranean, the British fleet entered the Dardanelles. Under Russian pressure the Sultan refused permission for the ships to proceed; but on February 15 the British fleet arrived at Constantinople, having been ordered there without the Sultan's consent.

agreement with Russia which would satisfy both countries' ambitions had been a fear of Turkey's ever since Tzar Nicholas I visited England in 1844. At that time his proposal that Britain and Russia should agree to a joint dismembering of the Turkish possessions failed to endear itself to the British government, which preferred to preserve the "sick man of Europe" as a barrier to a Russian advance. The British government had little love for Ottoman rule, but the prospect of a Russian outlet on the Mediterranean was even more disquieting. In spite of the clause in the Treaty of Paris of 1856 which formally avowed the decision of Britain, France, and Russia to respect the existing possessions of Turkey, the Sultan's suspicion of British penetration remained. The Druze-Christian war in the Lebanon in 1860 provided France with her opportunity to intervene and occupy the Lebanon for an original six months' period which was later extended by four months. Although Napoleon III withdrew his troops in 1861 the French foothold in the Lebanon and Syria was firm and Britain's determination to advance her own cause in the area was strengthened. Her opportunity came, and was grasped, in 1876 when Disraeli purchased the Suez Canal shares of Khedive Ismail, the bankrupt grandson of Mehmet Ali, on behalf of the British government. In the Cyprus Convention of 1878, Britain formally guaranteed Turkish Asian possessions but in practice forced Turkey to acknowledge Britain's supremacy. Driven by a strange combination of imperialism for its own sake, by reasons of imperial strategy, by the economic need to expand the demands for the products of British machinery and the cotton and wool industries, but also by the often sincere belief that it was almost the divine destiny of Britain that she should bring the benefits of her rule and civilization to the world, in the ten years 1879 to 1889 Britain's empire grew by well over a million square miles. Burma, South Africa, Egypt, were all for over half a century to be colored "British red" on the maps of the world; and the security of all depended largely upon the newly acquired Suez Canal.

The Bulgarian revolt of 1875 with its accompanying Turkish atrocities had given rise to a tide of Turkophobia in Britain which Gladstone in his pamphlet "The Bulgarian Horrors and the

Question of the East" (London, 1876) fully exploited. Thus with Gladstone's rise to power in 1880 the Sultan became even more antagonistic to any British proposals. Certainly it was clear to the Ottoman rulers that the concept of a British protectorate was motivated partly in some cases, and wholly so in others, by the desire to safeguard British lines of communication and interests in the Middle East. The scheme of Edward Cazalet, a British industrialist with interests in Russia, to establish a Protectorate of Palestine financed with private capital made as little headway as had the plans of Oliphant. His idea of a railway from the coast to the Euphrates served if anything to increase Turkish suspicions. No modification which he suggested—even to the extent of offering to accept any suitable area within the Ottoman Empire—could allay the fears of the Ottoman government. The succession of schemes—of Gawler, Oliphant, Cazalet, Crybbace, Bradshaw, Mitford, Ashe, and others—which emerged throughout these years came to naught. The birth of a Jewish Home could be achieved only with the help of the great powers, and the climate for such action was rapidly being created. The writings of Lessing, Moses Hess, Dumas fils, Marx, Engels, and Lasalle, the Italian Risorgimento, and the whole complex of the emancipatory movements all served to produce such a climate. However, the driving force had to come from the Jews themselves and a succession of outbreaks of violent anti-Semitism, particularly in eastern Europe, was soon to provide the stimulus.

2. THE EUROPEAN BACKGROUND

The assassination of Alexander II of Russia on March 1, 1881, may well have been indirectly one of the most decisive factors in the history of Zionism. On the morning of the day of his murder Alexander had signed the Loris-Melikov constitution. Though in no way a true democratic constitution, it provided nevertheless some basis from which a more democratic regime might have emerged. The accession of Tzar Alexander III—a shrewd, despotic autocrat—resulted in a period of reaction which by its harshness and lack of foresight was to plant the seeds of the Revolution. For the Jews of Russia it marked the beginning of a reign of persecution, pogroms, and terror. No doubt can exist that even when not actually instigated by the local authorities these outrages had at least their tacit approval and frequently that of the Church and of the central government.

Pogroms were no new phenomenon to Russian Jewry. Odessa had been the site of outbreaks in 1820, 1859, and in 1871. However, the attacks under Alexander III were so widespread, so frequent, and so violent that it became clear that they followed an organized pattern instigated from above. The report of the Austro-Hungarian Consul in Kiev to his Foreign Minister in Vienna states without reservation: "The entire behaviour of the police leads one rightfully to the conclusion that the disturbances are abetted by the authorities." [1]

Within a few months well over 200 pogroms occurred in southwest Russia; and while actual cases of murder were few, the prospect of violent attack, rape, and looting confronted much of East European Jewry.

Appeals for aid both to the central and local authorities met with little response and even with accusations that the blame for the pogroms should be laid at the doors of the Jews themselves. Ignatiev, the Minister of the Interior, stated that the outbreaks were natural reactions of the exploited masses who were bitter about Jewish monopoly of the financial affairs of the country and about their control of the land—a charge which must have sounded strange to the ears of the largely impoverished, landless Jewish masses. As a logical consequence of this baseless accusation, Ignatiev used the pogroms as a pretext for the imposition of new and severe legal disabilities on the Jews. The movements of Jews within the already highly restricted Pale of Settlement were further constrained and additional economic burdens were imposed. The governors of the provinces were ordered to set up committees to investigate the problem of the Jewish community.

[1] Gelber, "The Russian Pogroms of the 80's in the Light of Austrian Diplomatic Correspondence," *Historische Schriften* [in Yiddish], II, 466-96; quoted in L. Greenberg, *The Jews in Russia* (New Haven: 1951), II, 21.

With the proceedings held in camera, with their delegates denied every elementary right of questioning, and with the anti-Semitic prejudice of the judges obvious at every turn, the Jews were reduced to yet further depths of despair. Hitherto it had been felt that the violence which they had suffered might yet be stopped by the forces of authority; it was now clear to all that that hope was a vain one.

The position continued to deteriorate throughout the 1890's; and under Nicholas II, who succeeded Alexander III in 1894, the scale of the anti-Semitic outbreaks increased. Denied the right to almost any form of higher learning and to entry into the professions,[2] hampered at every turn from carrying on business by the malicious rulings of police chiefs and governors, expelled and deported from their homes—often overnight and frequently in chains—the Jews turned from despair and misery to panic. The massacres in Nikolaev in 1899 and in Kishinev and Gomel in 1903 finally convinced the mass of the Jews that flight was the only alternative to annihilation.

This growing conviction of the need for emigration was, however, not merely a simple reaction to persecution. The fear of the Jews was compounded with disillusion, their panic with a profound sense of disappointment and shock. From the middle of the nineteenth century there had grown up in Russia a movement, begun in Germany in the previous century by Moses Mendelsohn and in Galicia by Krochmal and Rappoport, which was designed not only to acquaint the Jewish world with secular thought but also to fit the Jews for civil and legal integration by having them adopt the language, customs, and culture of their surroundings. The members of this movement of enlightenment, the *Haskalah,* firmly believed that intellectual and social advances within the Jewish community would inevitably produce a more liberal attitude within government circles. The movement also included within its ranks, however, such early representatives of Jewish nationalism as David Gordon, Perez Smolenskin, Eliezer

[2] A law of November 8, 1899, required the confirmation by the Minister of Justice of the application to practice of every non-Christian lawyer. During the first six years of this law's operation not one Jewish attorney was admitted to the bar (Greenberg, II, 38).

ben Yehudah,[3] and others, who envisaged the rebirth of Jewry and of the Hebrew language and culture in Palestine well before the days of the pogroms. However, it was without doubt the "shock of recognition" that the apparent liberalism of Alexander II could so soon degenerate into the coarse brutality of his successors and that not one of the liberal publications of Russia put up any fight against the anti-Semitic acts of the government, that finally shattered the illusions of the "enlighteners": not until after the Kishinev pogrom of 1903 did even Count Leo Tolstoi deplore the brutality of the previous two decades. Among the Jews the feeling mounted that no longer would the Jewish intellectuals sacrifice themselves and their culture upon alien altars. However, unanimity upon the problems confronting them and the methods for dealing with them has rarely been one of the outstanding characteristics of Jewish groups at any period and Russian Jewry at this time was no exception. Moreover, between the experiencing of an emotion and its translation into practice stand many barriers. The disillusion with Russia, though often voiced as a disillusion with all lands in which the Jews lived as minorities, did not, indeed could not, result in a mass emigration to Palestine. Zionism was still for the idealist few. For the majority the simple economic facts of life still came first, with the result that it was to America, France, and England that the refugees turned. For many, too, their theoretical intellectual disillusionment rapidly became a compromise in practice. While many henceforth devoted their energies to Zionism, others continued to sacrifice "on alien altars" by participating in those movements which promised a better world for all men, and still others resumed positions in their new lands which, apart from a lessened anti-Semitism, differed but little from their previous existence. Already in 1881 the first wave of emigration from the region was under way, but a considerable body of opinion was to oppose such a move for many years. It is a common feature of minority groups that they are not only actively zealous for their reputation as patriots, but also that they fear greatly any act of

[3] Smolenskin's essay on Jewish nationalism "Am Olam" (The Eternal People) was written as early as 1873, while Ben-Yehudah in 1879 had argued for a return to Palestine and for the revival of Hebrew as a language.

the members of the group which might arouse the suspicions or even the disapproval of the majority in whose midst they live. Unable or unwilling to face the realities of the present and afraid to discern the trends of the future, many Jewish leaders felt that any large-scale emigration would destroy such emancipatory progress as had been achieved and would also produce a new mood of antagonism which would lead to new discriminatory measures.

Repeatedly Jewish individuals and Jewish newspapers pleaded with the Jews to have faith in the better feelings of Russia. Clinging to the belief that full rights and freedom would be granted them soon, they urged the Jews to wait patiently, to fight for their rights, to "place their trust in princes" and in those from whom they hoped salvation would come.

By 1882, however, the masses in eastern Europe were no longer, at least in theory, split upon the emigration issue. With the most elementary rights denied them and with their looted homes and dead before them, they had no real alternative. But mere physical flight was not the only question which posed itself at that time. The Jewish community was so tightly knit a unit, so rich in culture, learning, and traditions, so much the heart and center of every aspect of Jewish life, that the whole problem of the spiritual survival of Jewry was involved. Clearly from the point of economic possibilities, of civil rights, and of freedom of immigration barriers, America was the light which beckoned with increasing attraction. However, Jewry needed more than physical freedom at this stage. The yearnings for a true independence from the whims of governments, the desire for a total self-assertion, the wish to live as the masters of their own fate again, was a basic impulse. For the group which shared these feelings, whether they themselves went there or not, only Palestine—the historic homeland and the symbol of independence—could serve as any secure and *permanent* solution. In support of their thesis they pointed not only to Russia but also to Germany, the center of rationalism and culture, where in 1882 an international anti-Semitic congress had been called in Dresden. In almost every Balkan country the situation was the same—the Jew carried anti-Semitism on his back wherever he went; in Christian

Europe he had no future. Leo Pinsker's *Auto-Emancipation*, which appeared in 1882, analyzed and crystallized the whole situation. He felt that a legal emancipation granted even out of humanitarian instinct was useless to the Jew. Only self-emancipation could produce any lasting results; self-liberation alone could avail the wandering Jew. But Pinsker did not see Palestine alone as a possible solution—any "land of our own" could be a haven. But to most Jews a rational analysis of the problem was not enough. Any move to self-emancipation had to draw upon wells of emotion for its strength. For many,[4] Palestine alone was the theoretical answer, and throughout the Pale of Settlement Zionist groups called *Hoveve Zion* (Lovers of Zion) were founded.

Nevertheless, while Palestine may have been the only theoretical answer and while it attracted a few hundred of the politically conscious elite, it was to the U.S.A. that the main stream of immigrants flowed. Not only were the economic prospects in Palestine extremely bleak and discouraging, but the Turkish government also discriminated against Jewish immigration.[5] Into America, on the other hand, the tide of settlers flowed with growing force, some 160,000 Jews entering the country in the decade after 1881.[6]

One of the problems involved in attaching a name such as Zionism to an idea is that we inevitably tend to ascribe to the movement, throughout the whole period of its existence, those

[4] While no analysis exists of the members of the Zionist movement on the basis of their economic and social status, it is generally considered that it was to the lower and middle classes that the movement appeared most attractive. Change is usually resisted by those who are most secure and by those who are economically well off.

[5] While in 1874 the Turkish Ambassador in London had informed the Palestine Colonization Fund that his government welcomed settlers in all parts of its dominions, the accession to power of Gladstone in 1880 produced an attitude of suspicion and fear in the Ottoman government. When, in 1890, the Russian government approved the setting up of a Society for the Relief of Jewish Agriculturists and Artisans, the Turkish government became even more apprehensive of outside intervention in the supervision of Jewish groups, and prohibited the immigration of Russian Jews or the purchase of land by them. (See Greenberg, II, 72; and Hyamson, *Palestine* [London: 1917], pp. 96 ff).

[6] See Joseph, *Immigration of Jews into America* (New York: 1914), pp. 93 ff.

features which characterize it in our own time. Admittedly with the founding of the Hoveve Zion, Zionism began to assume certain features of a political movement. However, it was still a movement without any real semblance of political organization; it still subsisted almost entirely on emotional drives: hope, fear, despair, and self-sacrifice. The faith which had been wasted on the Haskalah, on governments, on the liberal and socialist movements, found a new home in the struggle for the Holy Land, in the fight for a holy cause. The birth of new hope in the Jewish people was a vital need for those who had lost faith in themselves and in those institutions for which they had fought. The disillusioned youth of Russia was ready material for any mass movement. Weizmann in his autobiography mentions this highly illustrative story. He describes his mother as saying, "Whatever happens, I shall be well off. If Shemuel [the revolutionary son] is right, we shall all be happy in Russia; and if Chaim is right, then I shall go to live in Palestine."

Throwing themselves whole-heartedly into the ranks of the early revolutionaries, the Jewish youth readily transferred their zeal to Zionism when the socialist parties[7] either took no stand against—or even participated in—the pogroms. Some twenty-five Kharkov University students, adopting as their motto the verse from Isaiah, "O house of Jacob, come, let us go forth," and calling themselves "Bilu" after the Hebrew initials of the verse, toured Russia seeking recruits for their cause of immediate settlement in Palestine; in 1882 they established Rishon le Zion, near Jaffa. For these settlers the move to the Holy Land was more

[7] The *Bund*, the Jewish Workingmen's party, had been formed in 1897. The Social Democratic Workers party had been founded in 1898 and the Social Revolutionary party in 1902. After the Odessa pogrom the Moscow executive of the revolutionary *Narodnaia Volya* issued an appeal directed against Jews, the landlords, and the Tsar; and throughout the last two decades of the century *Raszvet,* the Russian-Jewish paper, pleaded for help from the liberal elements of the country. As early as 1883, the Hebrew author M. L. Lilienblum had tried to point out to the Jewish socialists that they could hope for little from any political movement. (*HaMelitz,* 1883, No. 60 [in Hebrew]). Although the anti-Jewish appeal was later withdrawn, S. M. Dubnow states (*History of the Jews in Russia and Poland* [Philadelphia: 1918] II, 280): "Nevertheless, the champions of 'The People's Freedom' continued for some time to justify theoretically the utilization of the anti-Jewish movement for the aims of the general social revolution."

than a simple migration; they took with them not only their ideals for a national rebirth but also hopes for a new order in society. Seeing the system of land ownership as the root of evil in Russia, they envisaged the renaissance as one which should take place not only along national but also along economic lines. Zionism was to be more than a national movement, it was to be also a social revolution within Jewish society.

It would be wrong to give the impression, however, that political Zionism captured the hopes and imagination of the whole of East European Jewry from its commencement. From the very beginning Zionism met with opposition within Jewry for a variety of reasons. While many of those whose initial sympathies lay with the socialists transferred their allegiance to Zionist groups, the opposition of many of the Bundists was still strong. For them Zionism could be no lasting solution; the problem of Jewry was but one aspect of the class struggle within society, and a diverting of hopes and energies into other fields could only delay the final necessary outcome. Inevitably, too, those who saw a total assimilation of the Jews into society as the only solution objected to Zionism as being yet another factor which distinguished the Jew from his neighbor and which, therefore, must militate against his ultimate welfare.

Yet another group was to voice its opposition to Zionism. Though possessing little strength in eastern Europe, Reform Judaism had grown considerably both in Germany and in America. While there can be little doubt that much of the opposition of Reform Judaism stemmed from socio-economic motives, nevertheless this group also based its antagonism upon theological grounds. Arguing along much the same lines as had the Cromwellian supporters of a Jewish resettlement in England in 1656, the Reform group stressed the universalism of Israel and maintained that the propagation of prophetic Judaism was the mission of Jewry. Such a mission not only demanded the dispersal of Jewry rather than their centralization in Palestine, but also Zionism, in their view, was a secular, nationalistic ideal essentially opposed to their concept of Judaism.

Such a view was not new to Judaism. Isaiah, too, had maintained that the political status of Palestine was of little concern to the Jewish religion. The Jewish mission was bound by spiritual ties and was not dependent upon purely physical conditions. The rabbis of the first century had also seen the virtues of bowing before the storm of physical domination so as to preserve the essentials of Judaism. However, as with the Reform group, it would appear that all were making a virtue of necessity. Lacking a national home and deprived of all national and international status, it was perhaps inevitable that Jews would construe these failings as the very assets of Jewry. Thus in 1897 the Central Conference of American Rabbis passed a resolution which stated:

> Resolved, that we totally disapprove of any attempt for the establishment of a Jewish State. Such attempts show a misunderstanding of Israel's mission which from the narrow political and national field has been expanded to the promotion among the whole human race of the broad and universalistic religion first proclaimed by the Jewish prophets. Such attempts do not benefit, but infinitely harm our Jewish brethren where they are still persecuted, by confirming the assertion of their enemies that the Jews are foreigners in the countries in which they are at home, and of which they are everywhere the most loyal and patriotic citizens.[8]

Even within Zionist ranks controversy raged. While the practical achievements of the *Hibat Zion* movement (whose adherents were the Hoveve Zion) were comparatively small, its effects upon the morale and outlook of Jewry were profound. The trends and developments for which it paved the way were growing increasingly apparent and it was with these trends that Asher Ginsburg (better known by his pen-name Ahad Ha'am) took issue. In an article in *HaMelitz* of 1889 entitled "Lo zeh Ha-Derech" (This is not the way), he powerfully attacked the thinking and methods of the new movement. Denying any great physical potential to Palestine and criticizing the attempt to achieve too rapid a growth of nationalism, Ahad Ha'am saw in Palestine not so much a home for Jews as for Judaism. While deeply concerned with the physical conditions of European Jewry, he saw an even greater danger in the spiritual decline of the Diaspora. Only in Palestine could Judaism flourish, only upon

[8] *Yearbook of Central Conference of American Rabbis* VII, xli.

its national soil could it develop freely; the stress, however, had to be placed on Palestine as a spiritual center and not as a political entity. While in his view the fund-raising and settlement activities of the Odessa committee of the Hoveve Zion were essential bases, it was a slow but steady development that was the keynote of his "cultural Zionism": the full realization of the national ideal had to be conceived in terms of the fulfillment of the spiritual center.

3. THE BIRTH OF POLITICAL ZIONISM

In 1897, in the same year that the Reform Rabbis of America formulated their anti-Zionist resolution, there was held in Basle the First Zionist Congress; its president was a man named Theodore Herzl.

Born in Budapest in 1860 into a comfortable and assimilated background, Herzl, after receiving his law degree from the University of Vienna, decided upon a literary career and in 1891 was posted to Paris as the correspondent of the *Neue Freie Presse*, at that time perhaps the most influential paper in Europe. In this capacity Herzl attended the trial of Dreyfus and the ceremony at which he was ignominiously dismissed by the army and exiled to Devil's Island. Though actively aware of the strength of contemporary anti-Semitism, Herzl was nonetheless profoundly shocked at the cries of "Death to the Jews" which resounded through the parade ground during Dreyfus's public degradation. Although Herzl himself stated in 1899 that the Dreyfus affair had made him a Zionist, it appears that he was overstating the case. While Herzl had no doubt realized that the pressure of the anti-Dreyfus charges was due largely to the fact that Dreyfus was a Jew, it was not until he had written *Der Judenstaat*—the manuscript of which was not completed until January 1896—that the real anti-Semitic overtones of the Dreyfus case became apparent to Herzl.[1]

[1] Dreyfus was arrested on October 15, 1894, and on January 5, 1895, was publicly degraded at the Ecole Militaire in Paris. It was not until well into the following year, after the completion of the manuscript of *Der*

Herzl saw anti-Semitism as a prejudice so widespread and so deeply rooted that no process of assimilation, small-scale emigration, or legal change could eradicate it. Convinced that as a minority the Jews could find security and rest in no land, Herzl pleaded for a territory to satisfy the homelessness of the Jew. "Let the sovereignty be granted us over a portion of the globe large enough to satisfy the rightful requirements of a nation," he wrote, "and the rest we shall arrange ourselves."

The publication of *The Jewish State* produced an immediate reaction in both Jewish and non-Jewish circles. At first the opposition within Jewry was more vociferous and widespread than its supporters. Writers in *HaMelitz* accused Herzl of being an inexperienced novice in the field of Zionism with no real understanding of the problems involved. Orthodox rabbis decried his attempt to do the work of the Messiah and Reform rabbis proclaimed their opposition to his negation of the Jewish mission. The assimilationists saw in the creation of a Jewish state a setback in their fight for the consideration of the Jews solely as a religious minority and not as a national group, while Zionists such as the influential Nahum Sokolow feared that Herzl's plans would give the Turkish government an excuse to stifle any further immigration and the development of the existing settlements.

In the light of these reactions it was not surprising that Herzl's call for a World Congress of Jewry should meet with much opposition. With patient argument and persuasion he set about dealing with his opponents and with those who, while not actively opposing him, nevetheless doubted his methods. Although the majority of the Zionists were in eastern Europe and Germany, Herzl felt that it was to London and Paris that he had to turn to advance his plans. But with the influential London Jews he met with little success. Claude Montefiore and Frederick Mocatta, the representatives of the Anglo-Jewish Association, rejected his plans. From Sir Samuel Montagu and from Colonel Goldsmid he received initial encouragement, but Herzl's insistence on rapid and dramatic measures as opposed to the slow and con-

---

Judenstaat, that the use made of anti-Semitic feelings became clear. In his diaries of the period in 1895 when he deals with the birth of the Zionist idea in his mind, Herzl makes no mention of Dreyfus at all.

servative settlement policies of Baron Rothschild and the Hoveve Zion antagonized them. Herzl's attacks on Rothschild's schemes were violent; his natural inclination was not toward patience and calm discussion, and his exercise of these qualities was a tactical concession on his part which frequently vanished when his zeal overcame his political acumen. While his offer to withdraw if Rothschild would assume the leadership of the movement removed some of the suspicions against him, it was not sufficient to win over the Anglo-Jewish aristocracy. Their opposition to Herzl's plan was a genuine one, based not only on a personal disapproval of the man himself. They foresaw the growth of active hostility if thousands were to enter Palestine in an uncontrolled mass movement.

Overcoming his pride, Herzl sought an interview with Baron Rothschild in Paris on July 18, 1896.[2] Ten days previously, Sir Samuel Montagu had told him that the Hirsch Foundation[3] had at its disposal a "liquid sum" of approximately ten million pounds sterling. Herzl's aim was to enlist the Baron's support to secure about half this amount to enable him to proceed with his schemes[4] in Palestine. However, Colonel Goldsmid had written

[2] Previously he had rejected the suggestion that he do this as being "beneath his dignity," declaring that if "a dinner at Rothschild's is the victor's prize . . . moi, je m'en fous" (entry in his diary, July 5, 1896).

[3] Baron Moritz de Hirsch was one of the wealthiest and most charitable Jewish philanthropists of his day. Particularly disturbed by the troubles of East European Jewry, he set up, in 1891, the Jewish Colonisation Association (ICA), and during the course of his life he gave it some forty million dollars. Convinced that, for political and economic reasons, Palestine was unsuitable for large-scale colonization, he purchased land in the Argentine in the hope of successfully settling there large numbers of Russian and Polish Jews. By 1895, when Herzl met him, there were only some 3,000 Jews who had been resettled by Hirsch. Despite the lack of success, Hirsch persisted in regarding the solution of the problems of Jewry as a philanthropic, as opposed to a political, task, and gave Herzl no help. Hirsch died in 1896 before Herzl could secure a second interview. From Herzl's account of his contacts with the Baron, it would seem that a more temperate approach, coupled with a greater acknowledgment of Hirsch's achievements, might have led to a more cooperative arrangement.

[4] By 1861, the Turkish national debt had reached 253 million pounds sterling. Even after consolidation in the same year it still amounted to well over 100 million pounds, a state of affairs which allowed foreign powers to exercise considerable control over the affairs of the weakened Ottoman Empire. Herzl's proposal to the Sultan (with whom he was unable to secure

to Rothschild warning him against Herzl and his dangerous-sounding plans. Even without this warning it is highly unlikely that Herzl's passionate and emotional analysis of his proposals could have failed to antagonize the Baron, who neither believed in Turkish promises nor in Herzl's ability to feed the "150,000 schnorrers" (beggars) who would pour into Palestine in the unlikely eventuality of Herzl's succeeding.

Rothschild's refusal to help was definite and Herzl's reaction was equally firm and determined. On July 18, Jacob de Haas had written from London offering his services as Herzl's honorary secretary. Three days later, Herzl wrote to him: "There is only one reply to the situation: let us organize our masses immediately." From then on the plan was the same in Vienna, Paris, and Berlin: to organize meetings, to secure local leaders in the various districts to work in support of Herzl's schemes, and thus to convince the wealthy Jewish aristocracy that not only were these schemes capable of being carried out but that they also already had the support of the mass of Jewry in Europe.

Already on his return from Constantinople, Herzl had seen the adulation showered on him by vast crowds of Jews. The oppressed always seek a Messiah at the time of their direct distress; often the seemingly impossible appears more feasible than the merely difficult. Herzl was freely reported as having had audience with the Sultan after his first visit (when he actually did not succeed in gaining entry to him), and at every train stop he was met by Jews who saw in him the salvation of their people. In the East End of London the pattern was repeated.

---

an interview until 1901, though he had visited Constantinople for that purpose as early as 1896) was that he would enlist the support of Jewry to raise the large sums needed to strengthen the Turkish economy; he also offered 1½ million pounds to cover the immediate deficit. To obtain a cover for this sum, Herzl sought the help of Andrew Carnegie and of Cecil Rhodes; with neither, however, did he succeed in obtaining interviews. In spite of the fact that Herzl had not yet actually succeeded in raising the money, the Sultan had no reason to suspect that his plans were faring badly and summoned him to Constantinople in 1901, when Herzl openly stated his desire for an offer of "immigration rights without any restrictions." He met with refusal and with the suggestion that immigration would be permitted, under Turkish control, outside of Palestine. "A Charter without Palestine!" wrote Herzl. "I refused on the spot."

Herzl was proclaimed a new Moses, a Messiah, and, perhaps a little strangely in such company, a Columbus. On July 14, 1896, Herzl had said to one of his aides, Rabbinowicz, "Organize me the East End!" By the end of the year "the masses" were being organized in most of Europe's capitals. Rothschild's refusal had shown Herzl where his real support lay, and on Oct. 27, 1897 Herzl finally convened a three-day conference in Basle, Switzerland. In spite of their initial doubts and disagreements the Russian Jews sent some 90 delegates out of the total of 204 who gathered from all parts of the world. Even Ahad Ha'am, the future inveterate opponent of political Zionism, attended. For the first time in nearly two millennia the representatives of Jewry had convened to debate the rebirth of their national home.

Assisted by Dr. Max Nordau, a brilliant orator, psychiatrist, and writer, who had encouraged Herzl during his early doubts about *The Jewish State,* Herzl dominated the Congress. Every detail of the arrangements was his concern. Realizing that the majority of delegates had no clear picture of what was expected of them or of the Congress as a whole, Herzl saw that his function was as much one of setting a mood and of channeling the emotions of the delegates as the production and endorsement of a detailed political program. Perhaps above all he felt the need to impress the delegates with a sense of dignity; they were to be present at a ceremony marking the rebirth of their nation, and they had to be made to feel that they were the representatives of a whole people. To achieve this end, Herzl insisted upon the strictest decorum and even on the wearing of a frock coat and white tie by all. On the organization of the Congress, Herzl spent much of his own fortune. By 1899 he had spent most of his money, on his travels, on Congresses, and on the newspaper *Die Welt* which he founded in 1897; and he attempted, with some success, to write for the theater in order to provide for himself and for his children.[5]

Herzl had no illusions about the problems and personalities which confronted him at Congress. He recognized, and met, the great variety of groups and interests; the Orthodox and the so-

[5] For details of his literary and theatrical works see Alex Bein, *Herzl, A Biography* (Philadelphia: 1942).

cialist-atheist; the conservatives and those who sought rapid development; the assimilationists as well as the most nationalistic. While for many Herzl's strength as leader lay in Alexander Herzen's dictum that "leadership consists in thinking other men's thoughts more vividly than they," for others Herzl had to implant and control the very ideas he wished to promulgate. On August 24, 1897, only three days before Congress opened, Herzl recorded in his diary: "The fact is—which I keep to myself—that I have nothing but an army of *Schnorrers* . . . I stand in command of striplings, beggars and sensation mongers." This impatient conceit reflected Herzl's passionate concern with the success of his plans; perhaps correctly, he felt that he alone could ensure their success. Of his personal triumph at Congress there could be no doubt.

> . . . Before us rose a marvellous and exalted figure, kingly in bearing and stature . . . a royal scion of the House of David . . . everyone sat breathless as if in the presence of a miracle . . . and then wild applause broke out; for 15 minutes the delegates clapped, shouted . . . it was as if the Messiah, Son of David, confronted us . . .[6]

Such extravagant-sounding statements have to be accepted at their face value if one is to succeed in capturing the atmosphere which prevailed among Jews at the time; out of despair new hope had come and it had not yet crystallized into hope for the success of a movement; it rested upon one man alone.

This first Congress and the two which followed in 1898 and 1899 laid the basis for the future of the Zionist movement. With the formulation of the Zionist Program, the establishment of the Zionist Organization and the Actions Committee, and with the determination of Herzl to raise the issue from one of slow settlement of pioneers to the obtaining of a charter from Abdul Hamid for an autonomous settlement, the whole picture of Zionism changed. For the first time it was now a political movement. Herzl had succeeded in making the problem of Jewry and Palestine a political issue whose solution demanded the attention of the major powers of European politics. At the end of the 1897 Congress, Herzl wrote in his diary for September 3:

[6] Ben Ami, "Erinnerungen an Theodor Herzl," *Die Welt*, 1914, p. 688; quoted in Bein, p. 231.

. . . at Basle I founded the Jewish State. If I were to say this today, I would be met by universal laughter. In five years, perhaps, and certainly in fifty, everyone will see it. The State is already founded in essence, in the will of the people to the State.

However, in spite of all his powers, diplomatically Herzl's efforts appeared to bear little fruit. His interview with the Sultan, as we have seen, brought no result. His discussions with Joseph Chamberlain for a settlement in Cyprus[7] failed since Chamberlain feared the opposition of the Greeks and Muslims. In addition, his plan for a Jewish colonization of the Sinai Peninsula, though supported by Lord Lansdowne, the Foreign Secretary, was also in vain, owing to its rejection by Lord Cromer, the British Consul (actually the Vice-Regent of that country) in Egypt at the end of 1902.[8]

In all these negotiations Herzl acted almost entirely on his own. Even Nordau, his closest collaborator, was often kept uninformed as to what was going on. No doubt Herzl was convinced that should any one of his plans meet with any real success, he could win over his opponents to his side. One factor which he undoubtedly considered to be in his favor, should such a course become necessary, was the fact that in both the Cyprus and the Sinai schemes he had the support of Lord Nathaniel Mayer Rothschild, who was opposed to any large-scale Palestinian settlement. The full strength and intractability of the majority of Zionists was not brought home to Herzl until the Uganda project was put forward. In particular the Russian Zionists made it clear to Herzl that no "*Nachtaysl*" (a temporary shelter for the night) could be considered.

[7] On June 20, 1896, Herzl noted in his diary: "Izzat Bey [the Sultan's chief adviser] advises me the following: The Jews should acquire some other territory and then offer it to Turkey in exchange for Palestine (with additional payment). I immediately think of Cyprus." The idea of Cyprus as an alternative to Palestine was put to Herzl by David Trietsch a year earlier.

[8] The main reason for Cromer's rejection was the fact that the water required for irrigation was too great to be drawn from the Nile. Herzl, possibly quite correctly, saw this only as an excuse; however, since he regarded Cromer as "the most disagreeable Englishman" he had ever met, some degree of prejudice must be admitted!

Nevertheless, though the East European delegations were the most powerful at Congress and were therefore able to win the day, some delegates, notably Israel Zangwill and Nachman Syrkin, signified their approval of the British scheme by resigning their membership of the Zionist Organization. Maintaining that the Zionist movement should support Jewish autonomous settlement anywhere in the world, they set up an organization called the Jewish Territorial Organization (the I.T.O.). Their attempts to found settlements in Australia, Cyrenaica, South America, and Angola all failed and at the end of the 1914-18 war the organization was dissolved.

Following the Kishinev pogroms of April 1903 and the order of Plehve, the Russian Minister of the Interior, that all Zionist meetings were to be made illegal, Herzl visited St. Petersburg in order to attempt to change Plehve's policies. While traveling through Vilna, Herzl received the offer from the British government of an autonomous territory in East Africa to be administered by a Jewish governor. The mere fact of his consideration of this project met with a storm of criticism at the Sixth Congress in August of that year. Herzl had miscalculated the passion and fervor which Palestine alone engendered in the hearts and minds of the delegates. Declaring his unaltered belief in the fact that only in the Holy Land could a lasting solution be found, he stated that he viewed the East Africa project as but a temporary measure to ameliorate the immediate situation. In pursuance of this policy, Herzl journeyed to Italy to seek the aid of the King and the Pope on his behalf. While the good will of the former was forthcoming, from the Pope he received a complete refusal. "We cannot prevent the Jews from going to Jerusalem—but we can never favor it."

Though profoundly shocked by Herzl's death some months after his Italian visit, the Zionist world continued to grow both in numbers and in organization. Problems such as the secession of those who supported the East Africa scheme, the question of the religious character of the movement, and the attitude toward socialism among the members arose and continued to confront Congress on each occasion of its meeting. But the trend was clear; whatever the actual convictions and special pleadings of the various groups, political Zionism had by now taken a firm and unshakable hold on world Jewry. Even in its earliest days, when its progress was impelled purely by emotional drives its forward surge was great. By the time of Herzl's death, when this force was placed within the political framework of Zionist organization, it was apparent that his vision of the future State was no mere dream.

Opposition to Zionism among the Jews still existed. In Britain, where the Jewish community was as yet comparatively small and where the vocal, representative section of the population consisted largely of the well established, distinguished families, a certain amount of concern existed lest the actions of the Zionist Organization should prove inimical to their interests. Inevitably too the rapid rise in immigration from eastern Europe was a cause for concern. However, with a long tradition of active humanitarian interests on behalf of their less fortunate brethren, the leaders of Anglo-Jewry took no steps to oppose Zionism, even if few of the earlier political schemes met with their approval. In Russia, where the critical period in Zionism following Herzl's death coincided with the rapid growth of revolutionary feeling, the situation was different. Passionately attracted by the ideals of liberty for which the Revolution stood, Jewish youth was drawn to it in ever increasing numbers. While for many it appeared that a choice had to be made between socialism and Zionism, between an apparent universalism and narrow nationalism, for others a combination of the two seemed possible. Even the outbreak of new pogroms during the days of the 1905 October Revolution did not shatter their illusions, though it did produce a marked increase in *Aliyah*.[9]

The old pattern of tsarist rule showed no change with the passage of time; and during the period of radical reaction under Stolypin, anti-Zionist legislation was intensified. In 1907 a Senate law made all Zionist groups illegal and a number of their leaders were prosecuted in spite of Plehve's assurance to Herzl that while their activities were confined to Palestine no restrictions would be imposed. Plehve raised no objections to practical Zionism.

[9] *Aliyah*—literally "ascent," but traditionally and in modern Hebrew usage it signifies, almost as a religious act, immigration into Palestine.

Any measure which reduced the number of Jews in Russia met with his approval.

In the light of Herzl's abortive negotiations with the Sultan, the revolt of the Young Turks in 1908 was welcomed by the Zionists, who hoped for a more sympathetic attitude on the part of the new regime. Their hopes were in vain. Having already felt the surges of Balkan and Armenian nationalism, the new government had no desire to see any additional nationalistic groups within the empire. Their fears of Zionist intentions were further increased by the misrepresentation of these aims by a group of assimilated Jews within Turkey who feared that their own status might be endangered by the inclusion of a Jewish state under Turkish rule.

It was becoming increasingly apparent to many of the Zionist leaders that for the time being at least, the main progress to be attained lay in the field of practical achievements and not in attempts at far reaching political decisions. By the Tenth Congress in 1911 the adherents of this policy had captured the executive and by 1914 some forty-three agricultural settlements with a population of 12,000 had been founded.[10] However, it was not merely the numerical value of the settlements which characterized the developments of the time. This period saw the emergence of ideas and practices which were to influence the whole mode of life of the country and the attitudes of its future inhabitants. The firm establishment of Hebrew as the language of settlers, the cultivation of the concept of physical labor as an ideal, the emergence of a socialist, democratic society—all these grew and took root. The Zionist ideology of the National Home, an ideology so passionate and deep that it was to create almost a new type of Jewish youth, was molded. However right the "practical Zionists" might have been at the time in their avoidance of seeking final political settlements, the events of the 1914–18 war and those which followed upon the peace settlements were to galvanize the political aspects of the situation.

[10] At this date the total population of the country was *ca.* 700,000, of whom perhaps 90–100,000 were Jews (see Great Britain, Foreign Office Historical Section, Syria and Palestine, *Peace Handbook No. 60* [London: 1920], p. 15, fn. 1; also N. Bentwich, *Palestine* [London: 1934]). These figures are only approximate, as no official census was taken until 1922.

The outbreak of the war caused a serious setback to the Zionist Organization of Europe and proved almost disastrous to the Jewish economy in Palestine. With the two most important sections of the Organization split by the state of war between Germany and Russia, and with its members scattered throughout the lands of all the combatants, the Zionist movement transferred its headquarters to neutral Copenhagen, where it attempted to maintain some contact wtih the various parts of the movement.

From the time when Turkey entered the war on the side of the Central Powers the prospects facing the Yishuv were alarming. While the cessation of exports and the flow of Chalukah (see p. 135) into the country was extremely serious, it was the measures taken by the Turkish government which gave the greatest cause for concern. Suspecting, with considerable justification, that the Jews supported the Allies, Djemal Pasha, the Turkish governor of Syria, set out to eradicate every Zionist activity. Though perhaps this policy was justified in principle, his methods were unnecessarily harsh. The use of Jewish National Fund stamps was made a capital crime, the Anglo-Palestine Bank and the watchman's force "*HaShomer*" were ordered to cease all activity. The many Jews in Palestine who were still legally subjects of any of the Allied Powers were given the choice of adopting Ottoman citizenship or else of leaving the country. When in 1917 Allenby began his advance into Palestine, the restrictions were intensified. The Jews of Tel-Aviv and Jaffa, among them some who had taken Ottoman citizenship, were evacuated under conditions of extreme hardship to the north. Thousands fled to Egypt and many more were deported to Syria; in many cases only the material relief which came from America saved the bodies and spirits of great numbers of the population. These measures only served to increase Jewish support for the Allies, to whom the Jews gave information concerning Turkish military movements. In certain Zionist circles the idea of pro-Allied action spread and with it the idea of organizing a fighting unit representing the Jewish people among the Allied nations and in the Allied forces. One of the earliest protagonists of such a scheme was Joseph Trumpeldor, a Russian Jew who had emigrated to

Palestine and, at the beginning of 1915, had succeeded in forming the Zion Mule Corps of 900 men. This force, which served at Galipoli, was disbanded in March 1916. A more ambitious scheme was proposed by Vladimir Jabotinsky,[11] who throughout 1916 had been agitating for the formation of a Jewish Regiment. Three battalions of Jewish volunteers were recruited and they arrived in Palestine in February 1918, when they took part in the final repulsion of Turkish troops from the country. By September of that year, the whole of Palestine had been cleared of Turkish forces and four hundred years of Ottoman rule had come to an end.

4. THE LAND OF PROMISES

At the Fourth Zionist Congress held in London in 1900 Herzl, in one of his frequent prophetic analyses of the future political scene, declared that it was upon England that Zionist hopes should be focused. "England will understand us and our aim," he proclamed in his inaugural address, perhaps little realizing how completely the events of the war were to make of his dreams a reality. One of the members of the British War Cabinet, Mr. Herbert (now Viscount) Samuel, had for long been interested in Zionism and in the fate of the Ottomon territories. At the end of 1914 Samuel had met Weizmann (see below) and early the next year he had placed a memoir before the Cabinet. In this memoir he proposed that in the postwar dismembering of

[11] Vladimir Jabotinsky was a Russian-born journalist who took part in the formation of the Zion Mule Corps. In 1920 he became a member of the Zionist executive but resigned from it in 1923 because of his lack of sympathy with the moderate methods and policies of Weizmann. Two years later he founded the Revisionist Group which, at the 1931 Congress, demanded a Jewish State on both sides of the Jordan. In 1935, Jabotinsky resigned from the Zionist Organization and set up the New Zionist Organization. This group even withdrew its support from the "labour dominated" Haganah and established its own military force called the Irgun Z'vai Le'umi (National Military Organization). This group, more militant in its retaliatory attacks on the Arabs and later against the British, became the basis of the political party Herut after the establishment of the State of Israel.

the Turkish possessions, Palestine should be annexed by Britain as the future home of persecuted and scattered Jewry. He argued that apart from humanitarian motives Britain needed to have friendly inhabitants in the region. Sir Edward Grey and David Lloyd George were in favor of the scheme. Grey went so far as to seek Russian support, but the British Ambassador in Petrograd received little encouragement.

Throughout the period of the war, as we have seen, there had been present in London Dr. Chaim Weizmann, a member of the Actions Committee of the Zionist Organization. Brought into contact, through his official position, with Cabinet members and with others influential in the formulation of British policy, he succeeded in convincing many of the virtues of the Zionist cause. There exists some debate as to the degree to which British policy was influenced by Weizmann's discovery of a new process for the production of acetone at a time of a severe shortage in the munitions industry. Certainly his labors helped him to win over Lloyd George, who had already given him a sympathetic hearing. Referring to his work Lloyd George wrote:

> Dr. Weizmann enlisted my adhesion to his ideals at a time when, at my request, he was successfully applying his scientific skill and imagination to save Britain from a real disaster over the failure of wood alcohol for the manufacture of cordite.[1]

In his *Memoirs*[2], the former Prime Minister records the following conversation:

> I said to him, "You rendered great service to the State and I should like to ask the Prime Minister to recommend you to His Majesty for some honor." He said, "There is nothing I want for myself." "But is there nothing we can do as recognition of your valuable assistance to the country?," I asked. He replied, "Yes, I would like you to do something for my people." He then explained his aspirations as to the repatriation of the Jews to the sacred land they had made famous. That was the fount and origin of the famous declaration about the National Home for Jews in Palestine.

In addition Lloyd George also stated in Parliament in June 1936 that the motivating force behind the Balfour Declaration

[1] *Memoirs of the Peace Conference* (New Haven: 1939), II, 722.
[2] (London: 1938), I, 349.

was the conviction on the part of the British that some step had to be taken which would win the sympathetic support of Jewish communities throughout the world. Nevill Barbour[3] and others have correctly pointed out the contradictory nature of these two accounts, and have also stressed the unreliability of recollections made twenty years after the event—particularly when one authority offers two incompatible versions. The doubts of Barbour are clearly justified and the inaccuracies of Lloyd George's *Memoirs* on this point are corroborated by the fact that Weizmann denies the story point-blank, remarking: "History does not deal in Aladdin's lamps."[4] He also adds that for his five years' work for the government they "gave me a token reward for my work, amounting to about ten shillings for every ton of acetone produced, a total of ten thousand pounds."[5]

In his work at the Admiralty Laboratories, Weizmann renewed his contact with Arthur (later Lord) Balfour, then First Lord of the Admiralty, whom he had already interested in Zionism some years before. Britain had for some time given close consideration to the position of the Middle East in the postwar world. Sir Mark Sykes, the head of the Middle East Department of the Foreign Office, as we have seen in Part I, had already secretly negotiated in May 1916 the Sykes-Picot Agreement whereby Britain was to take over Haifa and Acre, the northern territory (i.e., the *Vilayet* of Beirut minus the sanjaq of Nablus and Acre) was to go to France, and the south and the Holy Places were to be internationally administered. Zionist aims received no consideration; and when, on February 17, 1917, Sykes gave his sympathetic support to Zionist aims at a meeting in London, no mention was made of the agreement whose contents were unknown to the Zionist leaders.

In the summer of 1917 Balfour, with the support of the Prime Minister, began conducting negotiations with Lord Rothschild, the president of the British Zionist Federation. With Russia's position greatly weakened since the general mutiny of the army on March 10, support for French policy in the Middle

[3] *Nisi Dominus* (London: 1946).
[4] In *Trial and Error* (New York: 1949), p. 150.
[5] *Ibid.*, p. 174.

East was weakened and Britain, less afraid of Arab discontent in this matter, was freer to act as she pleased. Under prompting from Supreme Court Chief Justice Brandeis and Stephen Wise in America, President Wilson voiced his support of Jewish claims to Lord Balfour. On November 2, 1917, modified as a result of extreme pressure from a group of anti-Zionist Jews in England,[6] the Foreign Secretary sent Lord Rothschild the communication that became known as the Balfour Declaration (quoted on pages 63-64 above).

British government policies had not been determined solely by gratitude to a brilliant chemist, nor were they brought about by the persuasiveness of Zionist leaders alone. Though these factors were undoubtedly present, and though considerable sympathy existed in England for the plight of Jewry in Europe, there were more pressing considerations. With Russia no longer in the war and American forces not yet employed in full strength, the situation of the Allies was shaky. No doubt overestimating the power and influence of Jewry, Allied leaders nevertheless believed that if the sympathies of American Jews and of those Jews living in enemy territory could be won, the Allied cause would be considerably strengthened. In his testimony before the Royal Commission on Palestine in 1937, Lloyd George declared:[7]

"The Zionist leaders gave us a definite promise that, if the Allies committed themselves to give facilities for the establishment of a national home for the Jews in Palestine, they would do their best to rally Jewish sentiment and support throughout the world to the Allied cause. They kept their word.[8]

Throughout Jewry the Balfour Declaration was hailed with joy. In homes and synagogues it was discussed and analyzed; each word and phrase was examined and dissected. Was there any significance in the phrase "a National Home"? Did it imply

[6] Among the leaders of this group were David Alexander, president of the Board of British Jews; Claude Montefiore, president of the Anglo-Jewish Association; Lucien Wolfe; and Edwin Montagu, Secretary of State for India.

[7] Cf. p. 75, above.

[8] No doubt sentiment was aroused in favor of the Allies, but apart from those Jews living in Allied countries who were already taking a full part in the war effort, it is difficult to find any evidence of the Declaration's having had any practical, calculable effects.

full autonomy or was it different in principle from "Jewish State"? How much did this difference imply a concession to allay the fears of the anti-Zionists, and how much did it reflect a subtle modification of British policy? Thus in a letter to the *Jewish Chronicle*[9] Leon Simon asked: "What is a 'National Home'? . . . and 'since nothing shall be done which may prejudice the civil and religious rights of existing non-Jewish communities in Palestine,' what precisely will be the civil and political status of the Jewish People [sic] in their 'National Home'?" For years these questions were to remain a source of acute dissension.

By some, however, the government's statement was held to be a retrogressive act. The struggle for Jewish rights in England had brought almost complete political freedom to the Jewish community. Socially, too, a number of Jews had attained to the "upper crust" and some saw their position endangered and their loyalty to Britain become questionable as a consequence of the Balfour Declaration. "Judaism is a religion and not a nationality," they repeatedly declared, and protest meetings—dignified and graced with venerable names, but often sparsely attended—were organized. At a meeting of the Anglo-Jewish Association on November 30, 1917, Mr. Claude Montefiore, the president of the Association, declared: "The Zionist movement was caused by anti-Semitism," and his expression of repudiation of the Balfour Declaration was supported by such men as Sir Philip Magnus, H. S. Henriques, Dr. Israel Abrahams, and Lucien Woolf.[10]

Less than three weeks after the publication of Lord Balfour's letter to Lord Rothschild, there was set up a "League of British Jews," one of whose aims was "to resist the allegation that Jews constitute a separate political nationality," and again many of the leaders of the Anglo-Jewish Association were in the

[9] (London), November 23, 1917.

[10] Nevil Barbour, p. 59, quotes, almost in full, the letter to the *London Times* of May 24, 1917, of the Conjoint Committee, which, he states, "officially represented Anglo-Jewry," and in which the authors, Alexander and Montefiore, stated their opposition to Zionist aims. Barbour neglects to point out that this letter was written without consultation with the bodies which these men represented. As a result of the letter, Alexander was censured by the Board of British Jews and was forced to resign.

vanguard of the new movement. Their inclusion as another of their aims being "to facilitate the settlement in Palestine of such Jews as may desire to make Palestine their home" did little to deceive their opponents as to their basic anti-Zionism, and the pages of the *Jewish Chronicle* of November and December 1917 reflect the powerful and widespread opposition which they aroused. The vast majority of England's quarter million Jews were passionately in support of Zionist aims. Daily meetings, packed to overflowing, were held throughout London and the provinces. With little conception of the practical problems involved, the enthusiasm of British Jewry was fervent.

While in England the opposition to Zionism was voiced largely by a section of the "Anglo-Jewry aristocracy," in Russia the Bund was the strongest source of anti-Zionist agitation. Seeing their future as irrevocably bound up with the progress of the class struggle, the Bundists reiterated their opposition both to religious and nationalist Jewry. Thus, on November 16, 1917, the *Jewish Chronicle* correspondent from Petrograd reported that a meeting of the Bund at Homel had condemned Hebrew as an "aristocratic language" which therefore had to be opposed along with any religious or Zionist basis of Jewish life.

While today there may be little point in re-examining in great detail all the suggested implications of the Balfour Declaration, it is nevertheless instructive to attempt to discover the interpretations placed on it at the time. To the Zionist movement, in the words of Dr. Weizmann, "it meant a National Home, 'national' meaning in contradistinction to living on sufferance anywhere else . . . something which will be as Jewish as England is English." [11] Also during his evidence before the Royal Commission on Palestine in 1937, Lloyd George declared:

> The idea was, and this was the interpretation put upon it at the time, that a Jewish State was not to be set up immediately by the Peace Treaty without reference to the wishes of the majority of the inhabitants. On the other hand, it was contemplated that when the time arrived for according representative institutions to Palestine, if the Jews had meanwhile responded to the opportunity afforded them

[11] Weizmann had first stated this at the Versailles Peace Conference in 1919 and he repeated it in his evidence before the Palestine Royal Commission in Jerusalem on November 25, 1936 (Cmd 5479).

by the idea of a national home and had become a definite majority of the inhabitants, then Palestine would become a Jewish Commonwealth.

Further in this connection he wrote,[12] ". . . the notion that Jewish immigration would have to be artificially restricted in order that the Jews should be a permanent minority never entered into the heads of anyone in framing the policy. That would have been regarded as unjust and as fraud on the people to whom we were appealing."

It was clear that the words of the Declaration, decided upon only after months of thought and discussion, "were the outcome of a compromise between those Ministers who contemplated the established of a Jewish State and those who did not." [13] The interpretation placed upon it by the press, however, clearly accepted it as recognition of the right of Jewish autonomy in the land. Thus the *Manchester Guardian* commenting at the time wrote: [14] "What it means is that . . . our deliberate policy will be to encourage in every way in our power Jewish immigration . . . with a view to the ultimate establishment of a Jewish state."

Nevertheless, the ambiguities of the document became increasingly apparent. More far reaching, however, were the consequences of other British commitments which had been made some two years before to Sherif Hussein of Mecca.

The British government always maintained that "the whole of Palestine west of the Jordan was . . . excluded from Sir Henry McMahon's pledge," and in a letter to the London *Times* of July 23, 1937, McMahon confirmed this view: "I feel it my duty to state, and I do so definitely and emphatically, that it was not intended by me . . . to include Palestine in the area in which Arab independence was promised. I had also every reason to

[12] *The Truth About the Peace Treaties* (London: 1938), 1135 ff.

[13] Cmd 5479, p. 24.

[14] December 3, 1917; see also *The Times* (London), November 3, 1917, and the *Manchester Guardian* of the same date. In this connection it should be borne in mind that the leader-writer of the *Manchester Guardian* at this time was Herbert Sidebotham, a prominent non-Jewish Zionist. Like C. P. Scott, the editor of the *Manchester Guardian*, Sidebotham had become converted to Zionism by Weizmann while the latter was Lecturer in Chemistry at Manchester University. It was through Scott that Weizmann was introduced to Lloyd George and to Herbert (now Viscount) Samuel.

believe at the time that the fact . . . was well understood by King Hussein." T. E. Lawrence also held that Palestine had been excluded and expressed his view on the conflict of policies in the McMahon-Hussein correspondence and the Sykes-Picot Agreement in a letter to *The Times* of September 11, 1919. However, while the issue may have been settled in the minds of the British,[15] the Arabs castigated them for having broken their pledges to Hussein. To them the role of "perfidious Albion" was clear; it appeared opportunistic and hypocritical.

There exists more than a little justification in the charge that through the whole of this period and later the Zionists paid too little attention, not only to the legal claims of the Arabs, but to their actual feelings and views. That this attitude was not a conscious one is clear; there was a sincerely genuine desire to obtain an atmosphere of conciliatory cooperation. It was perhaps all too easy for the Jews, accustomed for so long to having their fate decided by governments, to see Palestine as merely a piece of territory whose future could be settled by any one or more of the Great Powers. Nevertheless, the fact remains that in all the planning which went on from 1916 and which ended with the Balfour Declaration, the Zionist leaders displayed but little concern for Arab reactions. Thus Dr. Eder, acting chairman of the Zionist Commission, in his report before the Commission of Inquiry to investigate the causes of the riots of May 1921, stated[16] that in his view there could only be one National Home in Palestine and that in Jerusalem, and no equality in the partnership between Jews and Arabs, but a Jewish predominance as soon as their numbers were sufficiently increased. Moreover, the Commission's report stressed that Dr. Eder was speaking in his official capacity and as such was putting forward the official Zionist view of the time.

It is clear that either the Zionist leaders felt that Arab opposition was overrated, or else that it could be safely ignored; certainly they seemed prepared to make no concessions to it.

[15] Nevertheless, it is clear from his speech in the House of Lords of March 27, 1923, that Lord Grey, the Minister whose agent McMahon was, was much disturbed by the apparent inconsistencies and double dealing of British policy.

[16] Cmd 1540.

While it is perhaps idle to conjecture at this time upon what other steps might have been taken to produce an attitude of cooperation and Arab-Jewish good will, the unfortunate consequences of this lack of rapport are all too apparent today. While the Jews fell all too easily into that practice (which was so marked a feature of British colonial policy in the nineteenth century) of disregarding the views and aspirations of the inhabitants of the area, the Arabs were, and are, too prone to see in Zionism little more than yet another extension of western imperialist policies.

One of the problems confronting the Jewish leaders was that (as will be discussed more fully in Part III) there were few if any Arabs in a position to speak authoritatively on behalf of the Arab peoples. Internal struggles for power, rival dynastic and tribal claims all served to crystallize the Zionist attitude of too great concern with the acts of Britain and too little with the view of the Arab world. It is all too clear from Weizmann's autobiography that he saw the real center of decision to be London rather than any of the Arab capitals.

In April 1918, while the northern part of the country was still in Turkish hands, a Zionist Commission composed of members from Britain, France, and Italy, and with an accredited British government member, Major Ormsby-Gore, visited the country. American Jewry was not represented as America was not at war with Turkey, and the Russian delegates were prevented from attending because of the turmoil of the Revolution. One of the objects of the Commission was to help to establish harmonious relations with the Arabs. Weizmann records that on the morning of departure from London Sir Mark Sykes stated that he "had received some 'very disquieting' telegrams from Cairo, to the effect that the Arabs were beginning to ask uncomfortable questions . . ." Weizmann's reaction and his assessment of the strength of these stirrings in the Arab lands is indicative both of his underestimation of these feelings as well as of his own determination to proceed. "I remember maintaining with much emphasis and warmth that if we were going to be deflected from a considered line of action by such things as telegrams vaguely indicating some stirrings of the Arab world, our work in Palestine would be utterly impossible, and we had better not go out at all." [17]

In June 1918, Weizmann visited Emir Feisal in an attempt to obtain his agreement on Zionist plans, and to convince him that Zionist policies offered no threats to Arab aspirations and that full cooperation was his sincere wish.[18] Though Feisal could certainly not speak on behalf of the Arab world, it was nevertheless Weizmann's opinion, as it was that of the British, that Feisal was the most representative spokesman at the time. Personally powerful, the commander-in-chief of the Arab army against the Turks, and backed by British gold, Feisal wielded great influence.

As we have noted above, Feisal was fully conscious of French opposition to the rise of Arab nationalism, and he no doubt hoped that by accepting British advice on the issue of Palestine and by showing reticence over the question of French control of Syria he would be able to effect some more favorable compromise over the latter issue. With this in mind and convinced by Weizmann of the possibilities for mutual benefits from Zionist ideals, he signed an agreement which presupposed the separation of Palestine from the Syrian state and accepted in full the Balfour Declaration —the only condition being that the Arabs should secure their independence in accordance with the terms previously agreed upon with the British government.

Although Feisal had signed the agreement with Weizmann as the representative of the "Arab state," it soon became clear that he did not speak for the whole of the Arab world. Though in his letter of March 3, 1919, to Mr. (now Justice) Frankfurter and also in statements at the Peace Conference, Feisal reiterated that "we Arabs, especially the educated among us . . . fully acquainted with the proposals submitted by the Zionist Organization . . . regard them as moderate and proper . . ." other Arabs were to express their opposition in equally strong terms. On February 13, 1919, Chekri Ganem, as head of the "Syrian Delegation," made the following statement:

[17] Page 214.

[18] For an account of Feisal's discussion with the Zionist representatives see M. Perlmann, "Chapters of Arab-Jewish Diplomacy 1918–1922," *Jewish Social Studies* (New York) VI (1944), 123 ff.

Palestine is incontestably the southern portion of our country. The Zionists claim it. We have suffered too much from sufferings resembling theirs not to throw open the doors of Palestine . . . Let them settle in Palestine, but in an autonomous Palestine, connected with Syria by the sole bond of federations.

Chekri Ganem's position, however, appears to have been a questionable one. Harold Nicholson states[19] that Ganem was "a Syrian poet of Paris, who, although he had not set foot in Syria for twenty years, had been produced by M. Pichon as the spokesman of the Syrian Arabs." The fact that his statement on Palestine was followed by a plea for a Syria which would be under French protection speaks volumes on his position.

The legal triumph of Zionism came at a time when the movement was ill equipped to take full advantage of the opportunity which presented itself. The economic and political problems which beset Europe at the end of the war, and the disruption of Russian Jewry after the Revolution, provided little basis for the kind of constructive work which was demanded. Russian Jewry was now split in two. The three million Jews under Bolshevik rule were, as today, largely cut off from contact with the rest of the world. In the three years after the war a wave of pogroms swept through the Ukraine and western Russia on a scale even greater than that of those at the beginning of the century.

Polish Jewry, though not suffering in the same way, was so materially impoverished and dislocated by World War I and by the Russo-Polish struggle that their contribution, too, was severely limited. While the potential force of the five million Jews of eastern Europe was to remain for long one of the mainsprings of action in the Zionist world, it was to the western Jewish communities that Weizmann turned for further political action. However, it was not so much the actual material improvements and changes which were made in Palestine which were to influence the growth of the movement as the profound effect upon Diaspora Jewry of the new way of life and thought that was being evolved. Into the lives of European and American Jewry a new dimension had entered. For many young Jews to whom religion

[19] *Peacemaking 1919* (Boston: 1923), p. 143; quoted in P. L. Hanna, *British Policy in Palestine* (Washington, D. C.: 1952).

had become a symbol of the ghetto and as such was to be discarded, Zionism became invested with religious fervor and zeal. Zionist societies sprang up in every country. Aliyah became the symbol of every fine sentiment of self-denial and national assertion. Jewish religious and secular activities took a new lease on life. Schools, evening classes, folk songs, study groups, and political clubs of every description arose and flourished. Hebrew was studied as a living language by thousands for whom it had been but a vehicle of prayer. The feeling of belonging, of having roots and a home affected the outlook of even the least Zionist-inclined Jewish communities. The pent-up revolutionary zeal of those Jews who were cut off from and disillusioned with the Revolution was now channeled powerfully into Zionist as well as other political activities. Social and cultural institutions wholly non-Jewish in purpose found large numbers of Jews among their members. While the economic and political problems of Palestine were still vast, their solution was being made inevitable by the passionate driving force which was being created throughout the Jewish world.

5. INTERNAL CONFLICTS

The end of World War I saw the beginning of a period of great change in Palestine. For the first time immigration took place on a large scale, with some 150,000 Jews entering the country between 1919 and 1933.[1] Though economically still very weak, particularly since the majority of the immigrants brought no capital with them,[2] the collective settlements were gradually becoming more self-supporting, though they were for long to remain dependent upon outside help. The *Histadrut*, the Fed-

[1] This constituted about 22 per cent of the Jews who left Europe at this period.

[2] By 1930 only 4 per cent of the immigrants possessed capital of £4,000 or more (information taken from 1938 Report of the Palestine Department of Migration).

eration of Jewish Workers which had been set up in 1920, itself established numerous other institutions. Perhaps no other union in any country has secured so strong a hold over political and economic affairs. The nation-wide health service, the *Kupat Holim,* was organized by the Histadrut; it maintained a newspaper, schools, and it owned considerable property. Its say in political decisions grew with the passage of time until today its power—though essentially democratic in origin and practice—has been a source of concern to many who fear the accumulation of too great strength in any one institution.

The political structure and motivation of the European scene were also having a profound effect upon the pattern of the Jewish National Home. The great difference between the labor and the bourgeois Zionist groups was apparent from the earliest times. For the socialist section any attempt to exclude political and cultural attitudes from the terms of reference of the movement constituted a denial of all their beliefs. Any attempt to make of Zionism a movement whose sole function was the ingathering of Jews from the Diaspora without constructing a new way of living was almost heretical. Zionism had to serve not only as the provider of a new home, it had also to infuse into the lives of the people a new approach, a new way of thinking. Of supreme importance was the decision made at the Zionist Congress of 1919 at which the Jewish National Fund (J.N.F.) was set up and at which it was decided that "the fundamental principle of Zionist land policy is that all land on which Jewish colonization takes place should eventually become the common property of the Jewish people."

Because of its fundamental importance to the whole concept of resettlement of the land, it might be of value here to mention the basis upon which J.N.F. allotted land to groups on a 49-year lease and at an almost nominal rental. The basic principles were 1) Jewish national ownership of the land; 2) prohibition of the use of hired labor—the land had to be worked by the tenants themselves; 3) mutual assistance among those using J.N.F. properties; 4) buying and selling to be carried out on a cooperative basis.

The settlements consisted of two main types: a) *Kvutzot/Kibbutzim*—wholly collective settlements—and b) *Moshavim*—collective settlements of small-holders.

The Kibbutz was collectively owned by its members with no property being possessed privately. All meals, clothing, etc., were communally administered and all profits were plowed back into capital improvements.

The Moshav sought to increase the degree of privacy and generally to lessen the communalism of the group. Each family unit possessed a small home and piece of land, though all sales and purchases were made by a central authority.

These developments within the movement soon highlighted the basic ideological differences between the various groups. Though for a time only apparent in the practical policies pursued within Palestine, the dichotomy of opinion gradually emerged at Congress. With the growth in power of the American Zionist Organization under the leadership of Justice Brandeis, the views of this section of the movement assumed greater importance; fundamental differences of approach between the American delegates and those from eastern Europe became apparent. With the differences between them growing constantly, it became clear that the Washington of Brandeis and the Pinsk of Weizmann were worlds apart. Weizmann himself describes his quarrel with Brandeis as "a revival, in a new form, and a new country, of the old cleavage between 'East' and 'West' in Zionism and Jewry,"[3] and he further states,[4] "The propositions of the Brandeis group, dealing ostensibly with formal matters, with organizational institutional rearrangements, actually reflected a denial of Jewish nationalism; they made Zionism simply a sociological plan—and not a good one, as I shall show—instead of the folk renaissance that it was."[5]

[3] *Trial and Error* (New York: 1949), p. 267.

[4] *Ibid.*

[5] For an analysis of this cleavage, based on the powerfully documented suggestion that the controversy did not really arise from a difference in their conceptions of how the Zionist movement should proceed with its practical tasks, see Rabbinowitz, *Fifty Years of Zionism* (London: 1952), pp. 75 ff.

The real key to the controversy[6] was outlined in a speech given by Weizmann in New York in 1921, in which he declared: "The fundamental question is who shall control the work in Palestine. The American leaders wish to make themselves the rulers of Zionist movement." Weizmann maintained that "the Brandeis group envisaged the Zionist Organization as henceforth a purely economic body. Since, in their view, it had lost its political character by having fulfilled its political function." An additional point of controversy was the fact that Weizmann's group set their budget target at about two million pounds a year, realizing that most of this would have to be raised in America. Brandeis maintained that the most that could be obtained from that source was in the region of one hundred thousand pounds. Weizmann's reply that he would have to go to America and try for himself, brought the personal conflict tween the two men to a head. "I doubt," wrote Weizmann, "if Justice Brandeis ever quite forgave me for that challenge."

At any rate this struggle, with Weizmann seeing himself as the real representative of the Yishuv while regarding Brandeis as the leader of the Diaspora Zionists of America, was the beginning of the whole process of seeking out what was to be the relationship between Diaspora Jewry and the Yishuv—a problem which still confronts the government of Israel and the Zionist movement today.[7]

While this struggle was developing within the Zionist movement, Britain proceeded with the appointment of Sir Herbert

[6] While it is not possible to be fully aware of all the factors involved, one nevertheless gains the impression that Brandeis's actions were on a higher moral plane. Weizmann, too, undoubtedly had the welfare of Zionism at heart, but that he also felt his personal position to be at stake seems clear. Brandeis emerges less as the shrewd politician, but as the man with the greater integrity.

There is, however, room for a fuller examination of the relationship between the two men.

[7] The most interesting recent development in this connection was the setting up, in May 1957, of the American Jewish League for Israel. This new group, which was formed out of the former Independent Zionists of America, seeks to separate American Zionists from direct affiliation with Political parties in Israel.

Samuel as the first High Commissioner for Palestine in 1920. Though wholly logical in the light of fulfilling the terms of the Mandate and the Balfour Declaration, this appointment naturally served to increase Arab fears of Jewish domination. However, in attempting to demonstrate his intention of fully safeguarding Arab rights, Samuel exhibited an almost pro-Arab policy in making his appointments and succeeded in giving the Arabs the hope that some reversal of British policy was a possibility. The post of Head of the Political Department he gave to E. T. Richmond, who had freely in the past expressed his strong anti-Zionist feelings. In an attempt to achieve a balance of family interests in the capital, Samuel then appointed Hajj Amin al-Husseini—an organizer of the anti-Jewish riots of 1920—as Mufti of Jerusalem.

By these acts and by others concerning the sale of land, Samuel succeeded, not in pacifying the Arabs, but in persuading them that by sufficiently violent actions and protests they could alter the course of events in their favor. At the same time he gave the Jews the feeling that the British authorities, once quit of their legal requirement in establishing the Mandate, no longer had the real interests of the Jewish National Home at heart. The actions of the dominantly Arab police force in the May Day rioting of 1921 served further to produce feelings of anger and apprehension among the Jews, and the order that immigration should cease pending a revision of legislation increased Jewish fears and Arab hopes. One of the deeper causes for anxiety among the Jews was their conviction, whether correct or not, that much of the Arab opposition was being artificially fostered by the wealthy effendis and absentee landlords who feared the weakening of their hold over the country with the introduction of European ideas and standards of living.

Throughout 1922 and 1923 the British followed a policy of vacillation and weakness which only served to incur the mistrust and dislike of both sides. Unwilling to adopt an openly anti-Zionist policy, allegedly for fear of incurring the disapproval of the international body which had allotted her the Mandate for the express purpose of setting up a Jewish National Home, and determined to retain the friendship of the Arabs, Britain hesitated from one position of weakness to another. Somehow at no stage during the whole Mandate period was she prepared to admit the basic truths of the situation. Apparently so determined was she to maintain her position in the area, that she remained convinced to the end that a compromise between two irreconcilable ideologies could be achieved.

6. THE SEEDS OF CONFLICT

In spite of growing Arab resentment, to which Zionist leaders were still paying little attention, Jewish immigration continued during the 1920s on a growing scale, with the annual rate rising from 5,500 in 1920 to 34,000 in 1925. Largely for economic reasons[1] this number fell to 13,000 in 1926 and only 2,713 in 1927. Though weak economically, Palestine saw a period of political peace until 1929, when, after the incident at the Wailing Wall discussed in Part I, an atmosphere of tension prevailed which led to rioting in which some 250 Jews and Arabs were killed. A series of official inquiries followed, and in spite of the High Commissioner's statement which condemned the "savage murders perpetrated upon defenseless members of the Jewish population," the Labour government of Ramsay MacDonald, as we have seen above, issued the Passfield White Paper which made further concessions to the Arabs. So strong was the outcry of the Jewish Agency leaders, as well as of leading non-Jews, that the Prime Minister felt it necessary to write a letter (February 13, 1931) to Weizmann denying that the government had any intention of not fulfilling its mandatory obligations, and that "H.M.'s Government . . . does not contemplate any stoppage . . . of Jewish immigration in any of

[1] Apart from internal instability within Palestine itself, more important was the fall of the Polish government of Grabski in November 1925. This government had succeeded in stabilizing the currency after taking power in 1923. Its fall led to a period of economic and political confusion during which emigration was difficult.

its categories." He further stated that the policy of the government "did not imply a prohibition of acquisition of additional land by Jews."

Again the government had succeeded in antagonizing both sides. At first it incurred the disapproval of the Jewish Agency with the restrictions and tone of the Passfield White Paper and later that of the Arabs with MacDonald's so-called "black-letter" to Weizmann which appeared to remove any concessions which they had won. Once again the moral appeared to be that only violence, agitation, and influence could secure results. We have seen in the history of this period that the moral once learned was never forgotten.

The rise to power of Hitler in 1933, the growth of anti-Semitism in Germany, and the tensions produced by the Italian invasion of Ethiopia in 1935 served to turn the tide of Jewish immigration into a flood. In 1933, 30,327 Jews entered Palestine; 42,359 in 1934; and 61,854 in 1935.[2] In addition to these figures there must be added a number probably not short of 25,000 "illegal" immigrants who entered the country without British entry certificates—some, it is thought, being transported by Syrian and Lebanese Arabs. British attempts to prevent such entries were largely to no avail. With the whole-hearted backing of every Jew in Palestine, there was little that could be done short of the sort of full-scale operations which were resorted to in the immediate post-war years. Thus, by the time of the 1936 troubles, the official figure of the Palestine population was 1,336,518 of whom 370,843 (or approximately 28 per cent) were Jews. For the Arabs the possibility of becoming a minority in the country was no vague event of the distant future. Zionist acts in raising the standard of living, of spreading the benefits of a technical civilization, of providing an economic well-being along with the development of political institutions were no answer to Arab claims for independence. The rationale of material progress was no answer to a deep emotional desire.

For the Jew, however, the position was more urgent and desperate than ever before. Even before the major Powers were able, or perhaps willing, to foresee the terror which was soon

[2] Col. 94, 104, 112.

to break out from Germany, the Jews realized the measure of the task ahead. Legally justified in developing every aspect of life in Palestine under the terms of the Mandate, and fired with justifiable pride in their achievements, they were now also driven by the belief that upon their efforts depended the actual survival of European Jewry.

Throughout these years Arab attacks upon the Jews and British continued and on April 26, 1936, an Arab strike was declared. As we have seen, this situation led to the sending of a Royal Commission to Palestine to investigate. The Commission found the Mandate unworkable in the light of the situation which had developed in the preceding years. It did not accept the growing attitude which held that the Mandate owed equal obligation to both Jews and Arabs. It stated categorically that "unquestionably . . . the primary purpose of the mandate, as expressed in its preamble and its articles, is to promote the establishment of the Jewish National Home." However, since this task had to be carried out without prejudice to the existing inhabitants who were unwilling to accept the Zionist ideal, the Mandate had to be abandoned. Moreover, to entrust the fate of the 400,000 Jews in Palestine to the rule of the million Arabs was also out of the question. Arab actions over the previous decade had made that clear, and the only alternative appeared to be to partition the country into independent Jewish and Arab states. The British clearly intended to maintain their hold over the political, military, and economic life of the country, by remaining in Haifa, Jerusalem, Tiberias, Acre, and Safed. The Commission also suggested the restriction of Jewish immigration to 12,000 per year and the imposition of severe limitation upon land purchases.

The Twentieth Zionist Congress was split over the issue of partition, and it was only after a violent debate that, while rejecting the scheme as unacceptable, it nevertheless empowered the executive to negotiate with the British on the basis of "ascertaining the precise terms of His Majesty's Government for the proposed establishment of a Jewish State."

However, by now almost no action of the British was accepted at its face value. Every move of the authorities was regarded by both sides—Arabs and Zionists—as concealing an ulterior motive—at the best of self-interest, but, more often, of supporting the other side. To the Yishuv the fact that for so long the administration had retained the strongly anti-Zionist Mufti as head of the Supreme Muslim Council implied a tacit approval of his anti-Jewish terrorist acts. The proposal to limit immigration at a time when the Jews of Germany were attempting to save their lives by entering Palestine naturally intensified suspicion of British actions. The motives of the administration were even suspected at home. In Parliament the government was accused of making the conditions of partition so stringent that the scheme could never be put into practice. It was evident that without Arab consent the plan could never succeed, and since the government was not prepared to use the necessary force to effect it, the severity in the terms of reference prescribed for the Partition Commission was seen as yet another step in the appeasement of the Arab world.

When the conference of both parties called by the British on February 8, 1939, failed to reach any agreement (the Arabs refusing to sit and discuss with the Jewish leaders), the government proceeded to act of its own accord. The policy which Britain decided upon was set out in a White Paper published on May 17, 1939.[3] Britain proposed that a maximum of 75,000 Jews should be allowed to enter Palestine over the next five years. After this time no further immigration would be permitted without Arab consent. This happened at the time that Hitler moved into Czechoslovakia and while "coffin" boats hopelessly overloaded with Jews fleeing from the German terror sailed up and down the Danube and the Mediterranean seeking refuge.

The decision aroused powerful opposition in Parliament and produced a reaction of shock and fear among the Jews. On behalf of the Labour party, Herbert Morrison declared that if a Socialist government were elected it would not consider itself bound by the White Paper. Time was to show how easy it was to make promises when the power to implement them lay in other hands.

A fortnight before Hitler moved into Poland, the Zionist

[3] Cmd 6019.

Congress met to consider the situation. Weizmann, whose faith in Britain throughout the interwar years had brought him into constant conflict with his fellow Zionists,[4] was shattered and humiliated by what was considered as the betrayal of the terms of the Mandate. The Mandates Commission of the League condemned the White Paper as being contrary to the original terms under which the Mandate had been granted.

Before the Council of the League could meet to debate the question, the war, during which millions of Jews of Europe were to be murdered, broke out.

With little immediate prospect of having to honor them, promises could now be made freely. The Jews, whose allegiance to the Allied cause was unquestioned,[5] could be kept quiet with vague promises for the future. The question of oil supplies and communications made Arab good will essential. While the Zionists looked to the end of the war for the building of "a State of three to four million Jews in Palestine," [6] the Arabs assumed, as they were entitled to do after the 1939 White Paper, that all further major Zionist expansion would be prevented. For the present, however, the gates of Palestine were closed.

7. THE WAR AND THE BILTMORE PROGRAM

The war, however, brought no halt to Zionist aims and planning. It served only to spread the conviction that complete independence in a Jewish state was essential to Jewish survival.

[4] It was Weizmann's so-called "pro-British" policy which was to lose him the presidency of the Zionist movement at its first postwar Congress in 1946.

[5] Ben-Gurion had stated: "We shall fight the War as if there were no White Paper, and the White Paper as if there were no War"; quoted in Litvinoff, *Ben-Gurion of Israel* (London: 1954), p. 132. The Yishuv did, in fact, devote its manpower and resources whole-heartedly to the Allied cause.

[6] Chaim Weizmann, *Trial and Error* (New York: 1949), p. 419, in a conversation with Churchill, who replied, "Yes, indeed, I quite agree with that."

Few families in Palestine were without relatives in Europe, and it was not long before news filtered through of the Nazi policy of extermination. The Yishuv was also kept in a state of shocked tension by the callous policy of the British, who refused to allow those refugees who escaped from Europe to land in Palestine. In September 1939 a ship which reached the shores of the Promised Land was fired on and three victims of Nazi persecution lost their lives. During the following months the human cargoes of those few vessels which got through were either interned or deported to Mauritius. In November 1940, two ramshackle boats, the *Milos* and the *Pacific,* arrived off the Palestine coast with some 1,770 Jews on board. The latter ship, whose normal complement of passengers was 60, had over 1,000 on board. Their voyage, which had taken two months, had been one of unmitigated horror. There was neither heat nor drinking water on board. On arrival the passengers were transferred to the *Patria* prior to deportation. On November 25 the *Patria* exploded in Haifa harbor and over 200 lost their lives. While there is no conclusive proof of the following assertion, it appears clear today that the Haganah planned the explosion—intending only to immobilize the ship. However, the story spread through Palestine that the immigrants had blown themselves up in desperation rather than be deported. In spite of the statement of the administration that "as an exceptional act of mercy" the survivors would be permitted to remain in Palestine,[1] the 1,584 visa-less survivors were deported to Mauritius on December 8.[2]

In Europe frantic attempts were being made by the Jewish Agency and other representatives to salvage a few thousand lives from the Nazi holocaust.[3] For these people to be told on arrival in Palestine that they were "illegal" was incomprehensible. Was the technical lack of a British immigration visa to mean they should have remained in Europe? In any case the 1939 White Paper had allowed for 25,000 certificates to be granted to

[1] New York *Times,* Dec. 6, 1940.

[2] *Davar* (Tel-Aviv), Dec. 9, 1940; also *Qol Ha-Am,* illegal publication of Palestine Communist party.

[3] In 1937 there had been set up in Tel-Aviv the Committee for Illegal Immigration (*Mossad le'Aliyah Bet*). The truly amazing story of this group, which continued to save Jews from the Germans throughout the

victims of persecution.[4] To the Zionist leaders British action reflected the deeper implications of that Paper and only served to intensify their plans to fight it.

Perhaps the most tragic case of all was that of the *Struma.* This vessel, leaking and without power of its own, had broken down in the port of Istanbul. In spite of all requests, the British authorities refused to grant the visas to allow the 769 on board to enter Palestine; and without an assurance that these were forthcoming, the Turkish authorities also refused to permit their landing. In imminent danger of sinking, the ship was towed out into the Black Sea; within a few hours she drifted into a mine and sank. There was one survivor. (See *New Judaea,* March and April, 1942.)

These events might have had no place in this account were it not for the fact that they produced a considerable hardening in Zionist feelings. For over a year Zionist circles had debated the desirability of demanding a Jewish state at the end of the war. The time when they would place their trust in promises and alternative schemes had now passed. Neither humanitarian pleas nor the zeal with which the Yishuv had thrown itself behind the Allies appeared to move the Mandatory power. Repeatedly Zionist leaders stressed that an Allied victory did not necessarily entail a solution of the Jewish problem; their struggle would continue after the German defeat. Accordingly the Emergency Zionist Council, at its conference in May 1942 at the Biltmore Hotel in New York, demanded "that the gates of Palestine be opened; that the Jewish Agency be vested with control of immigration into Palestine with the necessary authority for upbuilding the country, including the development of its unoccupied and uncultivated land; and that Palestine be established as a Jewish Commonwealth integrated in the structure of the new democratic world."

In the eyes of the British, this resolution only served to cast doubts upon the loyalty of the Zionist leaders. Weizmann's public acceptance of the Biltmore Program (though in private

[4] It is interesting to note (Kimche, p. 29) that in 1937 Schumburg of the German Foreign Ministry held that Britain was determined to set up a Jewish state. Moreover, von Hentig, the Middle East expert of the Foreign Ministry, stated that if Britain were so determined, the Arabs would "not

he expressed serious misgivings) was but another step in his decline as the supreme moderating force in Zionist politics. It marked Ben-Gurion's final arrival as the new leader of the movement. Five years before, at the time of the Royal Commission, Ben-Gurion had openly conceded that some form of partition was inevitable. It is perhaps difficult to decide how much his new extremism was due to a realization that his own political rise resulted from Weizmann's weakened position. In view of the fact that it was precisely within his own party that Ben-Gurion met with the strongest opposition, one might more easily concede that he was moved by the nobler motive. A closer examination of his intraparty rift, however, shows that he made no concession to the left-wing element within Mapai on this issue, and that he saw the opportunity to purge the party of its dissidents and to assert his total authority.[5]

Toward the end of 1942, as a fuller picture of Nazi exterminations in Europe became known to the Yishuv, in spite of British censorship attempts to prevent such news from getting through, the tension in Palestine grew and Zionist policies assumed an air of desperation. By 1943, resistance to British plans became more pronounced and violent in word and deed. The administration appeared to the Jews to swerve from an attitude of great correctness and restraint to one of anti-Zionism and callous stupidity. At times, in the face of what was often great provocation, the military behaved in a way which was exemplary. On other occasions, such as during the trial of two Jews for possessing arms, the government counsel was permitted to indulge in the most virulent anti-Jewish statements. The sentences on the two prisoners of seven and ten years respectively aroused a tide of resentment in the Yishuv,[6] particularly since, in a recent case when a British soldier was tried for selling arms to an Arab, the Arab was not even allowed to testify. Perhaps the

[5] At the Mapai Conference which followed the adoption in New York of the Biltmore Program, the "Bevanite" wing of the party, under the leadership of Zisling and Tabenkin, broke away from the main body and reconstituted their "Fraction B" under the old name of the *"Achdut Avodah."*

[6] Report on Minutes of Electoral Assembly (*Asefat HaNivharim*), August 1943.

flow of events was such that no action on the part of the authorities could have removed the tension. Nevertheless, some reduction in it might have been achieved if a more enlightened attitude had prevailed.

Anti-British acts were henceforth to take place on two levels. First, a calculated policy involving determined resistance and careful planning, but with an eye to the political implications of any action, was carried out by Haganah. This body, which had grown out of the HaShomer (Defence Force) of the 1920s, could now be considered the official army of the Yishuv. Under the leadership of Jacob Dostrovsky (later Dori), the Haganah had been completely reorganized after the 1939 White Paper, and by 1943 it was a well-disciplined and comparatively well-armed group which included within its ranks a striking force—the *Palmach*—of some 3,000 men and women. The existence of the Haganah had always been known to the authorities, and in 1937 at a meeting of the Mandates Commission, the Colonial Secretary had paid a tribute to its restraint against Arab attacks. The de facto recognition of the Haganah was also implied when, in 1942, some 15,000 of its members were being trained and armed by the British.

The second type of opposition to the government was that of the terrorist groups. As early as 1938, in protest against the policy of "*Havlagah*" (self-restraint) of the Haganah, one section had seceded from official defence forces. This group, the *Irgun Zvai Leumi* (National Military Organization), differed from the Haganah not only in its political thinking (it was composed largely of Revisionist followers of Jabotinsky), but also in its belief that only an active military fight against both Arabs and British could achieve results. Weizmann's policies of moderation and compromise were anathema to them. Even Ben-Gurion's early policy of attempted cooperation with the Arabs was a political blunder in their eyes.

At the beginning of World War II terrorist activities ceased. However, by 1943, not only had the Stern Group—the splinter party of about 200 under the leadership of Abraham Stern—broken away from the Irgun, but also under the new leadership of Menahem Begin the Irgun itself began to resume its activities. After the attempted assassination of the High Commissioner, Sir Harold MacMichael, on August 8, 1944, and as a result of the murder in Cairo of Lord Moyne, the British Resident Commissioner in the Middle East, the Jewish Agency leaders and the Haganah broke openly and officially with the terrorist groups. However, while genuine disapproval and horror existed concerning the actions of the Irgun and Stern groups, and while the Haganah made several attempts to prevent or control their activities, the attempts were only half-hearted. The enemy was still the government and no attempts on the part of London to increase differences between the two groups could succeed. The Haganah leaders were admittedly against the terrorist methods; nevertheless, they could not fail to note their effectiveness. However, even on those occasions when they took an active part in opposing the Irgun, such as on June 20, 1948, when the Irgun vessel *Altalena* containing arms was set on fire by the Haganah, their actions were perhaps dominated more by a fear of the growth of a new military-political party within the country than by other motives.[7]

The left-wing press saw in the terrorist organizations the rise of a new right-wing fascist party and repeatedly attacked Irgun and Stern Group raids. Thus *HaMishmar,* of August 24, 1944, declared in an editorial: "We have powerful allies in the struggle against World Fascism; but who will be concerned if our own Fascism devours us entirely?" Thus from the end of 1944 until March 1945, the Jewish Shadow Cabinet, foreseeing the dangers to internal stability, as well as the likelihood of antagonizing world opinion, went so far as to hand over to the British information concerning terrorist hide-outs and arms stores. However, throughout the period it was clear that, whatever the future actions of the Irgun might be once the Jews had gained their independence, the activities of the terrorist groups were largely dominated by despair. It was apparent too that the military and the Palestine police were prepared to deal

[7] After the *Altalena* incident the Irgun and Stern groups were officially incorporated into the Israeli army. The Irgun reappeared as a political party Herut which, in 1949, polled some 12 per cent of the votes and in 1955, with a similar percentage, became the second largest party with 15 seats out of a total of 120.

with these acts only on an ad hoc basis. The administration was to make no attempt to apply itself to the deeper causes underlying the whole situation.

8. ANGLO-AMERICAN REACTIONS

At the Chicago Convention of 1944, the Democratic party declared: "We favor the opening of Palestine to unrestricted Jewish immigration and colonization and such a policy as to result in the establishment there of a free and democratic Jewish Commonwealth." In February 1944, the Arab States had protested against resolutions of the United States Congress which had called for unlimited postwar Jewish immigration. The personal protests from Abdullah of Trans-Jordan and from Ibn Saud of Saudi Arabia to President Roosevelt produced assurances from the President that no fundamental changes would be made in the Palestine situation without consultation with both Jews and Arabs. However, in October 1944, in his statement to Senator Robert Wagner to be read before the Convention of the Zionist Organization of Amcrica, Roosevelt declared his acceptance of the Democratic party's policy statements, and also added his own personal commitment that: "if re-elected I shall . . . help bring about its realization." Even after his meeting with Ibn Saud, Roosevelt stated—just three weeks before his death—and at the timc of the ratification of the constitution of the new Arab League that: "I made my position on Zionism clear in October. That position I have not changed."[1] Two weeks later, Roosevelt again notified Ibn Saud that he "would take no action which . . . might prove hostile to the Arab people."

The effect of these apparently conflicting statements was most unfortunate. To the British authorities they gave the impression of being too subject to business interests and voting blocs. At the same time British officials noted that the American government was unprepared to take any direct steps to help solve the problems which she herself was helping to make more

[1] Quoted in Bartley Crum, *Behind the Silken Curtain* (New York: 1947), p. 38.

acute. To both Arabs and Jews it appeared that the U. S. government was as subject to the charges of "double-dealing" as Britain had been over its promises to both sides.[2]

Opposition to the Biltmore demands came not only from the Arabs. Throughout the interwar year Jewish anti-Zionist sentiment had existed among a small but wealthy and influential minority in England and America. Particularly in England, where the non-Zionist Anglo-Jewish Association had hoped that Palestine might enter the British Commonwealth as a Dominion, was opposition to the extremist demands of the Zionist Organization strong. Fearful of a spread in anti-Semitic sentiment after the war (Sir Oswald Moseley, the head of the Fascist Organization in Great Britain, had been interned for "the duration"), the demands for a Jewish state were attacked by some on the basis that the Jews constituted a religious group and not a nation.[3] However, the 1939 White Paper and the mass murder of European Jewry had popularized active Zionism;[4] and, though vocal, the views on Zionism of the Anglo-Jewish Association represented but a small fraction of Anglo-Jewish public opinion.

In the United States a similar situation existed. While naturally not favoring the inclusion of Israel in the British Commonwealth, the American Council for Judaism, refusing to acknowledge the implications of "dual loyalty" which it held to be involved in an acceptance of Zionism, repeatedly declared that American Jewry should have no part in the national and political affairs of Palestinian Jewry. "We are definitely opposed

[2] In his book *Behind the Silken Curtain* (pp. 36-37) and in a private communication to the author dated May 21, 1956, Bartley Crum has stated that, when serving as a member of the Anglo-American Commission of Inquiry on Palestine in 1945, he was shown a confidential State Department file the "existence of which even President Truman had not known. According to this file, since September 15, 1938, each time a promise was made to American Jewry regarding Palestine, the State Department promptly sent messages to the Arab rulers discounting it and reassuring them, in effect, that regardless of what was promised publicly to the Jews, nothing would be done to change the situation in Palestine." Mr. Crum added that the contents of this file, to his knowledge, have never been made public.

[3] Anglo-Jewish Association, *Memorandum on Palestine* (London: 1944).

[4] The Zionist Federation of Great Britain increased its membership by almost 500 per cent from 1943-45. (Figs. from Zion. Fed. of Gt. Britain, 77, Gt. Russell Street, London, W.C. 1.)

to a Jewish State," it declared[5] as well as to "a Jewish flag or a Jewish army. We are interested in the development of Palestine as a refuge for persecuted Jews; but we are opposed to the idea of a political state under Jewish domination in Palestine or anywhere else." In the minds of many Jews who had little sympathy with the religious reform attitudes of most of the members of the Council and who questioned their sincerity as well as their motives, it appeared that the Council wished ultimately to deny both the religious as well as the national character of Judaism.

9. POSTWAR AND ECONOMIC PLANS[1]

In the years of the first Royal Commission on Palestine, the phrase "absorptive capacity" had been attacked by the Zionists as implying an illegal limitation upon the numbers of immigrants permitted to enter the country. Certain it was that little agreement was ever reached by the British and the Jews as to what was the economic potential of Palestine. In the face of the 1939 White Paper and confronted with the immediate need to bring in the survivors of European Jewry, the Jewish Agency's Planning Committee tended to accept this principle of saving lives as the criterion for Jewish population growth.

At the beginning of the war, economic life in Palestine came almost to a standstill. Particularly after Italy entered the war the shortage of shipping space brought severe losses to the citrus industry.[2] A similar problem involving an acute shortage of supplies of all kinds prevented the growth and normal functioning of almost every industry. Only toward the end of

[5] Statement of Rabbi Wolsey of Philadelphia on the occasion of the establishment of the American Council for Judaism, Philadelphia, 1947.

[1] See below, Part IV, for more details.

[2] In 1941-42 total citrus exports (including bulk shipments) were equivalent to only 0.6 million prewar cases, and in 1942-43 only 1.3 million (See R. Nathan, O. Gass, D. Creamer, *Palestine, Problem and Promise* [Washington, D. C.: 1946], p. 211).

1941, when military requirements injected new financial life into the country, did the situation change. The settlements, as the chief agricultural producers, prospered[3] since the British Middle East forces were prepared to take all food that could be spared. Machine shops for the repair of British Eighth Army vehicles were set up and light machinery—lathes, drills, automobile spare parts, and scientific instruments—were produced in Palestine for the first time.[4] By 1944, when military demand began to drop, these new "mushroom" industries were able to be successfully turned over to peacetime use. In preparation for new immigrants, housing projects were undertaken and different types of prefabricated buildings from several countries were examined.

From the standpoint of any large-scale expansion of agriculture—and eventually of population—the development of the Negev was essential. On November 4, 1944, Churchill had assured Weizmann (at an unofficial luncheon) of his acceptance of the fact that the Negev should be included in any future partition scheme.[5] The Jewish authorities had begun planning earlier, however. Of the forty settlements which had been established during the war period, ten had been placed in the Negev; in the light of any future settlement, their position would play a large part in the allocation of territories. The most heartening factor, from the Jewish point of view, was the scheme put forward by Dr. W. Clay Lowdermilk of the U. S. Bureau of Agriculture, for the establishment of a Jordan Valley Authority. This plan, which presupposed cooperation with the neighboring Arab states, envisaged the possibility of absorbing up to two million more immigrants into the territory west of the Jordan.

Upon such schemes as this, no disagreement existed among Jewish groups in Palestine. Whether it was wholly feasible or not, the Zionists insisted that given the time, energy, and money, the land could absorb all those Jews who might wish to come—

[3] By 1943 the national income had increased 200% over 1939. However, 90% of the agricultural increase was due to inflation, only 10% to increased output (Nathan, Gass, Creamer, p. 156).

[4] *Ibid.*, p. 235.

[5] *Trial and Error* (New York: 1949), p. 436.

should the political situation allow it. On the political front, however, the rift between Weizmann and Ben-Gurion was widening. Weizmann, still placing his trust in Britain and particularly in Churchill, wished to see a five- to ten-year transition period before a State was born. Ben-Gurion, with perhaps a more shrewd grasp of the contemporary political trend, warned the Jews to be prepared to fight the White Paper should no decision reversing it be put into force.[6]

With the return of the Labour party to power in July 1945, it appeared that the Zionist movement would need to fight no longer. Throughout its history the British Labour movement had gone on record as being strongly in favor of Zionism and a Jewish State for both political and humanitarian reasons. In 1939 its opposition to the White Paper had been loud and bitter. At its conference in June 1943 it reaffirmed its statements in favor of the Jewish Home. In its report on *Palestine Post-War Settlement* in 1944, the National Executive had called for a Jewish majority in the land and for the transfer of willing Arabs to neighboring countries. It had even spoken of extending the boundaries "by agreement with Egypt, Syria and Trans-Jordan." The Zionists themselves had never called for such radical policies.

It was four months before the new government made its pronouncement on the Palestine question. The two months preceding this statement had seen a new outbreak of anti-British activity in Palestine. No longer restricted to terrorist activities, the Haganah too now declared that the gates of Palestine would at all costs be kept open to allow the pitiful survivors of the concentration camps to enter. On August 31, in a letter[7] to the British Prime Minister, President Truman appealed for the immediate granting of 100,000 certificates to the displaced Jews of Europe. The vast majority of these Jews, as the UNSCOP Committee was later to confirm, wished to go to Palestine. They would entertain no alternative. The survivors of Teresienstadt, Dachau, and Buchenwald were going to the one place they could call home. To attempt to start their lives anew in their old lands was unthinkable. Of the few who attempted

[6] *Jewish Agency Digest of Press and Events,* No. 61 (March 21, 1945).
[7] Published in the New York *Times* on November 13, 1945.

to return there, the majority found a population imbued with an anti-Semitic prejudice which became all the more marked when the returning Jews made any attempt to regain the homes which had been taken from them years before.

The British reaction to the American proposal was cold. Resentment was strong over what was felt to be essentially a vote-catching gesture, wholly unsupported by any American offer of troops to help put the proposal into effect. British resentment went deeper, however. American oil holdings had grown enormously and Britain's financial grip in the area had correspondingly declined. Thus Britain, thrown on the defensive in the face of nationalist movements throughout the East, was in no mood to receive kindly American advice which involved neither troops nor money.

On November 13, 1945, the British Foreign Secretary, Mr. Ernest Bevin, announced to the House of Commons the setting up of a joint Anglo-American Committee to report on Palestine. Within 120 days the Committee would give its findings and Mr. Bevin stated his intention of abiding by its decisions should they be unanimous. At a press conference following the statement in Parliament he also remarked that he staked his political future on his ability to reach a settlement of the problem.

Ernest Bevin's advisor on Palestine was Harold Beeley, a Foreign Office official who was also appointed a member of the above-mentioned Committee. Beeley saw the Palestine issue in the light of powerful Soviet expansionist plans. Convinced too of the strength and importance of doing nothing to antagonize Arab good will in the Middle East, he constantly urged Bevin to take no steps which might weaken Britain's position in the area. Bevin needed little urging not to be pro-Zionist. Sensitive to the anti-British criticism in the United States, readily persuaded by the mass of briefs from the Foreign Office, the War Office, the Middle East Office in Cairo, and from the Palestine administration, that the Arabs were both powerful and necessary allies, and engaged as he was at the time of the Committee's report in the struggle with Russia over the evacuation of Persia, Bevin was in no mood to accede to any Zionist wishes.

The report of the Joint Committee urged the abrogation of the 1940 land laws and the immediate admission of 100,000 Jews from Europe. Prime Minister Attlee's statement in Parliament on May 1, 1946, argued that in order for such a number to be admitted, American help was essential. This remark was largely conditioned by Truman's impulsive statement greeting the report, in which he gave the suggestion of the admission of the 100,000 and the removal of the land laws his immediate approval, while he made no mention of any other points in it. Attlee's other demand, that before any immigration could be permitted the Haganah must be disbanded and disarmed, was to destroy any hopes of the findings' being implemented. To demand this was, at that moment, to ask the impossible—as Attlee well knew. Judge Joseph Hutcheson, the American chairman of the Committee had stated explicitly: "I will not, under any circumstances, be a part to any recommendation which would strip the Jews of Palestine of the right to defend their lives." [8]

The effect in Palestine of Attlee's statement was catastrophic. Only the position of the extremists among Jews was strengthened. The Haganah, which had been passing through a period of conciliation with the British and had swung over to a mood of strong anti-terrorism, was put in an impossible position. Determined to show that its cooperation had not been due to weakness, the Haganah now went into the attack in the hope of forcing some concessions from the British. On June 16, 1946, almost every bridge connecting Palestine with its neighbors was blown up. But it was one of the few occasions in Palestine when force failed. The British welcomed the opportunity to meet strength with strength. Almost all the Jewish Agency leaders were interned at Latrun. Settlements were searched for arms; and although on this, as on most occasions in Palestine, the British officers and men behaved with discipline in the face of the understandable hostility of the population, some troops took the opportunity to work off their feelings against the Yishuv with acts of unnecessary brutality and destruction.[9] With the

[8] Quoted in Bartley Crum, *Behind the Silken Curtain* (New York: 1947), p. 279.

[9] See *Mishmar,* June 30, 1946 (HaShomer HaZair Hebrew daily).

blowing up, on July 22, by the terrorists[10] of the King David Hotel—the east wing of which housed the headquarters of the administration—a situation of almost open war between the British and the Jews existed. Lacking any policy which would appeal to either side, and heir to a tradition of bowing before those who showed the most determination, the government often appeared to behave with a viciousness born of weakness. Henceforth little or no distinction was made between Haganah and Irgun attacks, though the rift between the two groups was now wide. British troops, and especially the Palestine police, caught between a policy which they did not understand and the bullets of those who opposed that policy, became more brutal, as did the acts of the terrorists. Meanwhile anti-British sentiment was further increased by the steady arrival of immigrant ships, the majority of which were intercepted by the Royal Navy and their passengers deported to Cyprus.

For a brief period in the fall of 1946, some rapport between the British and the Jewish Agency seemed to exist. Britain put forward the "Morrison Plan," which proposed the partition of Palestine into Jewish and Arab cantons. However, the Agency was in no mood for such sacrifices[11] and the plan fell through.

On February 14, 1946, Mr. Bevin announced his intention of referring the Palestine problem to the United Nations, and the following month Britain called for the setting up of a UN Commission of Inquiry. Following Bevin's announcement, British repressive measures were intensified. All British women and children were evacuated. Deportations of Jews to Kenya and Eritrea were increased and death sentences and floggings were carried out. Irgun reprisals were equally brutal.[12] However, with only

[10] Originally Begin had proposed a joint Irgun, Stern, and Palmach attack. The Haganah turned this down but agreed not to prevent it if it was carried out at night and with a warning to prevent loss of life. The Irgun broke its agreement and nearly 100 Jews, Arabs, and British were killed.

[11] The Agency had put forward secret details of a scheme for "a viable State in an adequate area of Palestine" based on the 1937 Partition plus the Negev (Jewish Agency Political Survey, 1946-47).

[12] In reply to the flogging of an Irgun member, a British officer was flogged. One week later the British abolished flogging. During twenty-five years of peace the Agency had urged that this be done—with no success. The moral seemed clear.

a small fraction of the Yishuv supporting terrorist policies, the mass of the population was forced, by the total lack of understanding on the part of the administration, to sympathize with any anti-British act. In retaliation for the hanging of terrorists, two British sergeants, chosen at random, were hanged by the Irgun in July 1947. The wave of horror which swept Israel was sincere; that which overtook Britain was naturally even more profound and its results were immediate. Somehow in keeping with the whole history of the problem, this emotional force was to influence political action more than all the legal considerations and deliberations had done.

The British decided they were through with Palestine.

"Mr. Bevin's earlier assertions that British control over the Middle East was vital, and that the withdrawal of British troops from Palestine would adversely affect the pay packets of the British workers, were swept aside as irrelevant. Strategic, economic, and political arguments were impatiently overruled. It was one of those rare moments when the public mood and emotion really made British policy. Public opinion sounded the retreat from Palestine. The Labor Party had done with Zionism." [13]

However, the condition under which Mr. Creech Jones, the British Colonial Minister, announced that Britain would implement the decisions of the UN Assembly, were apparently designed to ensure their failure. Though nominally declaring a British refusal to continue to administer the mandate without UN aid, Britain stated that her help would be forthcoming only if any UN decisions were acceptable to both Arabs and Jews. Britain, it must be assumed, was convinced that the UN could not but fail to solve the problem which she had failed to solve in thirty years. With no coherent Cabinet policy of her own, with decisions largely in the hands of the military on the spot, and with the Palestine administration largely free from Foreign Office control, Britain's Middle East diplomacy seemed bankrupt. However, the failure of the UN would serve greatly to strengthen the British hand, weaken the attacks of the United States, and allow Britain to attempt to continue to administer the territory in her own fashion.

[13] Jon Kimche, *Seven Fallen Pillars* (New York: 1952), p. 161.

10. A UNITED NATIONS SOLUTION: THE STATE IS BORN

As we have seen in Part I, on November 29, 1947, after certain amendments in the UNSCOP original partition plan had been made[1] the UN General Assembly voted by 33 to 13 in favor of partition.[2] The British Mandate was to end by August 1 at the latest and an international commission was appointed to supervise the implementation of the Assembly's plans.

The Arab threats of war which were made at the initial talks before the setting up of UNSCOP were not merely verbal. In accordance with "treaty obligations" British military mission and arms supplies were arriving in Trans-Jordan, Egypt, and Iraq. In September 1947, the Cairo French-language daily, *Le Journal d'Egypte,* reported the purchase from the British of fifty-seven tons of munitions, and during the succeeding months the Palestine press contained several reports of British supplies of tanks and heavy artillery to the Arab states. Following the United Nations decision of November, Arab preparations became more intense. On January 9, 1948, some 800 armed members of the "Palestine Liberation Army" crossed into Palestine from Syria. Some two weeks later, a second force of approximately the same size joined the first group at its headquarters at Tubas. The absence of any British move to prevent their entry convinced the Yishuv of British partiality. With an estimated 40–50,000 troops in the country, the Foreign Office explanation to the press[3] seemed barely convincing. It appeared that it was mere coincidence that the road from Syria to Tubas was one of the first to be evacuated. However, the fact that no military action against the Arab troops was even contemplated, the excuse being that the British no longer had sufficient forces, did little to remove

[1] The Jewish state was reduced by about 500 square miles from an originally proposed total of 6,000. The reductions consisted of a) the transfer of Jaffa to the Arab state, as well as b) about 500,000 acres of the Negev near Beersheba and along the Egyptian frontier.

[2] UN General Assembly, *Official Report 2nd Session PM,* II, 1424-25.

[3] Quoted in Jon Kimche, *Seven Fallen Pillars* (New York: 1952), p. 214.

Jewish apprehensions about the situation.

Once it was clear that the British intended to leave Palestine (Mr. Creech Jones informed Parliament that the Mandate would end on May 15, 1948), the Jews set about consolidating their already efficient organization covering every department of the central and local administrations. Admittedly many refused to believe that the British would actually go—they held that some last-minute excuse for retaining a hold on the country would be found, and certainly many British actions at the time were puzzling to the observer. Britain refused to put into effect any of the UN requests concerning the establishment of armed police forces, the reopening of Jewish immigration, and the demarcation of the proposed boundaries. Nor would she allow the UN Supervisory Commission to enter the land before May 1. To the Jews it seemed clear that a strongly pro-Arab policy was being followed, the suggestion being made by the Jews that Britain was banking on an Arab victory on such a scale as to solve, once and for all, the political question of the Jewish state. Thus the UN Commission reported that the Arabs alone were being armed by the Palestine government, and while British forces were able to prevent the landing of immigrants despite the active support of the whole Yishuv,[4] Britain maintained that "the nature of the border country makes it extremely difficult to secure the entire frontier against illegal immigration, especially at night."

Even if, as many Jews felt, the British scheme was intended to give the Arabs a head start in the proposed war, it is difficult to see precisely why Britain did not take more decisive steps to hinder the development of the Jewish administrative and military organization. That Britain had the troops at hand to carry out such a policy must be agreed. Had Britain in July 1947 possessed the clear intention of so weakening the Yishuv that an Arab attack must succeed, then the hanging of the two sergeants provided precisely such a situation. Public outcry in England would have been absent. One can only conclude that at that time British policy did not consider either that an Arab attack

[4] UNPAC, First Special Report to Security Council, UNSC S/676 (A/AC.21/9), p. 7; and UNPAC, Report to General Assembly, OR, 2nd Special Session, Supp. No. 1, pp. 17, 35, 36.

would come, or that if it did come it would be on such a scale as to have any chance of succeeding. And, by 1948, when it appeared to the Jews that Britain was more than somewhat interested in helping Arab preparations, she was sufficiently concerned with the force of world opinion (and in particular that of the United States) that she should only indulge in comparatively mild pro-Arab measures.

Whether this analysis is correct or not, it certainly appeared to the Jews of Palestine in 1948 that a distinctly pro-Arab policy was being followed, and that this plan was succeeding. During March the Arab troops, thought by many to have been non-Palestinian and to have numbered seven to eight thousand,[5] had entered the country and occupied positions dominating the Haifa–Tel-Aviv and Tel-Aviv–Jerusalem roads. Settlements in the Negev were attacked or isolated. On March 11 the Agency building in Jerusalem was blown up and two weeks later a Haganah force was ambushed and forced to surrender. Arab elation over these events was further increased by a United States proposal on March 30 that the partition scheme be abandoned and a UN trusteeship set up instead.

Gradually, however, the Haganah was recruiting and training, and at the end of March the first trickle of supplies from Czechoslovakia began to arrive.[6] By April the tide was turning.

[5] New York *Times,* March 12, 21, 29; also *Palestine Press* for March 12, 13, 16, 21-29.

[6] In December 1947, the U. S. stopped the sending of any arms to the Middle East. With the Arabs receiving arms from Britain, the Jews tried frantically, and with some success, to buy arms illegally in the U. S., and purchasing missions scoured Europe for the same purpose. The money for purchases made in the U. S. was raised by donations from Jews in America. Where other countries demanded payment in dollars, the money was obtained in the same fashion.

While it is not yet possible to document statements on the arming of the Haganah, it is perhaps reasonably safe to assert that from 1944 onward attempts had been made to build up the military strength of the organization. Every means was used, from the stealing of arms from Middle East dumps, the taking over (in a wide variety of ways) of ex-German equipment, the purchase of materials from the large numbers of dealers in these goods in Italy, France, and Greece, even to the purchase of equipment from Egypt and Iraq. Kimche (p. 243) quotes Israeli military leaders as claiming that on May 15, 1948, they possessed: 10,000 rifles, 450 light machine guns; 180 heavy machine guns; 670 2″ mortars; 96 3″ mortars; 2 pieces of artillery

With the occupation of the Arab villages on the road to Jerusalem, the highway to the beleaguered city was reopened. Within weeks Haifa, Jaffa, Safed, Acre, Tiberias, and the New City of Jerusalem were firmly in Jewish control.

At 9:50 on the morning of May 14, 1948, the Union Jack was lowered in Haifa port; the British Mandate had ended. At 4:00 P.M. on the same day, Ben-Gurion announced the establishment of "the Jewish State in Palestine, to be called Israel."

11. EAST AND WEST: THE PROBLEM OF ABSORPTION

Israel's problems did not end with her Declaration of Independence. Even apart from the military attacks which began at midnight on May 14, with the bombing of Tel-Aviv by Egyptian aircraft followed by invasion by the armies of the major Arab states, Israel was faced with social, legal, religious, and economic difficulties of a unique kind. Many of these derived from the problem of the absorption of the new immigrants, who, it was now declared, had an absolute right to enter the State and become full citizens. In addition, the Zionist movement was faced with the need for an "agonizing reappraisal." What was to be its function now that Israel was an independent state with its own democratically elected government? Was the movement to serve merely as a fund-raising institution, or were its members throughout the world to exercise any more direct influence upon the course of events in Israel? The masses of the Zionist movement had always been in the main "philanthropic Zionists"—tied to the ideals of the movement by little more than their purse strings and a fount of emotion. The war years had produced a certain change of attitude, however. The Zionist organizations had become far more of a political movement, articulate and active. For Israel

without sights; an adequate supply of Sten guns but an inadequate supply of ammunition.

This figure may very well be correct. However, towards the end of May, a second batch of arms arrived from Czechoslovakia.

the problem was now to keep the financial, moral, and political support of these groups while retaining full independence of action, in all fields, within the state itself. These, and other dilemmas confronted—and still confront—the State of Israel.

Table

IMMIGRATION TO ISRAEL ACCORDING

(Figures taken from

COUNTRY	May 15-Dec. 31 1948	1949	1950	1951
ASIA				
Iraq	15	1,709	32,453	89,088
Iran	43	1,778	10,519	9,444
Yemen	270	35,422	8,650	698
Other Countries	46	6,351	3,699	2,899
AFRICA				
Libya	1,064	14,352	8,956	6,570
Tunisia	6,821 (Tunisia, Algeria, Morocco)	17,354 (Tunisia, Algeria, Morocco)	4,792	3,469
Algeria			457	269
Morocco			4,213	7,631
South Africa			179	43
Other Countries	179	307	—	56
EUROPE				
U.S.S.R.		2,579	2,286	566
Poland	28,789	47,343	26,499	3,505
Rumania	17,678	13,596	46,430	40,208
Greece		1,364	437	113
Germany	1,817 (Germany, Austria)	6,953	1,352	643
Austria				
Czechoslovakia	2,115	15,689	632	295
Hungary	3,463	6,844	2,721	1,273
United Kingdom		758	345	187

From the day that the State was founded until May 1956, some 786,000 Jews have entered the country, about 140,000 more than the total Jewish population in 1948.[1] With over 40 per cent of the immigrants coming from Asia and North Africa,[2] and with

[1] *Jewish Agency Digest of Press and Events* (Jerusalem), Vol. IX., No. 36.

[2] During 1954 and 1955 the immigrants from these areas constituted approximately 90 per cent of the total (statement of Dr. G. Josephthal, Treasurer of the Jewish Agency, before the Zionist Congress in Jerusalem, April 26, 1956).

an estimated minimum of 100,000 Jews in North Africa wishing today to enter Israel,[3] it is clear that the make-up of the Yishuv has undergone a fundamental change. Moreover, unless there should be a radical change in the policy of the Soviet Union,

1

TO COUNTRIES OF ORIGIN
Israel Annual)

1952	1953	1954	TOTAL	Percent of Total 1948-54	1919-48
961	421	250	125,896	17.0	1.0
4,187	1,091	472	27,534	3.7	0.5
87	27	584	45,738	6.2	4.3
1,113	695	355	12,790	1.7	—
1,187	236	186	32,552	4.4	—
2,688	606	2,628			
95	81	220	67,226	9.1	0.7
4,777	2,941	8,185			
17	22	29	683	0.1	—
1,260	1,023	940	19,630	2.7	—
156	173	151	8,277	1.1	
615	398	268	107,393	14.6	40.9
3,627	180	99	121,715	16.7	6.3
67	93	40	2,309	0.3	
260	185	129	11,335	1.6	13.9
84	30	39	18,880	2.3	1.9
218	224	55	14,796	2.0	0.9
159	112	97	2,157	0.3	20.9

which today allows no emigration to Israel (apart from a few, usually elderly individuals, permitted to join their children), the proportion of oriental Jewry in the country must grow for some time to come. For not only does western Jewry show no indication of emigrating to Israel on any scale, but also the birth rate of the oriental communities[4] is appreciably higher, while the

[3] *Ibid.*

[4] "The Jewish families in Morocco with more than three children are 3½ times more numerous as among American Jews, and 7 times as numerous

health facilities of the new state keep their death rate low.

That the operation of the "ingathering of the exiles" has been a remarkable success on the whole, cannot be denied. No country before has ever increased its population by 250 per cent in so short a space of time. However, difficulties have arisen—and still exist—and these difficulties are by no means confined to the physical and financial problems of resettlement alone.

The disparity between the cultures of the new immigrant groups and that of the predominantly European Yishuv is enormous. The gulf separating the Yemen and Iraq from Poland and Germany is bridged only by the tenuous strand of a common Judaism. The existence of this racial tension is attested by both *Ashkenazim* and *Sephardim* (these terms are used, somewhat loosely, to represent the Jews of European and Middle Eastern origin respectively). The Ashkenazim see in the unlimited immigration from the oriental communities a threat, not only to their material standards of living, but also to the very ideals and practices of western civilization. Few, however, over the last few years, would have refrained from bringing in those Jews from Arab lands whose lives were in danger; but more are prepared to argue today that perhaps North African Jewry should be kept out. To admit this publicly in Israel today would take courage and would court severe criticism. The citizens of Israel have made enormous sacrifices—even of their lives—in order to save their brothers abroad. The accusation that a color bar is in the making in Israel would be fought with strength and with sincerity. Many believe it does not exist; others, that the slight inequalities which are present today were inevitable but are fast disappearing. However, the Sephardim, seeing themselves as second-class citizens, accuse the political parties, the government, the whole Ashkenazi community, of fostering this color bar. While, admittedly, legally no restrictive practices are permitted or practiced, their charge has some justification. The feelings of Ashkenazi superiority, of condescension and pity toward the Sephardim, the lack of trust and confidence in their abilities and

---

as among native born heads of American Jewish families" (J. Lestchinsky, *Palestine Year Book & Israel Annual,* IV (1949), 57.

in their idealism, are all factors whose existence—while fought against—cannot be denied.

Thus even the liberal, independent, center newspaper *Ha-Aretz,*[5] argued that the ingathering of too many Jews from the more backward countries constituted "a threat to the existence of the State of Israel." The new problem, as seen by the newspaper, was "to bring Western culture to Oriental Jewry."

The problem is, perhaps, as acute as the Ashkenazim fear. With a strong probability of the Yishuv's being from 60-75 per cent oriental in origin within twenty years, the dread—and it is no less—that Israel might become another "Levantine" state is real and understandable. The true credit side of the question lies in the fact that the solution is seen, not in any way as demanding the suppression of the Sephardim, but as the successful transmission to them of western culture. The ethnic problem has to be removed via the democratizing process of the army, the schools, the settlements, and by free social intercourse. No section of the population envisages the establishment of legal disabilities or of any type of "apartheid."

However, yet another danger exists. While western standards of health, education, housing, etc., are essentials in this acculturation plan, the whole fabric of oriental society may not be too rapidly broken down in the process. The effects of deculturation in Africa have been all too apparent. The positive cultural elements of the Sephardim have to be preserved. Their contributions, particularly those of the Yemenites, are held to be a gain to the Yishuv, and every attempt is being made to ensure their retention. The difficulties in this process are very great. To undertake the selection of certain cultural characteristics of a group for absorption into another culture, to seek out that which is worth while and retainable and to separate it from the unsuitable, is, at best, a difficult and speculative task. Tensions and tragic mistakes occur, for the problem goes very deep. Thus, in his essay, "Yemenite Jews in Israel,"[6] S. D. Goitein states:

The general difficulty with the Yemenites, and their real tragedy, is

[5] *Ha-Aretz,* April 15, 1952 (author's translation).

[6] In Davis (ed.), *Israel: Its Role in Civilization* (New York: 1956).

the fact that the whole economy of Israel is so different from that with which they have been acquainted. Not a single one of the sixty-six arts and crafts practiced by them in the Yemen could be applied in Israel without profound changes. The Yemenite Jew, who had been in his country of origin a skilled master, found himself in the new country an unskilled laborer. The greatest tragedy of all, perhaps, was the fact that the religious sector of working Israel was far too small to cope with the exigencies of the mass immigration of religious Jews. The result was that the instructors and other agents who molded the occupational and communal life of the new Yemenite communities necessarily had to be chosen largely from nonreligious circles, a fact which naturally gave rise to many problems.

It must be realized, however, that a subconscious distinction has for long been made in Israel, between those who came there in the early *Aliyot* imbued with a strong, idealistic Zionism, and those who followed later because of persecution, or fear of it, in their own countries. This distinction reflects the ever present underlying assumption that the building up of Israel is a task to be carried out only on a moral and ideological basis. Thus, to this extent, the oriental immigrants share in the implication—common to all later immigrants—that their motives in coming were not of the purest and highest, and especially that they do not as yet fully comprehend the community's approach and attitude to social and political affairs.

The zeal for work, the romantic aura surrounding manual labor, which was so characteristic of the earlier pioneers, was inevitably lacking among the oriental immigrants. To expect the peasant from Morocco or the stall-keeper from Iraq to be imbued with the same passion for social change as the product of revolutionary Russia or of the European Enlightenment, was to demand too much. Moreover, for thousands of the Sephardim, their Aliyah was not a political act but a sign of the Messianic Age. Their arrival at Lydda Airport "on the wings of eagles" was but a symbol of the fulfillment of the divine promise. The immediate hardship of life in Ma'abara (the temporary camp in which immigrants were housed—often for long periods—pending the availability of a more permanent home) seemed almost a betrayal. Their whole attitude to the problems which faced the State was one of unreality. When demands for physical labor were placed upon them, they usually responded by working only long enough to satisfy their immediate frugal needs. The driving ambition of the European middle class for material and cultural improvement was unknown to them. Although there was no actual ill will, their fundamentally different set of values at first puzzled and antagonized the Ashkenazi settlers. Thus, in her article on the "Oriental Jews in Israel," [7] Marie Syrkin writes:

> Complaints are frequently voiced by administrators of immigrant camps that the Oriental Jews work only three days a week, instead of six; because in three days they earn enough for their very modest needs. Accustomed for generations to a spare diet and to primitive living conditions, they cannot suddenly and artificially increase their requirements—and they see no point in further labor.

In this connection, the settlements themselves merit some degree of criticism. Though in many ways the leaders in democratic-socialist ideas, it would appear that in the field of making a great contribution to the solution of this social problem they have been found wanting. Thus while some Kibbutzim have made every effort to absorb and integrate oriental immigrants, many have merely reflected the discriminatory practices of the rest of the country. In an analysis of the question made by Koren,[8] it appears that of the 87 Moshavim established in 1949-50, none included a mixed Sephardi-Ashkenazi group. When it is borne in mind that some 75,000 immigrants in that year came from oriental and North African lands, this lack of integration can be explained away only with the greatest difficulty.

In the towns, too, this policy of separation was frequently practiced, and a tacit equation of the oriental immigrants with the departed Arab population was common. The less satisfactory portions of the evacuated cities and villages soon became the residences of the Sephardim. Examples exist, of course, where Ashkenazi settlers were frequently allocated the homes of the former Arab inhabitants; such a "distributive fall-out" was inevitable. However, the tendency was clear: the "wrong side of the tracks" was readily given over to oriental groups, and those

[7] *The Jewish Frontier*, April 1952.

[8] *The Settlement of Immigrants in 1949-50* (Tel-Aviv: 1951—in Hebrew).

areas predominantly occupied by Sephardim soon became "the wrong side" by virtue of the country of origin of the newcomers.

The existence of this problem is recognized in Israel; its dangers are clear. All too often, however, an ostrich-like attitude of refusing to acknowledge its presence endangers its early solution. For a country so dependent upon the highest ideals for its national and international justification, anything but the utmost honesty of thought and liberalism of practice could prove disastrous.

The development of a social system in which all Jews are equal but some are more equal than others would signify the death of the Zionist ideal. The crux of the problem lies in the fact that unlike most acculturation situations in the past, it is not so much a question of how the new immigrant group is to acclimatize itself to the existing norm, but rather which cultural pattern is to become the norm, since one does not yet really exist.

To reduce the problem to one of material standards of living is to obscure the issue. The State of Israel and the Zionist movement were more than simple reactions to anti-Semitism, even if their coming into being was largely directed by such factors. Many of the members of the immigrant groups of the twenties and thirties differ as fundamentally from the native-born "*Sabras*" [9] as do these latter from the new oriental immigrants. The pattern of culture as it existed in the 1930's lies far from that which will exist in 1965—by which time the present generation of European-born leaders will have largely disappeared while the full impact of oriental migration will probably not yet be fully felt. The question must remain: to which norm will the society of 1975 adjust itself? No doubt some compromise solution will emerge; but closely linked up with this resulting social pattern is the whole problem of whether Israel is to regard itself—and be regarded—as a western, European state, or as a semi-Levantine, Asiatic country. Merely to talk of Israel as a cultural "pressure-cooker," to compare Israel's problems with those of America

[9] A "Sabra" is a Jew who was born in Palestine or Israel. The name is taken from the common cactus of the land—hard and spiny on the outside, but soft and sweet inside. It is thus taken to illustrate the characteristic features of the native-born Israeli.

at the height of its immigration era, is to obscure the scope and difficulty of the task. However, the energy and thought which Israel has so far devoted to the question gives more hope than would at first seem reasonable.

12. POLITICS IN ISRAEL

Throughout the latter years of the Mandate, a Jewish shadow cabinet had been emerging. With much of the internal organization of the Yishuv already carried out by Jews or Jewish organizations, the passage from Mandatory control to autonomy within the Jewish state was smoothly and efficiently carried out. For months before the British left, their policy of turning the country into an armed camp had, in practice, shut them off completely from all social and administrative life, and had given the Jews the possibility of taking over almost all the essential means of running the State.

From the time of the Declaration of Independence, the republic was governed by a provisional government whose members had been appointed by agreement between the major political factions within the Zionist movement. In January 1949 the first general elections were held on a basis of proportional representation, to elect a Knesset of 120 members. No distinctions of sex, race, color, or creed were permitted among citizens of the State, and some 1,288 candidates, representing the surprising range of 21 parties, presented themselves to the electorate. This highly overdeveloped party system, in conjunction with the system of proportional representation in one constituency compromising the whole country, still today allows for 12 of the 19 parties to be represented in the Knesset. The three elections which have been held since 1949 have produced the results shown in Table 20. The consequences of such an electoral system are obvious. No one party has been able to secure an overall majority and every coalition has been made up of uneasy alliances of groups, each participating in the coalition in order to further its own political ends. "Within the coalition, portfolios are not assigned objec-

Table 2[1]

ELECTION RESULTS

	1949 Knesset	Seats	1951 Knesset	Seats	1955 Knesset	Seats
Eligible to vote	506,567	120	883,000	120	1,057,609	120
Total vote %	87%		79%		83%	
Mapai	155,274	46	256,456	45	274,735	40
Herut	49,782	14	45,651	8	107,190	15
Gen. Zionists	22,661	7	111,394	20	87,099	13
Hapoel Hamizrahi }	32,982	6	46,347	8	77,936 (Hapoel Hamizrahi and Mizrahi)	11
Mizrahi }		4	10,383	2		
Ahdut Ha'avoda }	64,018 (Ahdut Ha'avoda and Mapam)	19	86,095 (Ahdut Ha'avoda and Mapam)	15	69,475	10
Mapam }					62,401	9
Agudat Israel }		3	13,799	3	39,836 (Agudat Israel and Poalei Agudat-Israel)	6
Poalei Agudat-Israel }		3	11,194	2		
Communists	15,148	4	27,334	5	38,492	6
Progressives	17,786	5	22,171	4	37,661	5
Arab Parties (affiliated to Mapai)						
Arab Democrats	7,387	2	16,370	3	15,475	2
Progressives & Labor	3,214	—	8,067	1	12,511	2
Agriculture & Development	2,812	—	7,851	1	9,791	1
Sephardim	15,287	4	12,002	2	6,994	—
Yemenites	4,339	1	7,965	1	—	—
W.I.Z.O.	5,173	1	—	—	—	—
Halohamim	5,363	1	—	—	—	—

tively to the best men, but to whomever the party chooses and in proportion the number of votes the party brings into the coalition."[2]

Some of the reasons for the adoption of such a system are clear. The semiserious jest that for every three Jews there will always be four political viewpoints, is only one reflection of the desire for individuality of beliefs and views. Moreover, the religious, geographic, cultural, and economic differences between the various groups in Israel were so great that their viewpoints have to be heard. Yet another factor—unique to the Israeli political scene—is the fact that Diaspora Jewry still exercises, though only indirectly, considerable influence on the tenets of some of the Israeli political parties. The political system

[1] Figures taken from Hadwin, *Politics in Israel* (London: 1956).
[2] Hadwin.

of the State grew largely out of the sections within the Zionist Congresses—sections which themselves reflected social, economic, and ideological differences within European Jewry. Many leaders and participants in the early Zionist political conflicts are today leading figures in Israeli national politics. Their views and attitudes often reflect their origins. In many cases the bitterness and distrust of the motives of the other parties is justified. The charges of nepotism and "*protectzia*" at the expense of serving the best interests of the country, have some basis. Though Israel is undoubtedly a democracy in the accepted sense of the word, uncomfortable signs of relics of East European political practices, and even of "Levantinism," must be acknowledged.

The tradition of the "*Shtetl*" (the small village community in Poland or Russia in which the Jews lived) dies hard. Subconsciously many Jews have retained certain attitudes which they adopted in eastern Europe (with considerable justification) and still apply them in Israel today. The concept of the "public weal" is not one which is adopted easily by many of the older generation who grew up with the idea firmly ingrained in their minds that "the state is against us" and that they had to look after their own welfare largely regardless of whatever the state claimed to be the public interest. To tell the tsarist police the truth, whether it concerned the date of birth of one's child, or a correct statement of one's income, was dangerous or even unthinkable. Similarly today the public interest in Israel tends all too often not to be taken seriously; the State and its officials are fair game for all.

However, it is an accepted psychological fact that loyalty to and identification with larger groups beyond the family (and the Jewish concept of the "*mishpoche*" includes far more than the immediate circle of parents and children) is natural and necessary. With any minority which is unable to assimilate or identify itself wholly with the majority, a particularization of loyalties is substituted. Thus in Israel today, among the older generation who grew up in Poland or in Russia where the governments neither merited nor invited Jewish support or identification, some of the older attitudes persist. However, the smaller group has ultimately no power. Law, legislation, and major administration are never within its province. Thus there results a fierce internecine struggle and enmity between the various groups. Political parties, newspapers, different religious sects, all war against one another with a bitter vehemence which rarely reflects the actual degree of the differences between them. They are, in the final analysis, in no way unpatriotic. Basically they are firmly united and devoted to the ideal of the State: but the "Shtetl" has always been unrestrained in its attitudes, and its influence still persists. Moreover, it is clear that the perpetuation of such a system must, and in fact has, weakened the force of the central government. All too often the effective working power is in the hands of a multiplicity of groups. To calculate the resulting loss of efficiency is impossible, but that it must exist is certain. Further, with any system of government depending so largely on knowing the right people, on having influence, and on comprehending the workings of the "unwritten laws" of the constitution, it is clearly inevitable that the new immigrant is in fact partially disenfranchised. Nominally he has his vote, but he is in a far less powerful position to use it than the established citizen.

That such a situation, admittedly not the most efficient, mildly corrupt, and partially discriminating, can continue to exist is made possible largely through the perpetuation of yet another of the old traditions upon which the Yishuv was built. Earlier we mentioned how the Yishuv of the pre-Zionist era was supported by the Chalukah system—the organized collection of money throughout the Diaspora—originally intended to support mainly the rabbinical students and their families. Gradually the system was extended to include a far wider section of the population than was originally envisaged. The collection of the Chalukah money became a minor industry in itself and the distribution of the funds inevitably gave rise to situations where privilege, nepotism, and patronage prevailed.

Without going in any detail into the quantity and administration of the present-day contributions from world Jewry to the State of Israel (the economics of the State will be discussed below), it is clear that, while the tradition of *giving* has persisted with an admirable lack of restraint, so too has the tradition of *taking* been perpetuated in Israel. So much so that the subsidizing of Israel's economy from various sources has been running at a conservatively estimated $300,000,000 per year. This money is freely given. World Jewry feels the need to support Israel and realizes that its participation can, short of actually going to settle in Israel, only be demonstrated by financial aid. However, the multiplicity of organizations receiving an outside subsidy, the pressure groups clamoring for a larger share, the inefficiency which results from the spending of unearned money, all contribute to the perpetuation of the system which pervades Israeli political life today.

Naturally criticism exists in Israel of this attitude and of the resulting malpractices. Perhaps indeed more exists within the country than without, though even within the State too many of these faults are taken uncritically for granted. However, outside Israel, within the Zionist movement all too often the expression of such criticism is taken as anti-Zionism; the questioning of any aspect is taken to imply the casting of aspersions on the whole. So frequent, so violent, and so immediate is this reaction that one is led to the conclusion that it reflects a basic, subconscious desire to deny the possibility of any faults in order to avoid admitting their existence at all, or even to avoid thinking honestly about the whole problem.

Bearing in mind the complex connection between the internal political structure of the Zionist movement and the party system in the State of Israel today, and in addition when considering the dependence of Israel's economy upon contributions from Zionists throughout the world, it is necessary to examine more closely the relationship between the State and the Diaspora.

Throughout the Zionist movement there exists agreement that a fundamental change came about with the establishment of the State. However, this agreement in principle appears to have been little reflected in actual practice. Whether through inability, or the natural desire to retain prominence within the movement —and few persons are willing to vote themselves out of existence —or whether through a lack of realization of the profound rethinking required, the Zionist movement today resembles extremely closely its structure in 1948.

It has, of course, been readily conceded, by and large, that the Zionists outside Israel have no claim or right to intervene in the internal running of the country. Thus the raising of funds—the bulk of which comes from America—has no direct political strings attached. No serious suggestion has been made that elections or political acts of the State are controlled from without. Nevertheless, it is true that different sections of the Zionist movement abroad reflect and influence the views of their counterparts in Israel. It is true, however, that the reverse is not equally the case. Antagonism has existed between the fund-raising bodies in the United States and the Israeli authorities over the bond-selling drives and the United Jewish Appeal in 1948 and 1949. Ben-Gurion's views on the Diaspora, and in particular on America, have been received with little enthusiasm outside of Israel. Strangely the fear that American Jewry, because of its financial gifts, would attempt to influence, and perhaps even to dominate, Israeli affairs, did not materialize. Rather was the reverse true. Seeing themselves as the only true Zionists as opposed to the "armchair" Zionists, many Israelis have felt it necessary to state frequently their views and demands of world Jewry.

The readiness with which Diaspora Jewry relinquished any claims upon internal Israeli affairs illustrates perhaps not so much their understanding of the problem as their desire to free themselves of any real responsibility. In this connection it is interesting to speculate whether Zionism in itself is not, for many Zionists, but a means whereby they seek to free themselves from the responsibilities and stresses of a historical Jewish past. That the burden of Jewish history is a heavy one for many Jews is undoubted. Some feel that Zionism allows them to start off on a clean sheet; they are relieved of the pressure and tensions of a historical Judaism. After the establishment of the State the giving of economic aid and verbal moral support alone involved no problem of "dual loyalties." An easy conscience toward Israel and toward America could be purchased for dollars, in the expenditure of which the donors showed remarkably little interest.

Thus the hard-headedness of the American, British, and South African businessman seems to undergo a surprising "softening up" process where his donations to Israel are concerned. He displays little or no interest as to how his donation is to be spent;

he appears unconcerned as to whether or how his bonds will be redeemed, and he is prepared to place his money at the disposal of men whose religious, political, and social views often bear no relationship whatsoever to his own.

The Zionist movement after 1948 reverted somehow to the days when it depended upon the wealth of a well-established and wealthy Anglo-Jewish aristocracy. Once again a Zionist was becoming one who collected money from another Jew in order to send a third Jew to the Holy Land. The idea that the donations of world Jewry to Israel are increasingly becoming guilt offerings cannot be ignored.

In addition there is one factor which reflects directly upon the structure of the Jewish communities outside Israel, and perhaps particularly strongly upon that of America. It can hardly be denied that much of the amazing generosity of world Jewry stems from the noblest of motives. However, the very act of giving and the organization which has grown up around it has given rise to a whole social hierarchy within the community. For the active Zionist, the collection of funds often becomes his dominating interest—again, and the point cannot be overstressed, with the finest of motives. However, often too his Zionist activities become for him his seal of social status. The amount he gives largely determines his social acquaintances; it decides his—and perhaps even more significant, his wife's—circle of friends and their standing within that group. Should he be active enough, wealthy enough, or generous enough, the V.I.P. treatment given him on a visit to Israel, in addition to his natural delight with what he sees and is shown there, is sufficient to fill him with enthusiasm for continuing his work with renewed ardor. His after-dinner speechs are henceforth those of the expert who is "in the know"; the illuminated address given him by some Israeli official to mark his past labors is ample reward. He asks no more; he does not even ask if the money has been spent constructively; whether it has been spent to create more working places for the future; whether it has gone to maintain the existing standard of living or to increase future productive facilities. He has done his duty: his not to reason why.

That Israel fails fully to grasp the motivating forces in

American and British Jewry is also clear. Financially and even more, ideologically, there is a growing gap between Israel and the Diaspora; a gap which today Israel does not fully comprehend and which tomorrow she may be afraid to face. The flow of contributions continues; the flow of tourists grows.[3] Unless these tourists, or a high proportion of them, were to return as settlers, they would tend to highlight this gap rather than act as a proof of its nonexistence.

In spite of the increased donations and in spite of the growing tourist traffic, it must be clear that for the mass of Diaspora Jewry Zionism is not an ever present, active factor in the running of their lives. Rather one should perhaps say that fund raising and tourism is no real Zionism; it is merely the manifestation of a pro-Israel sentiment. Few would suggest that the philanthropies of Montefiore and Rothschild were Zionist activities in any political sense. But is the situation so different in the West today? Admittedly the pro-Israel sentiment is infinitely more widespread and practical; the sum of the gifts to Israel is vastly greater; instead of a lone Montefiore visiting Palestine thousands go annually; but it is merely a difference of degree. It is hardly anticipated today that many of these tourists will settle. Without the stimulus of anti-Semitism, the Jewries of the West show no inclination to leave their adopted homes.

Immediately the problem of immigration facing Israel appears to be one of moving and absorbing North African Jewry. Basically and from the long-term point of view, the problem is how Israel is to induce immigration from the West. Admittedly it might be argued that such immigration cannot be expected today. Economically and politically secure, it is maintained, western Zionism must today be only "pro-Israel." However, if this is to be accepted, then Zionism must admit its failure in the face of contemporary conditions. If Israel has nothing to offer the western Jew when his status is assured, then the movement is ideologically bankrupt. If Jewry (and not only Israel) is

[3] 21,479 tourists entered Israel in the first six months of 1956. This is 9.3 per cent less than for the corresponding period of 1955, though this drop is put down to the increased tensions in the area (*Jewish Agency Digest of Press and Events* [Jerusalem], Vol. IX, No. 44 [July 20, 1956]).

unable, in the next decade or two, to establish the State on such a basis that economically, socially, and from the point of view of political liberalism it becomes attractive to western Jewry, then Zionism will have failed in part of its aim.

This conflict between Israel and the Diaspora, this whole problem of the future of the Zionist movement, has been emerging more clearly with every Zionist Congress of recent years; however, though the problem has become clearer, no constructive action has followed. At the Twenty-fourth Zionist Congress held in Jerusalem in April 1956, it was apparent that the meeting, described as an emergency one, illustrated that there was as much an emergency within Zionism as within the international situation. Repeatedly statements were made decrying Israel's coldness toward the Diaspora. Dr. Nahum Goldman, aptly called the Prime Minister of Diaspora Jewry, was ready to remind Israel that while Zionism was in no way attempting to interfere with the State, Israel was forgetting that its existence was not the culmination of Herzl's vision, but only one step toward his goal. Though verbal concern for the Diaspora and its relationship with the State was forthcoming, it was clear that Jewry outside Israel is being "written off" from the point of view of practical Zionism. The implications of this, together with the scale of oriental immigration, were felt but not openly discussed. There is a marked tendency within Zionism to be oversensitive to criticism—even to self-criticism. It has yet to face with full frankness a total reassessment of its position today and of its future function.

One of the major implications of the Israeli attitude of "writing off the Diaspora" stems from the fact that it conceals the phenomenon that assimiliation is proceeding in Israel itself at a rate which is perhaps even greater than that which is taking place in the Diaspora. Admittedly the process of Jewish assimilation has always tended to presuppose a Gentile environment. However, if the essence of the process is recognized to be a secularization of Judaism, then its existence in Israel is apparent. The transformation of the remaining religious symbols into secular ones is a clear characteristic of life in Israel today. For the religious parties the fight appears to define itself into the clash over the use of cars on the Sabbath and over similar issues. In reality the very setting up of a political party solely on a platform of the introduction of religious practices into state law, was the ultimate in the secularization of Israel, while the whole concept of a "Ministry of Religions" runs contrary to the very grain of Jewish thought.

That this process is taking place within Israel is rarely considered by Diaspora Jewry, while to the majority of Israelis the idea that assimilation is occurring within the Jewish state is in itself paradoxical.

Exactly how much of this lack of contact between Israel and the Diaspora is due to the climate of opinion in Israel created by the "Sabra" mentality is hard to say. That it is a major contributory factor cannot be overlooked or denied.

The return of the Jew to his homeland has been described as having produced a certain relaxation of his whole person "in the sense that a steel spring may be said to relax from bending."[4] Certainly it is true that the Jew feels more free there than anywhere else—often even when his material well-being in Israel is at a lower standard. Occasionally one is led to wonder whether, in the process of unbending, a little of the steel of the spring has not entered into the heart of the Sabra. Such a view might well be attacked as harsh or untrue. Alternative reasons and explanations for it might be easily found. The bowed, gentle, timorous, cultured Jew of Europe cannot easily be the product of the freedom of Israel. One may regret it, but it cannot be. The Sabra is a new type; a product of idealism and of a despairing determination. Freed from the oppression of a European past, he often rejects the finer characteristics of that past along with its faults. Confident of his own and his country's power, he often tends toward conceit. Imbued with a passionate love of his land, he often combines this with a chauvinistic parochialism. Brave in his emulation of the heroes of Israel's history, he seems to have lost a degree of the gentleness and softness of his European-born parents. Potentially the finest product of a highly cultured and socially conscious society, events have also made him a member of the Irgun or Stern group.

[4] Edmund Wilson, *Black, Red, Blonde & Olive* (Oxford: 1956), p. 492.

Certainly it must be apparent, if indeed such illusions still exist, that no stereotyped picture of the "Jew" can any longer remain. As much as the European Jew and the Yemenite Jew was a product of his traditions, so too with the Sabras. Their lives have been molded as much by their lack of inhibitions and by the absence of anti-Semitism as those of their parents were dominated by self-consciousness and sensitivity in the face of social and political oppression.

When the children of immigrant societies grow up it is a commonplace that they tend to reject the traditions, standards, and practices of their parents. With the Israel-born generation a similar development occurred, but with some important differences. The "great divorce" between the generations has been a divorce of physical contacts as well as of mental attitudes. The Sabra who drifts away, or who consciously removes himself from his parents' milieu, does not do so in a negative manner. He constructs for himself a wholly self-contained society. He is away from his home during almost all of his spare time, including the vacation months. He has evolved for himself a comprehensive group of institutions in which he is involved: youth movements, sports clubs, school clubs, paramilitary training, arrangements with Kibbutzim for periods of work, etc. Part of this reaction was a simple defense mechanism. The inevitable nostalgia of the bourgeois merchant who had been driven from Warsaw, or of the disgruntled academician from Vienna—neither of whom was able to resume life on the same level in Israel—romanticized many of the features of their prewar lives. The outside world of cosmopolitan Europe was constantly being contrasted with the harsh realities of life in Israel. The grass is always greener on the other side of the fence. To this attitude the resistance of the Israel-loving Sabra became increasingly one of "we're not interested; we don't want to know."

More and more one feels that the Sabra tends not even to admit the reality of the world outside Israel. He is not curious about it; the tourist is rarely questioned about his own country, but is expected to show interest only in Israel. The considerable numbers of Jewish delegates and officials from abroad are either resented or else shrugged off as an unreal group who refuse to recognize that Jewish history ceased 1,800 years ago and only began again in 1948. Geography for the Sabra is real; he has walked and traveled up and down the land. Demography for him is alive; he knows the problems involved for they are his own. He appreciates the relationship between water, transport, and people's employment. But "world geography" is important only because it involves the proximity of enemy Arab forces; basically the subject lacks meaning and reality.

Moreover, this rejection of the outside is a total one; it is a rejection not only of the stories of the cultured, comfortable past of the older generation, but also of everything for which that generation stood and of what it could teach the Sabra. As one observer put it: "if the parents correct their manners, they reply by correcting their grammar." Gradually the community of interests between parents and children is broken; the less they have to tell each other, the more the worlds in which they live become separated. The one group drifts back increasingly among groups of friends with the same memories and nostalgias, while the other becomes more absorbed in the interests, excitements, and stresses of a wholly young society. It is perhaps only in the religiously Orthodox families that there is a continuing community of interests between the two generations.

It would perhaps be strange if the youth of Israel were to conform to any accepted pattern of normality. No Israeli under the age of thirty has grown up free from an ever present atmosphere of emergency, and few Israelis of any age group have lived their lives free from the stresses of war, anti-Semitism, the concentration camps, Mandatory rule, and "illegal" immigration. Moreover, it was not the tensions alone that produced the new type. The lack of security and continuity would have affected any group, but there was also present a permanent demand for self-sacrifice, for the channeling of interests and energies into the service of the settlement, of the youth movement, and of the State. The type which emerged from this highly indoctrinated background was, in spite of his chauvinism and parochialism, possessed of noble ideals, honest and unselfish. However, even by the end of World War II a change was noticeable, and this change has been accentuated by the influx of immigrants from Europe, North Africa, and the Middle East.

The change was inevitable and can be traced directly to the move from a predominantly agricultural community to an industrialized one with the accompanying growth of large towns. The rate at which the new type is emerging has been accentuated by the fact that the youth movements themselves have largely been at a loss to know how to cope with the problem. Hitherto their aims had largely been directed toward instilling an attitude of *Chalutziut,* of self-sacrifice and the pioneer spirit. The *Noar Saloni* (literally drawing-room youth), the town-bred, swing-loving, apolitical youth so typical of any modern large city, has found the movements largely at a loss. It must be emphasized, however, that it is still the idealistic section which predominates and which typifies the youth of the country.

This new type, physically as well as mentally different from his parents, is reflected in every sphere of life in Israel; in politics and literature, in the writings of Berdichevsky and in the movement of the "Canaanites." Berdichevsky's characters, restless and rebellious, stand in perpetual revolt against the whole of their historic past: a past which, in their eyes, enslaves and crushes the Jew. As into the writings of Saul Tchernichovsky, so a note of Nietzsche-like pantheism creeps into Berdichevsky's work. Like Tchernichovsky, too, he seems more at home "Before the Statue of Apollo" [5] than before the Scrolls of the Law.

The Canaanites, also known in Israel under the name "*Aleph,*" are one of the most interesting groups to have emerged in the State. Though small in number, the group, which is almost entirely Sabra in composition, is highly articulate and includes within its ranks a goodly number of professional writers. The opposition to them in Israel has been strong; politically reactionary, they have been decribed as "fascists" by many who see in them a danger far out of proportion to their actual size. Certainly their closeness to Koestler's "Hebrew Tarzans" is uncomfortable. Whereas those Hebrew writers who revolted against the Jew and Judaism of Europe wished to see a return to the ethical

[5] The title of one of Tchernichovsky's poems, depicting the clash of loyalties between the traditional and the new in Judaism.

Judaism and political independence of the period of the prophets, the Canaanites desire a return to the "Hebrew culture" of the earliest Biblical period. This in no way implies their wish for a purer, non-Rabbinic Judaism. Their opposition to all accepted Jewish religious values is total. Already today they claim that Israel is a theocracy, in the grip of the Orthodox Zionists. The ultimate aim of the Canaanites is the establishment of an "*Eretz HaPrat*" (The Land of the Euphrates): an area in which the present national boundaries are to be removed, and in which Islam and Judaism have relinquished their hold. In alliance with the Lebanon, where they feel the Christian community is apprehensive of Islam, the two countries could then introduce western democracy—presumably as interpreted by the Canaanites—into the whole area. The theocratic Arab and Jewish states would break down, and be replaced with the new Hebrew culture. The underlying assumptions of ethnic superiority and of cultural exclusiveness make it sufficiently clear why the charge of "fascism" is leveled. For the first time in Jewish history a distinction between "Jew" and "Hebrew" is being made. The charge of the Canaanites that Zionism has failed merits consideration. They see in it, rightly or wrongly, the bearer of Judaism, of an outdated religious creed. They maintain it has failed to induce any western immigration, and that it has no hold upon Israeli youth. Both in practice and as a theoretical philosophy, they claim, Zionism is dead. For further progress in the Middle East, they demand also the death of Judaism. Even though numerically the Canaanite movement counts very few in its ranks, it nevertheless reflects a far more widespread attitude which prevails among the youth of Israel. For them, the Jewishness of Zionism either lacks meaning or is unacceptable. Moreover, it is not merely a question of rejecting certain aspects of religious Judaism; Reform Judaism has made less progress in Israel than anywhere else. They seek an entirely new path; which way they will go, is still to be seen.

13. RELIGION AND THE STATE

The establishment of the Maccabean state in the second century B.C. acted as a catalyst upon Jewish life. In that period were sown the seeds of those forces which were to create the "classical" Judaism as it is understood today. At that time too there began to emerge the spiritual power of the early Hasidim and Pharisees, groups which, when properly understood, can be seen to have influenced almost every concept of western culture and of its social system. It was with hopes for a similar revival that many Jews looked to Zionism in its early days and look to the State of Israel today. It is both futile and mistaken to dismiss this as a mere pious wish totally divorced from the issues of practical politics. It is often the intensity and passion of such "pious wishes" which, for good or ill, influence the very course of political events. While today it is too early to attempt to evaluate the spiritual potentialities of Israel, some understanding of the religious problems confronting the modern republic is necessary for an appreciation of the lines along which the state is developing.

One of the questions facing the State of Israel at the time of the making of its constitution, was whether Israel was to be a secular or a religious state. It was a question upon which every Jew had the strongest feelings. For the very few, a totally secularized state with no religious background whatsoever was the desired policy. For many, even for those who personally had few religions convictions, some integration of religious thought into the fabric of the State was the only logical justification for much of Jewish history and of Zionist endeavor. For them "a Jewish state organized permanently as a secular policy with no constitution to bind it to the authentic Judaism of the Torah, a state dependent upon political rivalries and the ephemeral interplay of political parties and their coalition, a Jewish state whose supreme source of law is a secular parliament, is a logical absurdity. . . .

A *permanently* secular Jewish state is an anomaly."[1] The final outcome of all the deliberations on the draft constitution was the establishment of Israel as a secular state whose supreme legal authority was not the Torah but the Knesset. Certain questions of "personal status" (marriage, divorce, birth, death, certain laws of inheritance, etc.) were left under the jurisdiction of special "religious courts" of the Jewish, Christian, and Muslim communities. For the citizen who in no way considers himself a Jew, Christian, or Muslim, there is no provision for his jurisdiction in any of the above matters. The Jew desiring a wholly civil marriage has no authority who can perform the ceremony. There is no secular body with any jurisdiction to legalize his divorce, arrange for his burial, probate his will, and divide up his estate. The situation is additionally complicated by the existence of communities such as the Druze who fit into none of the three main religious groupings. Moreover, within Jewry itself there is considerable variety in religious practice. Conservative practice, and even more Reform practice, is often contrary to Orthodox Jewish law. At present no allowance is made for this lack of homogeneity; the successes won by the Orthodox will not lightly be given up. For them these are not merely political triumphs; they are the very raisons d'être of the Jewish state.

Perhaps the fundamental problem, however, is not the clash between those who favor a secular state and those who wish for a religious one, but the fact that there is no recognized Orthodox body in Judaism capable or willing to engage in any constructive thought on the question of relating religious practice to the problems posed by the establishment of the state. For centuries the rabbinical authorities have been able to legislate on Jewish practice without any concern for questions involving political responsibilities. The need to pass judgment upon such issues as might involve economic ruin for a state (e.g., *Shemitta,* whereby all land must remain fallow each seventh year; or the prohibition against using electricity on the Sabbath—a law which would demand the closing down of all power and water stations) was not necessary as long as the Jews lived in foreign

[1] Bergman, "The Phenomenon of Israel," in *Mid-East, World Centre* (New York: 1956).

lands. Today this responsibility can no longer be avoided.

One of the main reasons contributing to the impasse in religious legislation is the fact that, with the existence of political parties such as the Mizrachi and Agudat Israel, whose main platform is the establishment of a "Torah-State," religion has become a party issue. This religious bloc has, in spite of the concessions and gains it has won in the Knesset, probably done more harm than good to the very ends for which it strives. In particular, by their political maneuverings and threats of leaving the coalition in order to gain concessions, they have succeeded in alienating the sympathies of large sections of the Yishuv, and particularly the youth. In addition, by turning religious issues into a question of party politics, they have compelled their political opponents to oppose any extension of religious legislation, even when they might not have done so for other reasons.

The issue today is no longer a question of detail; it is no longer merely a question of whether trains should be permitted to run on the Sabbath, or whether pig breeding should be made illegal.[2] For the majority of the citizens of Israel, freedom of religious practice necessarily entails also the freedom not to be controlled by laws whose validity they no longer accept.

"It is not within the province of organized religion to acquire political power, and to use that power in order to make the state its secular arm, thus coercing the population, in whole or in part, into the acceptance of beliefs, restrictions and observances which are unacceptable to the religious, or, for that matter, to the irreligious conscience of any group of citizens. Cuius regio eius religio is an essentially antireligious principle, regardless of whether it is pronounced by a king, by a militant church, by a powerful minority, or even by a great majority of the people themselves. True observance, commanded and guided by true faith, can be based only on freedom of assent, or consent; otherwise it loses its intrinsic religious value. Religion, which is transcendental, must not use the tools, the weapons, and the political strategy of the temporal." [3]

[2] In May 1956, by a vote of 55-29, the Knesset rejected three motions calling for the enactment of a law banning pig breeding. The Prime Minister promised, however, that a bill would be introduced to allow local authorities to pass legislation should they so decide. Thus in June, 1957, a total ban on pork was passed by the Tel-Aviv Council.

[3] Greenberg, "Religion and the State in Israel," in Davis (ed.), *Israel: Its Role in Civilization* (New York: 1956).

Part III. THE ARABS AND PALESTINE

by William R. Polk

1. "THE EXISTING NON-JEWISH COMMUNITIES"

"Arab" is a word foreign to the vocabulary of the Balfour Declaration. It is even more conspicuous by its absence from the Mandate charter. Both of these documents refer to the 80 per cent or 90 per cent of the Palestine population which then thought of itself as Arab and spoke Arabic as "the existing non-Jewish communities in Palestine."

What lay behind the avoidance of the term and what assumptions have been made in subsequent writings according to various definitions of it?

Like many other aspects of the Palestine issue, the word "Arab" seems disarmingly simple. But here as elsewhere we find that not the least of complexities is the ease with which one may be correct yet not truthful. It has been possible to build factual arguments dealing with the Arabs of Palestine by simply ignoring that which doesn't fit the desired train of thought. Any observer must constantly question all concepts which cast sharp shadows in this otherwise murky atmosphere. Thus what the word meant to Zionist writers was obviously not what it meant to Arab nationalists; we who are far from the scene may have even more hazy notions. Therefore, it will be well to survey the ground before going deeply into the development of Arab self-consciousness or Arabism and the emotional attachment of Arabs to Palestine.

When we read of the French or the Germans "doing" or "thinking" something, we have a reasonably clear notion of a spokesman, a government, or some organization or person appropriate to the subject at hand, recognized as being entitled to speak for the whole population. This of course also implies our having a fairly clear notion of whom we mean by the French or the Germans. For convenience, in spite of great and obvious diversity, we have ascribed to these groups a more or less homogeneous outlook, a national identity. This we can justify by contrasting them with their Polish or Spanish neighbors. The unity they attain, then, is not so much internal as in contrast to the outside: the Frenchman is never so French as when in Germany. It is the presence of this ready contrast which makes it possible for us to sum up a diversity of opinions and mores and dialects in France as something distinct from European, something we can call French.

Precisely the lack of this contrast with neighbors is what raises the first problem in discussing the Arabs of Palestine. In recent centuries they could not readily be contrasted with the populations in the surrounding areas who were also Arabic-speakers and also heirs to the Arab heritage. As has been shown in Part I, Palestine as such did not exist, nor had the population as a whole any single spokesman. The reasons for this state of affairs are simple in broad outline and are basic to an understanding of many facets of recent developments.

The "Arab" period of Palestinian history is usually dated from 636 A.D.; and this, like many dates, provides a convenient *aide memoire*. The year 636, however, is not a clean slice in the loaf of Palestine history. Arabs lived in Palestine before that date, and others than they have continued to live there up to the present time. Yet, all too often, writers on Palestine have attempted to build elaborate chronological scales in which to weigh rights of tenure. This is of course simply propaganda and can only be considered to merit our attention because attention to a chronology of habitation has itself become a datum of the controversy.

That the Arab period of Palestine began in 636 is correct in the sense that the tribal armies which carried the banner of Islam did, in that year, break the power of the Byzantine Empire and incorporate the area now divided between Syria, Lebanon, Jordan, and Israel into the Empire of Islam. But, it is by no means true to say that the year 636 began the Arab period in the sense that the ancestors of those people whom we call Palestinian Arabs all came to Palestine in that year.

Some writers have suggested that in Palestine, Arabs were coevals of the ancient Israelites. The English writer Nevill Barbour has pointed out[1] that the Hebrew text of the Book of Exodus contains a word which is usually translated as "multitude"

[1] *Nisi Dominus* (London: 1946), p. 73.

but which, he suggests, could also be interpreted to mean "Arabs."[2] For textual reasons Mr. Barbour's interpretation is unlikely, but even if he were correct we know little more for it. The Hebrew word *arev,* like the Arabic word *Arab,* until fairly recently meant only "nomad" or "dweller in the desert." It does seem probable on other evidence, however, that Arabic-speakers were known all over "geographical Syria" before Greek times.[3] The figure of the nomad—who probably spoke Arabic—was surely a familiar one from the earliest recorded times. In the Roman and Byzantine period there are references to Arabs which are unequivocal. The province of Arabia, set up in 106 A.D., had its capitals at Bostra and Petra and covered most of what is now southern Israel and Jordan.[4]

Some Arabs—that is, people who spoke a language identical to or similar to classical Arabic—occupied posts in the Byzantine administration and many were enrolled in the army. The Byzantine government continued the old Roman practice of subsidizing the "inner barbarians" as a means of controlling the outer. No particular effort seems to have been made to Romanize them, but inevitably they were influenced by the settled communities and whole tribes became Christian. However, references to them in Arabic poetry indicate a strong awareness on their part of being Arab and of participating in Arabic cultural life. In practical political terms the fact that they felt themselves in the seventh century to be Arab was demonstrated by their desertion of the Byzantine army to join fellow Arab (Muslim) invaders.

Until modern times, the population of Palestine included a large proportion of nomads—about 12 per cent in 1921[5]—yet both in modern times and in the Byzantine period the bulk of the population was neither bedouin nor urban but settled peasantry.

[2] For a millennium after the text was written, Hebrew had no way of indicating vowels, so in the original no distinction could be made between the words *erev* (multitude) and *arev* (Arab).

[3] René Dussaud, *La Pénétration des Arabes en Syrie avant l'Islam* (Paris: 1955), p. 17.

[4] A. G. Wright, "Formation of the Provinces of Syria and Arabia," *Palestine Exploration Fund Quarterly,* 1895.

[5] Of the total estimated population of 750,000 about 100,000 were bedouin (Cmd 3686, pp. 24-25).

For some centuries after the Arab invasion the peasantry was Christian, which some of it still was in this century, and Aramaic-speaking. The peasant's Monophysite Christianity was heresy in the eyes of the government-supported—mainly urban—Orthodox, and consequently internal religious intolerance was a feature of Palestinian life under the Byzantine administration. Moreover, in his language and customs the peasant was Semitic, whereas his rulers were Greek. To them, he was little more than an entry on tax registers. These were the peasants' main contact with the administration, since to "cover his enormous debts Heraclius had been compelled to put on the fiscal screw to its utmost tension."[6] And this fact, obviously, had much to do with the ready welcome the local population gave to the incoming Arabs.

At the time of the Conquest, it is doubtful that the Arabic-speaking invader and the Aramaic-speaking peasant could have understood one another—their speech would have differed somewhat more than French and Spanish—but time was to merge their languages into the Arabic dialect of Palestine which was grammatically Arabic but enriched by borrowings from the vocabulary of Aramaic. In spite of a certain linguistic problem, the two groups as Semites were heirs to a general body of culture and had many similar customs.

For religious reasons as well as for raisons d'état, the invading Muslim Arabs little disturbed the peasantry. The popular image of the Islamic invasion is that of a savage horde spreading the faith with fire and sword, but surviving records discredit this notion. In the first place, Islam regarded the "People of the Book," those who had accepted the unity of God and had in turn received a part of His Scripture, as potential Muslims. In the Koran, Islam is identified as "the religion of Abraham" and is regarded as formally identical with Judaism and Christianity, not as these religions are practiced but as they are meant to be practiced. In Part I we have seen how social and political factors in Mohammed's lifetime helped to shape this attitude. The fact that Christian Byzantium was the main enemy of Islam caused occasional periods of friction and persecution, but probably in no

[6] C. Becker in *The Cambridge Medieval History*, II, 345.

known society before modern times were dissidents allowed greater internal autonomy. Thus, in some ways, the Islamic invasion tended to freeze the religious structure of the community and to preserve the traditional pattern of life. In the Islamic invasion of Palestine, Christian and Jewish groups, unlike the Jews and Moriscos in the Spain of the Reconquest, were constrained only to surrender to the civil hegemony of Islam, not to apostatize.

Moreover, the Muslim Arab armies were small indeed in relation to the task they undertook. Those who fought at the battles for what came to be Palestine were soon needed for the invasion of Egypt, for further fighting in what is now Iraq against the Persians, and to resist the expected Byzantine counterattack. Therefore, the Islamic government was at some pains to keep its armies from melting away as they would inevitably have done had they been allowed to seize land. From this they could only be prevented if they were kept in military camps, away from the civil population, and were paid. Whole tribes of warriors were settled in such garrison points as grew into the cities of Kufa, Basra, Qum, and Cairo. In Syria the government was able to rely on the existing Arab tribes of the steppe to a large extent. It did all it could to keep them from the sown land.

Partly to satisfy this martial jinn it had summoned from the steppe, the government desperately needed revenue, and this it could draw most easily by continuing the old Byzantine taxation practice with whatever modifications were needed to bring it into accord with Islamic custom. Like Byzantium so the caliphate had to be a rentier. In its earliest days Islam had evolved a tax system in which non-Muslims, in the first instance Jews, paid a special tax in lieu of military service. Converts ceased to pay the tax. Thus, it was to the direct benefit of the treasury to have the non-Muslim population remain non-Muslim; and if this did not lead the government to actively oppose proselytizing, it did at least keep the government from encouraging any violent spreading of the new faith.

For these reasons—smallness of the Arab forces, their seclusion, religious principles, and the vested state interest—it would appear likely that the average peasant of the Levant seldom saw a Muslim Arab in the period of the Conquest. In all truth, the modern Palestinian peasant would probably have about the same chance of finding any of his ancestors in the conquering army as would the average American of finding his among Washington's army at Valley Forge.

Easy it is, of course, to carry this train of thought too far. Just as few Americans would be so extreme as to look upon members of the D.A.R. as the only *real* Americans, so the Arabs, with many more centuries of reasons, would minimize the problem of origins. Of whatever origin, all *became* Arabs. That is to say, the Aramaic-speakers of Palestine, like their counterparts in Egypt and Iraq, merged into the cultural heritage and largely into the religion of the fellow-Semite invaders. This Arabization was a slow process and in the beginning, as we suggest, was not encouraged by the government. But the lure was strong. By joining the Islamic-Arabic community, one escaped the extra tax and gained that sense of security to be obtained only from membership in the dominant group. In the Middle Ages, when most conversions took place, one also came to participate in what was one of the three or four great civilizations of the world. Thus, over many generations, the peasantry of Palestine became Arab in the ultimate sense that it thought of itself as such and lost the awareness of having a different origin.

In only one important sense were the peasants outside of the main stream of the Arab cultural heritage.

To a people whose cultural tone had been set by a nomadic life, as was that of the Arabs, land had only a temporary value. In Arabic poetry, the "Register" in which the values of Arabic culture have been preserved, one reads of camp sites which evoke memories of romances and friendships, of desert landscapes as the background for the wonders of a storm or the trial of wild beasts, and of a few pleasant valleys made verdant by spring rains. But in man's relationship with the land there could be no fixity: what one used today was used by another tomorrow. Camp sites and graves alike were erased by wind, sand, and flash floods. Emotional ties were to people, the folk or *Quawm,* not to the *watan* or territory on which one happened to be born. Man, the herdsman, put little of himself into the land. For him, one might say, land was not enriched by the dimension of time.

For the settled peasant, land obviously has quite a different value. Land is one's *own* land, where ancestors were born, where they built, tilled, are buried, and where sons will be born. Land is a visible extension of man—as it were, the summary of life. In its terraces, holy places, and graveyards, the individual achieves a sort of immortality. This is a feeling which is almost as foreign to modern Americans as to the bedouin herdsman, but it is perhaps the strongest emotional attachment known to peasants the world over.

The "nation" of the peasant was the village community. In the village he lived, kept his animals and farming tools, stored or processed his goods, and daily went forth to work in the surrounding fields. In Ottoman times the village was an administrative unit not dissimilar to a New England township; but more than the township, the village constituted a corporate unit. It was a miniature world in which the peasant married and "belonged"; with the other members, who were likely to be kinsmen, the peasant joined to oppose the great outer world. Feuds between villages were tiny international wars, so that the internal ties of kinship and neighborhood were compounded by the sense of difference from outsiders. Land was rarely owned by outsiders, and outsiders who came to live in a village normally were grafted onto the lineage of one of its families. Finally, during the centuries of insecurity of travel, when the Ottoman Empire failed to secure internal peace, commerce either broke down or became so expensive that single villages or small clusters of villages became autarchic. Handicraft industries to satisfy local needs became economic; these, although on a much smaller scale and obviously not competitive with what is today revolutionizing the society, tended to integrate village life and to stimulate village economy. Travelers' accounts of the villages of the early nineteenth century portray a life much more prosperous and active than it became when the competition of European industry came to be felt. Prosperous or not, however, the village community provided a satisfying whole life and wedded man to the land. Land, indeed, became the graphical representation of society. In the configurations of land holdings can often be seen the web of social relationships, and in the records of land transfers over the years the marital history of the people. Indeed, man built himself into the land.

If the peasant's nation was the village, then his world was a small cluster of villages. For him there was no "Palestine" in the sense we have spoken of a France. His emotional attachment was closer to home and his administrative commitments to the Ottoman Empire were not collected into a state or province of Palestine. In late nineteenth-century usage, if the villager lived more than a few miles north of Jaffa he was a resident in the province of Beirut, or if he lived south of the Dead Sea he was a resident of the province of Syria—little more than the triangle of Jerusalem, Jaffa, and Gaza was administratively tied to Jerusalem. Thus, if the people in the fertile and thickly settled areas around Haifa had any sense of "belonging" (in the sense an American might to being a Texan) to a district, it would have been to Beirut rather than to anything like the country as created by the League of Nations Mandate. It must be admitted that Palestine has long been a vague geographical notion and that it would seem that attempts to find an Arab nationalism for Palestine in the last century are simply projections of modern feelings into a different context. The villager's loyalty was first to the family, then to the village, and perhaps then to the faith. Contacts beyond the village were largely governmental, involving the payment of taxes and the sending of young men to the army, and commercial, involving especially after the 1830s the sale of local products and the purchase of European goods. The latter was increasingly significant as we approach this century, but probably the most significant tie with the outside, for our present purposes, was that established by the collection of taxes.

Taxation in the Ottoman Empire, as in some former governmental systems, was often not directly administered; rather, it was farmed out to private factors. In this way the government could economize its power resources, could be sure of a steady return not dependent upon vagaries of the weather, and traded rights over elusive, numerous, and scattered poor peasants for rights over a few rich settled merchants. On its part, the government gave the tax farmer a free hand to squeeze what he could from the peasants and, when needed and convenient, would give him the sanction of troops. In return, besides paying the set tax assessed on his area, the tax farmer took over many of the police duties of the government. The recipient of this lucrative favor could be counted upon to grease the palms of the local government officials, and upon this extra source of income depended the low-salaried administration.

Theoretically the tax farmer had no rights over the land as such; his rights were over the peasants on the land. Time, however, was on his side. In an area of poor communications and weak central government, the tax farm, like many other functions of provincial administration, tended to become hereditary in families of wealth and influence. Over the years, the factor who added to his official functions the private undertakings of crop purchase and money lending at rates that may have averaged 60 per cent or more—both easily geared to the collection of taxes at the peasant's poorest season—could in time gain mastery over the illiterate and isolated peasantry. Moreover, title to land was so complex as to be open to considerable manipulation. Full ownership or *mulk* was, by right of conquest, vested in the state. In Palestine most of the land was held by the tenure known as *miri*, "which resembles a lease of indefinite duration, in which the rental, so to speak, is represented by the obligation to pay land taxes and land registry fees."[7] On certain lands, for example those of religious foundations, other types of tenure obtained; and on others, for political reasons, local custom was the de facto law. Where the government had the power to exercise authority, it was often possible for influential men to lease from the government whole groups of villages. For example, J. L. Burckhardt wrote in 1812:

. . . at present the chief man at Nazareth is M. Catafago, a merchant of Frank origin, born at Aleppo. He has rented from the Pasha about twelve villages situated in the neighborhood of Nazareth and the

[7] *Survey of Palestine* (Jerusalem: 1946), I, 255. Probably no aspect of Ottoman administration is more complex than land rights.

plain of Esdrelon, for which he pays yearly upwards of £3,000. His profits are very considerable . . .[8]

In local custom, which prevailed wherever the Ottoman administration was weak and the farmer strong, land belonged ultimately to the village and then to that member of the village who worked it. The villager could, theoretically, sell his land to a foreigner, but the chances are that the foreigner could not obtain irrigation water rights, which belonged to families rather than to individuals. The outsider with the power to extort, be he bedouin raider or government factor, was admitted to have the rights of a privateer. Custom gave him a share in the fruits but not rights in the land: his was a power to avoid if possible and placate if necessary. To exhibit wealth before the factor or bedouin was to invite extortion; beyond him was no appeal and toward him passive resistance the main weapon.[9]

Yet bad as he was, the tax farmer was at least known and was already partially satisfied. The distant and unknown government might well be—and often was—infinitely worse. The Arabs have a parable of a peasant with some honey covered by bees. A friend comes along and chases off the bees, at which the owner is furious: these bees, he points out, have already eaten but now their places will be taken by hungry ones.

Also, whereas the tax farmer wanted only the produce of the soil, albeit as much as he could get, the government began to want the sons of the village. And since boys taken off to the army were often, and often correctly, written off as dead by

[8] *Travels in Syria and the Holy Land* (London: 1822), p. 341. In a footnote, Burckhardt notes that in the district comprising northern Palestine and southern Lebanon (the area around Acre) the villages were all assessed for set sums "which each is obliged to pay, whatever may be the number of its inhabitants. This is one of the chief causes of the depopulation of many parts of Syria." On Catafago also see F. Perrier, *La Syrie* (Paris: 1842), p. 42, fn. 1.

[9] Sir Hamilton Gibb and H. Bowen, *Islamic Society in the West,* Vol. I, Pt. I (London: 1950), p. 209: "From time immemorial the governing class had lived on a percentage of the produce of the land, supplemented by various duties on goods, and the social structure of the other class had accommodated itself to this situation . . ."

their grieving families, the villagers went to great lengths to avoid losing them. Thus, when in the nineteen century the Ottoman administration came to be reformed on quasi-western lines and an attempt was made to simplify the maze of rights in law and custom to provide a definite tenure system so as to encourage economic development, the peasants saw this merely as a mask for conscription.[10] To avoid this, which in their terms meant a probable break in the immemorial continuum of father-to-son tenure of the land, the peasants had recourse to a device which had occurred to their counterparts in the decadent Roman Empire in Italy: to register the land in the name of any important and influential man who could seem to offer some protection. Large numbers of peasants in Palestine simply hid and did nothing. In any event, the result was usually much the same: title frequently passed out of the hands of those who worked the land and into the hands of influential city merchants. In the eyes of the villager, the wealthy Muslim, Jewish, or Christian families of Damascus, Beirut, or Jerusalem which thus acquired large de jure holdings were no different from the old tax factors.

But little aware of the meaning of the new concept of ownership, the peasant clung to his land with that stubborn determination which can be understood only by men who live on the soil. Land was the ultimate value to be saved at all sacrifice; in the peasant's mind it *was* saved so long as he worked it, buried his dead in it, and raised his sons upon it. To him it was incomprehensible that through the edicts of a distant government, whose authority he had hardly ever felt, the land had ceased to be his. But, as the British Mandate government had to interpret legality, from surviving Ottoman records and western legal concepts, such was indeed the case. Long before the Balfour Declaration, which is so often seen as the fount of

[10] The 1858 Ottoman Land Code was effected between 1867 and 1873 by village roll calls without survey. ". . . it soon became apparent to the cultivators that the registers were being used as a means of identifying properties for the purpose of taxation and of disclosing the existence of persons subject to military conscription . . ." (*Survey of Palestine,* I, 237-38).

all the contention over Palestine, the inarticulate but ancient peasantry had slipped a rung on the ladder which was to lead them down into the refugee camps in 1948.

How this came about deserves to be better understood.

Jewish land purchases in Palestine were mostly, perhaps as much as 80 per cent,[11] from large owners of whom the majority were absentees and many had derived their titles in the manner described above. Since the purchase of land by Zionist organizations, as distinct from such previous ventures as that of Baron Rothschild, was for the sole purpose of settling Jewish immigrants, the Arab peasants obviously had to be evicted. The Arab version of the plot of the *Grapes of Wrath* became a national preoccupation. One fairly well-documented example will illustrate why the Arabs were disturbed.

In 1872, the Beirut Christian family of Sursuk acquired *miri* title to a whole district in the Vale of Esdraelon near Haifa. One plot of approximately fifty thousand acres containing some twenty-two villages was purchased from the Ottoman government, apparently when the villagers could not or would not show title. This was one of the most fertile and best-cultivated areas in Palestine,[12] but Sursuk was an influential and wealthy man and so the purchase price was said to have been only about £20,000, of which probably a fraction was actually paid. In the usual pattern, Sursuk was able to combine the choice functions of tax collector, usurer, and purchaser of shared crops to the extent that he must have made 100 per cent profit yearly. In fact, in April 1883, Sursuk told the English traveler Laurence Oliphant that the cost of transporting the goods, in which he

[11] Dr. Ruppin, who represented the Jewish Agency before the Shaw Commission as its land expert, noted that nine tenths of the land bought by Jews to that date came from absentee landlords (Cmd 3530, p. 114). By the end of 1937 the figure had fallen to eight tenths (A. Grannott, *The Land System in Palestine* (London: 1949), p. 277). After 1936 and up to 1947, of the 460,000 acres acquired by various Jewish groups, the sales of peasants accounted for 27 per cent.

[12] In 1838 Edward Robinson wrote: "The prospect was charming for its rich fertility and beauty. Yellow fields of grain, with green patches of cotton and millet interspersed, checkered the landscape like a carpet" (*A Journal of Travels in 1838* [Boston: 1856], p. 319). On bedouin raids and insecurity see van Horne, pp. 36 ff.

had collected the fruits of his various labors, to the coast was $50,000. The land, wrote Oliphant

> is at this moment in the highest state of cultivation . . . It looks to-day like a huge green lake of waving wheat, with its village-crowned mounds rising from it like islands; and it presents one of the most striking pictures of luxuriant fertility which it is possible to conceive.[13]

And though it goes without saying that the peasants enjoyed only a small fraction of their produce, they had benefited from the increased security which Sursuk and his neighboring fellow owners (including the Ottoman sultan himself) were in a position to provide; moreover, Sursuk had the capital to enable the farming craftsmanship of the peasants to be utilized.

As early as 1903 the Emeq, as the Vale is now called, was noted by Zionist agents as suitable land for purchase. Negotiations were begun somewhat later and were interrupted by the First World War. At the end of the war, Haifa was no longer a part of the *vilayet* or province of Beirut but had been incorporated into the British-occupied, later Mandated, area of Palestine. Thus Sursuk, as a resident of the town of Beirut, was in a French-mandated territory (subsequently the Republic of Lebanon) and his land in the British Mandate of Palestine. In 1920, three years before the Mandate was officially issued to Great Britain and while the territory was in a sort of shadow zone legally between international recognition as a part of the Ottoman Empire, and so subject to the provisions of the Hague Convention—i.e., that no political changes were to be made—and the Mandate, the Palestine government issued the Land Transfer Ordinance.[14] The following year, agreement between Sursuk and the Zionist purchasing group was reached. Sursuk was to receive £726,000 for the block of villages and their lands. According to the Land Transfer Ordinance, approval of the government of Palestine had to be obtained for the title transfer, but this was assured by the terms of the Balfour Declaration

[13] L. Oliphant, *Haifa, or Life in Modern Palestine* (London: 1887), p. 60.

[14] Text in *Survey of Palestine* I, 238-39.

which were subsequently incorporated in the Mandate.[15] Both the buyer and the seller had cause for satisfaction. At a time when liquid capital was very short in the Middle East and when many had been ruined by the long years of war, Sursuk had multiplied his investment over thirty-five times and could take advantage of new opportunities closer to his home. The buyer had acquired a large block of rich and well-farmed land.

The losers were the peasants. Some 8,000 of them were evicted from a land which had been theirs, in the only way they and their societies, the village communities, had understood ownership. Some refused to go, others got jobs in the cities, but the fate of most is unknown.

Their cup of bitterness had its full share of dregs. Those who lost their homes and whatever rights they had in the land could not even hope to work as landless laborers on their former lands. The first settlements in the nineteenth century by Jews did employ Arabs; but for a reason which is entirely creditable in itself, like so many factors in the whole of the Palestine tragedy, the Zionist purchasers of the land would allow only Jews to work it. The ideals of Zionism could hardly tolerate the creation of a Jewish rentier class over an Arab landless and exploited peasantry. The purpose of Zionism was essentially that noted in the Mandate: close settlement of Jews on the land. If this was to be accomplished, there was simply no room for the former inhabitants. To whatever fate, the peasants had to go.

The example of the Sursuk land sale certainly is glaring but it is not exceptional. The government of Palestine was aware of this and of the implications. For example, in the Palestine Partition Commission ("Woodhead Commission") report of 1938, it is pointed out:

[15]Article 6 of the Mandate subsequently enjoined the facilitation of "close settlement by Jews on the land [while] . . . ensuring that the rights and positions of other sections of the population are not prejudiced." Twenty-five years later the British Foreign Secretary, Mr. Bevin, pointed out that "The lack of any clear definition of this dual obligation has been the main cause of the trouble which has been experienced in Palestine during the past 26 years" (in a speech to the House of Commons, November 13, 1945; quoted in *Survey of Palestine,* I, 99).

The gulf between the Arabs and the Jews has widened year by year. The Arabs look upon the Jews as foreigners invading their country, who are able and ready to spend money regardless of values if only they can acquire land occupied by Arabs on which to settle Jews. Further they believe that the Jews intend to oust them from employment. They know that Jews settled on land belonging to the Jewish National Fund are prohibited by the terms of their lease from employing Arab labour; they know of the pressure on Jewish employers to employ Jews and not Arabs; they know of the movement to intimidate Jewish farmers who employ Arab labour.[16]

As a matter of fact, as early as 1930 the danger was clearly pointed out by Sir John Hope-Simpson:

Actually the result of the purchase of land in Palestine by the Jewish National Fund has been that the land has been extra-territorialised. It ceased to be land from which the Arab can gain any advantage either now or at any time in the future. Not only can he never hope to lease or to cultivate it, but, by the stringent provisions of the lease of the Jewish National Fund, he is deprived for ever from employment on that land. Nor can anyone help him by purchasing the land and restoring it to common use. The land is in mortmain and inalienable. It is for this reason that Arabs discount the professions of friendship and goodwill on the part of Zionists in view of the policy which the Zionist Organisation deliberately adopted . . . The persistent and deliberate boycott of Arab labour in the Zionist colonies is not only contrary to the provisions of that article [six, quoted above in fn. 15] of the Mandate, but it is in addition a constant and increasing source of danger to the country.[17]

Until the Arab rebellion of the mid years of the 1930s, the government was unwilling to face up to this warning. Even then it simply tried to crush the revolt with exemplary punishments and tighter security. It was not until the eve of the Second World War that the government acted. The White Paper of 1939 announced that the "High Commissioner will be given general powers to prohibit and regulate transfers of land . . . [in order to prevent] such transfers of land [as] must be restricted if the Arab cultivators are to maintain their existing standard of life and a considerable landless Arab population is not soon to be created."[18] This was implemented by

[16] Cmd 5854, p. 84.
[17] Cmd 3686; and *A Guide to Jewish Palestine* (Jerusalem: 1930).
[18] Cmd 6019, pp. 11-12.

the Land Transfer Regulation of February 1940. However, the extremely high prices offered—one plot of 156 acres was purchased at auction in 1941 by the Jewish National Fund for £2,900 or roughly $14,500[19]—and the loopholes in the regulations allowed land transfers to be made. European Jewry was obviously desperate at this period and America may fairly be said not to have done all she could have to help them. The Arabs likewise were, if not desperate, at least seriously alarmed and they likewise founded a fund, the *'Umma* [Arabic: community] Fund to buy land of bankrupt Arabs to prevent its "extra-territorialization." One Arab broker who sold land to the Zionists was murdered in the streets of Jaffa.[20]

Those who sold were lucky. Some made fantastic profits but these were a very small minority of the Arab population. It can be argued—and it was true in the 1930s and early 1940s—that Palestine as a whole benefited greatly by the $50 million poured into Palestine in the decade the Emeq purchase was made, although it is obvious that much of this was immediately exported. But to the peasants this could matter but little. Not only did they not benefit over the long run (in spite of better prices for their crops) but many had obviously and terrifyingly lost. Legal as it and subsequent land sales were, the Sursuk sale and eviction sent a quiver of horror through the peasantry of Palestine and did much to set the tone for the following years.[21] In 1920, even in 1930, Palestine as a focus of Arab loyalties was still a weak symbol; but the family plot of land had an almost mystical quality, and it was in this quality that Arab tenure had come to seem so fragile.[22]

[19] *Survey of Palestine,* I, 269.

[20] *Ibid.,* 270.

[21] Cmd 3530, p. 152; and Cmd 3686, p. 17.

[22] In summary, it has been possible only to sketch the main outlines as these appeared to the Arabs. The impression should not be got that all the gentry sold their lands or that all peasants were dispossessed. Had such been the case, much would have been more simple. Such large resident families as the Husseinis held their lands to the end (Grannott, pp. 81-84), and the last official figures before 1948 indicated that Jews held only 5 per cent of the total land and about 16 per cent of the "cultivable" land (*Survey of Palestine,* p. 566). The Jewish arguments on the above are presented by M. Shertok in the *Jewish Case before the Anglo-American Committee of Inquiry* (Cmd 6808, pp. 101 ff., 119-22).

2. THE ARAB GENTRY

The other side of the Arab coin to the peasantry was the gentry.[1] The gentry was much more conscious—could be much more conscious—of an Arab lineage. Many of its big families could trace their ancestors back to the period of the conquests and had ties with similar families all over the Arab world. The gentry's roots were less in the land than in the cities and its members were comparatively cosmopolitan. Not only was the gentry as a group literate, with the contacts and the wherewithal for travel, but it was well within the main line of the Arabic cultural heritage. The *effendi,* or man of the gentry, felt no particular sentimental tie, in the sense described for the peasant, to the land; nor did he any more than the peasant conceive of Palestine as his nation. He was at home in the whole empire. No frontiers hindered movement between Jerusalem and Damascus, Cairo, Baghdad, and Mecca; in all the same language was used, all were heirs to the same cultural and religious legacy, and all had much the same sort of society. By moving from Jerusalem to Damascus, one moved only within the system and had no more reason to feel alien than does the American who moves from St. Louis to Chicago.

However, both the gentry and the peasantry participated in certain attachments which were felt by all Arabs, felt perhaps as strongly by Arabs resident in Damascus, or Baghdad, to Jerusalem, and which long predate the rise of anything like a nationalist sentiment; so it will be well to outline the religious element in the emotional background.

In the Ottoman Empire, to whose system of administration and law the Mandate government of Palestine fell heir, the population was divided into religious communities (Turkish: *millet*). Each *millet* was autonomous; its internal affairs were

[1] For brevity we are omitting the new merchant rich, the industrial worker, professional groups, et al. In general these groups may be taken as lying between the peasantry and the gentry on political attitudes.

governed by the head of its church or sect and each was accorded government recognition for its internal decisions. We have discussed the Islamic basis of this system above; so here we may deal with its development in Palestine. As Elihu Grant in the early years of this century wrote of the Christian communities:

> Church life in the country is political life, and church dignitaries are adepts in politics. The wealth and cleverness of the church are employed to hold fast all traditions and all concessions which favor the Communion and to hinder excessive injustice from overtaking the members. There results a firm bond of union between the native membership and the ecclesiastical establishment. The Communion is a religious nation, as it were.[2]

By equating religious affiliation with citizenship, the *millet* system tended to coalesce and preserve congregations. Members normally were not allowed to apostate except to Islam. The system had considerable merit, from an economic point of view, in the evaluation of the empire. It was not unlike the tax farm in the sense that it grouped a diffuse population into manageable units whose administration cost the government nothing and in that it provided responsible agents to keep public order and to assure the payment of taxes.

However, these *millets* were ready pawns and pretexts for foreign states. In the eighteenth century the Greek Orthodox *millet* came to be linked with Russian foreign policy just as the Catholic *millet* and clergy had been and would be linked at various times with the policies of Spain, France, Austria, and, subsequently and briefly, Germany. European consuls gave or sold passports to their clients and so the *millets* tended to become extensions of European states. The Ottoman Empire in its long period of weakness not only had to concede an autonomous status to the mainly Christian district of Mount Lebanon and to Jerusalem but had to relinquish the enforcement of its laws over some of the protected minorities in all parts of the empire. Foreign schools catered to these minorities and encouraged them to participate in European culture, in extreme cases even to lose their native culture and to develop a sense of affinity toward, if not citizenship in, the protecting state. Naturally this led to

[2] *The People of Palestine* (London: 1921), pp. 44-45.

their involvement in the attempts to shatter the Ottoman Empire in the nineteenth century. If the Eastern Question led to European rivalry, one can imagine the hostility it produced on the scene of the premature wake for the "sick man of Europe." And not only were Greek and Catholic engaged in their mutual hostility but all tended to be drawn further apart from one another and from the Muslim majority to an extent which is difficult to translate into the experience of a modern western society.

As one might expect in a land as religiously prolific as is Palestine, the assiduously cultivated cuttings of most major sects took root, developed a corporate existence, were protected, and grew apart from one another.

In the year 1931 the 88,907 Christians resident in Palestine, the vast majority of whom were Arabic-speaking, were found to include:

> adherents of the Orthodox, Roman Catholic, Greek Uniate (Melkite), Anglican, Armenian (Gregorian), Armenian Uniate, Jacobite, Syrian Catholic, Coptic, Abyssinian, Abyssinian Uniate, Maronite, Chaldaean, Lutheran, and other churches.[3]

To this extent, at least, we can see that the Mandate could rightly speak of the "existing non-Jewish communities." The Arabs, although essentially a single cultural group, were *not* in governmental or even in Islamic terms a single community. We shall see that it was only in opposition to Zionism that a sense of participation in "Arabism" grew on a nonreligious basis.

In large part the Christians were urban, many of them in the incipient middle class, and they tended to live in the north-central part of Palestine, especially in Nazareth, Jerusalem, Ramallah, Acre, and Haifa. It is difficult to make generalizations about the extent of their attachment to Palestine or their involvement in the Arab community. Some affected to speak foreign—i.e., non-Semitic—languages and to think themselves to be protégés of a European power. Others combined the attachments of the peasant with those of religion. For those who

[3] Government of Palestine, *Census Report* (Jerusalem: 1933); quoted in H. Luke and E. Keith-Roach, *Handbook of Palestine and Trans-Jordan* (London: 1934), pp. 38-39.

have not visited Palestine, a perusal of any traveler's account will indicate how pervasive is the religious symbol and relic: few towns lack the tomb of a saint or some monument evocative of an emotional contact with the past. Religion was, so to speak, in everyone's back yard.[4]

Every year thousands of pilgrims visited the Holy Land, and the several churches maintained there a large population of clergy. It is probably true that the foreigners were more conscious of the religious resources of Palestine than were the natives, and it is difficult in our age to appreciate the extent to which this was felt in recent centuries.[5] Yet, even in our age, both native and foreign Christian feeling has run high, and it is curiously true, as the Archbishop of York pointed out, that the issue of Palestine is "commonly discussed as though it were a problem which concerns only the Jews and the Moslems."[6] It would surely be a mistake to fail to weigh in the factor of Christian Arab attachment to the Holy Land in any assessment of the emotional attitudes which have gone into the making of the Palestine tragedy.

Of course, the Muslim community formed the vast majority of the Arab community of Palestine.[7] As we have seen in Part One, the Arab founder of Islam, Mohammed, had looked upon himself as the last in the sequence of prophets, which sequence includes those of the Old Testament, Jesus, and certain obscure Arab prophets. Islam is identified as the religion of

[4] T. Canaan, "Mohammedan Saints and Sanctuaries in Palestine," *Journal of the Palestine Oriental Society*, IV (1924), 2: "There is hardly a village, however small, which does not honour at least one local saint. But generally every settlement boasts of many."

[5] Kinglake, who did so much to create an image of the East in English minds, has a delightful description of himself as the sane, rational, balanced modern man trying to catch the ecstasy hidden in the rocks of Palestine (*Eothen*, [London: 1904], pp. 135-37).

[6] In the House of Lords, December 10, 1945. Also see Constantine Rackauskas and the "Committee on World Order," *The Internationalization of Jerusalem*, (Washington, D. C., n.d. [1956?]) for the Catholic position in summary.

[7] Small numbers of relatively recently arrived non-Arab Muslims also lived in Palestine, but most of these faded into the Arabic-speaking community. As we have suggested, "Arab" is a cultural rather than a racial concept.

Abraham and subsumes the religious heritage, as it understood this, of both Judaism and Christianity in a manner similar to Christianity's incorporation of Judaism. Islam charges the Jews with having corrupted their Scripture and the Christians with being mistaken in ascribing to Jesus divine parenthood;[8] but it was clearly indicated that these were, so to speak, errors in the family. Mohammed was enjoined:

> Then bear with them (O Muhammad) and say: Peace. But they will come to know.[9]

The first Islamic *Qibla,* or target of prayer, was not Mecca as it is today but Jerusalem, and Muslims generally believe that it is to Jerusalem that the Koran refers[10] as the place from which Mohammed ascended to Heaven.

> On Mohammed's mind the sanctity of Jerusalem had in his youth been impressed by those Jewish or Christian story-tellers with whom he had associated in his travels . . . And to him it had been portrayed as somewhat similar to the Bethel of Jacob's dream; the place where there was a ladder between heaven and earth, whereby visitors could ascend or descend. For him who was to be permitted to approach the Deity's abode Jerusalem was the starting point. Thither the Koran tells us the Prophet made a night journey from Meccah; and as dreamland is bound by no conditions of space or time, it was the Temple—long ruined and even polluted, but still the Furthest Sanctuary, furtherest from us and so nearest to Allah—whither he was taken; it was there that—according to the tradition—he mounted the Pegasus that was to convey him to the upper world and its seven stories . . . Jerusalem was to the followers of Mohammed what Sinai was to ancient Israel, more than the unknown Mount of the Transfiguration ever became to Christians . . .[11]

Outside of Jerusalem were other centers equally holy to

[8] Koran iv/171; but Islam does attribute to Jesus a Virgin birth (iii/145-47), says he was not crucified but was taken directly into Heaven (iv/157-58), spoke as a babe in the cradle (xix/29-34), received the Gospel from God (v/46), contained the Spirit of God (v/110), and performed miracles (v/112-16). Yet he was only a man and a servant of God (v/72, 116).

[9] Koran, xliii/89.

[10] xvii/1.

[11] D. Margoliouth, *Cairo, Damascus, and Jerusalem* (London: 1907), p. 196.

members of more than one faith, such as Hebron, the home of Abraham. The landscape of Palestine, like most Muslim lands, had its share of saints' tombs to which minor local pilgrimages were made and in which intercession could be expected. In fact, veneration was contagious: not only were the pre-monotheistic holy places incorporated into one or other of the religions, or into all three, but the objects of each tended to be venerated by the others, to such an extent that even a crusader period church has come to be venerated by Muslims.[12] And, of course, the joint Muslim-Jewish interest of the Wailing Wall was a source of trouble during most of the Mandate period, as we have seen in Part I.

In the Ottoman Empire administration there was never any question as to who was the recognized spokesmen for Christian and Jewish *millets,* and for itself Islam provided a similar organization. This organization, however, was a part of the Ottoman government. When the Ottoman Empire as such was destroyed by the First World War, the Islamic community was left without a recognized spokesman. Under the Mandate, the very idea of being but one *millet* among many was difficult to grasp. Moreover, the old notion of loyalty to religious groups was subverted by a new and growing awareness of being Arab.

If the English had their "spokesman" in the government of Palestine and the Jews, however much they might disagree internally, in the Jewish Agency, what of the Arabs? The government of Palestine offered to allow the Arabs to create an Arab Agency;[13] but this the Arabs were unable to accept because, they contended, Palestine was theirs, and any agreement to the formation of a parallel agency to the Jewish was to admit that they were at a par in rights. Lastly, this new consciousness of being more than Muslim, something different from Ottoman, and

[12] Grant, pp. 112-13.

[13] See above, Part I. The Supreme Muslim Council was created in 1921 to control religious courts and to administer the Pious Foundation Funds, but the Arabs would never accept the Religious Communities Ordinance which would have made them a sort of *millet* (or rather would have made them into several *millets* on the basis of faith) as administered by a non-Muslim government.

perhaps something slightly less than Arab, was disturbing their leaders. How were they to achieve some sort of unity and identity and how was that new identity to find a spokesman? These were crucial questions to the generation which grew to manhood under the Mandate and they were still partially unanswered in 1948. The developing answer, which of course affects a much larger area than Palestine, is such as to take us back into the cultural history of the Arabs to examine what can best be described as Arabism.

3. THE ARAB ELEMENT IN ARABISM

The essence of Arabic culture, the refinement of the ideals, the fears, and the emotions, which is the legacy of the Arab past is contained in the body of classical Arabic literature and especially in the poetry of the era immediately prior to the advent of Islam. In this poetry is mirrored the ideal past of all Arabs—that is, of all who regardless of racial origin or religion think of themselves as Arab. Since generation after generation has memorized vast assemblies of poems in youth, poetry has become the thread on which Arabic culture is strung. On poetry was concentrated virtually the entire artistic expression—what other societies have divided among music, art, and literature—of the Arabs, so that it has rightly been called the "Register" of the Arabs. Even today, in schools and homes all over the Arab world, children memorize, repeat, and savor the powerful linguistic virtuosity of the classics.[1] One can hardly overemphasize poetry's importance as a key to the emotional subconscience of the people.

From those of us, then, who have not grown up in Arabic society—the means by which one assimilates his own cultural

[1] The Royal Commission noted in 1936 that "at both the primary and secondary stages, the teaching is in Arabic only [in Government schools]: apart from scientific subjects, the curriculum is almost wholly devoted to the literature, history, and traditions of the Arabs" Cmd 5479, p. 96).

heritage—this poetry deserves special attention; indeed, since we cannot acquire by osmosis, we must if we are to refine our understanding of modern Arabs pay rather more conscious attention to their heritage than they.

In the body of classical poetry one would search in vain for any sort of "nationalist" sentiment. At most one could expect to find, and would find, a cultural self-consciousness. Language was a sort of frontier which enclosed all men whose immediate loyalties tended to separate them. Those who composed, repeated, and relished Arabic eloquence partook of a common set of emotions; and since Arabic pre-Islamic society was not historic, even poems of hostility toward one's own folk written by the foe eventually became one's own as the circumstances in which they were composed faded from the memory of men. Sometimes the names of men or tribes were changed to fit new situations, or lines were plagiarized by younger poets. Thus what had echoed tribal particularism came to express a supra-tribal culture.

Both this sense of a common culture and of apartness, a sense of being different from those who did not use Arabic, is expressed, as one might expect in a tribal society conscious of the family ties-in-depth, by a sort of family tree.[2] All Arabs, and ultimately every man, for it was traced back to Creation, had a place on the genealogy, and by that place was indicated his current relationship to one's own self. Arabs were the sons of Ishmael the son of Abraham, and therefore ultimately were a single branch of mankind, which in turn was divided and subdivided into two major branches, into tribal confederations, tribes, sections of tribes, clans, and single tents.

The basic unit of bedouin society was the clan or five-generation group (grandfather to self to grandson), which moved, raided, and worked as a corporation. The desert set its own limits and this was the group which could survive. The single household or tent could not; nor could such a large group as a tribe when assembled feed itself on scant pasturage. Thus, while one would be conscious of a tribal affiliation in dis-

[2] Taught today in such school texts as Taha Hussein et al., *al-Mujmal fi ta'rikhi'l-adabi'l-'arabi* (Cairo: 1949), p. 2.

tinction to members of other tribes, effective loyalty of daily life was to the clan. All of the clan members were bound by kinship or an acceptable social fiction—in the colorful Arabic phrase, the outsider could "put on the skin" of the clan. All were compressed by the hostility of the outer world. To the clan all owed loyalty. It is this sentiment which is echoed by one of the most widely known and often repeated of Arabic poems, the "Warning" of Duraid bin Simma. The poet and his clan, know as Ghaziyah, have been on a raid and while returning decide to stop. The poet then earnestly warns his fellows of the danger of pursuit, but they refuse to heed him until high noon, too late.

> Then when they refused to heed me, I was with them
> although I had recognized their error and that I
> wasn't wise in my course.
> For what am I except of the clan of Ghaziyah: if
> Ghaziyah goes astray, so I; and if Ghaziyah chooses
> the right way, so I.

So the poet stays, fights, and is badly wounded as he protects his brother's body from the enemy—"the fight of a man who deeply cared for his brother, knowing that man lives not forever."[3] This is the Arabic version of "my nation . . . right or wrong" and sums up the bedouin ideals of loyalty, courage, and the delight in the well-phrased grand gesture.

Since neither government nor police nor court existed to regulate relations between these social corporations, all of the duties of preserving life and property devolved upon the clan itself. Aggression against a clan member by an outsider obligated his fellows to retaliate either on the aggressor or against his clan. As Sir Charles Lyall, perhaps the West's foremost student of the Arabic literature of this period, has written:

> With no national centre of authority, the duties of enforcing justice and providing for self-defense lay upon each man and his brethren by blood or covenant. The strong man armed kept his house:
>
> Who holds not his foe away from his cistern
> with sword and spear, it is broken and spoiled:
> who uses not roughness, him shall men wrong.

[3] Diwan al-Hamasah of Abu Tamam (Cairo: 1951—in Arabic), pp. 812 ff.

The master-passion of the Arab was revenge. In its prosecution he was conscious of a burning fever, the only medicine for which was the blood of his foe. Language in this sense recurs constantly throughout the pagan poetry:

> Hearts are cured of rancour-sickness, whether
> men against us war, or we carry death among them:
> dying, slaying, healing comes.

The root of this thirst for 'wild justice' seems to lie in the strong affection by which men of the same kindred were bound together, an affection which is testified in the multitude of noble dirges which form one of the most attractive classes of the ancient poetry.[4]

The clansman who did not exact vengeance on the aggressor may be equated in our terms with the man who hides a murderer: he is himself an enemy of society. Ultimately the peace and security of every individual depends upon the certainty that vengeance will take its heavy toll. Only this certainty could produce a "peace of the feud."[5] If certainty alone gave the individual security, then every social pressure available to a corporate and chivalrous society was applied to ensure certainty. Upon each individual was the burden of honor and in his hands the law. Aggression is equated with the "stain of shame" (Arabic *'ār* or *Khuzi*) which is cast upon the honor (Arabic *'ird*) of the attacked group. *'ār* seems to have been thought of as a filth which had to be washed (Arabic *ghasala*) away by vengeance (*tha'r*). The sort of action the clan must take depends upon the source of the act. If aggression is from an outsider, then normally nothing short of blood will wash it away, but if from another group within the same tribe, retaliation can be taken in "blood money" (*diyā*). Whatever the form, retaliation reproduces at least theoretically the *status quo ante* in terms of the wealth and power of the two groups. Thus it provides a principle other than bloodshed by which disputes were capable of solution.

[4] *Ancient Arabic Poetry* (London: 1930), pp. xxiii-xxiv.

[5] The phrase is used by Professor Max Gluckman in a series of lectures reprinted in *The Listener* (Spring 1955). His interpretation was based partly on Arab tribal evidence. It has a modern counterpart in the concept of "massive retaliation" in Russo-American rivalry.

In many ways Islam was hostile to tribal ethics, and Mohammed was particularly hostile to the poets, but Islam took over the essential features of this aspect of corporate society; in Islam the "clan" was Islamic community. Within this, as within the clan, vengeance was not possible or permitted:

It is not for a believer to kill a believer unless [it be] by mistake. He who hath killed a believer by mistake must set free a believing slave, and pay the blood-money to the family of the slain, unless they remit it as a charity . . . Whoso slayeth a believer of set purpose, his reward is Hell for ever. Allah is wroth against him and He hath cursed him and prepared for him an awful doom.[6]

But without the religious "clan," the community of Islam, the traditional laws of society were retained in Islam.[7]

And there is life for you in retaliation, O men of understanding, that ye may ward off [evil] . . . O ye who believe! Retaliation is prescribed for you in the matter of the murdered; the freeman for the freeman, and the slave for the slave . . .[8]

If, however, a man were prepared to forego his right of retaliation, he could count this as an expiation for sin.[9]

The basis of the incipient Islamic community may be, probably by its founder was, regarded as a sort of supertribe in which the brotherhood of believers was the bond of kinship. Believers were not to take unbelievers as friends in preference to believers. In the "Constitution of Madinah," Mohammed tried to establish the principle that if a person wrongs another, he involves only his immediate family, not the whole community. However, as significant as the Islamic community concept became in the urban life of the Islamic Middle Ages, it was unable at first to make much headway against the mores and obligations of traditional tribal life. In fact, the immediate result of the coming of Islam was the great wave of conquest which involved, as we have seen, the establishment of garrison towns in the conquered territories. In these garrison towns, tribes

[6] Koran, iv/92-93.

[7] H. Lammens, "Le Tar chez les Arabes: son caractère religieux," *al-Machriq*, XXXIII, pp. 1 ff., 428 ff., and 557 ff.

[8] Koran, ii/179, 178.

[9] *Ibid.*, v/45.

as such came into effective being for the first time as different groups of clans were physically and proximately juxtaposed to one another. This led in the first instance to the intensification of a *tribal* loyalty and then to the formation of huge confederations of tribes. The obligations and sentiments of clan life were thus promoted to a higher scale of social organization.

One might have thought that the task of defeating two huge empires would have created a sense of an Arab "nation" in opposition to the foreigners. Such does not seem to have been the case, perhaps because the conquest of the Sassanian Empire was too rapid and because relatively few of the tribes were engaged against the Byzantine Empire in its home territory. Moreover, the several Arab tribes most commonly acted as free agents under the distant, overall command of the Caliph. Each tribe began to adopt individuals from among the conquered as clients whose interests it undertook to defend against other Arabs, and the several tribes tended to carve out of the defeated empires separate chunks of territory for which each undertook responsibility. Thus the tribes tended to grow apart from one another in that the experience and commitments of those in Egypt were different from tribes resident in Persia. Pure Arab lineage was still considered the mark of the citizen, while a certain stigma certainly attached to the non-Arab convert. However, in the course of time, not only had this sense of inferiority ceased to be apparent but the fully assimilated foreigners became the major contributors to Arabic civilization.

In the essential bearer of Arabic culture which had given a sense of unity to disparate tribes of Arabia, the Arabic language, was written the Koran. Of course the Koran was common property of all Muslims. Translation from the original was discouraged; but because Arabic developed in new directions after becoming an imperial language, reading the Koran became difficult for later generations. A special study of classical Arabic came to be necessary in the second and third centuries after the coming of Islam. In this study non-Arabs took a leading part. The first grammars, dictionaries, and collections of the old poets, the development of the system by which vowels could be written, and other contributions to the language were made by men who were not Arabs. Arabic culture came to be something different from Arab. Even the word "Arab" was used by cultured men only in the sense of "bedouin," [10] and to be called such was probably to be insulted.

To the memory of a tribe in which one's ancestors had real or assumed membership one might attach a certain pride; but loyalty was to the community, and the frontiers of the community in the settled urban world of the Islamic Middle Ages were religious. Men were far more likely to describe themselves and be described by their acts as Muslims, Jews, or Christians than as Turks, Persians, or Arabs. Indeed, the Arabs themselves were divided, as we have seen in modern Palestine, into several religious communities with conflicting loyalties.

Settled life changed other aspects of the Arab heritage. Unlike the clan, which had no "chief" but only a *primus inter pares,* who led his folk only by holding their respect, expressing their will, and being prepared to act as their generous host, the settled communities, be they Muslim or the *millets,* came to have rulers. The Muslims were ruled by those in whom the "dye of sovereignty had taken," and the Christian and Jew by state appointees. Men lost that magnificant anarchy of desert democracy, and perhaps partly because of this clung even more tenaciously to their ideal past. Whole generations of poets tried to re-create the great expression of the wild, free life of the past; the great philosopher Ibn Khaldun, one of the most cosmopolitan and refined of men, writes with mixed fear and wonder of those who have the force and recklessness to be the prime movers in what he knew of history. The bedouin became Robin Hood, Jesse James, and Rousseau's noble savage in one—even more, he also added to these the ringing power of sonorous and vivid language. Arabic never again duplicated the intensity and power of his expression. Lastly, in the centuries in which settled Arabs have been subject peoples, the bedouin stands out starkly and triumphantly as the conqueror of half the known world.

This in brief is the native element in what we have called Arabism. But what of the rest, what of the nationalism so much

[10] E.g., Ibn Khaldun, *Muquaddimah* (Cairo edition), p. 283 (Book V/21).

more familiar to us? This is a newer, perhaps less essential but certainly much more articulated aspect of the modern scene. It is the gift of the West, but to appreciate it in the form it has taken in the East we must see the circumstances in which it came to the East.

4. MODERN ARAB NATIONALISM

By most people, social systems are evaluated not by any abstract standards or even entirely by the sort of life they provide but by the degree of success and power of those who profess them. This helps to explain why Islamic society, even when it was aware, was so little affected by the Renaissance. Islamic armies plunged deep into Europe, threatening Vienna in the seventeenth century and for most of the eighteenth were able to contend in respectable terms with the Russians and Austrians. If Islamic culture was producing no great new masterpieces, it was preserving masterpieces and producing facsimiles which satisfied its cultural elite. Not until the middle of the eighteenth century, when the sultans Abdul Hamid I and Selim III came to realize their military weakness before militant Russia, did the Ottoman Empire hurriedly try to borrow from the West.

In 1793, Selim declared the New Order (*Nizam-ı Jedid*), Turkey's first attempt at Westernization, and instructed his ambassador in Paris to analyze what was happening in the West. Like many of those of the rulers of the Middle East to follow, Selim wanted to know the "secret" of western power in order that he might use it to defend the East. His ambassador wrote that men in France felt a new sense of love for their *vatan* and that this is what led them to success in war.[1] In Turkish the word *vatan* (Arabic: *watan*) simply meant the place where a man happened to live and had none of the emotional overtones of *patria* or homeland. Traditionally in the nomad-oriented Arabo-Turkish cultures of the East, it was a man's folk, not where

[1] See Bernard Lewis, "The Impact of the French Revolution on Turkey," *Cahiers d'Histoire Mondiale,* I (1953).

he lived, which stimulated his ardor and created social cohesion.[2] The folk had been delimited by lineage. Even in settled life the frontiers, as we have seen, were not geographical, for even villages had people of several separate, and separately governed, groups; rather the boundaries were religious as expressed by the *millet* system. Gradually in the nineteenth century we find the element of geography emerging among the gentry as it had always been dominant among the peasantry, as the focus of men's loyalty. In most of Syria, with the single exception of Mount Lebanon, this simply made no sense. Christians living in Damascus were as attached to Jerusalem as were those living just a few miles away in Bethlehem, and active or moderately wealthy men were apt to have lived in several parts of the empire. Indeed, there was only one obvious hatchery for territorial nationalism in the Arab world, and to this we must briefly turn to trace the rise of Arab *wataniyah* or nationalism.

Since being conquered by Sultan Selim the Grim in 1517, Egypt had continued to be ruled by a non-Egyptian, Turkish-speaking military elite known in history as the Mamluks. From time to time a strong man would arise among them and for a longer or shorter period would detach Egypt from the empire. In no sense even in pretense were these national movements. Then, when in 1798 he invaded Egypt and routed the Mamluks, Napoleon found it expedient to attempt to drive a wedge between the Egyptians and the Ottoman suzerain. He tried to organize a native government as a façade for French rule, but is alleged to have been told that Egyptians practiced other professions—government was the profession of the Turks. Napoleon tried to cast himself in the role of liberator; he spoke, in the newspaper he founded with a captured Vatican Arabic press, in terms of *the* Egyptian "nation," saying that "all men are equal . . . in future all Egyptians will be eligible for all [government] posts . . ." We know that such learned Egyptians as Gabarti understood Napoleon's propaganda but thought it unappealing

[2] Ibn Khaldun, who is one of the very few philosophers of history to come from a tribal society, coined the word *'asabiyah*—the sentiment which binds men closely to their *asabah* or agnates—as the motivating social force in pre-nationalist Arab affairs.

or even odd. It is easy, indeed common, in modern nationalist intellectual archaeology to magnify Napoleon's influence on contemporary Egyptians. On one person, however, we are certain of a powerful influence, and this person himself deserves the title "Founder of Modern Egypt."

Mehmet Ali Pasha was a Turkish-speaking Albanian adventurer from Cavalla, a man not unlike numbers of strong men in the Ottoman service whose careers have briefly engaged us. But he was a man of great cunning and willingness to learn. Having watched Napoleon's might in action, he perceived that real power in the contemporary world was the result of some features of European society, some "secret" which if discoverable would make its discoverer also powerful. To this end, he sent mission after mission of young men to Europe to study or apprentice, and these were the men who were to shape Egyptian destiny in the following generations.

Ironically the man who made perhaps the most important contribution to an understanding of this "secret" was not sent as a student but only as a Muslim *shaikh*—to make sure the other young men didn't lose their old "patriotism" in acquiring the tools with which to defend it. This was Rifa'a Rafi at-Tahtawi, who wrote what was the most widely read book in the Middle East of the first half of the nineteenth century, a study of the manners and customs of the people of Paris.[3] He followed this by a stream of translations from European literature and technical works, and such "how to do it" or better "how to be it" books as his guide to good manners for the young Egyptian—not for the young Muslim or even the young Arab, but the young Egyptian.[4] Among other attributes to be cultivated, he writes, is love of country. With something little short of desperation, Tahtawi tries to derive the notion of *wataniyah* or patriotism from the traditional sources of Muslim values, the Koran, the Traditions of the Prophet, and the corpus of pre-Islamic poetry.

[3] *Takhlis al-briz fi Talkhis Bariz* (Cairo: 1834). A Turkish version also sold and was read widely; see J. Heyworth-Dunne, "Rifa'a Badawi Rafi' at-Tahtawi," *Bulletin of the School of Oriental Studies*, IX and X.

[4] *Muhahij al-albab al-Masriyah fi mabahij al-adab al-'asriyah* (Cairo: 1869).

"Desire for bringing civilization to the country," he wrote, "comes only from love of it . . . just as the Sacred Law and the Traditions enjoin love of the country . . ." A series of confirming quotations follow which naturally only vaguely refer to the foreign idea. Finally, to clinch his point, Tahtawi points out that Mohammed is known to have loved his home town, Mecca, and that modern Egyptians should likewise love Egypt, which is the land of Noah and moreover has many natural advantages in comparison with its neighbors.[5]

These were bold, and however they may appear to us today, deft attempts to incorporate a European idea into Egyptian and ultimately into Arabic thought; but it is something of an indication of the narrowness of the scope of their influence that subsequent writers as late as the turn of the century were concerned not with philosophical refinements but with the basic question, "What is a *watan* and what is *wataniyah*?"[6]

Egypt, as we have seen, has time after time attracted in one way or another the Levant. In the 1830s the Levant was occupied by Egyptian troops and the Egyptian government encouraged the opening of schools by foreign missionaries. In Mount Lebanon and Palestine a sizeable percentage of the population was Christian and was therefore open to western Christian missionary activity. The missionaries found that they could make little headway if people could not read their tracts, and the best-educated people in the community were their opposite numbers, the learned men of Islam. Therefore the missionaries, particularly the American Protestants, devoted much of their energies to the spreading of literacy among the villagers. By 1860, just before Tahtawi's book on good manners appeared, the American schools in the Levant were attended by nearly 1,000 students. At the very least these schools provided the tools of literacy and in the subject matter they disseminated could not help but impart some of the ideas of Europe.

Partly through coming into contact with the ideas of the

[5] *Ibid.*, pp. 5-11. Tahtawi also wrote the first *Wataniyat* or poems of nationalism.

[6] Shaikh Hussein al-Marsafi, *al-Kalim ath-thaman* [the Eight words] (Cairo: 1880); and Mohammed Umar, *Hadir al-Misriyin* (Cairo: 1902).

French Revolution, but perhaps mainly through coming into close contact with foreigners as such, young men became conscious of themselves as also a national group and rediscovered their own cultural heritage. It is in this sense that the foremost Arab student of Arab nationalism, George Antonius, could say that "the story of the Arab national movement opens in Syria in 1847, with foundation in Bairut [sic] of a modest literacy society under American patronage."[7] It was a shadowy beginning in Syria without the statesmen, writers, and pronouncements, and the flags we can find so easily in Egypt, and it certainly affected fewer people. It was far less a Muslim movement in Syria than in Egypt. In fact, in Syria many of the key figures in the next generations of nationalists were Christians who found in the extra-religious idea of *wataniyah* a way of entering the dominant society without apostating either religiously or socially. In Syria, therefore, we can find a good deal more concentration on the Arab past, whereas Egyptian nationalism tended to be at least as conscious of its great non-Arab past and decidedly more conscious of Islam.

Christians of the Levant, moreover, could more easily drop the newer yet traditional forms of literature in that these were largely identified with Islam.[8] It was indeed a Christian by the name of Nasif al-Yaziji (1800-1871) who more than any other single man revived ancient Arabic literature as a popular interest and infected a younger generation with his passion for the classical heritage of the language.[9] One of his sons, Ibrahim, penned the famous lines, "Arise O ye Arabs and Awake! The

[7] *The Arab Awakening* (New York: 1939), p. 13.

[8] See H. A. R. Gibb, "Studies in Contemporary Arabic Literature," BSOAS, 1928-30; H. Peres, "Les premiers manifestations de la renaissance literraire Arabe en Orient au xixe siècle," *Annals de l'Institute d'etudes Orientales,* I (1934-35); and Luis Cheikho, *La Littérature Arabe au xixe siècle* (Beyrouth: 1926), Part II, pp. 27 ff. (in Arabic).

[9] Almost a century later a young Arab, writing on "the problem of Arab unity," echoed the same sentiments: "The Arabic language is the most unifying and lasting element which binds the Arabs of all countries and all religions and creeds" (Tawfiq Heineidi, unpublished thesis, American University of Beirut, 1943, p. 31; also see N. Faris and M. T. Husayn, *The Crescent in Crisis* [Lawrence, Kansas: 1955] pp. 21-22; H. A. R. Gibb, *The Arabs* [Oxford: 1940], p. 3).

cause flows full tide that its adherents may plunge forward."[10] Like many of his generation who followed his father's lead, Ibrahim gloried in the image of the Arab past, constantly suggesting that it required by an effort of the will to shake off the dust of ages:

And what are the noble Arabs but lance tips to whom at the furtherest points is a stance?
By your life, we are at the forefront of every virtue
. . .
Iraq has known us of old,
Syria could not ignore our sovereignty
And in the land of Hijaz we have an abundance
. . .
And over Spain float our banners.
. . .
So ask the West about the effects of our valour
. . .
But we are not content with the mere mention of this
Nor do we depend upon it as a support
But we will strive to uphold [this sense of honor]
Until it has for itself troop upon troop of fighting men.[11]

And at least as early as 1880 Yaziji and his followers in Beirut founded a secret society within a larger literacy society to promote the use of Arabic, to work for the unification of Syria (i.e., the modern states Syria, Lebanon, Jordan, and Israel) and to abolish censorship and spread free education.[12]

In spite of retrospective importance, this movement affected very few people. The Ottoman government was strong,[13] it exercised censorship, and most of the population was not only illiterate but was profoundly suspicious of the more fortunate urban dwellers whom it supported. There can be no doubt also that the direct and close connection of the proto-nationalists with

[10] Cheikho, p. 43.

[11] *Ibid.*, p. 41.

[12] Ettore Rossi, *Documenti sull'origine e gli sviluppi della questione araba (1875-1944)* (Rome: 1944).

[13] In spite of European contempt for the empire, the internal forces of the state were formidable. As Odysseus [Sir Charles Eliot] wrote, "practical contempt for the Turk exists mostly outside of the Ottoman dominions . . ." (*Turkey in Europe* [London: 1900], pp. 6-7). Abdul Hamid employed one of the largest secret police forces of his era.

foreign missionaries tended to isolate them still further. Lastly, at a time when nationalism was still in the embryo of a literary revival of a dim past, Islam was itself undergoing a similar and what must have seemed at the time more significant revival. In Egypt and Constantinople, the powerful voice of Jamal ad-Din al-Afghani (d. 1897) was raised against the foreigner and for a modernization within the faith. Unhindered by the approving Ottoman government, able to draw on the more recent and more widely known resources of an Islamic past, and assisted by an active cadre of Free Masons in various parts of the empire, Islamic modernism was to prove a strong competitor to nationalism. Indeed, the competition is today still unresolved.

Arab nationalism, however, got its major boost less from its internal resources than from an external set of circumstances. During the nineteenth century the Ottoman Empire was prey to separatist movements; and in this battle for survival, the core of the empire, the Turks themselves, lost belief in the multinational concept of the state and came to suspect all but Turks. We have noted in Part I how, ". . . one national movement brought another to life: Greek nationalism led to Armenian, Armenian to Turkish, and Turkish to Arab." [14]

We have already briefly mentioned the rise of Turkish nationalism and the nostalgic desire for a Turanian revival in the writing of Ziya Gök Alp. In Turkey this was partly directed against Sultan Abdul Hamid, who was the symbol of an old way of life—incapable of withstanding the onslaught of the West and yet vexatious to all within the Empire.

The Arab young men who also studied the West felt much the same way as the "Young Turks," and if one substitutes the word "Arab" for "Turk" their opposition programs read almost identically. In Paris in 1905 the young Syrian Christian Najib Azuri, who subsequently wrote *Le Reveil de la Nation Arabe,* here calling himself the "Higher Committee of the League of the Arab Nation," issued a manifesto. This deplored the "confiscations" of Arab land (presumably such as those we have described above in Esdraelon), the governing of Arabs by Circassians and

[14] Albert Hourani, "The Decline of the West in the Middle East," *International Affairs,* XXIX (1953), 36.

other foreigners, and the use of Arabs (whom it called "simple and vulgar spies") by the Ottoman government. Claiming to have committees in all the major towns of Palestine and other parts of the empire, the manifesto continued:

> Encouraged by our servility, the Turks pretend to preserve the remaining independent tribes of the Arab nation. [But] it is their intention to dominate the Hauran [a part of Syria] Yemen, Iraq, and the Nejd [Arabia] where they wish to construct railways . . . And what is even more degrading, they plan to do it with our money and our labor so that we ourselves will forge the chains of our own servitude . . .[15]

Azuri was more of a prophet than he knew because the railways were of great importance in the attempt of the Turks to put down the Arab revolt in the First World War, but the audience of the "League" was little interested.

Indeed the first important Arab organization was not founded until the end of the first decade of this century. It was after the Young Turk Revolt had hardened its lines and had become increasingly suspicious of even those Arabs who were prominent in the army circles from which the Young Turks emerged. The Young Turks in 1909 had banned the open, Turco-Arab brotherhood called *Ikha'l-Arabi,* and this perhaps did as much to arouse Arab suspicions as all the propaganda of the previous generation. In the new, secret, and wholly Arab societies which took its place, the younger generation was for the first time deeply committed. The first of these was *al-Qahtaniya* (the Arabs were called the sons of Qahtan), but this society was allowed to die of "wilful neglect" after it was suspected that one of its members was loyal to the empire. In its manifesto, which was subsequently published by the Turkish military governor of Syria, the Society heaps scorn on the Arabs by saying:

> . . . the Armenians, who are far fewer than you, have their autonomy while you remain slaves of the dynasty of Hulagu and Gengis [the Mongols] who have effaced the Empire of Baghdad, and of the sons of Tammerlane who in his campaign against Aleppo made a tower of eighty thousand Arab skulls. . . . What is a life without liberty and what guarantee does the Ottoman flag give you? To arms, Arabs! Sons of Qahtan, seize the sword and sweep from our sacred soil those

[15] Quoted in Rossi, pp. 3-6.

who exploit you, scorn you, and detest your race and your language! God has said: Tyrants are infidels!

Muslim Arabs, this despotic state is not Muslim. Christian and Jewish Arabs, unite with your Muslim brothers. Those who say that they prefer the [fellow Muslim] Turks-without-[true]-faith to you are imposters and enemies of our race.

Arabs, a group of Feda'is[16] has sworn to kill those who kill the Arabs . . . Our reform henceforth is to give rebirth to our glorious past; our program: An independent Arab State for one and all [de tout et de tous].[17]

At the same time, the Arab members of the Ottoman Parliament wrote to the Sharif Hussein of Mecca, who was of course an Ottoman government official and was known as a friend of the ruling Turkish group, offering to aid him should he decide to "succor the bondage which weighs upon the Arabs and to deliver them from tyranny and slavery." The letter was signed by thirty-five Arab members of the Ottoman Parliament, but it doesn't seem to have particularly attracted the Sharif at the time.[18] The reason is not hard to find. It is simply the result of a series of factors we have already alluded to: the Arabs had no effective overall identity, they were separated into religious *millets* with different social and political hopes and fears, they were exposed to differing degrees of western cultural and philosophical impressions, and they had a centuries-old association with the Ottoman universal empire which even in its decadence evinced remarkable strength and held the loyalty of the vast majority of the Arabs.[19] Moreover, the Arabs had no spokesman. We have seen how the first Arab "Higher Committee" was really one Arab Christian student, and how subsequent com-

[16] The word *feda'i,* plural *feda'iyin* or *fedayeen,* means a devotee or one who sacrifices himself for a cause. It constantly recurs in the modern period. See E. L. Woodward and R. Butler, *Documents on British Foreign Policy, 1919-1939,* First Series, IV (1919) (London: 1952), pp. 362-63.

[17] Rossi, pp. 6-9; also see K. T. Khairallah: *Le Problème du Levant: Les régions arabes libérées* (Paris: 1919).

[18] Khairallah, p. 19; and Rossi, pp. 9-10.

[19] The desperation of the literati and their inability to stir their people to their nationalist vision is perhaps best summarized by Maruf ar-Rasafi in his poem "Sleepers Awake!": "They never stirred; my words were profitless . . . To move a folk that slept like children there . . . Rocked in the cradle of their foolishness" (text and translation in A. J. Arberry, *Modern Arabic Poetry* [London: 1950]).

mittees were only small groups of young men with little community standing. The one man of sufficient prestige who was recognized, in 1911, as having some possibility of leadership was the Sharif of Mecca. And what could the disaffected offer him? Certainly nothing with which he could have withstood the armed might of the empire until that empire was distracted by a World War. The members of the various secret societies, although subsequently proven to be energetic and resourceful young men, probably numbered less than two hundred at any given time before the First World War; and even this small number was split between various groups without full agreement as to their aims. Some wanted merely reforms within the empire, others a single great Arab state, others a foreign-protected Christian Lebanon, and still others a Greater Syria. Even the two most important groups, al-Fatat and al-Ahd, had basic differences. The one was composed largely of westernized students and the other of Arab officers in the Ottoman army. However, vague as it was and lacking effective unity as the movement did, the Arabs certainly felt a welling discontent on the eve of the First World War.

About ten days after the entry of the Ottoman Empire into the war on the side of Germany, Enver Pasha, as de facto ruler of the empire, appointed Djemal Pasha military governor of Syria (which as we have noted included the whole Levant), telling him that "the news from Syria points to general disturbance in the country and great activity on the part of the revolutionary Arabs."[20] At that time, the Ottoman government could not have known the full extent to which Arabs were dealing with the western powers. A group of Syrian Muslims had visited Lord Kitchener before the war asking that Britain annex Syria to Egypt, and their "advances . . . were . . . tactfully received."[21] Another group had in 1913 toured European capitals to get support for reforms favorable to the Arabs.[22] And, of course, the emir (later King) Abdullah established contact with Lord

[20] Djemal Pasha, *Memories of a Turkish Statesman* (New York, 1922), p. 139.

[21] G. P. Gooch and H. Temperley, *British Documents on the Origin of the War, 1898-1914,* X (London: 1938), pp. 824-25.

[22] *Ibid.,* pp. 825, 826.

Kitchener in 1912. Soon after Djemal Pasha arrived in Syria, the papers of the French consulate in Damascus were seized—whether by omission or commission, the French officials had not destroyed them as had their British counterparts—and these revealed offers also made by Arabs to support France against the empire.

The Ottoman government, alarmed as it already was by the coolness shown to its declaration of a Holy War by the Sharif Hussein at Mecca, bided its time and replaced the Arab units which had garrisoned Syria. It has been suggested that had the British landed at some point in Syria rather than at Gallipoli, in their attempt to relieve the Russian front, all of Syria might have risen. Djemal Pasha, who should have known, wrote that he was "certain that to the executions [of Arab nationalists from Lebanon, Syria, and Palestine] in April 1916 alone do we owe the fact that there was no rising in Syria during the two-and-a-half years following Sharif Hussein's declaration of independence."[23] Yet these executions themselves probably did as much as anything else to crystallize Arab feeling in favor of the revolt.[24]

The negotiations conducted by Sharif Hussein of Mecca with Sir Henry McMahon, High Commissioner of Egypt, contained the terms upon which the Arabs entered the war on the side of the Entente. Much has been written about them. They promised to the Arabs roughly what is now divided between the Asian Arab states minus certain areas of British and French interest in southern Iraq and along the Mediterranean Sea (see Part I, p. 58). It has long been a moot point whether or not Palestine, as it came to be, was promised to the Arabs. British writers in general contend that it was not and Arabs that it was. The Arabs rest their case on the fact that Palestine is not specifically excluded from the area claimed by Hussein from Britain. This was to be a single "Arabia" of which Hussein expected to be king. Then, when the train of events went against the creation of a single Arabia, it was still the hope of those Palestinians who were involved in the nationalist movement to be a part of the kingdom of Syria which Hussein's son Feisal was elected to rule.

[23] Djemal Pasha, p. 219.
[24] Antonius, pp. 188-90.

Indeed at the Syrian Congress of 1919 an "Arab executive" for Palestine was appointed to defeat British attempts at annexation or enforcement of the Balfour Declaration.

Arab opinion divided between those who admitted a British right to dispose of Palestine, but who claimed the right to have been exercised to the benefit of Hussein, and those who have unconditionally opposed any form of British activity. The vast majority of the population were, of course, exhausted from the long and harrowing ordeal of the war and quite prepared to submit to him who would feed them. On only one question was there found to be a general area of agreement by the King-Crane Commission which had been sent to the Levant by President Wilson: opposition to Zionism. It was indeed henceforth to be Zionism itself which was the greatest leaven in Arab thought in Palestine.

5. THE REACTION TO ZIONISM

Beginning in the 1920s and heightened in the 1930s was a new element in the thought of young Arabs. It involved something more than the rather formal nationalism of the years before the war, something remarkably like the longings in Zionism before Jews returned to Palestine. Earlier we have noted how the tenth-century writer al-Muqaddasi extolled the physical attributes of Jerusalem and, in passing, how nine hundred years later Rafi extolled those of Egypt. Now we find the same sort of writing again about Mount Lebanon and Palestine by a group of men known in Arabic letters as "The Emigrant Poets" (the most famous of them in America was Gibran Khalil Gibran, who wrote *The Prophet*). Swept by the flood of emigration out of the frugal mountains of the Levant to the more hospitable and generous parts of the New World, these young writers yearned for their childhood homes. Mystical and deeply concerned with man's fate as their writings were, in this mysticism was an element of what was almost pan-theism. In the eye of longing the very rocks and jagged valleys of the distant homeland seem gouged out by the fingers of some god. In their exiles, these poets took the word *watan* and made it into mystical *patria.*[1] Their poetry was widely and intently read and recited. By throwing into sharp and vivid verse what had been rather less precise sentiments, it exercised an emotional leadership on the whole generation of young men who came to maturity in the 1920s and 1930s. These sentiments could not but be stimulated in reaction to Zionism just as earlier Muslim feeling had been stimulated by reaction to the Crusades.

Zionism was obviously a matter of intense interest for Arabs. In its report, the King-Crane Commission described what it understood to be Zionist aims and Arab reaction to them:[2]

> The fact came out repeatedly in the Commission's conferences with Jewish representatives, that the Zionists looked forward to a practically complete dispossession of the present non-Jewish inhabitants of Palestine, by various forms of purchase.

and

> the non-Jewish population of Palestine—nearly nine-tenths of the whole—are emphatically against the entire Zionist programme . . . there was no one thing upon which the population of Palestine were more agreed than upon this . . . More than seventy-two per cent—1,350 in all—of all the petitions in the whole of Syria were directed against the Zionist Programme . . . No British officer, consulted by the Commissioners, believed that the Zionist programme could be carried out except by force of arms.

In the second serious disturbance after this warning, the riots of 1921, the investigating Commission pointed out that "what is written on the subject of Zionism by Zionists and their sympathisers in Europe is read and discussed by Palestinian Arabs, not only in the towns but in the country districts."[3] Arab

[1] See Mohammed Abdul Ghani Hasan, *ash-Shi'r al-'arabi fi'l-Mahjar* (Cairo: 1955).

[2] The Commission has been subjected to critical inquiry by Elie Kedourie, *England and the Middle East,* pp. 140-41, 145. There is no doubt that Arab nationalists did, as Kedourie suggests, conduct a propaganda campaign to influence the commissioners, but subsequent events have shown that the report was in all its essentials correct.

[3] Cmd 1540, p. 56.

witnesses showed the commissioners such quotations as the following:

Hence the real key to the Palestine situation is to be found in giving to Jews as such, those rights and privileges in Palestine which shall enable Jews to make it as Jewish as England is English or as Canada is Canadian. That is the only reasonable or, indeed, feasible meaning of Jewish National Home, and it is impossible for Jews to construct it without being accorded a National status for Jews.[4]

This sort of statement necessarily threw down the gauntlet to the Arabs. To add further insult, as the Arabs must take it, Palestine was described by modern secular Zionists as it had been by Jewish pilgrims of old, as a "deserted, derelict land."[5] Both the official Zionist position and that of Jabotinsky, who was later to inspire the Revisionist (Irgun) wing of Zionism, agreed that Jews alone should be allowed to bear arms and were firm in publicly stating that in their view "there can only be one National Home in Palestine, and that a Jewish one, and no equality in partnership between Jews and Arabs, but a Jewish predominance as soon as the numbers of that race are sufficiently increased."[6]

In the following year, 1922, an unofficial Arab Palestinian delegation went to London to discuss the proposed Constitution for Palestine. In a letter to the Colonial Secretary, Winston Churchill, they established the principle on which all subsequent negotiation would founder:

In the preamble to the Palestine Order in Council "the declaration of November 2nd, 1917, in favour of the establishment in Palestine of a national home for the Jewish people" is made a basis for this Order [to set up a semi-representative Government of Palestine]; the People of Palestine cannot accept this Declaration as a basis for discussion.[7]

In reply Mr. Churchill (through J. E. Shuckburgh)

regrets to observe that his personal explanations have apparently failed to convince your Delegation that His Majesty's Government

[4] *Jewish Chronicle,* May 20, 1921; quoted in Cmd 1540, p. 56.
[5] *Palestine,* June 4, 1921; quoted in Cmd 1540, p. 56.
[6] Cmd 1540, p. 57.
[7] Cmd 1700, p. 2.

have no intention of repudiating the obligations into which they have entered towards the Jewish people. He has informed you on more than one occasion that he cannot discuss the future of Palestine upon any other basis than that of the letter addressed by the Right Honorable A. J. Balfour to Lord Rothschild on 2nd November, 1917, commonly known as the "Balfour Declaration".[8]

Further in the correspondence Mr. Churchill mentioned in passing that 25,000 Jewish immigrants had arrived in Palestine since the British occupation, and this was of course taken by the Arabs in alarming conjunction with such remarks as that of Dr. Weizmann that "the Question [of the fate of Trans-Jordan which was then separated from the Palestine Mandate] will be still better answered when Cisjordania is so full of Jews that a way is forced into Transjordania."[9]

It must be recalled that a sizeable proportion of the Jewish community of Palestine, especially those of long residence, were opposed to Zionism on religious and other grounds, and in the 1921 disturbances the Commission of Inquiry had reported

But for the considerations set forth above we feel convinced that there would be no animosity towards the Jews as such; that there is no inherent anti-Semitism in the country, racial or religious [sic].[10]

But it is lamentably true that in the heat of anger and frustration, political philosophy is replaced by cruder mental tools. "During the [May 1921] riots," the investigation found

all discrimination on the part of the Arabs between different categories of Jews was obliterated. Old-established colonists and newly arrived immigrants, Chalukah Jews and Bolshevik Jews, Algerian Jews and Russian Jews, became merged in a single identity, and former friendships gave way before the enmity now felt towards all.[11]

In summary, the report illustrated how rival political aspirations had explosively congealed what had been disparate groups of people of various religious and political opinions and backgrounds, speaking different languages, from all three religions,

[8] *Ibid.*, p. 5.

[9] Quoted in Nevill Barbour, *Nisi Dominus* (London: 1946), p. 104, fn. 1.

[10] Cmd 1540, p. 54.

[11] *Ibid.*, p. 50.

into two sharply divided and hostile groups. It is lamentable that in the heat of the many hostile moments to follow the Arabs did not distinguish between anti-Zionism, which they certainly had a right to espouse, and anti-Jewish feeling, which was no part of their own cultural background. We can understand how this feeling came about both in the historical context of the *millet* system, in which Jews of all sorts were members of one corporate community, and in the propaganda context in which the Jewish community of Palestine, by British mandate, was represented by the Zionist Organization which itself paid little attention to a distinction between Jew and Zionist. This is not, however, to excuse it, and many Arabs of the period felt deeply ashamed over attacks on all Jews whether Zionist or not.

In the middle years of the 1920s, Palestine was superficially quiet. The history of these years is dealt with in Part I, so here we only need allude to the fact that the Mandate government managed to incorporate some of the best minds in the Arab community and accomplished many praiseworthy works of benefit to the entire population. These works did not, of course, lie in a political field because, as we have seen, the Arab community could never negotiate on the terms necessary for British negotiation; nor would the British alter those terms. In a curious way, both the administration and the dual population seemed to shelve the basic question of the Mandate and to concentrate on lesser issues. The government, following the rebuff it had received on its plans for a representative government and for the creation of an Arab Agency, decided that the best program for the future was to allow everyone concerned simply to get used to the idea of a developing Jewish National Home under the Mandate. The Zionists were more circumspect after the Churchill definition of what the government would support by way of a National Home, and the Arabs went their several ways. A basic split developed in the Arab community and was known by its rival leaders as the Husseini-Nashashibi feud. This, like many political splits in Islamic history, is personalized and personified to the point that the underlying issues are only dimly visible and are sometimes forgotten by the contestants themselves. Briefly, around the Husseini family, which came under the leadership of the mufti

Haj Amin, who had been appointed by Sir Herbert Samuel, grouped those who had decided that in any form the Mandate was unworkable and who were uncompromisingly opposed to both British tutelage and Zionism. In the course of events, this decision was to lead Haj Amin to flirt with Communists and to support Germany in the Second World War. This later association has so tarred him as to obscure the original position on which he and his supporters stood.[12]

The main opposing party was far more moderate, being prepared to work with the British administration in hopes of putting the accent on the second half of the famous Balfour sentence, ". . . it being clearly understood that nothing shall be done which may prejudice the civil and religious rights of existing non-Jewish communities in Palestine . . ."

How thin was the veneer of calm, however, was shown by the new round of troubles touched off by a trivial event at the Wailing Wall in 1929. We have described this series of events in Part I. Their effect, quite clearly, was to translate the political struggle into a religious idiom and therefore to evoke emotions not easily quieted. The mask of calm thus ripped off was never again replaced.

In the subsequent history tempers and fears alike rose, but almost all the elements were already present: the peasant feared for his land, the Muslim for his shrines, the Christian for his, and all Arabs for their future in the face of British-supported Zionism which, as the Shaw Commission of 1929 noted, the Arabs felt "must inevitably result in the complete subordination of the Arabs as a race and the expropriation of their people from the soil . . ."[13] The one new element which appeared in the early 1930s is Arab disillusionment with Britain.

From the British documents it is clear that the government

[12] His central idea was to obtain the independence of Palestine and to that end he was prepared to work with anyone. See Laqueur, *Communism and Nationalism in the Middle East* (London: 1956), pp. 96-97. He was reputed to be a moderate (see E. L. Woodward and R. Butler, *Documents on British Foreign Policy, 1919-1939,* First Series, IV [1919] [London: 1952], No. 253) and was probably more controlled by the feelings of the community until the end of 1937 than he was in control of them.

[13] Cmd 3530, pp. 97-98.

was officially informed of the growing Arab alarm. In a number of cultural and social ways, warm ties had developed between the individuals in the British administration and the Arab literati. Many Arabs were, if not grateful, at least proud of the real progress of Palestine in the years of the Mandate. Even in opposition, moreover, Arabs admired the sterling qualities of British civil servants with their exacting public code of the "done and the not done." As a result, except for times of outbursts of mob violence as in 1920, 1921, and 1929, the moderate Arab party was in the ascendancy. We have described, in Part I, the events in which this moderate position lost leadership of the community in the early 1930s. To briefly recapitulate, they involved what seemed to be a pair of 180° turns in British policy. First, during Sir John Hope-Simpson's inquiry into land and immigration, Jewish immigration was temporarily halted. This gave rise to considerable and perhaps unjustified optimism on the part of the Arabs that the government was abandoning the "National Home." When the Hope-Simpson report was published, it recommended a halt to immigration until such time as the economic capacity of the country was greatly increased, and the government issued a White Paper (Cmd 3692) which embodied the Hope-Simpson report. The Arabs were elated. Then followed a series of strong attacks on the government by the Jewish Agency and others including Messrs. Baldwin, Chamberlain, and Amery. The government gave in to the pressure, and in a letter to Dr. Weizmann the Prime Minister virtually explained away the entire White Paper. This letter was thenceforth referred to by the Arabs as "the Black Letter," and an increasing number of Arabs decided that no confidence could be placed in the Mandate in the face "of the power which world Jewry could exercise in London." [14] This led to an Arab boycott of virtually every sphere of government activity, but in 1933 the number of Jewish immigrants tripled the number in 1932. For the first time in 1933, the Arabs began to attack the Mandate government (and oddly enough in the same year the Revisionist wing of the Zionist movement also first clashed with the police).

Three years later the great rebellion began. In those years,

[14] *Survey of Palestine,* I, 26-29.

yet another pro-Arab scheme died on the vine in London. This would have set up a quasi-representative government in which Arabs had a majority and would have given the High Commissioner authority to restrict immigration and land sales. In Parliament in February and March of 1936, the program "was strongly attacked from all sides in both Houses. The Jewish Press was jubilant . . . the Arabs regarded the result as an even more conclusive proof of Jewish influence in London than the 'Black Letter' of 1931." [15]

The Arabs were shocked into unity. For the first time they agreed on a spokesman. Arab National Committees were formed, first in Nablus and then in most towns and villages all over the country, in April of 1936; leaders of five of the six major Arab political parties called a general strike, and then the six parties joined together to form a Supreme Arab Committee under the chairmanship of the Mufti. This had all taken less than a week. It may be seen to have been the culmination of the events of the past generation in which Arabs had been unable to escape the divisive influences of their separate histories, differing religions, and mutual antagonisms. Now Palestine Arabs were a unit. Without leadership from the center, the population arose and created a movement. The "leaders" then hastened to put themselves at its official head, but it is doubtful whether they really controlled or were guided by it in 1936 or 1937. Their arrest and deportation did not end the revolt and they were from the beginning impelled forward by it rather than being its driver or guides.[16]

[15] *Ibid.*, 31 ff.

[16] When, in 1937, it was rumored that the Nashashibi National Defense party wanted to negotiate on the basis of the Royal Commission report, "they must have found that Arab opinion was too solid for such a course to be practicable [and so] The National Defense Party, in fact, continued to pursue the same policy as the coalition represented on the Higher Committee" (A. J. Toynbee [ed.], *Survey of International Affairs* (1937), I, 550; also see C.330.M.222 (1937) VI, 50-51, 97).

6. PAN-ARABISM

In the stormy events in Palestine after 1935 emerged another factor which was to grow in significance in the years before the war of 1948. Briefly stated it was the growing involvement of non-Palestinian Arabs and, to a lesser degree, of non-Arab Muslims with the affairs of Palestine. Actually this was not properly speaking a *new* factor; we have seen that one of the first acts of the Syrian Congress in 1919, before the French invasion, was the creation of an "Arab executive" for Palestine. We have also described the contacts maintained by residents of many parts of the Ottoman Empire with the Holy Places in Palestine and with its leading citizens; and lastly we have emphasized the fact that the new states created by the Anglo-French agreement of 1920 and by the League of Nations mandates were artificial in that their boundaries were determined less by local considerations than by Anglo-French interests and "historic connections." Therefore, while the endeavors of politicians were necessarily concentrated on the separate mandate states, and while these states tended to grow apart both because they were attracted to different cultures and because they fought against different foes, the loyalties of Arabs were not so divided. Men might say that they were Syrian as opposed to Egyptian; but by Syrian they would mean only that they were from some part of "geographical" Syria which included, as we have seen, virtually the entire Levant.

In the confusing years of the early Mandate period, moreover, there was a considerable "shift of population" of the ambitious young men who were to furnish leadership to the emerging Arab states. Iraq furnishes the best examples, with its king, many of its leading statesmen, and prominent citizens having been active in the Ottoman government, then in the Arab revolt, and in the short-lived Syrian kingdom. But Syria, Lebanon, and Palestine also had many public figures who won youthful fame in the Arab nationalist movement. Most of these men knew

Palestine, had friends or relatives living there, and felt toward it in one way or another the sort of emotions we have described. And, perhaps more significant, their generation was for the most part in the mid 1930s just emerging from a period of alternate struggle against European powers and tutelage by European powers. Iraq, in 1932, was officially declared "of age" by being admitted into the League of Nations. Egypt passed into treaty relationship with Great Britain in 1936. Syria, although still firmly under French control, was promised in 1936 that independence would be granted in a few years; and, even when they narrowly circumscribed anti-French nationalist activity, the French were not averse to permitting occasional expressions of anti-British feeling on the part of the Syrians.[1]

The Emir (later King) Abdullah was already recognized as an important friend of Britain, received a subsidy and, in fact, had received his country from Britain. Partly, no doubt, on that account he went out of his way to hold down Trans-Jordan popular sympathy with the Arabs on the other side of the Jordan.[2] Already at this early date leading Arabs accused him in scarcely veiled references of wishing to be made king of Jordan, roughly as that state is now constituted, as a result of some "deal" opposed to Arab aspirations.[3] Outside of government circles, there was a stronger feeling of concern with the fate of the Arabs. Protest meetings were held, students demonstrated, and in press articles and speeches by many respected elders and politicians a parallel was drawn between the Jewish National Home concept and the Latin Kingdom of Jerusalem. Most regarded Zionism as the final phase of the "madness of imperialism," against which a whole generation of Arabs and Asians in general had fought.[4]

When their own fight seemed to be going well—or indeed when they seemed hopeless—in their own areas, it was therefore

[1] Since the end of World War I, they had felt that the British were trying to "biff them out" of Syria (to use T. E. Lawrence's phrase).

[2] *Survey of International Affairs* (1936), p. 736.

[3] The Prime Minister of Iraq, Hikmet Sulaiman, warned of this in a statement to the press which was reprinted in the *Times* on July 14, 1937; quoted in *Survey of International Affairs* (1937), p. 551.

[4] For example, see *ad-Difa'a* (the most widely read Arabic paper in Palestine) for December 21, 1936; quoted in Cmd 5479, p. 96.

to be expected that other Arabs would join the fight in Palestine. Already in 1935 a band of Syrians under Shaikh Izzu'd-Din Qassam went to fight in Palestine. When he was killed in a clash with the police, Qassam became a sort of modern counterpart of Roland. In the following years, his lead was followed by large numbers of Arabs from Iraq, Syria, and Trans-Jordan.[5]

When the general strike was declared in October 1935, after the discovery of a Jewish arms shipment,[6] the rulers of Iraq, Trans-Jordan, and Saudi Arabia urged the Palestinians to call off the strike and by this intervention inevitably accepted a certain moral and public responsibility for the future of the Palestine Arabs. The Iraqi government cabled the League:

> The Iraqi Government thereby [*sc.*, by intervening] accepted the gravest moral responsibility towards the Arabs of Palestine and pledged itself to continue its efforts to assist them.[7]

The Arab Higher Committee, which had at first boycotted the Royal Commission (as the latter's terms of reference were thought to force the Arabs to accept as de jure the de facto situation), at the urging of the Arab rulers, met with the Commission. Following publication of the Commission Report, the Higher Committee sent requests to these same rulers for help and advice. Then, they sent similar requests to the heads of state in Egypt, Syria, Lebanon, and Yemen and to the Muslim communities in India, Tunisia, and Morocco.[8] For their own reasons, which need not detain us, Emir Abdullah and King Ibn Saud returned replies "which were cautious to the point of obscurity."[9]

[5] A. J. Toynbee (ed.), *Survey of International Affairs* (1935), p. 6; J. B. Glubb, *Story of the Arab Legion* (London: 1948), pp. 231, 235 ff.

[6] A shipment was discovered by government customs inspectors marked "cement" in Jaffa port which was consigned to a Jewish alias in Tel-Aviv. The "cement" proved to be 400,000 rounds of ammunition and various sorts of arms (see Col. 112, p. 12; and C.330.M.222, p. 63).

[7] C.330.M.222, p. 86.

[8] The Islamic Conference in Jerusalem had done a good deal to publicize the Palestine issue throughout the Islamic world (see H. A. R. Gibb in the *Survey of International Affairs* [1933]; also A. M. Goichon, "Le Panislamisme d'hier et d'aujourd'hui," *L'Afrique et L'Asie* (1950), pp. 18 ff.

[9] *Survey of International Affairs* (1937), p. 551.

Iraq's statements, on the contrary, indicated an open, intense, and popular emotional involvement. The Palestine general strike of 1936 led to "days of mourning in Baghdad, collections for Palestine martyrs, and deputations to the British Ambassador. Individual Iraqis, notably an ex-officer of Syrian origin, Fawzi al-Qawuqchi, sought guerrilla service in Palestine and returned as heroes . . ." [10]

Nuri Said, many times prime minister of Iraq, tried to mediate between the Arab Higher Committee and the British and even tried to negotiate with the Zionists. No man in Iraqi affairs was a more stalwart friend of Britain and none was more closely identified with her, yet his attempt at mediation failed when for various reasons the British government felt unable to "accept the mediation of a foreign Power in an internal dispute." [11] There is considerable evidence that, at this point, the Palestine Arabs might have accepted a compromise, and it is certainly true that Nuri's failure was not the least of the factors leading to the rise in pro-German-because-anti-British sentiments in Iraq and subsequently to the expulsion of Nuri and the pro-British Regent.[12]

In the fall of 1936, the Arab Higher Committee again requested the intervention of Saudi Arabia, Trans-Jordan, and Iraq when the rapid buildup of British forces indicated that the British were not going to tolerate Arab resistance. These states urged "our sons the Arabs of Palestine . . . to resolve for peace in order to save further shedding of blood. In doing this, we rely on the good intentions of our friend Great Britain, who has declared that she will do justice. You must be confident that we will continue our efforts to assist you." [13] "Confident" was perhaps not quite the right word but the organ of the activist wing of the Arab parties in the coalition, *ad-Difa'a,* took heart in its finding that "Palestine Arabs are recognized as part of the Arab federation and therefore they are no longer alone."

[10] S. H. Longrigg, *Iraq* (London: 1953), pp. 264-65. For a somewhat different view of the interest of the Iraq government see Majid Khadduri, *Independent Iraq* (London: 1951), p. 112.

[11] *Survey of International Affairs* (1936), p. 736.

[12] G. Kirk, *The Middle East in the War* (London: 1952), pp. 333-34.

[13] *Survey of International Affairs* (1936), p. 740.

> If [said the members of the Royal Commission afterwards] we were to pick out the feature of the late "disturbances" which on a general view seems to us the most striking and far-reaching, it would be the manner in which they roused the feeling of the Arab world at large against Zionism and its defenders.[14]

Britain, at long last, had realized that the Mandate was unworkable and that the two halves of the famous 68-word sentence could not be joined simply with a comma. As the Royal Commission pointed out, "It must have been obvious from the outset that a very awkward situation would arise if that basic assumption [*sc.*, "that Arab fears and prejudices would gradually be overcome"] should prove false . . ."[15] It had so proven, the Commission found, by 1936 and "it seems probable that the situation, bad as it now is, will grow worse."[16] Therefore, as we have seen, the Commission recommended partition, which it explained as the giving of Palestine to *neither* the Jews nor the Arabs. This is precisely how both Jews and Arabs felt about the proposal; each one saw himself as the loser, neither as the gainer. On the Arab side a new wave of hostility swept the country, mainly directed at the British administration, and the popular feeling was far too strong for any split in the leadership of the Arab parties to be tolerated. The Nashashibi and the Husseini factions were not friendly but both were adamant on Zionism while indicating a new willingness to negotiate on the basis of the pattern Britain had established in Iraq and Egypt—i.e., treaty ties with British recognition of Palestine as a sovereign state. On this basis they promised to protect the interests of the Jewish minority, which then amounted to about 31 per cent of the population. The Arab leaders tried, publicly at least, to restrain their followers from provoking the British, but they were unsuccessful. This time the British trigger was pulled and

> the British met arson, bombings and assassination with such stern measures as the curfew, wholesale arrests, the destruction of the houses of suspected incendiaries, the imposition of large fines and the quartering of military garrisons on towns where outbreaks occur. They

[14] Quoted in *ibid.*
[15] Cmd 5479, p. 31.
[16] *Ibid.*, p. 279.

have also dissolved Arab political organizations and sent prominent Arab leaders into exile.[17]

In the surrounding Arab countries, popular feeling was not less intense if targets were less vulnerable. The Syrian government sent a note of protest to the French Mandate High Commissioner, there were

> mass demonstrations in Baghdad; a one-day strike in the Holy Cities of Arabia; a protest of the "Muslim Youth" of Tunis to the British Consul; numerous demonstrations in India [where Nehru had previously spoken in defense of the Arabs of Palestine] . . . The Mandatory Administration found it necessary, on several occasions, to prohibit the entry of newspapers from Syria, the Lebanon, Egypt, and Iraq.[18]

This agitation was climaxed by a meeting in September 1937 of the Arab Congress at Bludan, a town a few miles out of Damascus. To Bludan came nongovernmental delegates from Iraq, Syria, Lebanon, Trans-Jordan, Egypt, Saudi-Arabia, and 119 individuals from Palestine. The delegates were by no means all Muslims—included among their number were Greek Orthodox bishops and Maronite clergy. The only foreign reporter who seemed to think it important enough to attend was, characteristically, the German *DNB* correspondent. However, the group appealed directly to audiences it still had some hopes of reaching, especially through the Pope[19] and Nehru. This of course points to the vagueness of the coalition upon which the Arabs had come sentimentally to rely: Arabs, of course; Muslims, for some; the Pope for the Catholics and Uniates; Nehru as the leader of a powerful anti-colonial movement; and finally, "the enemy of the enemy," Germany. All Arab delegates agreed upon the following program: the preservation of Palestine, without partition, was the duty of all Arabs, but the Jews were to be allowed to remain in Palestine as a protected minority.[20]

[17] Robert G. Woolbert, "Pan Arabism and the Palestine Problem," *Foreign Affairs Quarterly*, XVI (1937-38), 310-11.

[18] *Survey of International Affairs* (1937), p. 553.

[19] After an early approval of the Balfour Declaration, the Catholic Church had become increasingly hostile to Zionism; but see also the Pope's reaction to Herzl's plans in Part II above.

[20] See Woolbert, *op. cit.;* and Robert Montagne, "Pour la Paix en Palestine," *Politique Etrangére,* August, 1938.

It came as a certain surprise to many that Egypt, which had never seemed particularly interested in *Arab* affairs, having developed politically mainly along the Egyptian particularist lines indicated by at-Tahtawi,[21] sent four delegates to the Conference. On September 18, the Coptic Egyptian Foreign Minister, Wasif Boutros Ghali Pasha, informed the League of Nations Assembly:

> The Palestinian question is engaging the closest attention of the Egyptian Government and people, because of the neighbourly relations between Egypt and Palestine, and of the religious and historical relationship which unites Egypt and the Holy Places, the bonds of fraternity based upon a common language, religion and civilization that connects us with the people of Palestine, and also because of the close relations of alliance and friendship existing between Egypt and the United Kingdom, the mandatory power . . . Right and Justice require that Palestine should remain in the hands of the Palestinians. This is the natural law in its simplest and clearest form.[22]

It is and has been for some time fashionable to question the basis of such statements: are they genuine or are they just red herrings to lead discontent away from domestic issues? It has been suggested that the Syrian government called the Bludan conference simply to screen the fact that France had just amputated the Alexandretta province from Syria and given it to Turkey; thus, since the Syrian government was forced to be something less than nationalist at home, it could make capital by being supernationalist in an area where talk (which was all that was contemplated) would be taken as a measure of patriotism. Likewise the Egyptian government, with a goodly supply of domestic evils and not a little ruling-class corruption, was thought to find in the Palestine issue a convenient diversion for the discontent of its vocal and dangerous student and street agitators. There certainly is reason to think that the motives of politicians who spoke in righteous fury about Palestine were often not all they might have been, and such indeed has been the charge leveled by opposition movements in the Arab countries. However, even those Arabs who accept the truth of this statement

[21] For the evolution of Egyptian nationalism into Arab nationalism see Marcel Colombe, "L'Egypte et les origines du Nationalisme arabe," *L'Afrique et l'Asie* (1951).

[22] Quoted in Woolbert, p. 319.

are indignant only because those who used Palestine as a screen bungled both domestically *and* over the Palestine issue. It was, as we shall see, the Arab failure in Palestine which became a domestic revolutionary force in the Arab countries. Thus, while one may impute the sincerity of much of the official propaganda and press in regard to Palestine before 1948, he would be making a serious mistake who by extension argues that the emotions to which this propaganda catered were also superficial, insincere, or artificial. In the late 1930s, an American observer, after remarking that he did not agree that even the politicians were not sincere, pointed out that "there is no use dragging a red herring across the path unless the cat likes herrings."

Of course, as so often when we deal with Arab affairs, it is difficult for us to credit any analysis of "public opinion." This is the case both because the sorts of guides which we use in our own society are largely lacking and because upwards of 80 per cent of the population of some of the Arab countries was illiterate in this period. Moreover, even that part of the population which had the leisure and the means of communicating its sentiment in a way we could know of and understand, often failed to communicate effectively. Few western newspapers kept staff correspondents in the area—we have noted that the only correspondent to attend the Bludan conference was a German—and the Arabs were often regarded even by well-educated westerners virtually as savages whose underdeveloped minds were manipulated by a tiny minority of backward, corrupt, and sinister leaders. The Arab position on Palestine, resting as it always did on a single notion, "Palestine is our land and even if we don't use it efficiently, it is ours," [23] inevitably seemed stubborn and fit well with the popular notion of the "immovable East." No less shrewd or potentially well-informed observer than Churchill was ready completely to discount the intensity of this feeling in the various Arab countries when he took office as Prime Minister. He was warned by the High Commissioner of Palestine that even though the Arabs of Palestine were leaderless (their leaders hav-

[23] The Earl Peel "Report of the Palestine Commission," *International Affairs*, XVI (1937) 762; and W. E. Hocking, *The Spirit of World Politics* (New York: 1932), pp. 5-6.

ing fled or been exiled after the crushing of the Arab rebellion), the general populace was not less strongly attached to its position and not less opposed to Zionism.

German propaganda had of course catered to their antagonism to Britain, and Britain's seeming weakness in the face of Germany in Europe and Italy in Africa had given Arabs cause to think they might yet win if they held fast. The Mufti, having fled from Palestine to the French mandate of Lebanon went on to Iraq, where he found the ground well prepared for his message. The government granted him facilities and money. Iraqi youth, stirred by the violent speeches of the native proto-fascist Sami Shawqat, was ready to be convinced. Palestine seemed to the younger generation the perfect example of Shawqat's most famous speech, "The Art of Death." That nation, Shawqat told the youth of Baghdad, which does not master "the art of death with steel and fire will be beaten to death under the hooves of the cavalry and the boots of the soldiers." [24] This was simply the modern way of saying as the bedouin poet had,

> Who holds not his foe away from his cistern with
> sword and spear,
> it is broken and spoiled: who uses not roughness,
> him shall men wrong.

In a sense, the growing feeling of desperation over Palestine had produced a retreat from Westernization. It was the glorious days of the Arab Empire and the hardihood of the bedouin warrior which dominated the emotions of young men in those days; and for this reason the German emphasis on physical toughness, bravery, and violence appealed powerfully to the Arab audience. Germany blared forth on its Arabic-language radio service the announcement of the impending collapse of Britain; and soon France, the great colonial power, overlord of Syria, and destroyer of the Arab kingdom, went crashing to defeat before the *Wehrmacht*.

In those days, Britain spoke to Europeans as the bastion of freedom in a darkening world; to the Arabs, however, Britain seems to have thought it unnecessary to speak in the same terms.

[24] Subsequently published in *Ahdafuna* (Baghdad, 1939), p. 2 (in Arabic).

Consequently, while winning the respect and devotion of an enslaved western people, she remained for many in the East *the* colonial power par excellence, the old enemy, "perfidious Albion," and the supporter of Zionism. No manifestation of popular feeling or any appeals by friends in the Middle East was able to effect more than the White Paper of May 1939, which had only slowed down the tempo of the development of Zionism.

Once again in Middle Eastern affairs, the plaintive and unheard murmur of speech was to be translated into the definitive clatter of steel, as Britain found herself involved in a minor war in Iraq which, had it been better planned, might have lost to Britain her major source of oil. And immediately the British government awoke to the situation in the Middle East. The pro-German Iraqi government was put down by a British invasion and Egypt quieted by a show of force; then on May 29, 1941, Eden made a conciliatory speech in London in which he hinted that Britain would pay more attention to Arab desires. Privately Arab leaders were given grounds for hope in the future and were warned to do all they could to pacify their followers.[25]

Pacification proved an easy task. The more violent or outspoken Arab leaders were in one way or another silenced or calmed, and pro-German feeling rested on a rather unsteady foundation. It was largely the unfamiliarity of Germany, her absence from the Middle Eastern scene, which made her attractive. Most Arabs probably did not involve themselves with the issues of the European war as we in the West saw them, although it must be said that German anti-Jewish statements, even though these multiplied the power of Zionism, were by and large not unpopular in the Middle East. However, the Arabs had no desire to have Germany replace Britain and could not feel particularly content that Germany's principal ally, Italy, boasted among her military heroes a man known as the butcher of the bedouin of Libya. All in all, the Arabs were indifferent as to the outcome of the war and were left with leaders who were completely identified with the old colonial and mandate systems, not recognized as capable spokesmen, and whose essential weakness

[25] Kirk, pp. 237-39, 333-35.

could only thinly be veiled by their bellicose pronouncements. It was these leaders, after the suggestion had come from Britain, who were to make the first hesitant declarations of intentions to achieve some sort of unity.

We need not trace this evolution in detail for it can be summarized in all of its essential points. Late in 1942, the two most important premiers, Nuri of Iraq and Nahhas of Egypt, announced that Arab unity was "one of our first aspirations." But it was not until July of 1944 that the Egyptian government issued invitations for the conference which was to decide to create a league of Arab states. Iraq, Syria, Lebanon, Trans-Jordan, Saudi Arabia, and Yemen were invited, but Palestine was not. This antagonized many Palestine Arabs, who felt that they were, if anything, culturally more advanced than Arabs in the surrounding states. But it must be admitted that Palestine was not a state, on a par even with Yemen in international law, and that once again the Palestine Arab community lacked leadership and an accepted spokesman. The Mufti was then in Germany, his colleagues and assistants were interned in Southern Rhodesia, and no remaining politician could coalesce the mutually hostile parties. Not until the meeting was well advanced was a non-party Palestine Arab, Musa Alami, selected to attend the meeting, and after some discussion the other delegates decided to accept him as a member-delegate. Insofar as the meeting referred to Palestine, it decided that Palestine was to be considered an integral and essential part of the Arab world, that the rights of the Palestine Arabs must be defended to secure the peace and stability of the whole Arab world. While declaring that they fully sympathized with the Jewish victims of the Nazis, the group insisted that the problem of these people must be considered outside the context of Zionism. The several states, thus, albeit in guarded terms, had accepted responsibility for the Palestine Arabs. Then, the following February, Egypt again invited the several Arab states to a meeting, this time to draw up the constitution for the Arab League, and this time Palestine was permitted only to send an observer. However, in a special annex, the de jure independence of Palestine was recognized and it was stated that until de facto independence was achieved, the League would itself select delegates to represent the country.[26]

The end of the war brought the independence of Trans-Jordan, Syria, and Lebanon and the gradual withdrawal of the huge military force maintained by Great Britain in the Middle East during most of the war. Key points—the giant air bases of Iraq, the Suez installations, and the vast armed camp that was Palestine—were still in British hands, and because of this evident might Arab nationalists were wont to feel a certain sense of restraint. No overt action on Palestine was planned or could be planned until Britain announced her intention to relinquish the Palestine Mandate. Indeed, in the period immediately after the war, it was the Zionists, not the Arabs, who violently clashed with the British. After Lord Moyne was murdered by the "Stern Gang" in Cairo on November 6, 1944, there was a considerable cooling in the attitude of Churchill and other high officials toward Zionism. Partly because of this, the Arabs tended to feel more friendly toward Britain than they had for years. With some feeling that the British would not be entirely opposed, Arab Boy Scout formations and patriotic groups in Palestine began to train in paramilitary drill. But the Palestine Arab community had lost initiative and was disillusioned by the lack of implementation of the hopes which had led to the formation of the Arab League. In effect, it had through force of circumstances lost any control over its destiny. To counterbalance the large, well-financed, and organized Zionist Agency, its army, the Haganah, and the small but determined, capable, and ruthless Stern Gang and Irgun, the Arabs had nothing. No one who visited Palestine in this period could help but be impressed at the ineffectualness and sense of drift of the Arab community.

The surrounding Arab states came out of the war with a larger measure of independence than most of them had ever enjoyed. Iraq, it is true, during the middle years of the 1930s was master of her own fate, but most Iraqis felt that a sort of veto

[26] The inclusion of the special annex on Palestine drew a protest from Weizmann to Churchill; but the British government, though alleged to have tried privately to prevent inclusion of the annex, did not publicly protest (see Kirk, p. 342, fn. 1).

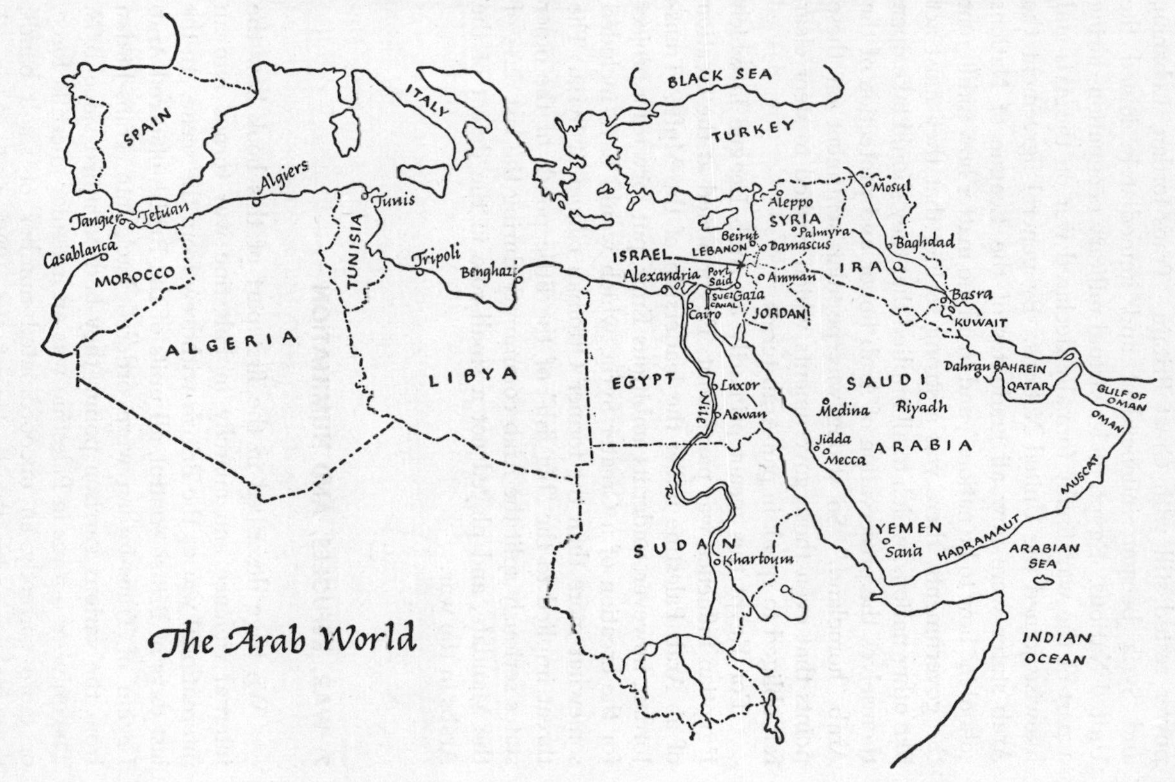

The Arab World

power rested still with Great Britain. Trans-Jordan, Lebanon, and Syria became independent and immediately joined the United Nations. Egypt, under virtual military occupation during a part of the war, finally formally declared war on the Axis and likewise joined the United Nations. By general agreement the Arab states were now all graduates of the League of Nations school in "how to be nations"; and in all, no matter how indifferent the governments, there was a strong feeling that they must act like other nations, which to all implied that they should take upon themselves the preservation of Arab honor and protection of the Arab "homeland." So strong was popular sentiment on these points that even those governments which wished to steer clear felt obliged to speak in pan-Arab terms.

For Egypt this meant primarily an Arab League in which Egyptian influence was paramount; Egypt aimed at the creation of an Arab Palestine under the leadership of the Mufti. Trans-Jordan, however, under its ambitious Emir, put forward a project for the creation of a Greater Syria, which would have included somewhat more than the former Ottoman *vilayet* of Syria. The threat implied to the "big fish" of the little ponds of the other states seriously split the Arab community during the last days of the Mandate, and played not a small role in the defeat of the Arabs in the war.

7. WAR, REFUGEES, AND HUMILIATION

We have described in the first part of this book how the internal violence and anarchy in Palestine was turned into an international war as the British withdrew from the scene. In the last days of British control, all units of the British-officered Arab Legion of Trans-Jordan were ordered back into Trans-Jordan from the various garrison points they had occupied since 1939. The only Arab force in Palestine was an irregular guerrilla force, or more correctly an uncoordinated number of small bands, theoretically under the leader of the 1936 Arab rising, al-Qawuqchi; and although these fought a number of bitter small engagements, the Irgun, Stern Gang, and Haganah picked off their objectives point by point as the British forces withdrew.

Still, for all their talk and assurances of Arab brotherhood, the surrounding Arab countries had not acted. Of course, they would not, could not, intervene until the date the British withdrawal became official, May 15, and by that time the resident Palestine Arabs may be said to have psychologically lost the war.

The invading Arab forces were actually not much larger than the Israeli army. Jordan, for example, had only four infantry battalions and one untrained new field artillery battery. The Arab armies were under different, often hostile, commands. Action by the Egyptians in the south was not coordinated with that of the Syrians, Iraqis, and Trans-Jordanians in the north and east; in numerous tactical ways this lack of coordination hamstrung the Arab forces,[1] and in the final instance King Abdullah and King Farouk fell out over the political future of the land of Palestine which both believed to be secure in their grasp. Trans-Jordan's King Abdullah made scathing references to his allies' poor military showing, but the real breaking point came when Egypt decided to recognize an Arab government of Palestine under the Mufti in September 1948. Thus Israel was able to operate singly and efficiently against small, and by this time ill-equipped, armies. From what had seemed an absolute certainty, the defeat of the irregular forces of a barely established state by five Arab states, the Palestine war drew to a humiliating close. The Arab armies, except for the British-commanded, -paid, and -supplied Arab Legion of Trans-Jordan, put up a very poor showing and no amount of excuses could cover the fact.

In their petty jealousies and conflicting aims, the Arab governments had allowed the entire Arab population of Palestine, except for a small minority, to lose what the Arab League had declared a few short years before to be an integral part of the Arab world. This resounding defeat threw into sharp focus

[1] For example, when the Arab Legion requested ammunition from Egypt, the ammunition was withheld by the Egyptians even though it was supplied by the British and would not deplete stores on which the Egyptians could rely (see O'Ballance, *The Arab-Israeli War, 1948* [London: 1956], pp. 137-38).

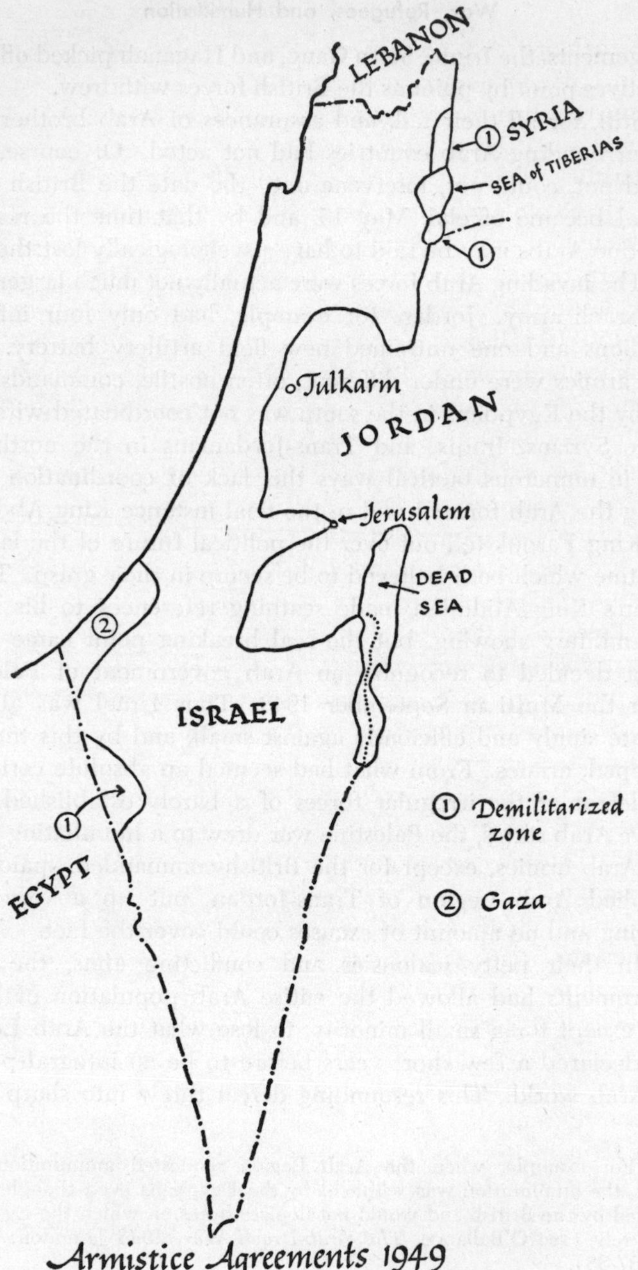

Armistice Agreements 1949

the inability and corruption of the ruling groups and led in short order to a series of coups d'état in Syria, to the murder of King Abdullah by an Arab from Palestine, and to the ousting of King Farouk by a group of young officers who had fought in Palestine.

The 1948 Arab-Israeli war, though a small-scale affair in comparison to European wars, was one of the most disruptive in modern times. Upwards of 80 per cent of the Arab population of Palestine was turned into homeless refugees; and an additional 125-150,000 villagers who retained their houses, and so were not technically refugees, lost the farmlands which had sustained them. The prewar pattern of economic and social relations was completely disrupted. Rain cisterns were sometimes to be found on one side of the frontier and those who had used them on the other; shopkeepers in Jerusalem lost the shops and tools which had given them a living; a village of railway workers was left on the Arab side and the tracks they had tended on the Israeli side. All of the tensions and fears which had been domestic to the Palestine Mandate now became international. Indeed, the new problems created by the war dwarf those which the Mandate had proved incapable of solving in its twenty-six years.

The refugee problem is perhaps the greatest challenge to the future peace of the Middle East, and the "frontier of hate" separating the displaced persons from their former homes and lands is the seed bed of the almost daily incidents which have become such a conspicuous feature of Middle Eastern affairs. But if the refugees are a focal point of general problems, they are also a focal point of propaganda; so before discussing the various facets of their impact on the current situation, it is necessary to establish a few important facts about them.

The first is the sequence of events which produced the problem.

In dealing with the actions of almost a million people, one obviously cannot hope to find any single, all-inclusive cause. The best he can do is to reconstruct the general situation in which the individuals and groups made their decisions. We have described in Part I how in Palestine from 1945 to May 15, 1948, public security deteriorated and then ceased to exist. In the latter part of this period, wealthy and middle-class Arab families, who had customarily vacationed in the cooler air of Mount Lebanon, began to go away or to send families away on extended "vacations." This is hardly surprising for this period saw an almost continuous parade of bombings, shootings, and military actions. The sound of distant firing, never distant enough, was a conspicious feature of daily life and made sleep a fitful and nervous affair. If deliberate attacks by terrorists were horrifying prospects, not much less disturbing were casual "mistakes" and accidents. It must be said in all honesty that the British forces were incredibly well held in line in most difficult circumstances, but they were naturally inclined to shoot first and question later as members of their units were shot or kidnaped and they discovered that it was impossible to distinguish the terrorist from the shopkeeper or laborer or even from the uniformed soldier. Virtually everyone in the country had access to arms. The cheap, badly made, unreliable, but murderous Sten gun was ubiquitous. One could not enter a bus, attend a cinema or even worship at Bethlehem on Christmas Eve without becoming accustomed to the continuous clatter of rifles and Sten guns being readjusted or dropped. The streets became rivers of barbed wire, and armored cars almost as common as taxis. Curfews, road blocks, check points, and the deterioration in public services made normal living difficult and relaxed living impossible. Moreover, the future looked darker yet. It was certainly obvious to everyone that as bad as the current situation was, worse was to come. It is not known how many people left the country during this period but estimates have run as high as 30,000.[2]

Then, on April 10, 1948, about five weeks before the end of the Mandate, the "refugee atmosphere" was fully developed by the Deir Yasin massacre.[3]

Deir Yasin was a small village to the west of Jerusalem. Its inhabitants were peaceful and independent. They wanted no

[2] See G. Kirk, *The Middle East, 1946-1950* (London: 1954), p. 263 (including fn. 4).

[3] See H. Lehrman, *Commentary*, VIII (1949), 529; R. Graves, *Experiment in Anarchy* (London: 1948), p. 179.

part of the troubles and were even reported, by the *New Judea* correspondent, to have driven out an Arab band which wanted to use the village as a base for anti-Zionist operations.[4] But for reasons which are still somewhat unclear, it was decided to take the village and the Irgun was entrusted with the task. Irgun failed to do so and had to call upon Haganah for assistance. Together the two groups captured the village, whereupon Haganah seems to have withdrawn from the scene, leaving the Arab captives to the tender mercies of the Irgun. Irgun then murdered the entire village population, men, women, and children, and called a press conference to announce its deed and to proclaim that this was the beginning of the conquest of Palestine and Trans-Jordan. A Jewish policeman who investigated the scene reported that *one* Arab had been killed but the details were privately communicated to the Jewish Agency, the Arab Higher Committee, and the government by the chief representative of the International Red Cross. Eye witnesses said later that it was not possible to go near the village without becoming nauseated. The full details, the fact that the villagers had been peaceful and neutral, that they had been attacked by terrorists with the active support of the Jewish Agency's own army, and that the population had been massacred, stripped, and robbed, and their bodies had been left unburied or thrown into wells, were widely circulated throughout Palestine.

Mr. Ben-Gurion immediately telegraphed a message of sympathy to Emir Abdullah and disclaimed any responsibility for the act. Yet it must be admitted that this could do little to reassure the population. The Jewish Agency itself could hardly be considered a blameless accessory. The government of Palestine had informed the general population in a paper presented to Parliament less than two years before that it knew that the Agency and the terrorists were cooperating. The Parliamentary paper contained intercepted telegrams from the Jewish Agency in Palestine to its representative in London. One of these reads as follows:

[4] *Ibid.*, p. 260, fn. 5.

We have come to a working arrangement with the dissident organisations [i.e., the Irgun and Stern Gang] according to which we shall assign certain tasks to them under our command. They will act only according to our plan.[5]

Then, just a month before the Deir Yasin massacre, the Palestine government issued a statement in which it condemned the Jewish Agency for condoning terrorism. The essential facts *seemed* to bear out the notion that the Jewish Agency was deeply involved. Haganah, which was of course the official military organization of the Agency, *had* assisted in the capture of the village and *had* entrusted its inhabitants to a group known to be terrorist. Under these circumstances a frightened and confused population could hardly be expected to grasp subtle distinctions.

Moreover, the general Arab population was well aware that Arab guerrillas were active against Jewish settlements and convoys. On April 13 a convoy of Jewish buses was attacked by an Arab band, which killed most of the passengers including a number of unarmed doctors and university people.[6] Reprisals were standard tactics in the incipient war, as they are in the truce which has followed it. The Arabs could expect that as the fighting became more bitter so would the reprisals. Lastly, it must be noted that even if the Arabs had agreed with Mr. Ben-Gurion that the Jewish Agency deplored the acts of the terrorists—and certainly they did not—they had no reason to think that the Agency could control the Irgun and Stern Gang. The events of the past several years had shown that these small groups of determined and ruthless men were a law unto themselves.

As the fighting grew in extent, there were numerous cases of population flights, evacuations, and ejections. On April 18, British forces evacuated the Arab population (47 per cent of the total) from Tiberias.[7] On April 21 the Haganah and Arab irregulars clashed in Haifa. Before this engagement neither side had used mortars. The Arabs had none and didn't think the

[5] Telegram 5, dated November 1, 1945 (Cmd 6873); see H. Sacher, *Israel: the Establishment of a State* (London: 1952), pp. 181 ff.

[6] Graves, pp. 179-80, 181-2.

[7] Kirk, p. 262.

Jews had any either. They were mistaken. As shells began to fall upon their positions, they jumped to the conclusion that the British army units still in Haifa had joined the Zionists against them and were using their field artillery.[8] A shell fell on the headquarters of the Arab irregulars and completed the confusion. The commander deserted his post, leaving the population battling from house to house. Leaderless, poorly armed, and sure that they were fighting the British army as well, the Arabs sued for peace and began to evacuate the city.

In this action and in others, the Arabic-language radio seems to have played an important role in leading the Arabs to decide to leave. News reports of course played up terrorists' activities and gave prominence to stories which made the Zionists seem utterly merciless and fanatical. This backfired in the same way that American propaganda on the Japanese after Pearl Harbor probably would have, had the Japanese landed on the West Coast. Instead of galvanizing action, it increased fear.

At the same time it seems certain that for tactical reasons the Arab leaders did advise evacuation of groups in dangerous positions and also called for a mass evacuation to clear the way for the Arab armies. This is a reasonable assumption in war. However, once begun, in these circumstances, evacuation turned into a flood.

This is not the whole story, however. During this period we also know of several instances of Israeli ejections of Arab populations of towns;[9] and by July, when the war had become general, eviction became common. The military historian of the war, Major O'Ballance, who is generally regarded as fair and informed, had this to say of the operations:

[8] At the time it seemed to make more sense than it does in retrospect. The Arabs identified Britain as the issuer of the Balfour Declaration, the supplier of arms to Zionists in 1929 and in the 1930's. Many members of Irgun and the Haganah had been in the British army, and during the gradual British evacuation there had been a certain amount of cooperation between the British forces and the Haganah. For example, during the last night of British occupation of Jerusalem, British sentries "doubled up" with Haganah guards (see O'Ballance, pp. 95-96).

[9] For example, from the villages of Beit Jiz and Beit Susin in June 1948 (See O'Ballance, p. 108).

Israeli vans with loudspeakers drove through the streets [*sc.*, of Lydda] ordering all the inhabitants to evacuate immediately, and such as were reluctant to leave were forcibly ejected from their homes by the triumphant Israelis whose policy was now openly one of clearing out all the Arab civil population before them . . . From the surrounding villages and hamlets, during the next two or three days, all the inhabitants were uprooted and set off on the road to Ramallah.[10] . . . No longer was there any "reasonable persuasion." Bluntly, the Arab inhabitants were ejected and forced to flee into Arab territory . . . Wherever the Israeli troops advanced into Arab country the Arab population was bull-dozed out in front of them.[11]

Those who have criticized this policy have often overlooked the fact that the war was a desperate, vicious, and bloody affair. The Arab population, after Deir Yasin, could certainly be expected to assist in the fight against the Zionists in every possible way. Tempers were high and incidents were never lacking as provocations for retaliation on both sides. Moreover, while this was a dramatic and brutal process, many had thought throughout the Mandate period that the Arab population would have to move over to make room for Jewish settlers. The moderate Zionists hoped to accomplish this by purchase of land and legal eviction. But it was admitted after the Royal Commission report that forcible transfer of population might be required. In the cold logic of hindsight, it can be seen that once the notion that Palestine was "an empty, derelict land" was exploded and it was realized, as it was already in 1919, that the Arab population would never peacefully accept the imposition of Zionism, war and emigration were inevitable. If Palestine was to absorb a million or more Jewish refugees, something had to give somewhere. Thus, in spite of their humanitarian feelings, moderate Zionists could hardly help admitting the strategic benefits of the Arab exodus.[12]

The position of those Arabs who elected to stay in the new state was not enviable. The Absentee Property Law authorized seizure of all Arab property whose owners were absent from their

[10] p. 147.

[11] p. 172; Kirk, p. 281.

[12] For conflicting views see J. B. Schechtman, *The Arab Refugee Problem* (New York: 1952); and F. A. Sayegh, *The Palestine Refugees* (Washington, D. C.: 1952). These two books contain most of the available information.

homes on November 29, 1947. Even a man who was away on business for a few days thus became an "absentee." Those who were able to escape this category were still liable to confiscation "for vital development, settlement, or security." An additional 5,491 Arabs were driven into Jordan between June 1949 and October 15, 1954. Martial law governed many Arab districts and in some areas it was up to the discretion of army officers even to evict whole villages. Those who won compensation in the courts were paid with tremendously inflated currency at 1950 prices. But even apart from material considerations, the Arab community was in a most difficult psychological position. In the first place, from being a part of the vast majority of the population, it was speedily converted into a suspect minority whose leaders had vanished and whose structure as a community was shattered.[13] In the second place, as long as war between Israel and the Arab states lasts, the Israeli Arab community cannot but be regarded as a potential fifth column within a Jewish state. And in the third place, its very existence in Israel has led Arabs in the surrounding areas to accuse the Arab community of collaboration with the enemy.

The bulk of the Arab population of the former Mandate, about 800,000, did not stay in their homes but fled as best they could to the surrounding Arab-held areas. In the summer of 1950, the estimates made by the UN Agency established to care for them estimated that 896,690 were drawing rations. Thirty-one thousand were in Israel and the rest scattered in camps in Lebanon, Syria, Jordan, and the Gaza strip.

It has been estimated that 120 died each night in the bitter cold of the Gaza strip in December 1948. Few had shelter or blankets, and mass starvation was not an unlikely prospect. Main credit for their preservation is due to private western philanthropic organizations, especially to the International Committee of the Red Cross, the League of Red Cross Societies, and the American Friends Service Committee. On November 19, 1948, the United Nations established the UNRPR (Relief for Palestine Refugees) to assist these private groups and began a study of

[13] See Don Peretz, *Middle East Journal,* VIII (1954), 139 ff.

ways to assist the refugees to resettle or to help support themselves. When the report of this committee, under Gordon Clapp of the TVA, had been made available in December 1949, the UNRWA (the "W" of which stands for Works) was established as an agency which could both keep the refugees alive and take whatever steps might become possible to resettle them.

To date resettlement has not become possible. The Arabs insist on the right of the refugees, under the UN resolution of December 11, 1948, to return to their homes or to receive compensation at their choice. Israel has been unwilling to consider return of the refugees until a general peace settlement is effected, maintaining, with truth, that the refugees would constitute an element in her population hostile to the concept of a Jewish state.[14] In March 1956, Israel notified the United Nations Conciliation Commission for Palestine that it had decided that it would no longer consider paying compensation for refugee property until the Arab states ended their economic boycott. The Conciliation Commission expressed "disappointment and regret" but is still trying to work out plans for compensation.[15] If compensation is difficult, return is impossible. Land has been realloted, houses turned over to immigrants or destroyed to make room for new buildings, and old means of livelihood modified or completely changed.

Meanwhile the refugees have existed in a "deplorable material and moral situation,"[16] scattered in camps around the frontiers of Israel (see map). When the author visited a number of camps in 1950 (and subsequently in 1952 and 1954), he found that except for medical care, which was probably better than that available to most before 1948, the conditions were beyond desperation—desperation is an emotion of one who still actively tries to control his fate. Most of the refugees live in ragged tents, some in caves, and many in public buildings converted into dormitories by burlap drapes. Less than $27 per person per year for medical care, food, shelter, and clothing is the total spent by UNRWA. The monthly individual food ration was valued on the

[14] UN Doc. A/1367.
[15] UN Doc. A/3199.
[16] UN Doc. A/SPC/9, February 11, 1957.

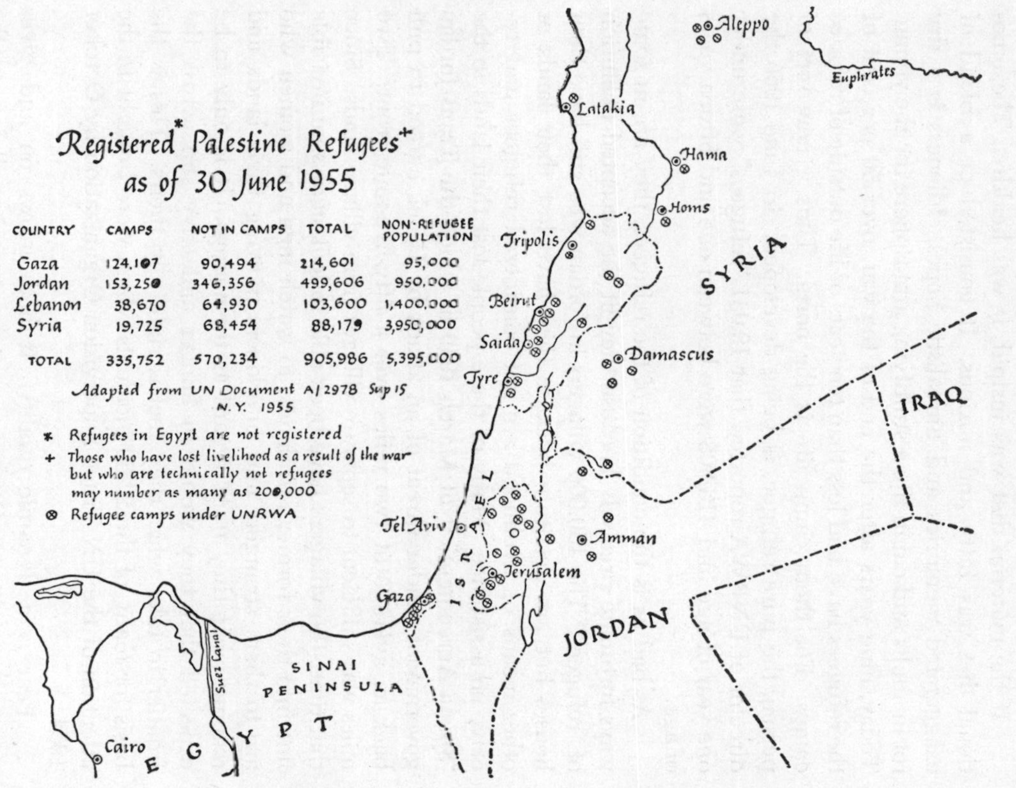

COUNTRY	CAMPS	NOT IN CAMPS	TOTAL	NON-REFUGEE POPULATION
Gaza	124,107	90,494	214,601	95,000
Jordan	153,250	346,356	499,606	950,000
Lebanon	38,670	64,930	103,600	1,400,000
Syria	19,725	68,454	88,179	3,950,000
TOTAL	335,752	570,234	905,986	5,395,000

local market at $1.80 and was estimated to provide a daily intake of 1,600 calories.

If the material diet was insipid, it was healthy. The emotional diet was fatty and noxious. It consisted of a blend of exaggerated memories and unrealistic hopes. Idleness is a dry rot in adults and camp life a stultifying atmosphere for the young. Today, nine years after the end of the war, over 50 per cent of the refugees have had less than ten years of life outside of refugee camps. For them camp life is the norm. Thus a new sort of person, the pure refugee, is being developed. In June 1956 the director of UNRWA reported that 19,031 "refugees" were under one year of age and 413,808 were between one and fifteen years of age.

As bad as is the condition of the refugees, they are in some ways fortunate precisely because they fit the accepted definition of "refugee." The 150,000 villagers in Jordan who still have their houses but are destitute because they have lost their lands or other means of livelihood are not considered refugees and receive no assistance. Many of these people lost their lands in the "Shuna Agreement" [17] of March 1949 in which the Trans-Jordan government, under threat of an attack by Israel, agreed to pull back an average of two miles over a fifty-five-mile front. Two miles was sufficient to separate villages from village lands. Since that time, the villagers have been able to look across an invisible line into their former farmlands, to watch men and women who are to them strangers and interlopers plowing their lands and reaping what they must regard as their crops. It is only to be expected that they would in hunger and envy slip across the frontier to take what they feel is rightfully theirs. This is the basis for many of the 2,960 incidents which were brought to the attention of the UN Truce Supervision Organization by October 1954.

Fear is a dynamic quality. It both grows on and gives growth to violence. One can see it in operation all around the frontier. The first thieving operations were probably relatively innocent, but both fear of being caught and the fury of the re-

[17] Kirk, pp. 298-99.

taliation which Israeli army units imposed on those across the frontier infected the sore. Raids have been forthcoming from both sides and the records of the UN Mixed armistice commission make sorry reading.[18]

The refugees interviewed by this writer—and his impression is confirmed by many observers including the director of UNRWA—are determined to return to their homes and "bitterly oppose anything which has even the semblance of permanent settlement elsewhere." In effect, the Arab refugees today are motivated by a Zionism as strong and compelling as that which motivated Jews. The Arabs today take the same position taken by the earlier Zionists in their refusal of such territories as Kenya, Sinai, and Cyprus as locations for the National Home. If anything, the Arab Zionism, combining as it does the peasant's attachment to a *specific* plot of land, the villager's feelings about a particular village, along with the religious and nationalistic sentiments common to both Jews and Arabs, may even be stronger and more personal than Jewish Zionism. The plight of the Arab refugee today is not less soul destroying than that of the Jewish D.P.s in Europe at the end of the Second World War. If the Arab lacks the impulsion of the specter of Nazism, he feels the attraction of childhood memories in well-known places.

The economic aspects of the refugee question are discussed below in Part IV. Here it only need be mentioned that they are formidable. Not only is the number of refugees large relative to the populations of the "host" countries, but the economies of these countries are weak. Lacking major economic developments, which are restricted for a number of reasons, it is difficult to see how the refugees could be absorbed, even if they were willing, into their economies, with the exception of Iraq. And apart from the cost of carrying out developments to provide them with work,

[18] Besides the UN documents see E. Monroe, "The Arab-Israel Frontier," *International Affairs*, XXIX (1953), 439 ff.; the Jordan Government Ministry of Foreign Affairs, *The Rising Tide of Terror* (Amman: 1952); Nancy Cranshaw, "A Frontier of Fear and Tension," *The Listener*, November 12, 1953; Hutchinson, *op. cit.;* T. R. Little, "The Frontier of Hate," Beirut *Star*, April 2, 4, 5, 1953; and Mizra Khan, "A Study in Frustration," *Midstream*, Spring, 1956.

it is estimated that merely providing them with permanent shelter would cost over $3 billion.

But the major problems are not economic. They are psychological. The refugees are materially and spiritually destitute. Their only remaining possession is their parcel of hope and memory. This, they absolutely will not part with. No one in responsible position has told them they must abandon this as well. This explains why refugees have even burned down camp buildings which seemed designed to be permanent. They feel that any indication of settlement will prejudge their chances of return. The Arab governments have encouraged this stand for various reasons which we must attempt to understand.

The attitude of non-Palestinian Arabs toward the refugee is ambivalent. If the refugee is a pitiful person, he is also the symbol of shame. One need not dilate on the reasons for pity, but the refugee as a reminder of Arab weakness and humiliation has yet to be fully appreciated.

It will be recalled that at the end of the First World War the Arabs were told that they had not yet reached a stage of development in which they could "stand alone." The mandate system was explained as a school in "how to be a nation." Graduation led to membership in the League of Nations. Iraq "graduated" in 1932, Syria was informed in 1936 that she had almost completed the course, and Egypt emerged from the status of a protectorate about the same time. However, in view of Britain's economic and military potential, few of the states felt really independent. Iraq was reoccupied in 1941 and Egypt was under de facto military occupation throughout the war. France did not quit Syria and Lebanon until forced to do so by American and British pressure in 1945. Trans-Jordan, although nominally autonomous in the 1920s, was still dependent upon a British subsidy until this year. The great events of the 1930s and the Second World War were not felt to be vital national issues. Indeed, the first task which confronted the Arab states as they really became states was the problem of Palestine.

All of the governments publicly announced that they were deeply committed to protect their fellows in Palestine and proclaimed Palestine to be essential to their own peace and security. Speeches were made, proclamations issued, encouragement given, and the Arab League even took upon itself the duty of deciding which group or person was a fit representative of the Palestine community. However, not only were the Arab states unable to intervene during the Mandate period, but on May 15, 1948, when they did intervene, it was a half-hearted gesture. The number of Arab troops committed was small, their equipment bad, their leadership inept. The only Arab force which made a good showing was the Arab Legion of Jordan. This exception was almost more humiliating than the lack of success in the other armies for the Arab Legion was under the command of an Englishman, many of its officers were English, and it was paid for and supplied by England.

Lack of success on the ground was compounded by a show of weakness and greed in politics. The figure of King Farouk became a symbol of corruption and degeneracy. King Abdullah was again charged, as he had been in 1936, with making some sort of "deal" with Israel to enhance his own ambitions. Many Arabs still believe that he ordered his army to halt in its advance so that the Israelis could more effectively attack the Egyptians. From a great show of bravado and a certainty of victory, the Arab states were forced to concede a humiliating defeat. They had failed miserably to keep the Arab population in Palestine and indeed were partly responsible for its exodus. Individual shows of bravery and devotion were not lacking, but these were swamped by the overall lack of performance. As the former Palestinian representative to the League of Arab States, Musa Alami, wrote:

> In the face of the enemy the Arabs were not a state, but petty states; groups, not a nation; each fearing and anxiously watching the other and intriguing against it. What concerned them most and guided their policy was not to win the war and save Palestine from the enemy, but what would happen after the struggle, who would be predominant in Palestine, or annex it to themselves, and how they could achieve their own ambitions. Their announced aim was the salvation of Palestine, and they said that afterward its destiny should be left to its people. This was said with the tongue only. In their

hearts all wished it for themselves; and most of them were hurrying to prevent their neighbors from being predominant, even though nothing remained except the offal and bones.[19]

Most Arabs found it hard to disagree, and the refugee is a constant reminder of the humiliating performance. This was a modern replica of one of the most famous of all Arabic poems, the taunt of Basus:

> . . . be not deceived! Protect thyself!
> This people for their clients have no care.
>
> But now such folk I dwell among that when
> The wolf comes, 'tis my sheep he comes to tear.[20]

It is a cardinal element of Arabic culture that failure to protect those one has undertaken to defend incurs public, humiliating shame. Arabs today feel this as much as their ancestors. So it is not surprising that immediately after the war most of the governments were violently shaken. Syria underwent a series of coups d'état; Lebanon had its spate of disorders and eventually its coup. In 1951 King Abdullah was murdered. In 1952 King Farouk was exiled by a group of veterans of the war.

These leaders were closely identified with the West. They had been identified with mandate governments and in some cases owed their positions to western support. Perhaps even more significant than their personal demise, however, was the fact that western government and political ideals were also questioned. Parliaments and other trappings of western democracy were seen to have failed to produce democracy in the East. Arabs came increasingly to feel that they had only facilitated corruption and led to weakness. The "secret" of the West had not been discovered.

But these things alone were judged not totally responsible for the "disaster" of Palestine. Some Arabs tried to take refuge

[19] Condensed from 'Ibrat Falastin (Beirut: 1949), in the *Middle East Journal,* III (1949), 373 ff.; the section quoted is on page 385 under the heading, "the main causes."

[20] This translation is taken from R. A. Nicholson, *Literary History of the Arabs* (Cambridge: 1953), p. 57.

in blaming the Palestinians for their own fate. The Syrian Mohammed Kurd Ali may be taken as typical:

> The weak soft-minded people in Palestine were jubilant when the Jews paid them such high prices for their land. . . . Many of those who bartered the heritage of their fathers deceived themselves with the thought that they had made unprecedented profit.[21]

But the vast majority of the Arabs blamed the West entirely for their defeat. As they saw it, Israel was the daughter of the West; Britain, the source of the Balfour Declaration and the power which undertook to carry out the Mandate. Gifts of money from the West had made possible the influx of Zionists. Arms had been given or purchased in the West. Israel itself was seen as the "last stage of Western imperialism—the creation of a Western nation in the East." Arab inability to stop this process had itself been a result of trying to become western. It is significant that the Egyptian prime minister who was known as a westernizer was murdered by the Muslim Brotherhood after the full extent of the military fiasco became known.

But even after all allowances had been made—to Britain, to America, to Russia, and to the refugees—the residue was still too great a load of humiliation. It had somehow to be averted or postponed. "The war is not over . . . there will be a second round," became the formula to preserve national honor. If retaliation was incumbent but impossible, talk could perhaps keep one from admitting the shame which traditionally was incurred by the folk which failed to preserve its honor by retaliating. All Arabs were agreed that Zionism and the creation of Israel constituted aggression and that they were committed to take vengeance. These are cultural responses which are perhaps even deeper than Islam in Arabic culture and which are even strengthened by Islam. It is not surprising that publications in this period lapse into the key words of classical Arabic poetry to express their deep emotional positions. Two publications began to appear under the name *al-Tha'r* (vengeance). No politician, even if he wanted peace and an end to the war, could

[21] *Memoires* (English translation, Washington: 1954), p. 221.

fail to pay at least lip service to the conduct required by Arabic culture. Those who did, and many Arabs felt that Abdullah was one, paid a heavy price.

If the war was not over, the refugees had to be kept mobile. If they ever were allowed to settle, then the problem was settled with them. A feeling that the West was never concerned with morality led many responsible Arabs to remark that they were "never going to allow Palestine to become a fait accompli or a chose jugée." They believed—and still believe—that the West would only be concerned with the rights and wrongs if the problem was real, present, and dangerous.

This it certainly is today.

Part IV. THE ECONOMIC FRAMEWORK OF THE PALESTINE PROBLEM

by Edmund Asfour

1. INTRODUCTION

In a review of this kind, where historical perspective tends to dwarf the events of the recent past, it may seem out of place to deal at any length with technical economic aspects of the recent history of Palestine. (This may seem particularly so if such aspects happen to require the use of statistics—a subject as confusing as it is dull to the layman—for the presentation of a fair economic statement.) Nevertheless it is unfortunately the case that economic reviews and appraisals related to Palestine have always acquired an exaggerated importance if only because they were supposed, whether rightly or wrongly, to hold some justification for more primary political aims. An analytical discussion of the subject is necessary at least to clarify this tangle by isolating the purely economic developments in Palestine from the more complex historical and political aspects of the problem which are dealt with elsewhere in this book.

This task is necessary mainly for two reasons. In the first place economic literature on Palestine has been written almost wholly either by British government officials or by Jewish writers who admittedly sympathized with Zionist political aims. The latter group, which is by far the larger of the two, seems particularly to imply that economic progress and material welfare, which are so welcome in themselves, also deserve moral and political support. Such an attitude, usually accepted with little question, if not whole-heartedly adopted in the western world, has been and is still easily capable of bringing an Arab to a boiling point of disagreement or even revulsion. This is not the place to discuss varying moral attitudes toward material progress[1] but we believe this to be a key point to the understanding of the strong feelings—and blind spots—which have been associated with economic discussions of Palestine. A review of the purely economic developments, as distinguished from

[1] On this question see W. E. Hocking, *The Spirit of World Politics* (New York: 1932), esp. pp. 5-6.

the political and moral, is thus useful in that it clarifies the issues by dealing with their simpler elements.[2]

In the second place, a review of the economic developments should shed some light on the question whether the economic impact of Jewish settlement on the indigenous Arab population of Palestine helped to smooth out existing sources of friction between the two communities, or alternatively to accentuate such elements of conflict. Since the settlement of Zionist immigrants in Palestine between the two world wars was as much of an economic venture as it was a political movement of population, Jewish settlers had to earn a living in their new location with the help of the capital they brought with them and the financial assistance made available to them from abroad. They built up an autonomous economy which in many respects had to be planned or directed. The manner in which that impressive task was achieved is an interesting story in itself. However, it is also important, from the point of view of understanding the development of what we have called the tragedy, to show how the construction of that economic edifice affected the life of the Arab population.

Nor is such a task a mere exercise in the study of economic history. For we can already see in the economic relations between the Jewish immigrants and the Arabs of Palestine before 1948 a replica, on a smaller scale, of the present economic relations (or their absence) between Israel and its Arab neighbors. Arab suspicions of the political aims of Zionism now, as before 1948, are partly based on the economics of Zionist settlement in Palestine and later of the consolidation of the Israeli economy. For both Zionist pioneer and Israeli citizen,

[2] The author of this section of the book, who is a western-trained Arab, is keenly aware of the difficulty of dealing with this problem. While attempting to present as fair and as technical a picture as possible he has been obliged, consciously, to emphasize some of its aspects which may appear to represent an Arab point of view, partly because the numerous English writings on the subject are almost completely devoid of reference to such a viewpoint. Arab writers contributed toward the production of only one work published in English and dealing comprehensively with the economy of Palestine, viz., S. B. Himadeh (ed.), *Economic Organization of Palestine,* (Beirut: 1938). The list of nine authors of that book includes five Arab, two British, and two Jewish writers.

in building up their economy, have shown vigor and zeal that are not motivated by material profit alone. Both have been heavily dependent on financial support from abroad. Both have given priority to non-economic aims, particularly the absorption of the largest number of Jewish immigrants. These same facts which are the pride of Zionists within and outside Palestine were and still are the source of the deepest suspicion to the Arabs. For, to the Arabs, an economy which is so dependent on foreign support spreads in its power far beyond its geographical boundaries; zeal to absorb more immigrants in a densely populated country, with only secondary reference to economic feasibility, means in their eyes an inherently unstable economy within which pressures to expand could easily prevail. Now, as in the past, the real or imagined clash of economic interests aggravates the more serious political conflict.

2. THE MANDATE PERIOD

Toward the end of the First World War, in 1917-18, when the British army invaded Palestine under General Allenby it entered a poor country inhabited by about 750,000 people, most of whom were Arab farmers who earned a simple living by tilling the land. There were meager signs of public administration or of essential public utilities. The whole country, an area slightly larger than the State of Massachusetts, had less than 300 miles of all-weather road and about half that length in railway tracks. It had no modern harbor on its long coastline and no significant irrigation or electric system. Economically it was a part of greater Syria, of which it had also been for centuries an administrative part under Turkish-Ottoman rule. It shared with the rest of Syria the same type of simple agriculture and traditional handicrafts. In general, it was a hinterland for Beirut and Damascus in the north. In addition, however, its unique religious position also attracted each year a small number of pilgrims who visited the Holy Places in Jerusalem, Bethlehem, Nazareth, and Tiberias.

By the end of 1947, that is to say thirty years later, the population of the country had multiplied two and half times, reaching 2,000,000. The area of cultivated land increased by about one third. Large tracts of land were irrigated and planted with oranges and other fruits. Towns and villages grew into populated cities served by most of the modern amenities of transport, electric power, and other municipal utilities. All-weather roads multiplied six times to about 1,700 miles, and railway tracts were roughly quadrupled in length. A modern port, one of the largest in the Mediterranean, was built at Haifa to handle the foreign trade of Palestine and its neighboring country Trans-Jordan. A sizeable manufacturing industry flourished; and an oil refinery was constructed, also at Haifa, which used part of the crude oil that moved by pipeline from Iraq. The standard of living, education, and health improved appreciably, particularly in urban centers.

The building up of Palestine over those thirty years was not the result of the efforts of one particular group alone within the country, whether Jewish, Arab, or British. All three parties did in fact contribute, each in its own fashion and within the limits of the resources available to it, toward achieving the final result. The British army and Mandatory government were responsible for developing the transport system, the port of Haifa, and many of the public services and utilities; a British concessionary company built the oil refinery. The Arab population directed its main efforts toward the development of agriculture (including citriculture) and to construction, and to a lesser degree toward creating a manufacturing industry. The Jewish and Zionist immigrants established a large number of agricultural settlements and shared equally with the Arabs in the development of citrus growing, but their main employment was outside agriculture. They were largely responsible for the development of a manufacturing industry in the country and for maintaining a relatively high standard of professional and commercial services.

There can be little doubt that the unique nature of Zionist immigration into Palestine and settlement there had a stimulating effect on the economy as a whole. For Zionist settlement was largely self-financed and it received the help of supporters from abroad. The associated inflow of foreign exchange into the country in the interwar period, when most of the other countries of the world were often suffering from restrictive international trade policies or from internal depressions, has certainly helped to maintain the rate of growth of the economy. However, the growth of the economy of Palestine and the pattern it followed after the First World War was due to more than one cause. To draw as simple and as broad a picture as possible, this growth can be said to have been stimulated by four interrelated but clearly distinguishable factors. The first is the establishment of a public administration which, by the standards of the defunct Ottoman Empire was incomparably more efficient. By introducing relative stability into the country and by creating the essential public services and utilities, the Mandatory government created a framework within which economic activity could flourish. Had the British administration not been there it would have been doubtful, to say the least, if the Zionist immigrants could have nurtured their economic system in its infancy. The second element is the growth of the Arab population and the fast development of its social, political, and economic consciousness. Although these may have been accelerated by the peculiar developments within Palestine, they were certainly paralleled and shared in varying degree by the rest of the Arab peoples of the Middle East. The third factor is the settlement of Jewish immigrants in Palestine largely in accordance with a Zionist economic and political program and with the support of capital and skills acquired abroad. The fourth major stimulus, and one which is easily comparable in its impact on the economy to the other three, is the Second World War and particularly what it involved in the way of large military expenditures and enforced trade protection.

Of course, in drawing such a rough and simplified picture, one should hasten to emphasize the interdependence of several of those major stimuli. Thus it is not difficult to show that the development of the Arab economy in Palestine was influenced directly by the policy of the British Mandatory administration and by its contact with the growing economy of the Jewish sector. Nor does it require much study to deduce that both the Jewish and the Arab sectors were strongly stimulated during and after the war by the large foreign-exchange expenditures of the British forces in Palestine. We shall go further into these interrelations at a later stage. At this point it is worth noting that it would be much too crude a simplification to deal with the economy of Palestine in terms of any one of the factors referred to. To deal with economic developments in Palestine as if they followed from the activity of one group alone, whether Jewish, British, or Arab would produce a picture which is as unrealistic as it is distorted.

3. THE LAND AND ITS PEOPLE

The emotional attitude of Zionists toward the notion of an independent Jewish state in Palestine tended often to hide from their view some economic realities of the country or to gloss over some others. This is true partially because the picture that was drawn of the economic potential of the country had always to adjust itself to the hopes and ideals of the many financial supporters of Zionism abroad. Indeed this was necessitated as much by the dynamic nature of the movement itself as it was by more down-to-earth needs and requirements of funds for its support. So we find that the outline of the economic picture of Palestine which was presented in the western world by Zionist supporters was of a country which is potentially very rich, a "land of milk and honey" but which in actuality had been neglected for many generations by its backward population, the few roaming bedouin shepherds and the suppressed tenants of feudal lords. Neglect, inefficiency, and feudalism were said have reduced the country to desolation. In its pursuit, Zionism was therefore pictured as pouring funds and effort, not only to reclaim the wasted land, but in fact to make a good investment and even to help to improve the lot of the hapless and exploited Arab inhabitants of Palestine.

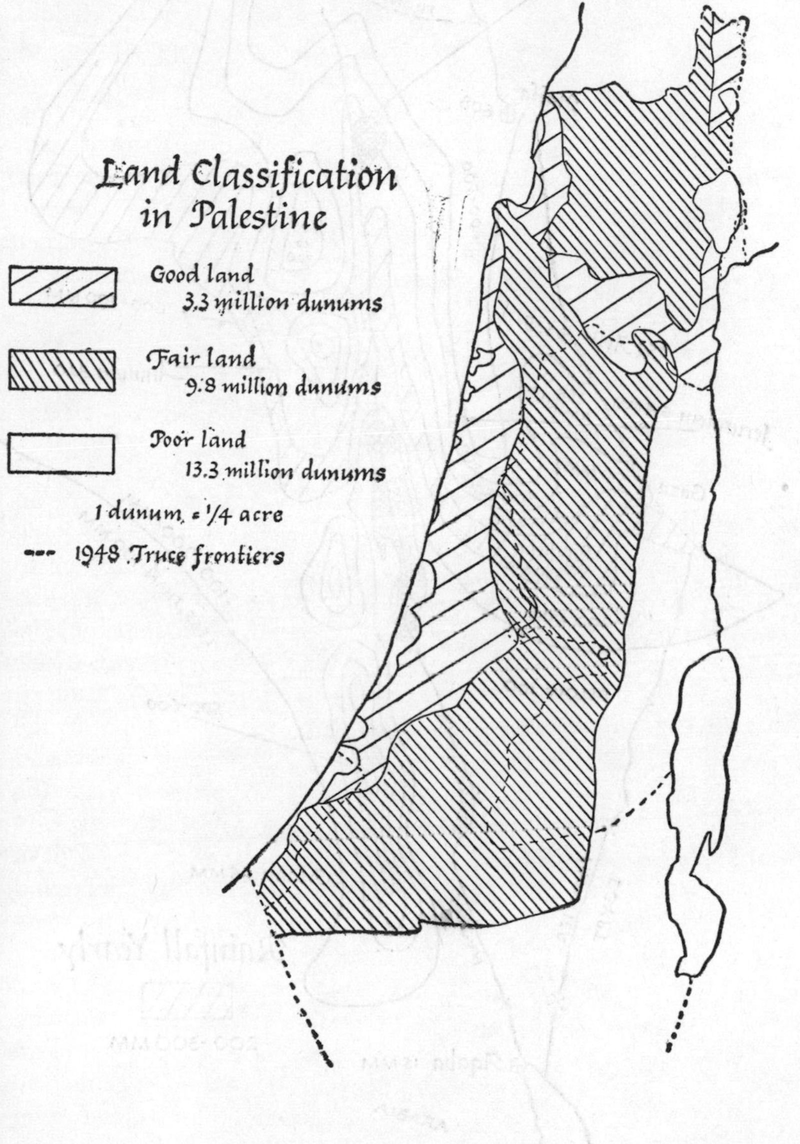
Land Classification
in Palestine
Good land
3.3 million dunums
Fair land
9.8 million dunums
Poor land
13.3 million dunums
1 dunum = 1/4 acre
1948 Truce frontiers

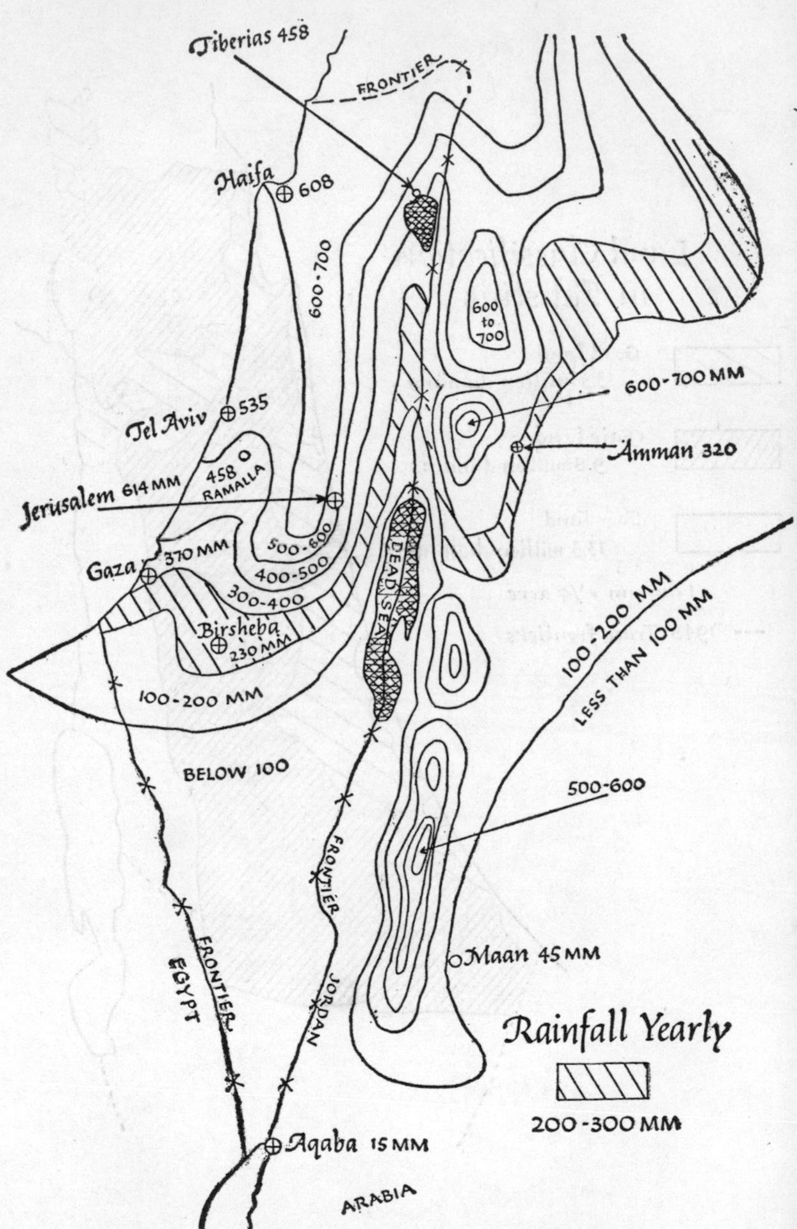

Tiberias 458
FRONTIER
Haifa
608
600-700
600 to 700
600-700 MM
Tel Aviv
535
Amman 320
458
RAMALLA
Jerusalem 614 MM
500-600
Gaza
370 MM
400-500
300-400
DEAD SEA
Birsheba
230 MM
100-200 MM
100-200 MM
LESS THAN 100 MM
BELOW 100
500-600
FRONTIER
FRONTIER
EGYPT
JORDAN
Maan 45 MM
Rainfall Yearly
200-300 MM
Aqaba 15 MM
ARABIA

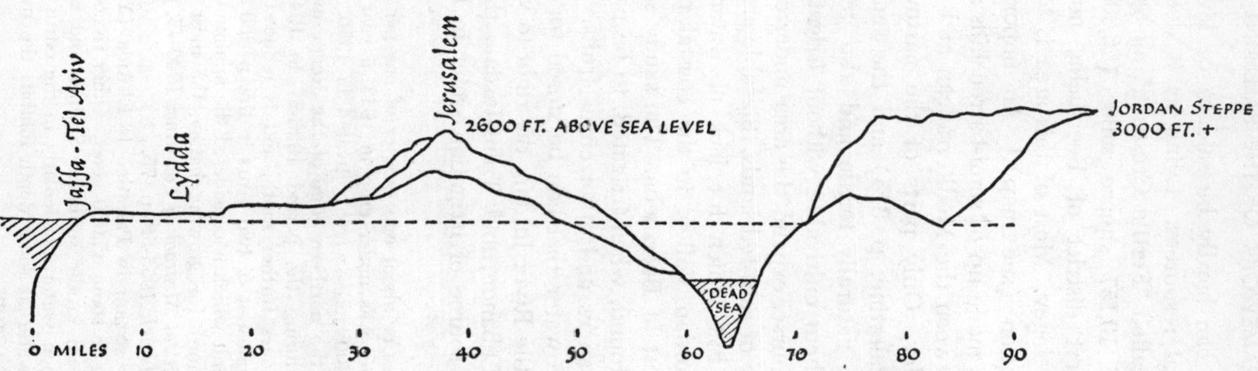

Source p16 J. L. Hurlbut: A Bible Atlas; N.Y. 1910/1947

Section of Palestine from West to East

Palestine, however, can hardly be said to be lavishly endowed with rich natural resources. Lying as it does at the southern tip of the so-called "Fertile Crescent," almost half of its small land area of 10,157 square miles (26,305 square kilometers) is the desert district of Beersheba, now better known as al Naqab or Negev. Most of this area is too dry to cultivate without irrigation (see map).[1] An important part of the remaining area is made up of semi-barren hills spreading from north to south between the Mediterranean and the great rift of the Jordan Valley. Only parts of the narrow coastal plain (see section of Palestine, p. 315) and the small inland plains of the north are naturally fertile and also get enough rain water to render them cultivable without irrigation.

Irrigation can, of course, expand the area under cultivation or raise the productivity of rain-fed lands. Sizeable areas which are potentially fertile, but which for lack of water are uncultivated, lie in the Jordan Valley, in the coastal plain, and south, in the large desert of Beersheba. The sandy soil of the coastal plain has been found, when irrigated, to be particularly suitable for growing oranges and other citrus fruits. However, the volume of available water that can be stored for irrigation is limited. Apart from the River Jordan, the right to which was also shared by Syria, Lebanon, and Trans-Jordan, there is no sizeable but unutilized source of irrigation water in Palestine.[2]

[1] Less than 10,000 acres or about one quarter of one per cent of the area of Beersheba subdistrict was under crop in 1943, a year of average rainfall, and less than 20,000 acres were cultivated in 1956. Rainfall in the town of Beersheba at the northern edge of the Negev averaged 220 millimeters (8.7 inches) during the period 1926-27 to 1943-44. Rain becomes scarcer as one moves further south, and is reduced to nothing near the Sinai border. In one out of two years in this period rainfall was below the 200-millimeter limit which is considered the minimum (assuming favorable distribution in time) for growing barley, the most resistant of the winter crops. See *Statistical Abstract of Palestine, 1940-45*, pp. 10, 224; and *Statistical Abstract of Israel, 1955-56*, p. 75.

[2] The other significant stream in Palestine is El-Auja (Yarkon), the waters of which could irrigate some 35,000 acres. Other rivers are mostly seasonal torrents that dry up in the summer. Springs and wells are an important source of irrigation water, particularly in the citrus grove area, but the cost of pumping water at some depth inhibits the unlimited use of this method for irrigating crops.

The Jordan itself has an annual flow of about 3 per cent of the Tigris River in Iraq or 1 per cent of that of the Nile in Egypt. According to the latest available studies and assuming half the Jordan water is used in Palestine there would be enough water from all sources to irrigate less than 100,000 hectares (250,000 acres) or about 16% of total area cultivated in 1945. Such an estimate of technically feasible utilization does not, of course, take account of the economic aspects of such utilization—i.e., the cost of storing and carrying the water to the land in relation to the benefits accruing from such utilization.

About the historical evidence of abundance in the Negev and its future potential, R. Nathan, O. Gass, and D. Creamer[3] have this to say:

> Enthusiasm and archaeological error have attributed to the Negeb a history of abundant population which modern hydrological engineering may give it in the future but which it has never supported. Judicious scholars such as W. F. Albright have concluded that the famed cities of the Negeb flourished at different times during a period of nearly 1,000 years. There were never more than one or two large towns at the same time, and these towns lived partly from the caravan trade. The desert was beaten back by ceaseless effort . . . In its most flourishing period, the Negeb may have supported a settled population of several tens of thousands of people.

Apart from land and water the main known natural resources of Palestine are the chemical salts of the Dead Sea, the dense water of which has practically inexhaustible amounts of common salt and magnesium chloride, as well as large quantities of potassium chloride and magnesium bromide.[4] Phosphate rock is also found in exploitable quantities in southern Palestine. And recently crude petroleum has been produced in small quantities in the Beersheba Desert near Gaza.[5] None

[3] *Palestine: Problem and Promise* (Washington, D. C.: 1946), pp. 21-22.

[4] See S. B. Himadeh (ed.), *Economic Organization of Palestine* (Beirut: 1938), pp. 57 ff. The salt content of the Dead Sea water is put at eight times that of average sea water. Exports of potash reached a maximum of 103,000 tons in 1943, valued at $3 million.

[5] In 1956, Israel mined 117,000 tons of phosphate rock valued at $0.5 million. Phosphate deposits are of low concentration (30 to 55% tricalcium phosphate) compared with those in neighboring Jordan (63-72%) (See

of these minerals, however, has so far contributed more than a very small share of national income whether of Palestine or of Israel. Large-scale production is hampered by the high transport cost involved in marketing the products. This is particularly true of the phosphates, which are of relatively poor quality and which have to compete with sources of supply such as Morocco and Jordan that also have cheaper labor. In the case of potash, while quantities are unlimited and production costs are relatively low, the world demand for the product does not justify large-scale production.[6]

Palestine, however, could have access to cheap sources of power within its boundaries and from neighboring countries. Hydroelectric power was in fact produced from the water of the Jordan during the period of the Mandate by a British concessionary, the Palestine Electric Corporation, but the power capacity was too small and production too costly to encourage wide use in industry. The Jordan River is capable of generating much greater electric power at cheaper cost for the countries that hold rights to it. More grandiose but so far speculative projects have been suggested to generate power by channeling the water of the Mediterranean into the Dead Sea, the lowest point below sea level in the world, part of the generated power being used to pump the water over the high point along its route. Such projects, however, have not gone beyond the general stage of a desk study and no serious and up-to-date attempt has been made to determine the cost and benefits of the scheme.

The population of Palestine at the end of the First World War was predominantly agricultural and overwhelmingly Arab. Of a population of 752,000 enumerated in the 1922 census, 84,000 were Jews and 660,000 Arabs. The latter included 71,000 Christian Arabs who were otherwise indistinguishable

---

Nathan, Gass, and Creamer, p. 114). Production of crude oil reached 30,000 tons worth $0.5 millions in 1956 (*Petroleum Press Service* February, 1957).

[6] It has been estimated that the Dead Sea has enough potash and bromine to supply the world for 2,000 years at the current rate of demand. Germany, the main world producer, has potash resources estimated at five times those of the Dead Sea but one-seventh the bromine deposits (Nathan, Gass, and Creamer, pp. 114, 495-505).

from the Muslims. At that early date about two thirds of the population lived in rural areas. Twenty-four years later—i.e., by the end of the Second World War—the population had multiplied by more than two and a half times to almost 2 million persons, or by an average of 5 per cent each year. Of the total number about half lived in rural areas, the larger part of the Jewish and Christian populations living in towns. This spectacular growth of population was due to two major factors: namely, Jewish immigration from abroad, and a high rate of natural increase of the whole population, particularly of the Muslim Arabs. The relative importance of the various factors can be seen in Table 1.

Table 1[7]

POPULATION GROWTH 1922-46
(Number in thousands)

	Arabs			*Jews*			*Total**	
	No.	%	% of Total	No.	%	% of Total	No.	%
1922 Population	660	52	88	84	12	11	752	38
Net Immigration 1922-46	33	3	7	431†	64	89	484	24
Natural Increase 1922-46	576	45	77	163	24	22	746	38
1946 Population	1,269	100	64	678	100	34	1,982	100

* Including 35,000 "others."
† Including 70,000 unauthorized immigrants.

The contention that is often made that the high rate of natural increase, particularly among the Arab population, was due to improved economic conditions, while true, is still an oversimplification. The rate of birth has a general tendency to fall rather than rise as the standard of living rises. This is borne out in Palestine as in other countries. Official statistics show that, except for a slight rise in the twenties—i.e., before any considerable economic change took place—the birth rate of all groups followed a continuous downward trend. The high birth rate of the Muslim population, said to have been

[7] Sources: Government of Palestine, *A Survey of Palestine* (Jerusalem: 1946), p. 142; and *Supplement,* pp. 10, 11, 17.

the highest in the world, was also paralleled by a high death rate, particularly among the infant group. The fast natural growth of population was in fact due to a considerable fall in the death rate of all groups in the country,[8] a fall which was most conspicuous among babies. There is little doubt that this was largely due to the improved health service as well as to the general improvement in living standards and knowledge of hygiene among the Arabs, particularly during the war period. Health service to the largely Muslim rural population was mainly supplied by the British administration, while the large number of private doctors (mainly Jewish but also Arab) helped to reduce mortality rates in towns to one of the lowest in the world, particularly among the Jewish population.[9]

As a result of the high rate of natural increase, and also because of the age composition of the Jewish immigrants who came to Palestine, the country had a rather young population. About 60 per cent of the Arab population in 1944 was below the age of 25. The Jewish population, on the other hand, included an unusually large proportion of young people of working age (between 25 and 49), who formed 43 per cent of the total as compared with the same group which formed only 25 per cent for the Arab population.[10]

[8] Birth and death rates, and the rate of increase, of the various religious groups of population changed as follows between 1922 and 1942 (per cent per annum):*

		1922-25	*1926-30*	*1931-35*	*1936-40*	*1941-42*†
Muslims:	Births	5.0	5.3	5.0	4.9	4.7
	Deaths	2.7	2.8	2.5	2.1	1.9
	Increase	2.3	2.5	2.5	2.8	2.8
Christians:	Births	3.6	3.9	3.6	3.3	2.8
	Deaths	1.6	1.8	1.5	1.2	1.2
	Increase	2.0	2.1	2.1	2.1	1.6
Jews:	Births	3.4	3.4	3.0	2.6	2.2
	Deaths	1.4	1.2	.9	.8	.8
	Increase	2.0	2.3	2.1	1.8	1.4

* Source: *Statistical Abstract of Palestine, 1944-45.*

† Figures for 1943-46 are not reliable. To avoid ration cuts during the war many deaths, mainly in rural areas, were not reported (see *Supplement*, p. 11).

[9] See Cmd 3686, p. 29.

[10] This was to an important degree the result of the selection policy

The employment of the various groups of the population is not known for the earlier years. Throughout the period of the Mandate the larger part of the Arab population, roughly two thirds, lived in rural areas and about half earned their living from the land. Only one quarter of the Jewish population, on the other hand, lived in rural areas and only one tenth worked on the land. The distribution of the country's population among various occupations and output per person in these occupations in 1945 is indicated in the following table:

Table 2[11]

ESTIMATED NUMBER ENGAGED IN EACH BRANCH OF PRODUCTION AND AVERAGE OUTPUT PER HEAD IN THE TWO COMMUNITIES IN 1945

	JEWS			*ARABS & OTHERS**		
	No. Engaged '000	*%*	*Output per Person (£ P)*	*No. Engaged '000*	*%*	*Output per Person (£ P)*
Agriculture, livestock, fisheries, and forests	24	10	400	152	50	167
Industry and handicrafts	66	27	452	19	6	352
Housing						
Building and construction	9	4	400	20	7	165
War Department, civilian employment	5	2	220	20	7	125
Palestine Troops	17	7	—	3	1	—
Transport and communications	12	5	425	14	5	228
Commerce and finance, hotels, restaurants, and cafés	43	17	379	31	10	284
Government and local authorities	12	5	267	32	11	165
Other	57	23	140	12	4	275
Total or average	245	100	333	303	100	205

* "Arabs and others" includes some non-Arab and mainly British employees of the government, oil refinery, etc.

The occupational and income distribution in 1945, the last year

followed by the Zionist Organization before the war, a policy which paid dividends in the fighting that occurred during and after the war.

[11] Source: P. J. Loftus, *The National Income of Palestine, 1945* (Jerusalem: 1948). Slight discrepancies in totals are due to rounding.

under the Mandate for which figures are available, were naturally affected by the conditions of the war. Government and army employment was unusually large and resulted in a diversion of some Jewish workers from the land. The shortage of both agricultural products and manufactured goods stimulated maximum production—except in the case of Palestine's major export crop, citrus, which could not be marketed because of shortage of shipping space. With this main exception, income was inflated, both in the agricultural and the manufacturing sectors, far beyond the general rise in prices during the war. Thus, while wholesale prices rose over three times and the cost of living over two and a half times in 1945 as compared with prewar, the value of output per person in agriculture rose eight times for both Jews and Arabs. Demand for manufactures more than doubled the employment of Jews in industry. These changes from the prewar period can be clearly seen from a comparison of the previous table with the following:

Table 3[12]

ESTIMATED NUMBER ENGAGED IN EACH BRANCH OF PRODUCTION AND AVERAGE OUTPUT PER HEAD IN THE TWO COMMUNITIES IN 1936

	JEWS			*ARABS & OTHERS*		
	No. Engaged '000's	%	*Output Per Person* (£ P)	*No. Engaged* '000's	%	*Output Per Person* (£ P)
Agriculture	32	19	52	162	62	24
Manufactures and handicrafts	30	17	130	22	8	90
Construction	14	8	111	8	3	39
Commerce and transport	32	19	141	32	12	107
Others	63	37	97	37	14	133
Total or average	171	100	104	261	100	56

It can be seen by comparing the two tables that the gap in output per person between Jews and Arabs was narrowed down from about one half in 1936 to about one third in 1945. This

[12] Source: Nathan, Gass, Creamer, p. 150; adapted from Ludwig Gruenbaum, *National Income and Outlay in Palestine, 1936* (Jerusalem: 1941). Slight discrepancies in totals are due to rounding.

is to a large extent due to higher prices for agricultural products, but also to the investment of larger savings in industry, construction, and other activities. It is a notable fact that while the gap in *output* per occupied person between the two communities was not very large, the difference in *income* per head was indeed great, the average income per head of the Jewish population being more than two and a half times that of the Arab, in both 1936 and 1945. While the difference in output reflects the greater use of capital and the greater efficiency of Jewish labor in some sectors, the difference in income is due in the main to the abnormal age structure, as we have noted earlier, of both Jewish and Arab populations. For Jewish labor had few dependents, one worker supporting roughly one other person, while the preponderance of young dependents among the Arabs resulted in one Arab worker's supporting three others on the average. In one sense, it could thus be said that the Arabs preferred large families to a higher material standard of living, while the requirements of pioneering Jewish immigrants restricted the number of unproductive members. This can be seen in the following table compiled from the previous two:

Table 4

POPULATION, OUTPUT, AND INCOME OF JEWS AND ARABS IN 1936 AND 1945

	1936		*1945*	
	Jews	*Arabs & Others*	*Jews*	*Arabs & Others*
Population ('000)	384	916	579	1,256
Working population ('000)	171	261	245	303
Average dependents per worker	1.24	2.51	1.36	3.15
Total output (£P million)	17.8	14.5	81.5	62.1
Output per worker (£P)	104	56	333	205
Income per head (£P current prices)	44	16	141	50
Income per head (£P 1936 prices)*			41	15
(£P 1936 prices)†			54	19

* Adjusted by the wholesale price index: 1936 = 100; 1945 = 344.

† Adjusted by the cost of living index: 1945 = 260 approximately. This index included a large number of food items with controlled or subsidized prices.

4. IMMIGRATION AND LAND

The fundamental conflict between the aims of the Zionist movement and those of the Arab population in Palestine centered on two basic questions, namely immigration and land. To create a "National Home" or state in Palestine the Zionist aim was to bring into the country as many Jewish immigrants as possible and in the shortest possible time. The Arabs, on the other hand, saw in every wave of immigrants a further threat to their majority and a growing obstacle to the future realization of their independence and self-rule. Similarly while Zionists aimed at consolidating their position and creating the basis for economic self-support by acquiring as much land as their financial means would allow, the Arabs saw in that same action a loss of the means of support for their growing number and an actual loss of territory under their control. Each party in its own way pressured the British Mandatory government to support its particular view. Soon enough the inherent contradiction in the two positions could not be disguised and was in fact brought out clearly following the serious disturbances of 1929 in the report of the Commission of Inquiry under Sir Walter Shaw, which attributed the outbreak to "the Arab feeling of animosity and hostility toward the Jews consequent upon the disappointment of their political and national aspirations and fear for their economic future." [1]

The main significance of the question of immigration in relation to Palestine was naturally political, since it affected the distribution and balance of power of the various groups within the country. However, its economic importance is by no means negligible. For many of the Jewish immigrants into Palestine brought with them some capital and/or skill which they utilized to support themselves in their new life.[2] Owing

[1] Cmd 3530, March 1930, quoted in Government of Palestine, *A Survey of Palestine,* (Jerusalem: 1946), p. 24.

[2] Immigration regulations required some categories of immigrants who

to the preponderance of middlemen and professional people among the newcomers, Jewish immigration resulted in the multiplication of services in urban centers. Naturally the consequent change in the pattern of supply of services affected the price of such services. It became difficult for many Jewish doctors who came in the thirties, for example, to make a reasonable living.[3] Indirectly, and until the economic rift was complete between the Jewish and Arab economies, this situation discouraged the fast growth among the Arab population of several types of professions that were abundant, as well as of specialized services that the Jews were better trained to supply.[4]

The inflow of skills which were unknown or in short supply into the country could not but affect the rest of the economy, whether by direct exchange or by simple example. However, the important effects that such exchange or example may have had on the Arab economy was largely limited, geographically, to cities and towns alone, where contact between the two groups was possible. But even there its effects were restricted as a result of the policies of exclusiveness and boycott that characterized economic relations between the two groups. Indirectly the appearance of new methods and products stimulated competition among the Arab entrepreneurs, although the separateness of the two markets did not allow this factor to come into full play.

As to agriculture, the traditional economic pursuit of Palestine's Arab population and the backbone of the economy as a whole, the lack of contact and exchange as between its Jewish and Arab sectors was almost complete and constant. Jewish agriculture was organized in settlements that were exclusively Jewish and which were surrounded by Jewish-held land that had no contact with Arab villages. Modern methods of agriculture used by the settlement farmers were seldom

---

had no assured job waiting for them in Palestine to bring in a minimum of £P. 500-1,000 ($2,000-4,000).

[3] In 1940 there was in Palestine 1 doctor to 676 people, compared with 1 to 797 in the United States (R. Nathan, O. Gass, D. Creamer, *Palestine: Problem and Promise* [Washington, D. C.: 1946], p. 139).

[4] See Cmd 3686, p. 29.

observed directly by Arab farmers. In addition, the small capital available to Arab farmers made it practically impossible for them to use such capital-intensive methods as were used in settlements even if they wished. Only in the intensively cultivated orange and fruit groves in the coastal plain, where Arab landowners could obtain capital, did modern methods of irrigation and fertilizing become common.

The land question and that of immigration had many ramifications that extended far beyond the economic field. For in the harsh and often one-sided propaganda war there was a tendency either to minimize the genuine opposition of the Arab population of Palestine to the political aims of the Zionist movement, or else to attribute it to the activities of a small self-interested group of large landowners.[5] While there were several landowners among the Arab population who possessed relatively large estates, the pattern of land ownership could hardly be described as semi-feudal and was in fact characterized by a predominance of small and fragmented land holdings. A wide survey of 322 villages, covering over half the cultivated area and with a population of 242,000 people, was undertaken in 1936 and revealed that "the smallest size of holdings is the most frequent and that the number of holdings decreases steadily as the size of holding increases. The result is that when a large-size holding is reached the number of such holdings in exceedingly small."[6] Only 27 per cent of the area was in holdings of more than 1,000 dunums (250 acres), and

[5] For example, Harold J. Laski, in J. B. Hobman (ed.), *Palestine's Economic Future* (London: 1946), p. 42, writes: ". . . the implication of a 'Jewish National Home' in Palestine is a thorough-going reorganization of the internal relations of a semi-feudal Arab society in which the privileges of a small group of rich *effendi* are deeply involved . . . This is the real source of resistance to large scale Jewish immigration . . . The Jew brings with him Western ideas, often Western socialist ideas, which cut right across a traditional historical pattern the beneficiaries of which seek at any cost to defend their claims. They therefore mobilize both religious fanaticism and nationalist passion to arrest changes in which they see the threat to their privilege and seek to use the dislike of the masses for change before they see that the change is to their advantage."

[6] P. J. Loftus, *National Income of Palestine, 1944* (Jerusalem: 1946), p. 42.

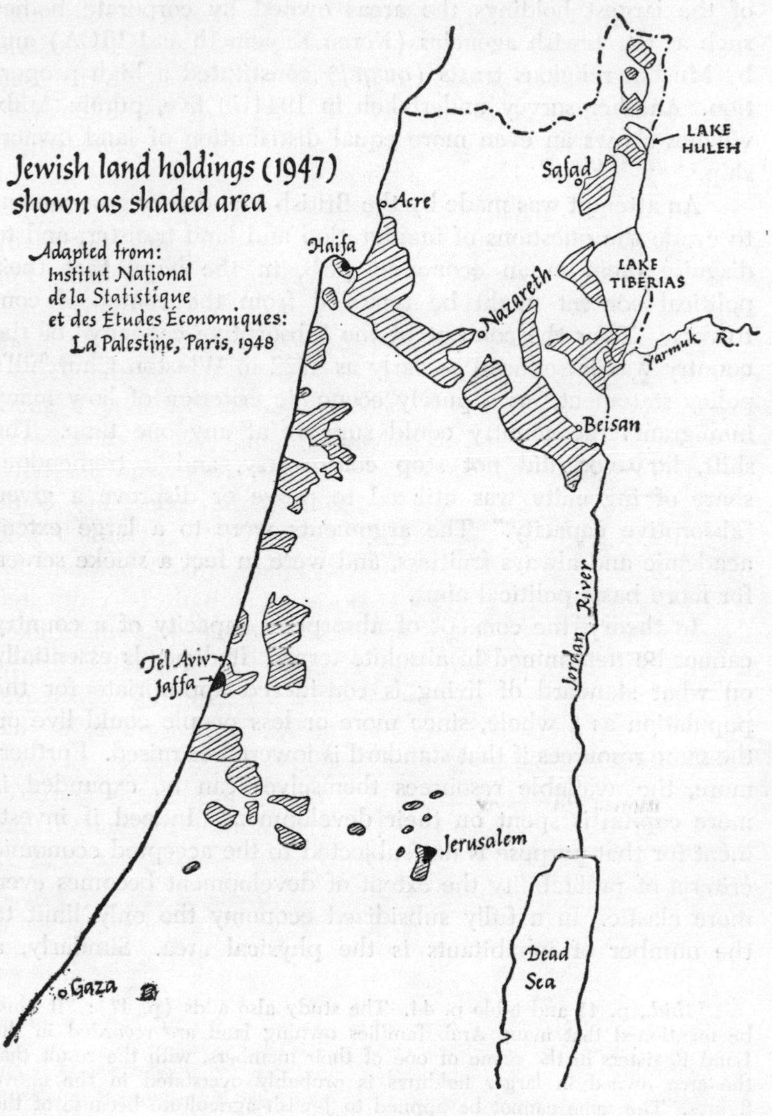
Jewish land holdings (1947)
shown as shaded area
Adapted from:
Institut National
de la Statistique
et des Études Économiques:
La Palestine, Paris, 1948
LAKE
HULEH
Safad
Acre
Haifa
LAKE
TIBERIAS
Nazareth
Yarmuk R.
Beisan
Jordan River
Tel Aviv
Jaffa
Jerusalem
Dead
Sea
Gaza

of the largest holdings the areas owned by corporate bodies such as the Jewish agencies (Keren Kayemeth and PICA) and by Muslim religious trusts (*awqaf*) constituted a high proportion. Another survey undertaken in 1944 in five, purely Arab, villages shows an even more equal distribution of land ownership.[7]

An attempt was made by the British Mandatory government to evade the questions of immigration and land transfer, and to disguise them in an economic garb, in the hope that their political content might be removed from the center of controversy. Thus the concept of the "absorptive capacity" of the country was introduced as early as 1922 in Winston Churchill's policy statement,[8] as a purely economic criterion of how many immigrants the country could support at any one time. The shift, however, did not stop controversy, and a tremendous share of ingenuity was utilized to prove or disprove a given "absorptive capacity." The arguments were to a large extent academic and always fruitless, and were in fact a smoke screen for more basic political aims.

In theory, the concept of absorptive capacity of a country cannot be determined in absolute terms. It depends essentially on what standard of living is considered appropriate for the population as a whole, since more or less people could live on the same resources if that standard is lowered or raised. Furthermore, the available resources themselves can be expanded if more capital is spent on their development. Indeed if investment for that purpose is not subjected to the accepted economic criteria of profitability the extent of development becomes even more elastic. In a fully subsidized economy the only limit to the number of inhabitants is the physical area. Similarly, a

[7] *Ibid.*, p. 41 and table p. 44. The study also adds (p. 47): "It must be mentioned that many Arab families owning land are recorded in the Land Registers in the name of one of their members, with the result that the area owned in larger holdings is probably overstated in the above figures. The same cannot be applied to Jewish agriculture because of the predominance of co-operative and communal farming."

[8] White Paper, Cmd 1700. Churchill, at the time, was Secretary of State for the Colonies.

change in the structure of the economy in favor of industry and services, which require relatively large outlays of capital, would also expand the size of the supportable population at a given standard of living though natural resources may remain constant. In the actual situation, however, the Arab population of Palestine was growing at a natural rate which soon produced a population pressure on the land which was available for cultivation. Land purchases by Zionist organizations increased the pressure of Arab farmers on land, while reclamation of uncultivated lands by Zionist Organizations did not benefit them. As to the structure of the Arab economy, although it was changing slowly toward greater employment in industry and services, yet it did not command enough capital to accelerate the process to an extent that would have absorbed the surplus population, or to reclaim new agricultural lands at the required pace. In this sense, therefore, there was a real and fundamental conflict of interest in the economic field between the Arab population and Zionism. They competed for strictly limited natural resources.

5. LAND AND CAPITAL

It is to be expected that a process of colonization in a country which is already occupied by a large settled population could not be carried out on the strength of purely economic incentives. Colonization has been economically successful only in very sparsely populated areas such as the Americas or Australia where the claim on the land and the natural resources was transferred to a right with little effective opposition from the indigenous population. In settled communities such as those of the recently independent countries of Asia, colonization largely took the form of commercial and administrative exploitation; only in a few cases did foreign colonizers there actually settle on the land and make a profitable and unharassed living out of it.

So in Palestine Zionist colonizers had to face the economic problem of settling on a land to which a relatively large and indigenous population had an ancient and well-established right, as well as an attachment. To acquire land they had either to pay for it or to obtain it through the administration in power. If all the land that Zionists now control had to be purchased, the financial burden would indeed have been staggering. In fact out of the total area of Palestine only about 6.6 per cent was actually acquired and held by Jews in 1946—i.e., toward the end of the Mandate. And not all of that area was purchased from the Arabs. A part was given in lease or concession by the British administration, as the power in charge of state domains. In particular little is known of land purchases before October 1920, when 40 per cent of the total area acquired by the Jews was already in their hands. After that date sale of land to Jews went on at a slow pace in the face of mounting Arab opposition, and almost came to a standstill following restrictions placed on land sale by the government White Paper of May 1939.[1]

Table 5[2]

JEWISH LAND HOLDINGS IN PALESTINE IN 1946

	Thousand Hectares
Holdings before 1920	65
Purchases 1920-46	97
Leased or conceded by government 1920-46	18
Total	180

However, this small area of land was located in the most fertile parts of the country, which generally coextended with the coastal and northern plains. Though most of it, outside

[1] The legislation of February 1940 which enacted the policy of the White Paper prohibited land sale to Jews except in a small zone where the Jews were already a majority or where there was a mixed population. This included a large part of the coastal plain and urban areas.

[2] Sources: Government of Palestine, *Survey of Palestine* (Jerusalem: 1946), pp. 244, 376; and *Supplement* (Jerusalem: 1947), p. 20. One hectare is equal to about 2.5 acres or 10 dunums.

urban areas, was cultivable, the part which was cultivated in 1944 reached 72,000 hectares[3] or about 12 per cent of the total cropped land in that year. As a proportion of total cultivable land Jewish holdings may have represented 20-25 per cent.

The largest part of Jewish-held land in Palestine belonged to organizations rather than individuals.[4] In particular two of them, the JNF (Jewish National Fund) or Keren Kayameth and PICA (Palestine Jewish Colonization Association), held between them three quarters of Jewish land. The PICA, initiated by Baron Edmond de Rothschild in the 1880s, acquired 45,000 hectares and established some forty agricultural settlements. The land and farms were generally given to individual settlers against repayment over fifty years of part of the original investment, and the farmers were free to dispose of them after repayment. The JNF, which was established in 1901, had acquired, on the other hand, some 75,000 hectares by 1946, which it held as the untransferable property of the "Jewish people." The Jewish Agency, which acted as the representative of the Jews in Palestine, managed these lands. Its constitution stipulated:[5] "Article (e) The Agency shall promote agricultural colonization based on Jewish labour and in all works or undertakings carried out or furthered by the Agency it shall be decreed to be a matter of principle that Jewish labour shall be employed". This principle was also embodied in the leases of land to Jewish colonists.[6]

The occupation of agricultural land by Jewish settlers resulted often in the displacement of Arab tenants.[7] The government reports reflected this problem early in the twenties and brought it out clearly following the riots in 1920 and 1921: "The Arabs regarded Jewish immigration not only as an ultimate means of Arab political and economic subjection, but also as

[3] *Ibid.*, p. 373.

[4] For a detailed and balanced description of Jewish agricultural settlement, see *Survey of Palestine*, p. 372 ff.

[5] Quoted in Cmd 3686, p. 53.

[6] *Ibid.*

[7] *Ibid.*, p. 51; and *Survey of Palestine*, pp. 297 ff.

an immediate cause of Arab unemployment."[8] Following the riots of 1929 and a thorough investigation by Sir John Hope Simpson the report concluded:

> It has also been shown that while an area of at least 180 dunums [43 acres] is required to maintain a fallah [farmer] family in a decent standard of life in the unirrigated tracts, the whole of the cultivable land not already in the hands of the Jews would not afford an average lot in excess of 90 dunums . . . It also appears that of the 86,980 rural Arab families in the villages, 29.4 per cent are landless.[9]

This was written in 1930. In the seventeen years that followed—i.e., up to 1947—the Arab population of Palestine increased by over 60 per cent and the Jewish population multiplied four times. The pressure of the basically agricultural Arab population on a shrinking area of agricultural land in these conditions created in itself an unhealthy political atmosphere. The fact that this condition was being created by the inflow of groups having conflicting political aims made it almost inevitable that the conflict should take violent forms. It is possible to see an almost direct connection between the inflow of immigration on the one hand and political and economic unrest on the other.

The conflict of economic interest and particularly the competition for limited agricultural resources between Arabs and Jews can be brought out both in negative and positive fashions in the economic history of Palestine before the war. Thus the tranquil period of the 1920s was associated with a considerable fall in the rate of immigration and indeed with a net emigration in 1927. Economic slump and unemployment in those years were relieved in that manner. Early in the 1930s, however, the increasing pressure of the Arab rural population began to be felt and the movement of unemployed labor toward urban centers gained momentum.[10]

[8] Paraphrase of the report of the Commission of Inquiry headed by Chief Justice Sir Thomas Haycraft, October 1921, quoted in *Survey of Palestine*, p. 19.

[9] Cmd 3686, pp. 142-43. The Simpson report was strongly criticized by Zionists.

[10] In 1930, in Haifa alone, unemployed Arabs were estimated at 2,000 (Cmd 3686, p. 134).

Consequently, when the European political developments led to an unprecedented inflow of Jewish immigrants, unemployment became rife.[11] A serious economic crisis began in the fall of 1935, before the Arab strike and the civil disturbances of 1936-39 took place. At the end of 1937 unemployment was estimated at 21,000 among the Arabs and 12,000 among Jewish workers[12]—i.e., about one tenth of the labor force. In this situation matters were improved among Jewish workers through a strict exclusion of Arab workers from employment in Jewish concerns. A Zionist writer declared "unemployment among Jews at the end of 1938 was much reduced owing to the replacement of Arab labour in plantations, increased security measures and public works . . . This year for the first time only Jewish workers are employed in Jewish owned orange groves. There are 25,000 of them, 10,000 more than usual." [13] Later, during the Second World War, tranquility was again associated with reduced immigration, improved prices of agricultural products, and large employment of labor by the British forces and administration.

It would thus seem prima facie that the Zionist claim that expenditures by Jews in Palestine and the purchase of land from the Arabs was of primary importance for the economic development of the Arabs is exaggerated. A more thorough study will only confirm this view. The total import of capital by Jews into Palestine during the whole mandatory period 1922-46 amounted to £162 million ($648 million at prewar rates).[14] The Jewish capital inflow, however, benefited the Arabs directly only to a small degree since the larger part of it was spent by the im-

[11] Between 1931 and 1939 more immigrants went to Palestine than to the United States, Brazil, Canada, Argentina, and Australia combined: A. E. Kahn, "Palestine, a Problem in Economic Evaluation," *American Economic Review*, September 1944.

[12] *Official Gazette,* No. 767 (1936); quoted in S. B. Himadeh (ed.), *Economic Organization of Palestine* (Beirut: 1938), p. 287.

[13] *The Jewish Frontier,* March 1939.

[14] P. J. Loftus, *National Income of Palestine 1944* (Jerusalem: 1946), pp. 21-22. The estimate includes £P 109 million in immigrants' property other than personal effects, £P 46 million in receipts of Jewish institutions in Palestine, and £P 9 million from Baron Rothschild through PICA. Part of this latter sum was sent before 1922.

migrants themselves to establish living quarters and to pay for imports required by them in their new homes. In this period Palestine's excess of imports over exports amounted to more than £P 245 million.[15] Transfer of Jewish capital to Arabs occurred mainly as payment for land or buildings purchased from the Arabs. About £P 10 million or 6 per cent of the Jewish capital inflow up to 1946 was made in payment for land, and part of this was transferred abroad by non-Palestinian landowners who sold such land to Jews.[16]

Much more important to the Arab economy in Palestine and also of great importance to the growth of the Jewish economy itself were the conditions created by the war. While Palestine avoided practically all destruction of war,[17] its agriculture and industry were highly protected by the shortage of foreign goods and shipping space. The greater demand for all types of products by the civilian and military population, and the large-scale employment of workers by the British forces led to high wages and a general prosperity. The Arab farmers were able to repay their age-old debts and invest in improvement of their farms. Industry, both Jewish and Arab, had a long period of protection with assured demand and thus built large profits and reserves for investment after the war. In comparison with the Jewish import of capital, expenditures of the British forces in Palestine in 1939-46 amounted to £159 million,[18] of which a substantial part went to the Arabs. Although prices during the war rose to about three times the prewar level, yet the significance of this expenditure in stimulating investment during the war in capital goods by both Arabs and Jews is great. It also enabled Palestine to save by the end of 1945 about £110 million in foreign exchange,[19] which it used to

[15] P. J. Loftus, *National Income of Palestine 1945* (Jerusalem: 1948).

[16] The Jewish Agency for Palestine estimated transfers to Arabs for land purchases at £P 8.5 in the interwar period. Purchases during the war and up to 1946 were less than 10 per cent of total Jewish land holdings in 1946 (see The Jewish Agency for Palestine, *The Palestine Economy, Achievements and Potentialities* (memorandum submitted to the Anglo-American Committee of Inquiry—Jerusalem: 1946), p. 5.

[17] A few air raids on Haifa by the Italians and French in 1941 did little damage and were generally ineffective.

[18] P. J. Loftus, p. 22.

[19] A. R. Prest, *War Economics of Primary Producing Countries* (Cambridge: 1948), p. 106, table.

import goods from abroad after the war at prices lower than those prevailing during the war.

With the large inflow of capital into Palestine before the Second World War, the Arab population could have benefited indirectly to an important degree had the economy of Palestine been normally integrated. But, as we have noted earlier, the economy in fact was split into two separate parts or sectors which intermingled rarely and only in urban centers. Practically no Arab labor was employed by Jews after the twenties except for seasonal work in the citrus groves up to the 1930s. On the contrary, professional and trade services were largely sold by the Jews to Arabs in the various towns. The Arab community, on the other hand, "exported" to the Jews some agricultural products, particularly wheat, meat, and vegetable oil.

The capital inflow into the country before the war was utilized by the Jews largely to build up their autonomous economy. The larger part of the capital was spent for that purpose on construction of houses and buildings, and the rest on developing the agricultural settlements, manufacturing industries, and commerce. For the period 1921-40 it has been estimated that investment in the Jewish sector outside communications totaled £P 86.6 million ($346 million), divided as follows:

Table 6[20]

	£P Million
Construction	42.3
Farms	14.6
Industry	12.0
Commercial	9.2
Land purchase	8.5
	86.6

The vital importance of this expenditure in enabling the Zionist immigrants to settle in Palestine cannot be exaggerated. Directly, of course, it enabled them to create shelter and the means of livelihood. However, the continuous expenditure of

[20] Source: Alfred Bonné, *The Economic Development of the Middle East* (Jerusalem: 1943), p. 74, except for the estimate of land purchases, which is the Jewish Agency estimate for the interwar period (see p. 334, note 16).

funds that came from abroad—i.e., that did not have to be saved out of current income—created additional employment and demand and thus maintained economic activity at a high level that the economy could not have otherwise supported. This was as true of the Jewish economy in Palestine as it is today of the economy of Israel, to which we will return in Chapter 7.

6. ECONOMICS OF THE REFUGEE PROBLEM

The military struggle in 1948 and early 1949 disrupted the normal economic life of Palestine and caused considerable economic losses to all parties involved. The political settlement that followed created new and more complex economic problems. In accordance with the individual armistice agreements in 1949 between Israel on the one hand, and Egypt, Syria, Lebanon, and Transjordan on the other, the armistice lines split Palestine into three main parts. One part representing 77.7 per cent of the total land area was declared the State of Israel. Another part representing 21 per cent was held by Trans-Jordan and was later, in 1950, incorporated into a unified Kingdom of Jordan. The remaining small part (1.3 per cent) formed the so-called Gaza Strip and was administered by Egypt. The parts which remained in the hands of the Arabs included a large part of the poorer lands of Palestine. Thus, Jordan occupied the semi-barren hills of Samaria and Hebron, and the Gaza Strip is largely covered by sand dunes that lie at the edge of the desert of Beersheba.

The population movement which resulted from the struggle was of an even more radical character. The Arab inhabitants of that part of Palestine which was occupied by Israel moved out of the area almost en masse. Of an estimated one million Arabs who lived there before 1948 only 160,000 remained in Israel. The rest took refuge in neighboring countries and most of them have been dependent since 1948 on international charity for their subsistence. Into their places, in the following few years, flowed an almost equal number of Jewish immigrants, some of whom settled in the vacated land and houses, and for whose final integration in the economy and for whose self-support Israel has been striving.

These two essential results of the military struggle between Zionists and Arabs, namely the armistice lines and the double movement of population, have since 1948 and up to the present dominated the economic as well as the political scene in the land that was Palestine. Just as the problems of immigration and security colored Israel's outlook, so did the impact of Arab refugees color the economic life of Jordan and Gaza, as well as influence the political atmosphere of all the Arab countries.

The Arab refugees from Palestine distributed themselves in unequal proportions among the neighboring countries. The number of Palestinian Arabs and their children at the present time reaches probably 1.6 million.[1] Of this number, over 920,000 are refugees registered with UNRWA and depending on its food rations for their subsistence. The total distribution of Palestine Arabs in 1956 was as follows:

Table 7[2]

ARAB POPULATION OF PALESTINE—1956
(in thousands)

Location	*UN Registered Refugees*[a]	*Others*
Israel	—	200[b]
Jordan	512	320[c]
Gaza Strip	217	100[d]
Lebanon	103	30[e]
Syria	90	20[e]
Egypt	—	5
Iraq	—	5
Others	—	20
Total	922	700

[1] Total Arab population in Palestine in 1947 reached 1.3 million. Assuming (conservatively) a net natural increase of 2 per cent per annum, the number would reach 1.6 million at the end of 1956.

[2] Sources: [a] UN, *Annual Report of the Director of UNRWA, July 1955-June 1956* (New York: 1956).

[b] *Statistical Abstract of Israel, 1955-56*, p. 7.

[c] Based on: International Bank of Reconstruction and Development, *The Economic Development of Jordan* (Washington, D. C.: 1957—mimeographed) II, 12.

[d] Based on UN, *Statement of the Director of UNRWA*, Doc. A/SPC/9, February 11, 1957, p. 2.

[e] Approximate figures based on enumeration of local governments.

In addition to the registered refugees, a substantial number of the Arabs who remained in their homes in West Jordan and the Gaza Strip lost their lands or means of livelihood. Although they are not entitled to UNRWA rations in accordance with the prevailing regulations, their condition is sometimes worse than that of the refugees. Thus, in Gaza, over 60 per cent of the indigenous population—i.e., over 60,000—cannot earn a source of livelihood in the desert strip.[3] In West Jordan, "150,000 or more inhabitants of the Jordan frontier villages . . . have been cut off from larger parts of their cultivable land."[4]

The Arab refugees have been maintained since 1949 by various philanthropic organizations which were succeeded in 1950 by the United Nations Agency. Since 1950, the mandate of the Agency has been renewed every year and appeals regularly made for contributions. The United States contributed about two thirds of UNRWA's budget; Britain, one fifth; and the remainder was supplied by a large number of governments—e.g., France, Canada, Saudi Arabia—and by private donators. The "host" governments—i.e., Lebanon, Syria, Jordan, and Egypt—have also made small contributions largely in the form of transport and other services, as well as buildings, land, and public utilities.

The aid and services extended by UNRWA to the refugees has largely been in the form of rations, the major component of which is 22 pounds of flour per person per month, but which also includes small amounts of fats, sugar, and soap. The total value of the food ration has varied with world prices but has always hovered around the $2 mark, or about 7¢ a day. It supplies around 1,600 calories per day per refugee. Additional services offered by UNRWA include valuable health services as well as primary education for a large number of refugee children. The total expenditure on relief, health, and education (including the cost of administration) per refugee has averaged about $2.80 per month, or roughly 9¢ a day.[5]

[3] UN Doc. A/SPC/9, February 11, 1957, p. 2.
[4] *Ibid.*
[5] The total expenditure on the relief and health program in 1955 amounted to $23.4 million and on education $2.5 million, while the number

The United Nations created in 1951 a rehabilitation fund of $200 million, also to be financed by contributions, which would be spent on resettling the refugees and making them self-supporting. Little success so far has been attained in achieving this aim. One major rehabilitation project, viz., the Yarmuk-Jordan Valley irrigation scheme, has been bogged down in the intricacies of international politics, as explained below in detail. The other big project, which envisages using Nile water for irrigating some 50,000 acres on the east side of the Suez Canal, has been studied but its implementation has been stated by Egypt to be dependent on water becoming available from the projected high dam in Egypt.[6] The only relatively large project that has shown a measure of success from the economic point of view is the Development Bank of Jordan, which has a paid-up capital of $1.6 million of which UNRWA contributed $980,000. The Bank, established in June 1951, has helped in financing small and medium development projects in Jordan on a purely commercial basis. The attempt to tie its operations in with the resettlement of refugees in any strict fashion did not succeed.[7] Other smaller projects implemented by UNRWA resulted in resettling a small number of refugees. The total number of refugees who have been presumably rehabilitated so far has not exceeded 2,000, of whom half have, in fact, been helped to emigrate from the area. UNRWA itself employs about 8,000 Palestinians and is, in fact, their major employer.

The difficulties facing the resettlement of Palestine Arab refugees outside Palestine is partly economic and partly political.

---

of rations totaled 838,000 (some of the 922,000 refugees receive only half rations). Thus the cost of the relief benefits from each ration averages $2.30 per month, and the average expenditure of all types and on each refugee amounted to $2.80 per month. (Based on the *Annual Report of the Director of UNRWA, 1955-56*), pp. 14, 34, 35.

[6] *Ibid.*

[7] The difficulty of creating a strict link between expenditure by UNRWA and ration reductions led the United States in February 1957 to introduce a resolution authorizing "the Director in his discretion to disburse such monies, as may be available, to the individual host governments for general economic development projects, subject to agreement by any such government that in a fixed period of time it will assume financial responsibility for an agreed number of refugees, such number to be commensurate with the cost of the project . . ."

Of the host countries that have given refuge to Palestine Arabs, Lebanon, Jordan, and Egypt are highly overpopulated and could, indeed, offer an opportunity of resettlement to the largely unskilled refugees only at the expense of reducing such opportunities for their underemployed populations. Syria has some agricultural projects which could absorb a small proportion of the refugees; but here, as well, the feeling is that the refugees would be competing for limited resources which soon would be needed to absorb the growing population. Iraq, Saudi Arabia, and Kuwait, all oil-producing countries, have very few refugees and their climate is too inhospitable to attract more except for short periods of employment in the oil countries. However, in addition to the natural obstacles, the refugees themselves present many difficulties in the way of resettlement. A very high proportion, about 80 per cent, of the refugees are small children and women. The men of working age are largely ex-farmers who have been idle now for almost nine years and whose unused skill and mental attitude make resettlement even more difficult. Some of those few who have special skills or education or capital found employment in the host countries or emigrated abroad.

But economic obstacles to resettlement are perhaps of secondary importance in solving the economic problem of the refugees. As the Director of UNRWA succinctly expressed himself on the subject before the United Nations:

> The question may be asked: why cannot UNRWA enable the refugees to settle and to work in peace in the countries where they are? The answer lies in the realm of politics, and in deep-seated human emotions. It does not lie simply in the field of economics. UNRWA can, to be sure, enable some hundreds of refugees to become self-supporting each year—through small agricultural development projects, grants to establish small businesses and the like. But it cannot overcome the fact that the refugees as a whole still insist upon the choice provided for them in General Assembly resolution 194—that is, repatriation or compensation. In the absence of that choice, they bitterly oppose anything which has even the semblance of permanent settlement elsewhere. Officials of the host Governments, with but few exceptions, openly support the refugees in this position and oppose large-scale resettlement projects. On the other hand, in the matter of repatriation and compensation, the Government of Israel has taken

no affirmative action. It is for all these reasons that, in my reports to the Assembly, I have repeatedly emphasized that unless the choice provided for in resolution 194 is given the refugees, or unless some other political settlement of the Palestine problem can be reached, UNRWA would be unable to implement the resolution of the General Assembly calling for the reintegration of the refugees into the economic life of the Near East, either by repatriation or resettlement.[8]

The United Nations has reaffirmed every year the right of the Palestine Arab refugees to "repatriation and compensation" first affirmed in its resolution 194/III of December 11, 1948.[9] The efforts of the United Nations Conciliation Commission for Palestine, established to implement that resolution in 1948, have not borne any fruit except in its mediation to transfer in 1952-56 about £2.6 million ($7 million) in deposits and safe boxes held in British banks in Israel to their owners among Palestinians.[10] The property of the Palestinian Arabs in Palestine has been variously estimated at one half to three billion dollars, and net income for that property during the last nine years would raise the figure substantially. In its last progress report[11] the United Nations Conciliation Commission notes a communication received from the government of Israel stating that: "The problem of compensation for abandoned Arab lands cannot be considered in disregard of the general context of Arab-Israel relations" . . . and that

> It is recognized that the payment of compensation for abandoned lands could be an important contribution to Arab refugee settlement. But the acceptance of such a burden at any one time would involve our population in a commitment beyond its powers. We were, therefore, interested in a proposal made recently by the Secretary of State of the United States under which an international loan would be made to enable Israel to discharge this undertaking.

It is noted that Israel refers only to compensation of Arab land and to no other form of income or losses.

[8] UN Doc. A/SPC/9, February 11, 1957, pp. 2, 3.

[9] See Fayez Sayegh, *The Record of Israel at the United Nations* (New York: 1957), pp. 14-17, for text of these resolutions.

[10] UN, Doc. A/3199, October 4, 1956, p. 8.

[11] *Ibid.*, Annex A, p. 1.

7. THE ECONOMY OF ISRAEL

In many ways Israel continued in its economic expansion to follow the path and pattern set by the Jewish community of Palestine. Only now the scale has been enlarged threefold as the inflow of Jewish immigrants since 1948 trebled the Jewish population in Israel and as financial assistance from abroad correspondingly multiplied. Similarly, the opposition of the Arab population to Zionism spread, in area and in intensity, with the spread of the refugees into the neighboring Arab countries. Thus it seems that the net outcome of the 1948 events has been to enlarge the arena by drawing in a larger number of contestants from a wider international field, rather than to do away with the source of conflict. As the political problem got more involved on the international level with the withdrawal of Britain from Palestine, so did the economic consideration grow less important and became more than ever before an instrument of political struggle.

The flight of one million Palestinian Arabs from the area which was occupied by Israel in 1948 solved many political problems for the new state. It also left space for, roughly, an equal number of Jewish immigrants and their children. Overpopulated as it was before 1948, Palestine could not have otherwise absorbed such an additional number of immigrants without creating both a political and economic upheaval. In its value for Israel the flight of the refugees was so great that it was described by Chaim Weizmann, the first President of Israel, as a "miraculous simplification of Israel's tasks." [1]

The development of Israel's economy since 1948 and until the present time has been dominated by three primary principles, all aimed, in the final analysis, at consolidating the position of Israel as a state in the Middle East within the armistice lines and, if possible, within the historical area of the "Land of

[1] Expressed to James G. McDonald, first U. S. Ambassador to Israel, and quoted in his book, *My Mission in Israel* (New York: 1951), p. 176.

Israel."[2] These principles relate to the absorption of Jewish immigrants, the maintenance of military forces superior to those of the Arabs, and the development of the production capacity of the country so as to reduce its dependence on foreign aid."[3]

The bulk of immigration took place in the period 1948-51 and was reduced to a few thousand in later years, but approximately 100,000 are expected during 1957. This was partly a result of a selective immigration policy introduced in 1952, but mainly because the potential sources of immigration other than eastern Europe had been exhausted. The change in the population of the area occupied by Israel and the origin of the immigrants are indicated in the following table:

Table 8[4]

POPULATION OF AREA OCCUPIED BY ISRAEL 1947-56
(in thousands)

End	Jews	Arabs and Others	Total	Net Immigration During the Year
1947	630	1,050	1,680	22
1948 Nov.	717	—	—	105
1949	1,014	160	1,174	235
1950	1,203	167	1,370	162
1951	1,404	174	1,578	167
1952	1,450	180	1,630	11
1953	1,484	185	1,669	−2
1954	1,526	192	1,718	11
1955	1,591	198	1,789	31
1956	1,667	205	1,872	

[2] The Israel *Government Yearbook 1955*, p. 320, under the title, "Boundaries, Area and Geographical position," states: "The State was established in part of the former British Mandated Territory of Palestine (Eretz Israel) and it occupies most of the historical Western Palestine (Eretz Israel) . . . It is called the 'State of Israel' because it is part of the land of Israel and not merely a Jewish State. The creation of the new State by no means derogates from the scope of historical Eretz Israel."

[3] Thus the Minister of Finance in *The Economic Report*, February 14, 1956, states: "The principles of our economic policy are: (1) Fortifying of the security framework to insure our existence and peace. (2) Continuation of immigration and absorption. (3) Development of the country and growth of production in all branches of economic and cultural life."

[4] Sources: *Statistical Abstract of Israel, 1955-56;* and *Statistical Bulletin of Israel,* February 1957; except for the estimated number of Arabs in the area occupied by Israel in 1947.

The inflow of some 720,000 Jewish immigrants between 1948 and 1956 had, of course, a profound impact on the social and political structure of the Jewish community of Palestine. It also influenced the pattern of economic growth. A large proportion, representing roughly half of the total, came from North Africa and the Middle East itself, and had a social and technical background different from that of immigrants from eastern Europe who formed the other largest group of immigrants in that period and the largest proportion of immigrants before 1948. In addition, the average age of immigrants after 1948 was lower than that of the Jewish population of Palestine. Their inflow, thus, raised the average number of dependents per worker, or to put it differently, reduced the proportion of the population of working age.

Table 9[5]

JEWISH IMMIGRANTS BY COUNTRY OF BIRTH AND EMIGRANTS BY COUNTRY OF DESTINATION

	1919-48		*1948-55*		*Total*		*Emigration 1948-55*
	'000	*%*	*'000*	*%*	*'000*	*%*	*'000*
All countries	452	100	772	100	1,224	100	63*
Asia	41	9	252	33	293	24	5
Africa	4	1	153	20	157	13	5
Eastern Europe (including Russia)	299	66	318	41	617	50	3
Western Europe	78	17	25	3	103	8	16
America	8	2	6	1	14	1	18
Others	22	5	19	2	41	3	4
Born in Palestine	170		223		393		6

* Including 16,000 Jews who emigrated in the first half of 1953 and the destination of whom is not disclosed.

By occupation the mass of working immigrants had previously worked in trade, professional, and other services, crafts and

[5] Source: *Statistical Abstract of Israel, 1955-56*, pp. 34, 46; and that for 1954-55, p. 41; except for the number of Jews born in Palestine before 1948. Figure may not add up to totals exactly due to rounding.

industry. Only 5.5 per cent of total immigrant workers in 1950-52 had been working in agriculture and 9.1 per cent were unskilled workers.[6] Employment surveys show that the Jewish labor force in Israel reached a total of 548,000 workers in June 1954 and 631,000 in November 1955. Of the labor force 8.3 per cent were unemployed in June 1954 and 8.2 per cent in November 1955, and the rest were distributed as follows:

Table 10[7]

Employed Jews by Occupation, June 1954

	Per Cent
Farmers and farm laborers	12.5
Craftsmen, production process	21.9
Operating transport	3.7
Professional, technical	8.9
Managerial, administrative, and clerical	14.1
Sales and service	16.5
Laborers, except for farms	12.3
Not specified	10.1
Total	100.0

Employed Jews by Branch of Activity, November 1955

	Per Cent
Agriculture, afforestation, and fisheries	15.3
Industry, mining and quarrying	22.5
Transport, storage and communication	6.9
Commerce and banking	14.4
Services	31.0
Construction and public works	8.6
Electricity, water, and gas	1.3
Total	100.0

Besides the evacuation and flight of the Palestinian Arabs from the area, the absorption of immigrants was facilitated essentially by the flow of financial aid from abroad in average volume per person that has seldom, if ever, been paralleled in other cases of resettlement. We have noted earlier that imports of capital and contributions to Jews in Palestine up to 1946 amounted to about $650 million. Between 1949 and up to the end of 1956, however, the total import of capital into Israel amounted to roughly $2.2 billion, or over $2,800 per immigrant.

Gross investment, which reached the substantial figure of £I 600 million in 1955 (about $330 million or 28 per cent of

[6] The Falk Project for Economic Research in Israel, *Second Annual Report, 1955* (Jerusalem: 1956), p. 11.

[7] Sources: The Falk Project, *Second Annual Report,* p. 21; and *Statistical Abstract of Israel, 1955-56,* p. 188. The two tables use different classifications and are not, therefore, strictly comparable.

the gross national income), was distributed among the various sectors of the economy in the following fashion:

Table 11[8]

GROSS INVESTMENT, 1949-1955
(per cent)

	Agriculture (in irrigation)	*Industry*	*Transport*	*Building and Public Works*	*Total (including others)*	*Total £I Million*
1949	23	14	10	43	100	80
1950	20	11	9	44	100	150
1951	12	12	4	56	100	214
1952	20	14	6	54	100	277
1953	23	19	10	40	100	325
1954	27	16	10	40	100	432
1955	25	15	10	42	100	600

The large-scale investment that has been going on in Israel since 1948 has obviously helped a great deal in raising output. A large part of the total investment went into construction of houses for immigrants, and perhaps another part in strengthening the military position of the country. Nevertheless, these types of expenditures, however necessary, do not raise the productive capacity of the economy to any appreciable degree. Investment in agriculture took the form, mainly, of expansion of the area under irrigation as well as of mechanization and the use of other intensive methods. Owing to the small cultivable area, however, and despite a 20 per cent increase in agricultural production per head since 1949[9] Israel remains dependent, to an important degree, on imports of food from abroad. Industrial development, on the other hand, included the expansion of such existing industries as cement, beverage, and diamond polishing, as well as the establishment of new industries producing superphosphates, sulphuric acid, detergents, plywood, rubber tires, and plastics. It has so far been found difficult for Israeli industries to

[8] Sources: UN, *Economic Developments in the Middle East 1945 to 1954* (New York: 1955), p. 121; and Israel Government: *The Economic Report of the Minister of Finance,* February 14, 1956, p. 30.

[9] UN, *Economic Developments in the Middle East, 1945 to 1954,* p. 127.

compete on a purely commercial basis with European industries in export markets, and the roots of the difficulty have been traced to various causes such as high wages, low physical productivity, high cost of raw materials and power, etc.[10]

It is perhaps neither easy nor profitable to try to determine the exact sources from which the absorption of immigrants was financed; nor, conversely, is it useful to try to distinguish between expenditures on the settlement of immigrants and other expenditures on projects that increase the production capacity of the country. An overall picture of national accounts supplemented by one of investment expenditures can give us a clear, though approximate, picture of both these points.

It is clear from the available estimates that the net product of the economy in 1954 and 1955 covered private consumption, but not both private and public consumption. To look at it differently, the net contributions from abroad were utilized to finance all investment in Israel as well as a part of government expenditure. This is a clear indication of the very serious dependence of the economy, as a whole, on foreign aid, a dependence that will continue so long as the total output of the economy cannot cover the consumption of both the private and the public sector.[11]

Of course, the gap between output and expenditure can be narrowed in one of several ways: such as by lowering the standards of consumption of the population; or by reducing Government expenditures on administration and defense; or lastly, by reducing the high scale of investment. None of these alternatives is pleasant, however, and some—e.g., lowering consumption levels or defense expenditures—are probably politically not

[10] For a thorough examination of industry in Israel see: Stanford Research Institute, *The Industrial Economy of Israel* (Menlo Park, California: 1955).

[11] A large part of the government budget revenue was received in grants from foreign sources: mainly from American grants-in-aid, Independence and Development bonds (largely sold in the United States), and from German reparations. Revenue from these sources represented 32 per cent, 34 per cent, and 28 per cent of the actual revenue of the fiscal years 1953-54, 1954-55, and of the estimates of 1955-56 respectively (Bank Leumi Le-Israel, *Review of Economic Conditions in Israel, June 1956* [Tel-Aviv 1956], table p. 9).

Table 12[12]

AVAILABLE RESOURCES AND THEIR USE 1954-55
(per cent)

	1954	1955		1954	1955
			Consumption: Total	83	81
Net product	79	78	private	(64)	(61)
Import surplus	21	22	public	(19)	(20)
			Net investment	17	19
Total	100	100		100	100
Value (in £I million at 1954 prices)	2,067	2,311		2,067	2,311

feasible at the present time. The pressure on resources, despite substantial foreign aid, has thus led to a serious money and price inflation that has beset the Israeli economy since its inception. The situation changed substantially, though by no means completely, after 1952 when immigration practically ceased.

The galloping inflation in 1951-52 was restrained through two measures. The first, introduced in November 1951, placed certain restrictions on organized and subsidized immigration, making it a condition that the immigrants should be physically fit and under thirty-five years of age. Priority was given to professional and skilled workers and those ready to work in agriculture. However, this measure seems to have coincided with a decrease in the number of people wanting to immigrate, and was helped after 1949 by the growing restrictions placed on emigration from eastern Europe and Russia by communist regimes. The second, more important measure was introduced in February 1952 and came to be known as the New Economic Policy. By reducing the budget deficit, restraining the issue of treasury bills and land bonds, collecting a compulsory fifteen-year loan amounting to 10 per cent of all but the smallest banknote issues and smallest bank deposits, removing some controls and subsidies, and other such measures, the rate of price rises was slowed down.

However, price inflation persisted after 1952 and continues at the present time, essentially because available resources are not

[12] Source: Bank of Israel, *Annual Report, 1955* (Jerusalem: 1956), p. 28.

sufficient to meet demands made upon those resources. Demands by the public sector are particularly influenced by the military budget, part of which is secret and cannot, therefore, be appraised. Demands by the private sector, on the other hand, have been kept high by the continued rise in money wages and hence in the cost of production. This price-wage spiral has been maintained by the link, established in December 1953, between wages and prices, which entitles the general Federation of Labor (Histadrut) to demand a proportionate raise in wages whenever the cost of living index registers a rise within a given period. It has not, so far, been possible to break this link, particularly since the General Federation of Labor, which includes in its membership practically all the workers, is the main supporter of the Labor party, which has been in power since 1948.

The rise in output cannot be clearly gauged in Israel mainly because of the price inflation and the consequent distortion of price patterns. In addition, government subsidies are paid to restrain price rises temporarily, a fact which makes deflation by indices not very significant. The best available estimates, however, show that while output in terms of Israeli pounds has increased spectacularly since 1950, the real increase in output is much more modest. It varied between 0.8 and 7.9 per cent in the period 1950-55 and averaged 3.6 per cent per annum during that period.

Table 13[13]

NATIONAL INCOME OF ISRAEL 1950-55

Year	National Income at Current Prices (£I Million)	National Income at 1952 Prices (£I Million)	National Income Per Capita at 1952 Prices (£I)	Per Cent Increase Over Preceding Year
1950	373	657	518	—
1951	585	791	529	2.1
1952	856	856	533	0.8
1953	1,130	919	557	4.5
1954	1,461	1,015	601	7.9
1955	1,663	1,070	611	1.7

[13] Source: The Falk Project, *Second Annual Report*, p. 37; except for 1955, which is based on estimates given in the Bank of Israel, *Annual Report, 1955*, p. 33.

The role that foreign aid and foreign loans play in the development of the economy of Israel is no doubt of crucial importance. The total net import of capital into Israel since 1949 has exceeded $200 million a year and reached $304 million in 1955 and probably $380 million in 1956.[14] All in all, it has reached $2.2 billion in the period 1949-56. About 44 per cent of this sum has been in the form of aid and grants and another 37 per cent in transfers that do not have to be repaid. Israel has, in addition, borrowed from abroad, mainly from United States banks and private individuals, to the extent of $350 million. The importance of all these forms of aid to Israel lies not merely in that they enable it to develop its resources as far as the nature of the land and the skill of the people allow. Nor is it only in the fact that they enable Israel to finance the resettlement of immigrants (a minor task in the last few years). From the economic point of view, the expansionist trend of the economy could not, probably, be maintained without the continued stimulation given to the economy by the expenditures on public works which are financed by the government from such aid. To look at it differently, a considerable part of the national income is created by the outlay of foreign funds and would disappear if such funds ceased to flow into the country. The significant fact at present is that despite the large expenditures on development projects and on new industries, productive jobs are still not enough to absorb all the working population. Unemployment persists, and though it fluctuates seasonally it has not fallen far below 9 per cent of the working population in recent years.[15] Expenditures on public works as a measure to relieve unemployment has thus come to be a permanent feature of the Israeli economy and its persistence in the midst of an inflationary situation is one of the serious aspects of Israel's economic problem.

Another equally serious problem facing the Israeli economy and related to the question of foreign aid is the fact that Israel's foreign indebtedness has been persistently increasing despite the expansion of the productive capacity of the country and the

[14] Statement of the Minister of Finance, January 14, 1957, reprinted in *Israel Weekly Survey*, January 24, 1957, p. 662.

[15] See above, Table 7, note.

large flow of foreign aid. By the end of 1955, the Israeli government foreign-exchange debts totaled $351 million,[16] while its total gold and foreign-exchange assets equaled $44 million.[17] Repayment of principal and interest on this growing volume of loans is becoming a heavy burden on the economy and may grow even heavier as more loans reach the date of maturity. In the 1957-58 budget, for example, there are provisions for £I 101 million ($56 million) for repayment of debts and interest on debts (partly internal) by the government alone. Similarly in the 1955 calendar year £I 55 million ($30.5 million) appeared in the balance of payments for "capital servicing" in 1955.[18] This

Table 14[19]

ISRAEL: NET IMPORTS OF CAPITAL AND CAPITAL SERVICING, 1949-55
(in millions of U. S. dollars)

	Net Import of Capital	Of Which			Capital Servicing
		*Grants**	*Loans†*	*Others‡*	
1949	206	69	18	119	—
1950	251	53	45	153	—
1951	312	46	84	182	—
1952	291	151	69	71	13
1953	258	155	36	67	19
1954	240	186	62	−8	19
1955	304	156	45	103	30
Total	1862	816	359	687	

* Grants under German reparations, U. S. aid, and Jewish institutions.

† Including U. S. Export-Import Bank loans ($121 million in 1949 and 1952) and "Independence," "Development," and "Consolidation" loans (238 million in 1951-55).

‡ Including releases of sterling balances accumulated during the Second World War ($98 million in 1949-51), sale of foreign securities ($16 million 1951-52), private capital import in kind ($392 million in 1949-55), and changes in foreign-exchange balances, etc. ($181 million during the period).

[16] Bank of Israel, *Annual Report, 1955,* p. 222. The figure includes $189 million in "Independence Loan" and "Development Loan" bonds, and $121 million in loans from the U.S. Export-Import Bank.

[17] International Monetary Fund, *International Financial Statistics,* (August 1956), p. 142.

[18] Bank of Israel, *Annual Report, 1955,* p. 41.

[19] Sources: Based on Israel *Government Yearbook, 1954* and that of 1956; Israel Office of Information, *Facts and Figures, 1954* (New York); American Financial and Development Corporation for Israel, *Prospectus,* (New York), March 28, 1951; Bank of Israel, *Annual Report 1955;* the Falk Project, *Second Annual Report, 1955,* pp. 48-49.

latter figure represented 3.2 per cent of the total national income. Payments on such a large scale can thus offset or even exceed the rise in real income unless it is met by further free contributions or loans.

The overall picture of foreign capital inflow and its main components are summarized for the reader in Table 14 on the preceding page.

8. ECONOMIC RELATIONS BETWEEN ISRAEL AND THE ARABS

With the background of political and military struggle between the Zionists and the Arab population of Palestine, and later between Israel and the members of the Arab League, it would be difficult to imagine any but strained economic relations between the two parties. Normal interchange across armistice lines which are more in the nature of front lines is not possible. Economic exchange will have to await a peaceful and final settlement of the whole question of Palestine in all its aspects, but particularly in relation to its political aspects including the refugee problem. In the meantime, economic relations between the two parties remain conspicuous by their absence.

Of course the immediate consequence of the strained political relations between Israel and the Arabs is for both parties to maintain a relatively large military machine, and to allocate a large part of the budget receipts to supply and enlarge military forces and equipment. On the Arab side, this is particularly true of Syria, Jordan, and Egypt, which, unlike other Arab countries such as Iraq or Saudi Arabia, have no rich oil resources. Both Egypt and Jordan, which have a serious problem of overpopulation and a relatively low per-capita income, can ill afford to spend extensively on large armies and expensive equipment. On the Israeli side, funds that flow from abroad are diverted in considerable proportions toward maintaining superior military strength. In any event, in spending on armaments, all parties concerned use funds that could otherwise be spent on increasing the productive capacity of their respective economies, and hence the income of the growing populations.

Armament races are, however, notoriously difficult to stop when a strong underlying suspicion or a real grievance or conflict of interest exists between the parties concerned. It is perhaps useless to try to blame either party for starting the race. Nevertheless, it is true that until 1955, when Egypt and later Syria purchased arms from the communist countries, several attacks were made by the armed forces of Israel on Syria, Jordan, and Egypt in retaliatory raids that the Arab countries felt they could not risk countering partly because of the lack of arms at their disposal. It also has been openly stated by the Prime Minister of Israel, David Ben-Gurion, that the latest campaign in Sinai, in October 1956, was meant to remove the potential threat of the new Soviet arms purchased by Egypt, a position which clearly implies that Israel, like Egypt, felt it always had a lead insofar as military preparedness and equipment were concerned.

There is also another rather curious economic sequel to the military preparations and tensions that exist between Israel and the Arab countries. For it is generally conceded that the vital financial support of Israel by world Jewry is stimulated by the fear that Israel is in military danger. In fact, it has been suggested that border clashes between Israel and the Arabs seem to acquire a greater degree of intensity, as well as publicity, in the period preceding the annual drive to sell Israel bonds and collect contributions by Zionist organizations in the United States. Whether this is true or not, there can be little doubt that there is a positive correlation between a sense of crisis surrounding Israel and the size of Jewish contributions to Israel. Thus, contributions were largest in 1948 and 1956–57, when large-scale military operations were involved, and dwindled between 1951 and 1954, when conditions were relatively stable (see Table 14). From this analysis it is the Arab contention that the practical politics of Israel require it to continue to maintain a highly expensive and superior military machine, and to use it persistently, in the hope that such a policy will render the Arabs more amenable to accepting peace on the basis of the status quo.

The alternative would seemingly be for Israel to risk a dwindling of financial support, and hence a weakening of her relative military position vis-à-vis the Arab countries.

It is of course speculative to ask whether the Arab countries would not have increased their armed strength had Israel followed a more peaceful policy toward its Arab neighbors. However, for several years after 1948 and until the arms deal between Egypt and Czechoslovakia in 1955, the Arab countries did little to retrieve the rights of the Palestine Arab refugees, in implementation of the relevant parts of the United Nations resolution of November 29, 1947, beyond denying to accept the status quo. The economic aspect of this generally negative attitude was for the Arab League states to boycott Israel and those foreign firms that deal with Israel.

The Arab economic boycott of Israel, in the final analysis, is a political weapon that the Arabs feel should be used in their attempt to help bring about the collapse of Israel. The boycott involves prohibition of trade and exchange between the two parties, and its application as a positive political instrument implies a gain to those who apply it or a loss to those against whom it is applied. It has often been said that in fact it causes losses to both parties and that economic exchange between the Arabs and Israel could only lead to profit for both. This approach, however, misses the crux of the matter by assuming that only *economic* considerations are behind the Arab decision.

That the boycott brings loss to Israel is open to little doubt, and is in fact openly stated by Israeli officials.[1] The loss, however, is largely potential rather than direct. That is to say, its absence would bring in profits that now are not forthcoming. These potential profits primarily arise from the possibility of obtaining access first to cheap raw materials and power and then to markets for Israeli manufactures and services.

The raw materials that the Arab countries could supply to Israel are primarily crude oil and foodstuffs but also cotton and oilseed which Israel is now importing from abroad at relatively higher prices mainly because of the higher cost of transport in-

[1] See, for example, the statement of Abba Eben to the UN, New York *Times,* Oct. 15, 1956.

volved. Other potentially cheap sources of power could be made available to Israel from the Litani hydroelectric project in Lebanon or from the Jordan Valley project. However, the potential loss incurred by Israel from having to import goods from farther afield are probably of minor importance. So perhaps is the loss of markets. For the demand of Arab populations for manufactured goods is small in relation to their number, although quite large when compared with the capacity of Israeli industry. If the boycott were removed, Israel would have to compete with other industrial countries for these markets that are becoming more and more protectionist-minded. In any circumstance, the advantage of Arab markets as compared with other Mediterranean, Asiatic, or African markets is only their greater proximity, which is not of vital importance in marketing manufactured goods.

The more significant effect of the boycott is probably the fact that it prevents Israel from profiting from its naturally favorable position as a country of transit. Thus, oil pipelines that carried oil from Iraq to Haifa before 1948 could be an important source of revenue as are their correspondents in Syria, Jordan, and Lebanon. In addition, Israel could compete with those transit countries for a greater share of the oil transit business.[2] In the field of trade, Israel's port at Haifa is more favorably situated to transport Jordan's foreign trade than is either Beirut or Aqaba, and could in fact regain its position as a starting point for transit trade across the desert to Iraq and Iran.

Also significant to Israel is the potential loss of income from services that it could supply to the Arab markets as a result of their proximity and because of its greater competitiveness. Such services would probably include tourism, entertainment, shipping, trading, and other professional services. Of course, this type of potential income, more than the preceding groups, re-

[2] This explains the great importance placed by Israel upon free navigation in the Gulf of Aqaba in recent months, since free navigation would enable Israel to build oil pipelines across the Negeb to the Mediterranean. A small (8-inch) pipeline joining the port of Eilat on the Gulf of Aqaba with Beersheba in Israel was completed early in 1957. It can carry half of Israel's own annual needs of crude oil and is not intended to carry oil in transit.

quires a far-reaching degree of peaceful coexistence and exchange together with freedom of travel.

Direct economic losses being incurred by Israel at present as an immediate result of the boycott largely arise from the difficulty of carrying goods through the Suez Canal. Such trading problems have been evaded in various ways in the past and it is doubtful whether such aspects of the boycott could be strictly enforced.[3] Since Israel imports by far the larger part of its goods from Europe and America, the importance of the Suez Canal and the Gulf of Aqaba lies essentially in their opening the markets of East Africa and the Far East to Israel exports. This is more of a future potential rather than an actual loss at present.

Let us now turn to examine the economic impact of the boycott on the Arab countries themselves. The most conspicuous losses to the Arab countries include the loss of revenue following the stoppage of the oil flow from Iraq via the twelve-inch pipeline to Haifa; the additional cost to Jordan of diverting its international trade via the ports of Beirut and Aqaba rather than through the more convenient port of Haifa; and the loss of a potential market for their goods and services. In addition, the policy of noncooperation that the boycott entails has created difficulty in implementing regional projects, such as the Jordan Valley development project, that could benefit both Arabs and Israelis.

The loss of oil revenue to Iraq, which produces the oil, and to Syria or Jordan, through which it passes, is proportionate to the quantity of oil that would have otherwise passed through, until alternative routes were created for it. On the basis of this principle, the loss to Iraq was of the order of $55 million and to Syria and Jordan together less than $10 million.[4]

[3] Thus since 1952 Israel has imported most of its crude oil via the Suez Canal, probably from Kuwait and Iran. The Arab boycott office has blacklisted a large number of tankers for carrying oil to Israel. Crude oil is by far the most important as well as most bulky commodity imported by Israel from Asia.

[4] The capacity of the completed pipeline to Haifa together with that of the incompleted pipeline would have amounted to 6 million tons per year. The 32-inch pipeline to Banias in Syria, which has over double the capacity of both Haifa pipelines, was completed in April 1952, four years after the closing of the Haifa pipeline. Iraq received royalties roughly at

The loss to Jordan from having to divert its foreign trade arises from the extra cost of transporting goods across Syria and Lebanon to the port of Beirut or south to the Jordanian port of Aqaba. The road distance between Amman and Beirut is about 220 miles, and between Amman and Aqaba 210 miles, as compared with about 140 miles to Haifa. The additional cost has, of course, been inflated in proportion to the growth of Jordan's trade, a growth that has been mainly due to the movement of Palestine's Arab refugees into Jordan. Against this, however, is to be set the fact that the boycott encouraged Jordan to develop its port of Aqaba, its natural outlet to the markets of Asia and East Africa, which otherwise would probably not have been developed. Lebanon and Syria have benefited from handling Jordan's trade where Palestine previously did.

As to the loss of market for Arab products, it is a loss that is commensurate with the importance of the Israeli market. Israel's demand for products that Arab countries could supply—e.g., dates and oil from Iraq, cotton and wheat from Syria, cotton and rice from Egypt—is of very minor importance compared with the total exports of these products by the respective countries. Alternative markets have so far been accessible. The same can be said of services that could be supplied by Arab countries to prospective Israeli clients. As we noted earlier, however, some of these goods are probably being obtained by Israel by devious means despite the boycott.

It would thus probably be correct to say that Israel would have a great deal to gain from the establishment of free economic relations and the Arab countries little to lose from the continuation of the boycott. It is probably such an appraisal that encourages the Arab countries to retain the boycott until the rights of the Palestine refugees are regained. Underlying this attitude and of a more basic nature is the fact that the political antagonism between the two parties does not allow of free exchange on

---

the rate of $1.65 per ton of exported oil prior to August 1950, and $2.45 up to the end of 1950, and $4.43 thereafter (see UN, *Economic Developments in the Middle East 1945-1954*, pp. 96-98). Syria received less than $1 million per year during the period in transit dues for the corresponding two Tripoli pipelines.

the economic level until the causes of the political conflict are resolved.

To exemplify this interrelation between the political and the economic, it is worth examining at some length the involved story of the plans to develop the resources of the Jordan Valley, plans that could benefit both Arabs and Israelis and which have the financial and political backing of the United States. It may not be clear at first sight how the hydroelectric and irrigation development of the Jordan Valley would be conducive to creating tranquility in the troubled area of the Middle East. Yet there seems to have been, until recently, a unanimous conviction in the American press as well as in the State Department that it is the best, if not the only practical, method of attacking an extremely thorny problem. The problem is that the Arab states and Israel, both of which have an interest in the Jordan River, are as irreconciled after nine years of uneasy truce and limited war as they were in 1948, when about one million Palestine Arabs had to move out of the country so as to leave space for roughly a million Jews gathered in from all over the world. The unanimous impression about the great value of the Jordan Valley development scheme is born of the belief that if the Arab states and Israel are brought together on the economic level, through a joint plan for exploiting the river, an important step would be made toward resolving the more knotty political issues between them. Otherwise the river system, which for a considerable part of its length forms the armistice boundary between Israel and the adjacent Arab states, may become a primary source of friction rather than a source of economic benefit.

It is the distinction of the River Jordan, a distinction claimed by few other rivers in the world today, that the manner in which its waters are to be utilized has been the subject of consuming interest and scrutiny for top-flight engineers and politicians, international as well as local. As many as eight different engineering plans (and many more amendments) have been prepared during the last fifteen years to deal with the problem of how best to exploit the waters of the river and its tributaries. A special envoy of the President of the United States, Mr. Eric Johnston, visited the Middle East four times in the last two years and conferred with leaders of five countries in an attempt to push through an overall development project in one form or another.

Yet this ancient river is only a small stream, measured by the standard equally famous rivers of the world. The interest and publicity it commanded is vastly out of proportion to its economic significance. For should every drop of water that pours annually through its basin be carefully collected and optimally distributed, it could irrigate a maximum area of 210,000 acres. This would be achieved at a capital cost of $120 million or at an average of about $500 per acre. In contrast, the comparable capital cost (i.e., excluding roads, public utilities, cost of settlement, etc.) of irrigating an acre in the vastly wider areas of the High Dam project in Egypt or the Euphrates Valley project in the northeast of Syria is about $200. Pure economic considerations are thus obviously relegated to a secondary position when this project is evaluated. Only incidentally has the project been energetically sponsored and carefully nurtured by the United States government as part of its drive to help people help themselves in underdeveloped countries.

Its value could lie more perhaps in the fact that it moves some way toward easing the problem of the Palestine Arab refugees. The double movement of population which resulted from the 1948 struggle in Palestine took place in a poverty-stricken area where resources are meager and overpopulation is a permanent problem. Its outcome was to increase economic pressures both in Israel and in the adjacent Arab states to which Palestinian Arabs moved for refuge nine years ago. The rehabilitation of the million Jewish immigrants and the creation of jobs in Israel was considerably facilitated by the utilization of farms and houses that belonged to the Arab refugees and by the expenditure of some two billion dollars obtained from grants, transfers, and loans from abroad.[5] The Arab refugees, on the other hand, are still dependent, almost wholly, on relief given by the United Nations Relief and Works Agency for Palestine Refugees (UNRWA), which is largely supported by the United States. It is worth noting in this respect that total relief ex-

[5] See UN, *Economic Developments in the Middle East 1945-1954*, pp. 137-39.

penditures on 920,000 registered Arab refugees varied between $22 million and $27 million per year (or an average of around $2 per head per month for food, shelter, and health services) when grants-in-aid to Israel by the U. S. government alone varied between $46 million in one year and $85 million in another. However, it must be added that the accusation that the "host" states have wished to keep the refugee problem alive as a political weapon is a fair one. A good proportion of Arab refugees are still living for their eighth winter running in surplus army tents, caves, and mud huts. They can find litle work, and then only by competing with Jordanians, Syrians, Lebanese, or Gaza inhabitants for wages that, in themselves, are a mere pittance. The "host" countries are struggling hard to accelerate the development of their few but unexploited resources, scattered at the edges of a wide desert, so as to maintain or raise the low level of income of their citizens. It is generally beyond their physical or financial resources to absorb large numbers over and above the natural increase of population. Except for some 5,000 who went to Iraq, no refugees moved to the more distant oil-rich countries of the Arab world.

In this setting the utilization of the waters of the Jordan River and its tributaries gains in importance. It is the major known asset of the poorest of the host countries, Jordan, which, with a population of 900,000 gave refuge to 500,000 Palestinians. The irrigation of the Jordan Valley will enable Jordan to settle some 160,000 persons on 120,000 acres of irrigated land.[6] To Israel it means chiefly more intensive agriculture and cheaper electric power for its industry, both of which lessen the serious dependence of Israel on foreign aid. The benefits that may accrue to Syria and Lebanon—the only two other parties who have riparian rights—are of minor importance and would mainly take the form of cheap electric power.

It is not clear, at present, whether the system of land tenure in the Jordan Valley and the present population living there will allow the absorption of all of the 160,000 persons from refugee ranks. At best, therefore, a maximum of one sixth of the total

[6] UN, *Annual Report of the Director of UNRWA 1955-56* (New York: 1956), p. 23.

registered Palestine refugees would be settled by the Jordan Valley development project and the proportion may turn out to be lower. Nevertheless, irrigation of the valley is of vital importance to Jordan and its only large development project. In 1952 that country had a plan known as the Yarmuk Project which did not require the cooperation of Israel. The project, which could irrigate 120,000 acres at a cost of $54 million, was elaborated by Mills E. Bunger, the American chief of the water resources department of the U. S. Technical Assistance Administration (Point IV). The plan envisaged storing and using to irrigate the valley most of the waters of the Yarmuk River, the Jordan River's chief tributary which carries 30 per cent of the combined flow. Jordan and Syria, who share the river, did in fact sign an agreement in June 1953 providing for the division of the water and electric power of the Yarmuk Project. The project was sponsored by the Jordanian government and UNRWA, which reserved $40 million until the end of 1954 for its execution. In fact engineering, aerial, and economic surveys were undertaken, an approach road to the dam site was built, an anti-malaria campaign was completed, and all in all $2 million were spent in preparation for the project's execution.

The project, however, was dropped when a plan, the "Unified Development of the Water Resources of the Jordan Valley Region," was published during August 1953. This plan, better known as the TVA plan or Johnston plan, was prepared at the request of UNRWA by a Boston engineer, Charles T. Main, under the direction of the Tennessee Valley Authority. It was submitted by U. S. Ambassador Eric Johnston to the governments concerned on his first visit to the Middle East in August 1953. Mr. Bunger, the originator of the Yarmuk Project, was subsequently transferred to Brazil but resigned before his transfer was due. The $40 million earmarked by UNRWA for the Bunger plan lapsed in 1954. Obviously some overriding consideration other than refugee welfare favored the "Unified" plan as against the Yarmuk Project—particularly since the latter could be started without prejudicing the future integration of such a project with a "unified plan." [7] Jordan, however, is completely depend-

[7] See M. Baker and Harza Engineering Co., *Yarmuk-Jordan Valley Project, Master Plan Report* (1955), 8 vols., mimeographed.

ent, for financing such a project, on the U. S., the British government, and UNRWA.

A "unified plan" has many attractive features from the point of view of U. S. foreign policy. A major consideration—that of creating jobs for refugees—could be satisfied by implementing a "partial plan" such as the one mentoned above which was supported indirectly by the U. S. through the UN Agency—a plan which did not raise a political hornets' nest as the Johnston plan did. But it is precisely because of its political implications that the "unified" Johnston plan has been favored by the U. S. By attacking the Israel-Arab impasse at a point where interests are not in open conflict and with a promise of U. S. financial aid as an incentive, it was hoped that a unified project would create an area of common interest between the two enemies. The construction of a system of barrages, canals, and hydroelectric power stations that cut across the present uneasy truce lines may change these into peaceful international boundaries. The people on either side, to whom the irrigation and power system would form the basis of livelihood, will have a vested interest in defending their livelihood by maintaining peace in the area. Conversely it is feared that if the Arabs and the Zionists each proceed with their own independent plans involving the use of the Jordan River and its tributaries then this may lead to a conflict that may deteriorate into a war. Indeed these fears are borne out by the recurrent crises that occur between Syria and Israel over the diversion of the Jordan waters by Israel in the demilitarized zone north of Lake Tiberias—crises that have received the attention of the UN Secretary Council more than once.

In his four visits to the area, the last in October 1955, Ambassador Eric Johnston used his diplomatic ability and the support of the President to bring both parties to agree on some amended form of the TVA plan. On his way back from his last visit he said that he had left the area

> "without the slightest doubt that both sides now recognize the plan as the only logical and equitable approach to the problem of developing a river system which belongs in some part to four sovereign states. These states have made it clear to me that the technical and engineering details of the plan—including a division of water—are now

satisfactory in the main. They believe the remaining differences can readily be reconciled. This is my opinion."[8]

The agreement on the technical points, as reported, includes an agreed distribution of the waters whereby Israel takes 35 per cent and the other three Arab states 65 per cent. A diminutive "Yarmuk Project" was accepted with a promise of future enlargement if the project was found feasible. There was also agreement that control of the division of water would be undertaken by a board of three members, one from each side and a third chosen by them from a list of neutral engineers.

Ambassador Johnston's progress in bringing divergent points of view to a partial agreement tends to bring out some of the basic problems inherent in the situation. The project in its final form is valuable in a negative way. It reduces the possibility of conflict between Zionists and Arabs by eliminating conflicting claims for a limited amount of water. Almost all the aspects of the original plan which called for cooperation between both parties have disappeared in the final plan. Israel will reportedly take all but a small proportion of the Jordan River waters, and Jordan all but a small proportion of the Yarmuk water. In its final form, the plan seems to be a combination of a Jordan plan and an Israeli plan both cut to size and presided over by a neutral board.

As it stands now, the story does not seem to have reached its conclusion. While technical points have been agreed upon, final approval has not yet been forthcoming. The Arab League, in its meeting on October 8, 1955, decided to study further the political implications of the plan. Israel, on the other hand, has declared its intention to proceed in diverting the Jordan River waters—whether a final agreement is reached or not—as soon as the end of the rainy season permits the resumption of work early the following spring. Since then more important events have held the interest of all parties concerned.

Recently seemingly successful attempts have been made by communism to penetrate into the Arab Middle East through sales of arms, offers of economic aid, and political support of

[8] The New York *Times,* October 15, 1955.

Egypt when it was attacked by the Israelis, British, and French in 1956. These moves enabled the Communists to generate enthusiasm in a population whose way of life is basically alien to Soviet communism. These events shifted the whole Arab-Israeli conflict to a more serious international level. They pushed the problem of the Jordan Valley to the background but served to bring into strong relief the basic forces that led to the partial failure of the project. To the Arabs, piecemeal progress toward peace—which is the aim of the Johnston plan—is not understandable. To them, fear of Israeli expansion, the injustice done to a million refugees, the show of force by Israel and its failure to compensate and allow refugees to go back to their homes in accordance with the resolutions of the United Nations—all these make an agreement with Israel an agreement with an unjust enemy. The immediate and tangible danger of Zionism impresses them much more strongly than the possible though unfelt dangers of communism. In this context the attempt of the Johnston plan to bring Arabs and Zionists together, without first correcting the basic conditions that gave rise to disagreement, is in Arab eyes to put the cart before the horse.

Part V. CONCLUSION

CONCLUSION

In discussing events of the past few years, the historian is deprived of the most reliable of his sources. Much of the reasoning behind acts is still shrouded in secrecy or covered by the veil of propaganda. The study of the earlier years, concerning which we know much more, is useful to us partly because it provides us with a framework. Events of recent months have tended largely to develop, not alter, this. The underlying pattern as sketched in the body of this book has merely been more fully amplified and thrown into sharper relief.

The gulf between Arabs and Zionists, and between Arabs and the native Jews of the various Arab countries, particularly in Egypt, has widened still further. However, the situation following Israel's attack upon Egypt in 1956 is not essentially different from that prevailing before except in degree of hostility.

Tho sense of shame, inability, and frustration which was a significant feature of the Arab emotional make-up before 1057 remains. The Egyptian failure before the forces of Israel, Britain, and France, has intensified the feeling.

The Arab hostility to the West as well was not created but was magnified by the Anglo-French intervention. The specter of colonialism again came to haunt the Arabs.

The Arab inability to find common leadership, in spite of the emotional attachment to a common set of ideals, a common language, and the notion of Pan-Islam, is as conspicuous a feature of the Arab scene—perhaps even more conspicuous—in May 1957 as it was in May 1948.

In Israel the logic of events has increased the tendencies toward "activism" which were in the ascendancy in 1945. Today the moderating influence of such "Old World" figures as Weizmann is diminishing. The pressure on Ben-Gurion's government from the far right has grown stronger, and the sense of frustration in being deprived of the fruits of the Sinai victory has put the government in a difficult domestic position.

The economic situation remains unproductive. The Arab

boycott of Israel has replaced the dual boycott within the old Palestine Mandate. The Jordan valley retains its mystical "mightiness" but provides little for the flesh.

Finally, the refugee problem is today even greater, more hopeless, more enervating, and involves more people than in 1948.

A few basic considerations emerge from our study of these problems. We offer them tentatively.

The first is that, even if some of the Arab governments wanted peace, as certain Arab senior officials have indicated in private, no government except the Egyptian was domestically strong enough or popular enough to entertain the idea of making peace.

There is some reason to believe that, in spite of its speeches and press statements (many of which were obviously designed for foreign consumption), the Egyptian government was interested in ending the state of war with Israel in 1952. At that time, the Egyptian government was deeply engaged in a domestic program of social and economic betterment for which it had high hopes. Its population was much less concerned with the issue of Palestine than were the people of Syria, Jordan, and Iraq. In these latter countries, the example of the murder of King Abdullah was fresh. It may be doubted that any Arab political figure would have dared to declare openly an interest in an end to the state of war.

The prospects of peace seem much less bright today.

The reasons are not obscure. High on the list is frontier friction. Such friction was inevitable when front lines dividing armies were drawn which separated men from what they regarded, rightly or wrongly, as their own property and upon which they depended to live. The conflict of rights produced a conflict of arms, and as raids and counter-raids grew more bitter and savage, on both sides, it became increasingly difficult for either side to back down or to call a halt. This was particularly true when the United Nations supervisors were few in comparison with the long frontier, when the acts of the raiders were condoned by (in many cases even ordered by) the governments, and when both sides felt a moral justification for their deeds.

Israel proclaimed that it would break out of the boycott and blockade and make the Arabs realize the price of war. To the Arabs, frontier attacks were perhaps never a matter of declared state policy. Although there is much that is still obscure concerning the degree of Egyptian involvement in the attacks by the Gaza strip *fedayeen*, the rationale of the raiders could be supplied by the heart of Arabic culture, the demand for retaliation and vengeance. In short, a psychological situation has been created which makes its own demands on both Arab and Israeli leaders.

The morality of preventive war, is dubious. However, no matter where one's sympathies lie, it is almost certainly true that the Israeli attack upon Egypt, whether provoked or not, has made the establishment of peace more rather than less difficult.

The Suez conflict, indeed, summarizes the essential elements of the train of events of recent years. Egypt had refused to make peace. Egyptian leaders encouraged and certainly did not stop raiders into Israel. It had organized a group of Palestine refugees into a military unit. As the Egyptian domestic program began to go awry, partly because increased tension with Israel diverted money to arms which could have been used for peaceful projects, the Government became increasingly desperate. It tried to play Russia against America in order to obtain large-scale grants of funds—and it was certainly not the first state to do so—but it refused to admit the realities of its position. Russia, for the moment not vitally interested in the Middle East, though ever ready to add to the existing troubles in the area, drove a hard bargain for the sale of arms. Although she tried to imitate India's neutralism, Egypt lacked India's bulk and India's relative isolation. In taking arms from the Communist bloc, it copied Israel but lacked the solid base of popular support which Israel enjoyed in the West. The fact that Egypt was a dictatorship, though not necessarily decisive in itself (as Spain and nationalist China show), provided a target for attack by liberals. Its attitude on the Suez Canal provided a similar target for conservatives. Egypt closed the Suez Canal to a nation with which it maintained it was in a state of war. Britain did the same in two World Wars, and did not object to the Egyptian move—which had been in effect since 1948—until Egypt nationalized the canal. But Egypt lacked Britain's power to enforce its policy. Egypt also infuriated France by encouraging, even arming, the North African anti-French rebels, thus violating the old Ottoman dictum of dividing the great powers: instead, she antagonized everyone at the same time. Finally, Egypt should have realized, but obviously did not, the psychological situation into which it moved in England. To a great many Englishmen—particularly to the Conservative "Back Bench," but by no means only to them—the actions which culminated in the nationalization of the Suez Canal took on an emotional value far out of proportion to their individual significance. Britain had been in retreat since World War II, and each negotiated surrender seemed to have led only to a new trouble spot. India was the first, but what would be the last: Kenya? Cyprus? Suez? Many Englishmen resented being "pushed around," and some Englishmen particularly resented being pushed by people who they were wont to regard as inferior Orientals. The Egyptian government should have realized that an anti-Egyptian move would be, ipso facto, popular to many in England. Suez was the last straw.

The Anglo-French invasion was a bad job, badly done. It not only clogged the canal, which had been functioning under Egyptian management, and caused a large number of Egyptian casualties, but it did infinite damage to the cause of peace. The Israeli invasion was in its way a much more effective military action and failed only in the general failure of the invasion before world opinion. But, if these invasions were aimed primarily at Colonel Nasser, as they certainly were, their effect was to make of Nasser a hero and a martyr throughout the Arab world.[1] Indeed, as the voting at the United Nations showed, the invasions rallied to Nasser's side the general support of Asia; for, however the West felt about Nasser, gun-boat diplomacy—especially when linked to old symbols of the "road of empire"—could only evoke recent and still painful memories of colonialism. Nasser was unquestionably stronger immediately after the invasion had been halted than he was on its eve. Materially he

[1] It appears today that his defeat at the hands of Israel in Sinai has, however, shaken his popular support to a certain extent.

had lost much, especially of his expensive war equipment, but he had won a world position and had weathered his most dangerous hour. The attack gave him a sort of personal grudge, quite apart from his nationalistic anger, against Britain, France, and Israel. It may be doubted that he will wish to try to make peace now.

We have suggested above that the parallel of the current situation with the Crusades is not historically accurate. Yet the partial parallel remains provocative. Because it is so often evoked by Arabs in discussing Israel and Zionism, it is at least valid as a key to the attitudes of some people in the Middle East today.

Like the Latin Kingdom of Jerusalem, so the State of Israel was born in war. Both came into existence because local inhabitants were too weak to prevent them. Both owed their existence to their military superiority over the Arabs. Both have been successful in the fissures of the Middle Eastern polity.

Will the parallel continue?

To the end of its days the Crusader kingdom depended upon the West. It was able to develop contacts with the surrounding area during the relatively frequent periods of peace, but it gloried in its military prowess. It never was able to clothe its existence in a morality which could render it acceptable to the society in which it had to live. To the end, the Latin Kingdom remained a symbol of Muslim division and weakness—until division and weakness were overcome sufficiently to destroy it. Finally, over its short history we can trace the inability of its European sponsors to sustain the contributions necessary for its maintenance.

At the present time, Israel is more than a match for any single Arab state and probably could again defeat the coalition. The coalition is, in truth, yet to be born. None of the Arab states assisted Egypt in the attack of last fall. The Iraqi government is openly hostile to Nasser. The Syrian government is untried, the Saudi government wavering, but apparently moving away from Nasser in defense of the principle of the monarchy. In Jordanian affairs it is difficult to improve on the parable in Genesis 4 of Abel and Cain. The bedouin element is attached to the person of the king (though how strongly remains to be seen should the flow of Saudi Arabian money dry up). The settled, largely Palestine-Arab element is strongly pro-Nasser.

In short, Israel is today in a position in which she can afford to try to convert some of her military advantage into an article of more lasting advantage. Such does not seem to be the course of current developments. The very success of her attack on Egypt last fall seems to have encouraged many Israelis to think and talk in martial terms. Withdrawal from Sinai and Gaza were unpopular in Israel even within the Cabinet, and the ability of Ben-Gurion to withstand popular pressure may be limited.

It is only Israel which is today in a strong enough position to make concessions which could lead eventually to peace. Though Israel is wholly convinced of the moral and legal rights of her position, it would seem that this is not the time for insisting upon them. No Arab government, smarting under the shame of defeat, is secure enough to be able to take the first steps to the peace-conference table. Israel, on the other hand, is becoming increasingly convinced that her only hope of peace and stability lies in her acceptance and integration into the Middle East and into the Asian Bloc. Economically, her natural outlets are not to the West, with whose industrial machine she can hardly hope to compete. Africa and the East are her natural markets. And increasingly since 1949 the feeling has grown within Israel (though as yet this has not been reflected in her actions) that a policy of activism cannot pay off in the long run. While little conclusive evidence of this can be adduced, it is generally accepted that the resignation and temporary eclipse of Moshe Sharett is due to his support of the policy of concession and rapproachement with the Arab states, as opposed to Ben-Gurion's more activist and belligerent attitude.

Exactly what concessions Israel could afford to make are admittedly open to much discussion. Admittedly, too, great risks are involved in any such actions. One might conclude, however, that greater risks are involved in her refusal to countenance such a policy. No nation has yet survived for long in a totally hostile environment.

In the world today, it is difficult to deal with such problems as these of the Middle East in their own terms. We have concentrated upon local factors precisely because they are often bypassed in favor of the more obvious struggle between the United States and the Soviet Union. It is toward this struggle and not toward the Middle Eastern situation as such that the Eisenhower Doctrine was aimed. And surely the Middle East has a value to Russia in the Cold War if only as a loss to Europe and America. However, it cannot be overemphasized that the problems of the Middle East would be there regardless of Russian plans, policy, or even existence.

In our world it is almost as difficult to deal with problems in disregard of material factors as it is to see beyond the Cold War. Western national success is so intimately bound up with technological improvement that we are wont to see the solution of all problems in terms of a better standard of living. However, it surely must be recognized, however much all may wish for a better life, that a more vigorous economic "plant" will not, alone, settle the problem of Palestine. Indeed, economic improvement could provide a new energy and so accentuate friction and hostility. The crux of Palestine is in the minds of men and in society—as much or perhaps more Western than Eastern.

The problem of Palestine is so intricately woven into our very lives as probably to be incapable of *solution.* As one reflects over history, it is striking how few problems have ever been solved. The very word "problem" seems to call for solution, but it is very likely that our real solution is only in learning how to live with and control the situation as we now see it.

The essential factor for the immediate future, whatever we may hope for the long-run, is a period of cooling off. Time is recognized in Arabic culture as a great healer. But time which is measured in units and decades of raids, counter-raids, threats, and fear counts for naught.

SELECT BIBLIOGRAPHY

I GENERAL

A) WORKS ON PERIOD BEFORE 1914:

1) Bibliography

Thomsen, Peter. *Die Palästina-Literatur, Eine internationale Bibliographie in Systematischer ordnung mit autorenun sachregister.* Leipzig and New York (Vol. I), 1908—Berlin (Vol. VI), 1953.

2) Histories and Special Studies

Bowring, John. *Report on Commercial Statistics of Syria.* (*Parliamentary Papers XXI.*) London, 1840. [Contains some information on life in Palestine]

Burckhardt, J. L. *Travels in Syria and the Holy Land.* London, 1822. [Excellent observations on area *ca.* 1810]

Caetani, L. *Studi di Storia Orientale,* Vol. III. Milan, 1914. [Indispensable for the period of the Muslim invasion]

Finn, J. *Stirring Times.* London, 1878. [Finn was British consul in Jerusalem]

Gibb, H. A. R., and Bowen, H. *Islamic Society and the West,* Vol. I, Part I. London, 1950. [The best study of Levant society in the eighteenth century]

De Goeje, M. J. *Mémoire sur la conquête de la Syrie.* Leiden, 1900. [Based on Arabic sources]

Gooch, G. P., and Temperley, Harold. *British Documents on the Origin of the War, 1898-1914,* Vol. X. London, 1938. [Contains a short section on the background to the Arab revolt]

Great Britain: Correspondence Respecting the Rights and Privileges of the Latin and Greek Churches in Turkey. London, 1854. [Deals with the dispute over Palestine Holy Places]

Heyd, W. *Histoire du commerce du Levant au Moyen-Age.* Leipzig, 1885-6.

Hyamson, A. M. "British Projects for the Restoration of the Jews to Palestine," *American Jewish Historical Society,* No. 26.

———. *The British Consulate in Jerusalem in Relation to the Jews of Palestine, 1838-1914.* London, 1939. [Uses British archives]

Lammens, H. *La Syrie, précis historique.* Beyrouth, 1921. [Perhaps the best general history but strong Catholic bias]

Le Strange, G. *Palestine under the Moslems.* Boston, 1890. [Translations from Arab geographers of Middle Ages]

Martineau, A. *Le Commerce français dans le Levant.* Lyon, 1902. [Deals with situation at turn of century]

Masson, P. *Histoire du commerce français dans le Levant au XVIIe siècle.* Paris, 1896.

———. *Histoire du commerce français dans le Levant au XVIIIe siècle.*

Paris, 1911. [These two works and Heyd *supra* give the best available account.]

Oliphant, L. *Haifa, or Life in Modern Palestine.* London, 1887. [Early Jewish and Protestant-German settlement in Palestine]

Parkes, J. A. *History of Palestine.* Oxford, 1949. [Perhaps the best general history; author is pro-Zionist Anglican minister.]

Puryear, V. J. *International Economics and Diplomacy in the Near East: A study of British commercial policy in the Levant 1834-53.* Stanford, 1935.

Runciman, S. *The Crusaders.* Cambridge, 1951-54. [Certainly the most readable history of the Crusades]

Smith, G. A. *Historical Geography of the Holy Land.* London, 1931.

Temperley, H. *The Crimea.* London, 1934. [Excellent study]

Verney, N., and Dambmann, George. *Les Puissances étrangères dans le Levant.* Paris, 1900. [Detailed and important study]

Volney, C. F. *Travels Through Syria and Egypt.* London, 1788. [Important source on late eighteenth century]

Wilson, C. T. *Peasant Life in the Holy Land.* London, 1906.

B) WORKS ON PERIOD AFTER 1914

1) Bibiliographies:

Bianquis, P. J. *Éléments d'une bibliographie française de l'après-guerre pour les états sous mandat du proche-orient.* Beirut, 1934.

ESCO Foundation for Palestine, Inc. *Palestine, A Study of Jewish, Arab, and British Policies.* 2 vols. New Haven, 1947. [A good reference work; pro-Zionist]

Faris, B. A. *Post-War Bibliography of the Near Eastern Mandates.* Beirut, 1932. [Covers only works in English]

Freyha, Anis. *Post-War Bibliography of the Near Eastern Mandates.* Beirut, 1933. [Covers only works in Arabic]

Udin, Sophie A. *Palestine and Zionism.* New York, 1949. [Covers the period January, 1946 to December, 1948]

Die Welt des Islams, Band IX (1927). [Includes a bibliography on Palestine]

2) Official:

a) Reports on Palestine Administration:

Command (Cmd) 1499: Interim Report on Civil Administration . . . 1 July 1920-30 June 1921. London, 1921.

Government of Palestine. *Report on Palestine Administration.* London, 1922.

Government of Palestine. *Report . . . 1922.* London, 1923.

H.M.G. Colonial Office (Col.) 5: Report . . . 1923, London, 1924.

Col. 9: First Annual Report to the Council of the League of Nations on the Administration of the Palestine Mandate. London, 1925.

Col. 12: Report . . . 1924. London, 1925.

Col. 15: Report . . . 1920-25. London, 1925.

Col. 20: Report . . . 1925. London, 1926.

Col. 26: Report . . . 1926. London, 1927.

Col. 31: Report . . . 1927. London, 1928.
Col. 40: Report . . . 1928. London, 1929.
Col. 47: Report . . . 1929. London, 1930.
Col. 59: Report . . . 1930. London, 1931.
Col. 75: Report . . . 1931. London, 1932.
Col. 82: Report . . . 1932. London, 1933.
Col. 94: Report . . . 1933. London, 1934.
Col. 104: Report . . . 1934. London, 1935.
Col. 112: Report . . . 1935. London, 1936.
Col. 129: Report . . . 1936. London, 1937.
Col. 146: Report . . . 1937. London, 1938.
Col. 166: Report . . . 1938. London, 1939.

b) *Permanent Mandates Commission of the League of Nations.* Minutes, passim.

c) *Documents*

Cmd 1700: Correspondence [of the Colonial Secretary] *with the Palestine Arab Delegation and the Zionist Organization.* London, 1922.
Cmd 1785: Mandate for Palestine. London, 1922.
Woodward, E. L., and Butler, R. *Documents on British Foreign Policy, 1919-1939,* First Series, Vol. IV (1919). London, 1952. [Dispatches and memoranda on the crucial period in the formation of British policy]
Cmd 5957: Correspondence Between Sir Henry McMahon and the Sharif Hussein of Mecca, July 1915-March 1916. London, 1939. [Contains the terms upon which the Arabs entered the war]
Cmd 5964: Statements Made on Behalf of His Majesty's Government During the Year 1918 in Regard to the Future Status of Certain Parts of the Ottoman Empire. London, 1939.

d) *Reports:*

Cmd 1540: Disturbances in May 1921: Reports of the Commission of Inquiry. London, 1921.
Cmd 3530: Commission on the Palestine Disturbances of August 1929. London, 1930.
Cmd 3686: Sir John Hope Simpson: Report on Immigration, Land Settlement, and Development. London, 1930.
Cmd 5479: Palestine Royal Commission: Report. London, 1937.
Cmd 5854: Palestine Partition Commission: Report. London, 1938.
Cmd 6808: Anglo-American Committee of Inquiry Regarding the Problems of European Jewry and Palestine: Report. London, 1946. [Also published by USGPO, Washington, 1946]
United Nations Special Committee on Palestine. *Report to the General Assembly of the United Nations.* Lake Success, 1947.

e) *Misc.*

Cmd 2559: Anglo-American Convention on Palestine. London, 1925.
Cmd 5974: Report of a Committee Set Up To Consider Certain Correspondence. London, 1939. [The Anglo-Arab attempt to evaluate the Hussein-McMahon correspondence]

Cmd 6180: Palestine Land Transfers Regulation. London, 1940.
Cmd 6873: Statement of Information Relating to Acts of Violence. London, 1946.
Cmd 7044: Proposals for the Future of Palestine. London, 1947.
Government of Palestine. *Col. 133: Memoranda Prepared for the Royal Commission.* London, 1937.
———. *A Survey of Palestine Prepared for the Anglo-American Committee of Inquiry.* Jerusalem, 1946.
———. *Supplement.* Jerusalem, 1947. [Prepared for UNSCOP]
———. *The Political History of Palestine under British Administration.* Jerusalem, 1947. [Memo to UNSCOP]

3) Works by Members of the Jewish Agency for Palestine (see below).

4) Memoirs:

Begin, Menachem. *The Revolt: Story of the Irgun.* New York, 1951. [Factually unreliable but psychologically important]
Djemal Pasha. *Memories of a Turkish Statesman—1913-1919.* New York, 1922. [He was military governor of Syria during the First World War.] [Vol. II contains information on Zionism and the Arabs.]
Glubb, J. B. *Story of the Arab Legion.* London, 1948. [Information on the Arab revolt of 1936]
Graves, R. M. *Experiment in Anarchy.* London, 1949. [Graves was the last mayor of Jerusalem before partition]
Lloyd George, David. *The Truth About the Peace Treaties.* London, 1938.
Oxford and Asquith, Earl of. *Memories and Reflexions.* Boston, 1928.
Storrs, Sir Ronald. *Orientations* (Definitive Edition). 1945. [Storrs was military governor of Jerusalem then first civil governor.]
Weizmann, Chaim. *Trial and Error.* New York, 1949.

5) Studies:

Abcarius, M. F. *Palestine Through the Fog of Propaganda.* London, 1946? [Presents an Arab view of the post-war situation]
Barbour, Nevill. *Nisi Dominus.* (American edition called *Palestine, Star or Crescent.*) London, 1946. [General survey, and a good, albeit pro-Arab, one]
Cummings, H. H., *Franco-British Rivalry in the Post-War Near East.* London, 1938.
Dugdale, Blanche. *Arthur James Balfour, 1906-1930.* London, 1936. [Some information on Balfour's interest in Zionism]
ESCO Foundation for Palestine, Inc. *Palestine, A Study of Jewish, Arab, and British Policies.* 2 vols. New Haven, 1947. [A good reference work; pro-Zionist]
Falls, Cyril. *Military Operations: Egypt and Palestine.* London, 1930. [The British campaign in Palestine: military aspects]
Hanna, P. L. *British Policy in Palestine.* Washington, 1952. [Strongly critical of British policy]
Hurewitz, J. C. *The Struggle for Palestine.* New York, 1950. [Excellent study of last years of Mandate; good bibliography]
Jeffries, J. M. N. *Palestine: The Reality.* London, 1939. [Pro-Arab]
Kedourie, Elie. *England and the Middle East.* London, 1956. [Well-written, penetrating, but dogmatic study of the crucial years]

Kirk, George. *The Middle East in the War.* London, 1952.
———. *The Middle East 1945-1950.* London, 1954. [A part of the Royal Institute of International Affairs *Survey.* Anti-Zionist in tone]
Laqueur, W. Z. *Communism and Nationalism in the Middle East.* London, 1956. [Contains a section on communism in Palestine and Israel. Uncritical use of sources]
Luke, Sir Harry, and Keith-Roach, Edward. *Handbook of Palestine and Trans-Jordan.* London, 1934. [Luke was chief secretary to the Mandate Government.]
Manuel, F. E. "The Palestine Question in Italian Diplomacy 1917-1920," *Journal of Modern History* (September, 1955).
Marlowe, John. *Rebellion in Palestine.* London, 1946. [Deals with the Arab revolt in the late 1930's]
Perlmann, M. "Chapters of Arab-Jewish Diplomacy 1918-1922," *Jewish Social Studies* (New York), VI (1944), 123 ff. [Uses Arabic press sources]
Rossi, E. *Documenti sull 'origine et gli sviluppi della questione araba (1875-1944).* Rome, 1944. [Collected and annotated documents]
Royal Institute of International Affairs (RIIA) Study Group. *Information Paper #20a: Great Britain and Palestine, 1915-1945.* London, 1946. [Restrained study of Mandate period]
Sacher, Harry. *Israel: The Establishment of a State.* London, 1952. [One of the best pro-Zionist studies]
Sykes, Christopher. "The Prosperity of His Servant" in *Two Studies in Virtue.* London, 1953. [An excellent study of the background of the Balfour Declaration]
Toynbee, A. J. (ed.). *The Islamic World Since the Peace Settlement.* (*Survey of International Affairs, 1925,* Vol. I.) London, 1927. [Subsequent volumes have articles on Palestine; note especially those for 1931, 1935, 1936, 1937, and see Kirk *supra.*]

6) Journals:
The Middle East Journal (Washington, D. C.). [1947 ff; contains bibliographies, chronologies, and articles]
Oriente Moderno (Rome). [1921 ff; the best journal on the modern period: translations of documents, speeches, newspaper articles, chronologies, and few, but excellent, articles]
Die Welt des Islams (Berlin). [1913 ff; good articles and bibliographies]
Cahiers de l'Orient Contemporain (Paris). [1945 ff; very full coverage]
The Times (London). [Indispensable for late 1920's and 1930's]
New York Times. [Good coverage from 1946]

II WORKS RELATING TO JUDAISM, ZIONISM, ISRAEL, AND THE HISTORY OF THE JEWS

A) OFFICIAL AND SEMI-OFFICIAL PUBLICATIONS RELATING TO THE JEWISH AGENCY:

Annual Reports to Secretary of the League of Nations, 1924-1939 (Jerusalem).
Jewish Agency Digest of Press and Events (Jerusalem, weekly).

The Statistical Basis of the Hope-Simpson Report, May 31, 1930 (Jerusalem). [See also in this connection the *Palestine and Near East Economic Magazine,* Vol. V, Nos. 21-22 (1930); Vol. VI, Nos. 2-3 (1931).]

The Jewish Case Against the White Paper of 1939, June 1939 (Jerusalem).

Documents and Correspondence Relating to the Palestine Question, August 1939-March 1940 (Jerusalem).

Jewish Agency Memoranda to the Anglo-American Commission of Inquiry, March 1946 (Jerusalem).

The Jewish Case for Palestine as Presented to the United Nations Special Committee, 1947 (Jerusalem).

[See also *Stenographic Reports of Zionist Congresses, 1897-1913,* Vols. XII-XXI. *Palestine Year Book* and *Israeli Journal.* New York: Zionist Organization of America, annually.]

B) STUDIES

Alon, G. *History of Jews in Eretz Israel in Mishnaic and Talmudic Period.* Tel-Aviv, 1955. [In Hebrew; a scholarly and fresh approach]

Baer, I. *History of the Jews in the Second Temple Period.* Jerusalem, 1953. [In Hebrew]

———. *Israel Among the Nations: An Essay on the Second Temple Period.* Jerusalem, 1955. [In Hebrew; a treatment of the Rabbinic struggle against Hellenism]

———. *Galut* [Diaspora]. New York, 1947. [Essay on the significance of the Diaspora]

Baron, S. W. *Social and Religious History of the Jews.* New York, 1952. [Among greatest contributions to subject; well-documented]

———. *Modern Nationalism and Religion.* New York, 1947.

Buechler, A. *Economic Conditions of Judaism after the Destruction of the Temple.* London, 1912. [To be read in conjunction with Baron *supra*]

Cole, G. D. H. *The Second International.* London, 1951. [Notes the influence of the Congress idea on Herzl]

Davis, M. (ed.). *Israel, Its Role in Civilization.* New York, 1956. [Essays on Jewish history and political problems of new State]

Dubnow, S. *History of the Jews in Russia and Poland.* Philadelphia, 1920.

Goitein, S. D. *Jews and Arabs.* New York, 1955. [An historical essay well drawn in bold strokes]

Graetz, H. *History of the Jews.* 6 vols. Philadelphia, 1945. [First published in 1891; the first major Jewish modern History; biased against East European Jews and against mysticism, but indispensable]

Granott, A. *The Land System in Palestine.* London, 1952.

———. *Agrarian Reform and the Record of Israel.* London, 1956.

Greenberg, L. *The Jews in Russia, 1881-1917.* 2 vols. New Haven, 1951. [Well documented]

Hoffer, E. *The True Believer.* New York, 1951. [Fascinating if erratic book on the nature of mass movements with occasional flashes of insight on Zionism]

Juster, J. *Les Juifs dans l'Empire Romain.* Paris, 1914. [The standard work]

Kimche, Jon. *Seven Fallen Pillars.* New York, 1953. [Fascinating account of the Middle East, 1945-1952. The statements are undocumented and therefore cannot be checked]

Lestchinsky, J. "Anti-Semitism," *European Ideologies,* ed. F. Gross. New York, 1948.

Lilienthal, Alfred. *What Price Israel.* Chicago, 1953. [In the tradition of Montagu: Judaism is not a nationality]

Margolis, Max Leopold, and Marx, Alexander. *History of the Jewish People.* Philadelphia, 1945. [Competent but difficult to read]

Namier, L. B. *Avenues of History.* London, 1952. [Essays on Wedgewood, Deedes, and Wingate]

———. *Facing East.* New York, 1948. [Essays on anti-Semitism, the Jewish Question, and Weizmann]

Nathan, Sir Matthew. *Jewish Travellers.* London, 1912.

O'Ballance, E. *The Arab-Israeli War, 1948.* London, 1956.

Roth, C. *Short History of the Jewish People.* London, 1948. [Best general outline available]

———. *The House of Nasi.* Philadelphia, 1947.

Ruppin, Arthur. *Die Landwirtschaftliche Kolonisation der Zionistischen organisation in Palästina.* Berlin, 1925. [Ruppin was the land expert with the Jewish Agency.]

Schechtman, J. B. *Rebel and Statesman: The Jabotinsky Story.* New York, 1956. [An informative account of the early years of the Zionist leader]

Stein, L. "Development of the Jewish National Home," in *Survey of International Affairs, 1925,* Vol. I. Oxford, 1927.

Starr, J. "Byzantine Jewry on the Eve of the Arab Conquest," *Jewish Palestine Oriental Society,* XV (1935).

Wilhelm, K. (ed.). *Roads to Zion.* New York, 1948. [Jewish travelers from the 15th to 19th Centuries]

III WORKS RELATING TO ARABS, ISLAM, AND ARAB PALESTINE

Alami, Musa. "The Lesson of Palestine," *Middle East Journal* (1949). [A condensed translation of the Arabic book; Alami was a prominent member of the Palestine Arab community.]

Antonius, George. *The Arab Awakening.* New York, 1939. [The standard work; indispensable, but should be read with critical notes by S. Haim in *Die Welt des Islams,* N.S. II (1953).]

Arab Office. *Palestine: The Solution.* Washington, D. C., 1947. [The 1946 Arab proposals]

Ashur, I. "Metayage in Syria, Lebanon, and Palestine," *al-Abhath* (1948).

Al-Bazzaz, Abd ar-Rahman. "Islam and Arab Nationalism," *Die Welt des Islams,* N.S. IV (2-3), 1954. [Based largely on Iraqi material; Bazzaz was dean of Iraq Law College and president of the Baath al-Arab.]

Canaan, T. "Mohammedan Saints and Sanctuaries in Palestine," *J. Palestine Oriental Society,* IV; V; VI; and VII (1924-27). [Illustrates the extent to which popular Islam was integrated into the landscape of Palestine]

Dennett, D. *Conversion and the Poll Tax in Early Islam.* Cambridge, 1950.

Dussaud, René. *La Pénétration des Arabes en Syrie avant l'Islam.* Paris, 1955.

Giannini, Amedeo. "La Questione Arabo-Palestinese," *Oriente Moderno,* I (1921). [Excellent early study]

Gibb, H. A. R. "Islamic Conference in Jerusalem in 1931," in *Survey of International Affairs for 1934*, ed. A. J. Toynbee. London, 1935.
———. *Mohammedanism.* New York, 1955.
———. *Modern Trends in Islam.* Chicago, 1947.
Goichon, A. M. "Le Panislamisme d'hier et d'aujourd'hui," *L'Afrique et L'Asie* (1950). [Good summary history]
Granott, A. *The Land System in Palestine.* London, 1949.
Grant, Elihu. *The People of Palestine.* London, 1921.
Haddad, E. N. *Blood Revenge among the Arabs, JPOS,* I (1921). [Sketchy, but confirms notion that Palestine Arabs retained, before the Mandate period, the classical ethics]
Haikal, Yusif. *al-Qadiyatu'l-filastiniyah.* Cairo, 1950? [Arab point of view; a history of Mandate Palestine]
Haim, Silvia G. "Islam and the Theory of Arab Nationalism," *Die Welt des Islams,* N.S. IV (2-3) 1955. [Based largely on the 1930's leader Sami Shawqat of Iraq]
Hourani, A. H. "The Decline of the West in the Middle East," *International Affairs* (1953-4). [Two penetrating articles on Arab-Western relations and reactions]
Khairallah, K. T. *Le Probleme du Levant: Les Regions arabes liberees.* Paris, 1919. [Aimed at the Peace Conference; important on early history of Arabism]
Lewis, B. *The Arabs in History.* London, 1950. [The best short history]
Montagne, Robert. "Pour la Paix en Palestine," *Politique Etrangère* (1938). [Describes mood of late 1930's]
Nuseibeh, Hazem Zaki. *The Ideas of Arab Nationalism.* Ithaca, 1956. [Thin treatment of Arab nationalism]
Pickthall, M. (trans.). *The Glorious Koran.* London, 1930. [Perhaps the best translation of the Koran]
Polk, W. R. *What the Arabs Think.* New York, 1952. [A summary survey of the background to the post-Palestine war period]
——— (ed.). *Perspective of the Arab World,* supplement to the *Atlantic Monthly* (October, 1956). [A collection of articles on various aspects of the modern scene by leading students]
Roberts, R. *Social Laws of the Qorân* [Koran]. London, 1925. [Comparison of the Koran with other Semitic codes]
Robertson-Smith, W. *Religion of the Semites.* London, 1923. [Stimulating essay on the common base of Semitic religions]
Sadaqah, Najib. *Qadiyat Filastin.* Beirut, 1946. [Arab-League blessed study of Mandate Palestine]
Said, Nuri. *Arab Independence and Unity.* Baghdad, 1943. [The pro-British answer to the pro-German feeling in Iraq]
Wilson, C. T. *Peasant Life in the Holy Land.* London, 1906.
Woolbert, Robert G. "Pan Arabism and the Palestine Problem," *Foreign Affairs Quarterly* (1937-38). [Result of trip to the Middle East and interviews; sound and sensible]
Ziadeh, Nicola A. "Recent Arabic Literature on Arabism," *Middle East Journal,* VI (1952).
Zurayq, Constantine. *Maana an-Nakba.* Beirut, 1948. [An assessment of the Palestine War by a leading Arab student of nationalism]

IV WORKS DEALING WITH ECONOMIC TOPICS

A) OFFICIAL DOCUMENTS (SEE ABOVE I B 2)

B) STUDIES

1) General:

Blake, G. S., and Goldsmith, M. J. *Geology and Water Resources of Palestine.* London, 1947. [A technical study of basic resources]

Bonné, Alfred. *The Economic Development of the Middle East.* Jerusalem, 1943. [Contrasts achievements of Zionists with those of neighboring Arab countries; full of generalizations]

Granovsky, Abraham. *Land Policy in Palestine.* New York, 1940. [Zionist critique of mandatory policy]

Himadeh, S. B. (ed.). *Economic Organization of Palestine.* Beirut, 1938. [Factual survey of pre-war economy]

Hobman, J. B. (ed.). *Palestine's Economic Future.* London, 1946. [Pro-Zionist view; photographs]

Horowitz, D., and Hinden, R. *Economic Survey of Palestine.* Tel-Aviv, 1938. [Description mainly of Jewish economy]

Institute of Arab-American Affairs. *Arab Progress in Palestine.* New York, 1946. [A poor answer to Hobman *supra*]

Kahn, A. E. "Palestine: A Problem of Economic Evaluation," *American Economic Review,* (September, 1944). [Technical article describing sympathetically economic implications of Zionist colonization]

Loftus, P. J. *The National Income of Palestine, 1944-1945.* Jerusalem, 1946 and 1948. [Short, valuable account of structure of economy and balance of international payments]

Lowdermilk, W. C. *Palestine, Land of Promise.* New York, 1944. [Optimistic review of economic potential of Palestine]

Nathan, Robert, Oscar Gass, and Daniel Creamer. *Palestine: Problem and Promise.* Washington D. C., 1946. [A thorough and generally balanced study of economic conditions and potential, mainly dealing with the Jewish sector]

République Française. Direction de la conjoncture et des études economiques. *La Palestine.* Paris, 1948. [A neat summary based on published economic materials]

Warriner, D. *Land and Poverty in the Middle East.* London, 1948. [The chapter on Palestine gives short but pithy account of agricultural conditions before 1948.]

Wood, G. E. *Survey of National Income of Palestine.* Jerusalem, 1943. [Short but valuable]

2) The Refugees:

a) *Official:*

United Nations. *Annual Reports of the Director of UNRWA.* New York, 1950-56. [Detailed description of the operations of UNRWA in supplying relief and in attempting to make refugees self-supporting]

———. *Quarterly Bulletin of Economic Development.* Beirut: Mimeographed.

United Nations. *Final Report of the United Nations Economic Survey Mission for the Middle East.* 2 vols. (Clapp Report) New York, 1949.

b) Studies:

Baster, James. "The Economic Problems of Jordan," *International Affairs* (January, 1955). [Discusses problem of refugees in relation to Jordan economy]

———. "The Economic Problems in the Gaza Strip," *Middle East Journal* (Summer, 1955).

———. "Economic Aspects of the Settlement of the Palestine Refugees," *Middle East Journal* (Winter, 1954).

Peretz, Don. "Problem of Arab Refugee Compensation," *Middle East Journal* (Autumn, 1954). [An incomplete review of a little-known subject]

Sayegh, Yusef. "Impact of the Palestine Refugees on the Economies of Jordan, Syria, and Lebanon" (Beirut: Mimeographed, 1953).

3) Economic Development of the Jordan:

Arab League (Technical Committee). *The Arabs' Plans for Development of the Jordan Valley.* Cairo: Mimeographed, March, 1954.

Baker, M., and Harza Engineering Co. *Yarmuk-Jordan Valley Project, Master Plan Report.* 8 vols. 1955.

Bunger, M. E. *Feasibility Yarmouk—Jordan Valley Project* (Amman: Mimeographed, 1953).

Burns, Norman. "Comparison of Recent Plans to Utilize Waters of the Jordan River and Its Tributaries," *UNRWA Bulletin of Economic Development* (Beirut), No. 14 (Mimeographed, 1956).

Cotton, S. *Plan for Development of the Water Resources of the Jordan and Litani River Basins.* Tel Aviv: Mimeographed, February, 1954.

Hayes, J. B. *T.V.A. on the Jordan.* Washington, D. C., 1948.

Ionedes, M. G. *Report on the Water Resources of Trans-Jordan and Their Development.* London, 1940.

Israel. *Data and Plans.* October, 1953.

MacDonald, Sir M., *et al. Report on the Proposed Extension of Irrigation in the Jordan Valley.* London, 1951.

Main, Charles T. *The Unified Development of the Water Resources of the Jordan Valley Region.* Boston, 1953.

4) Economy of Israel:

Israel. *Government Yearbook.* 1950 to 1956. [Annual official review of the general developments in Israel, including several chapters on economic affairs and a description of the activities of the various ministries]

Bank of Israel. *Annual Report, 1955.* Jerusalem; August, 1956. [A good technical analysis of economic and monetary developments in Israel in the last few years]

The Falk Project for Economic Research in Israel. *Second Annual Report, 1955.* Jerusalem; May, 1956. [A summary of various research projects and their result on the performance of Israel's economy in recent years]

Israel Economic Forum. *The Mineral and Water Resources of Israel.* Tel Aviv; March, 1954. [An optimistic review of natural resources of the area occupied by Israel]

United Nations. *Economic Developments in the Middle East, 1945 to 1954.* New York, 1955. [The chapter on Israel includes a balanced account of developments in Israel since its establishment]

CONCLUSION

Wint, Guy, and Calvocoressi, Peter. *Middle East Crisis.* London, 1957. [Provocative and balanced; contains fewer mistakes than any of the other recent works on the Suez crisis of the fall and winter of 1957]

INDEX

Abbasids, found Baghdad, 19
Abdullah, King (Emir), ambitions of, 301; British friendship, 274; intervention of, in riots, 94; quarrels with Farouk, 287
Abdullah Pasha, 37
Abrahams, Dr. Israel, and anti-Semitism, 163
Absentee Property Law, 294-295
Absorption, 197-205
Acre, battle of, 34-35; a British port, 60; capture of (1831), 38; fall of, 26; rebuilt, 33; rule of, 37
Advisory Council (1922), 80-82
al-Afghani, Jamal ad-Din, 260
Agriculture, experiments in, 51; and land production, 312; modern, 310, postwar, 188
el-Alamein, 107
Alami, Musa, on Arab states, 301; and League of Arab States, 283
Aleph, 217
Aleppo, 39
Alexander I, 45
Alexander II, liberalism of, 142; murdered, 51, 139
Alexander III, pogroms, 139
Alexandretta Province, and Bludan Conference, 279
Aliyah, 156; becomes symbol, 170
Allenby, General, and establishment of Mandate, 70; in Palestine, 158
Alliance Israélite Universelle, 51
Alp, Ziya Gök, 260
Altalena, 184
American Council for Judaism, opposes Biltmore program, 186
American Zionist Organization, 172
Amin, Haj, and communists, 270
Anatolia, and decline of Ottoman Empire, 32
Anglo-American Committee, 190
Anglo-American Committee of Inquiry (Refugees), 108-110
Anglo-American reaction, to Palestine, 185-187
Anglo-Italian Agreement (1938), 99
Anglo-Jewish-Arab Conference (1939), 104
Anglo-Jewish Association, opposes Biltmore program, 186
Anglo-Palestine Bank, 158
Anglo-Turkish Armistice, 65
Anglo-Zionist relations, and el-Alamein, 107
Anti-British acts, 183, 191-192, 278
Anti-Semitic Congress (Dresden), 143
Anti-Semitism, 135, 137, 143-144, 148-149, 186; in Germany, 176; Russian, 141; Zionist movement and, 163. *See also* Pogroms
Anti-Zionism, 163-164
Anti-Zionist legislation, 156
Anti-Zionist outbreaks, 123-124
Antonius, George, and Arab nationalism, 258
Antioch, siege of, 23
Aqsa Mosque, 84
Arab Congress, repudiates Feisal, 69
Arab Congress (Bludan), 278
Arab gentry, 241-247
Arab Higher Committee, 92-93; and Royal Commission, 275; and UNSCOP, 117
Arab-Israeli War, 287-289; economic effect, 336
Arab League, Egyptian influence on, 286
Arab Legion, 129; poor showing of, 287
Arab National Defense Party, on partition, 98
Arab revolt, in Palestine, 21
Arab States, League of, 283
Arabic literature, 258
Arabism, 54, 254-265; Arab element in, 247-254; French opposition to, 168; hostility to Zionism, 76-77; Nablus group, 92; pan-Arabism, 273-286

Arabs, and Advisory Council (1922), 80-82; aid Axis, 106; anti-Zionist outbreaks, 123-124; attacks by, 174, 177; and British "right" to Palestine, 265; culture of, 230, 248; definition of, 225; economy of, 334; education of, 256; and establishment of Israel, 194; feeling of subordination among, 270; and German propaganda, 281; homeland concept, 251-252; and immigration, 85-86; invade Palestine, 287; and Jewish persecution, 28-29; leadership lacking, 167, 367; nationalism, 273-284; pacification of, 174, 282; in Palestine history, 225-240; and Passfield White Paper, 90-92; population, 337; reaction to Zionism, 265-272; refugees, 337; revolt of (1939), 100; unity among, 272; and World War I, 263-264. *See also* Arabism

Arculf, Bishop, and Holy Land pilgrimage, 18

Armament race, 353

Armenia, nationalism in, 157

Arms, 353-354; shipments of, 275

Artisans, lack of, 325

Ashkenazim, 200

Ashley, Lord, and return of Jews, 40

Assyria, in Mediterranean, 3-5

Atrocities, 99-100; Turkish, 138. *See also* Terrorism

Attlee, Prime Minister, on American aid, 191

Azuri, Najib, 260

Babylonian captivity, 5

Baghdad, and Byzantine empire, 21; founded, 19

Bakr, Abu, and spread of Islam, 14

Balfour, Lord Arthur, 161-162

Balfour Declaration, 61, 63-64; and Advisory Council (1922), 80-82; British government interpretation of, 74; force behind, 160-161; and League of Nations Mandate, 64; and National Home, 162-163; and territorial limits, 165-166

Balkan wars, 52

Balkans, and decline of Ottoman Empire, 32; Jewish settlement in, 7; nationalism in, 157

Bar-Cochba, rebellion of, 6

Basil II, 18

Basle Conference, 152

Bedouin society, basic unit of, 243

Bedouins, 47-49

Beeley, Harold, and Soviet expansion, 190

Beirut, bombed, 39; pillage of, 33

Ben-Gurion, David, 107; and Arab-Israeli war, 291; and Arab League proposals, 129; on armaments, 353; proclaims State of Israel, 130; rift with Weizmann, 189; Zionist leader, 182

Benjamin, Rabbi, of Tudela, on Jerusalem (1163), 24

"Berlin-to-Baghdad" Railway, 51

Bethlehem, 46

Bevin, Ernest, on Anglo-American Committee, 190; on immigration, 110; on Palestine problem, 115-116

Biltmore Program, 107, 181-182; opposition to, 186

Bilu, 145

Birth rate, 319-321

"Black Letter," 88, 175-176, 271, 272

Bludan Conference (1937), 278-280

Bols, General, 63; urges Zionist program be dropped, 74

Bolsheviks, Jews under, 169

Boycott, Arab, 353-355; and Suez Canal, 356

Brandeis, Justice, 172; and Balfour Declaration, 162

British protectorate, 41

Brocquière, de la, on Palestine, 27-28

Buchenwald, 189

Bulgarian revolt (1875), 138-139

Bund, 145; in Russia, 164

Burckhardt, John, on commerce (1804), 35

Byzantium, conquered by Turks, 21; defeat at Damascus, 15; and Fertile Crescent, struggle for, 8; and Gaza raid, 15; peace treaty with, 21; and Sassanian-Persian war, 14

Cadogan, Sir Alexander, on British forces, 123

Cairo, and Byzantine empire, 21; effect of, on European life, 20
Canaanites, 3, 217
Capital, and land, 329-336
Capua, Prince of, 43
Catherine the Great, 44-45
Catholics, and Bethlehem, 46; in Holy Land, 43, 44
Cazalet, Edward, and protectorate plans, 139
Cesarea, Byzantine refuge, 15
Chalukah, 135
Chamberlain, Joseph, and Cyprus settlement, 154
Christianity, and Islamic religious heritage, 10; Roman conversion to, 7; philosophy, growth of, 6
Christians, and Advisory Council (1922), 80-82; expelled from Jerusalem (1099), 23; fanaticism among, 36; and Muslim conquests, 22; Persian-Jewish massacre (614), 8; population (1931), 243
Churchill, Colonel Henry, 136
Churchill, Winston S., coolness to Zionism, 284; and Constitution, 267-268; on "National Home" policy, 77-79, 88; on Negev, 188; on Zionism, 108
Citrus industry, loss to, 187
Civil disobedience, 93
Civil rights, in Syria, curtailed, 158
Clapp, Gordon, and UNRWA, 296
Colonization, economic factors, 329-330
Commerce (1804), 35; and dark ages, 19
Committee of Inquiry (refugees), 109-110
Communists, Haj Amin and, 270
Community, Islamic, 251
Congress of 1898, 153
Congress of 1899, 153
Colleges, support of, 135
Constantinople, fall of, 26; (1453), 44
Constitution of Madinah, 12
Contributions, financial, 208-209
Cotton, 32
Council of Clermont, 22
Creamer, Daniel, on Negev, 317
Crimean War, 47
Cromer, Lord, and Cyprus settlement, 154
Crusades, 22-29; brutality in, 25; France and, 42; importance of, 24-25; and Islam, 26; looting in, 23; motives for, 22; and Zionism, 26
Culture, absorption of, 197-205; Arab, 230, 248; disparagement of, 200-201; early Biblical, return of, 218; and trade, influence of, 9
Cyprus, deportation to, 192; settlement proposed, 154
Cyprus Convention of 1878, 138
Czechoslovakia, fall of, 178; supplies arms, 196

Dachau, 189
Dahir, 48
Dahir, Shaikh, 32-33
Damascus, Byzantine defeat at, 15; captured by French, 70
Dark Ages, pilgrimages during, 18
David, conquers Jerusalem, 3
Dead Sea Scrolls, 6
Debt, foreign, 350-351
Decembrists, 45
Declaration of the Seven, 65
deHaas, 151
Deir Yasin massacre, 290-291
Democratic Party (U.S.), on Palestine, 185
Deportations (1946), 192; to Cyprus, 192
Depression (1922), 82-93
Development Bank of Jordan, 339
Diaspora, 147
ad-Difa'a, 276
Displaced persons, 189; Arab, 331-332
Disraeli, Benjamin, and purchase of Suez Canal, 138
Djemal Pasha, 263-264
Dome of the Rock, 17
Dori, Jacob, 183
Dostrovosky, Jacob, 183
Dreyfus affair, 148
Druze-Christian War, 138
Druzes, and Maronite Christians, 39

Eastern Europe, migration from, 143-144
Essenes, 6
Economic plans, 189-193
Economics, Arab-Israeli, 352-364; conflicting, 332; during Mandate, 309; and refugee problem, 336-341
Economy, Arab, 334; after Mandate, 70; and World War II, 187, 324
Eden, Anthony, on Arab desires, 282
Education, Arab, 256; college, 135; growth in, 82; standards of, 201
Effendi, 241
Egypt, and Arab League, influence of, 286; bombs Tel-Aviv, 197; cooperates with Dahir, 33; decline of, 3; and Eighth Crusade, 26; Judah's alliance with, 5; and Levant, 257; Napoleon in, 34; and Pan-Arabism, 279; rise of Malmuks, 32; and Trans-Jordan, 83; under Mehmet Ali, 38
Eighth Crusade, 26
Elections, 205-207
Emergency Zionist Council, 181
Emigration, need for, 141
Employment, 345; census, 321-323
England. *See* Great Britain
English Jews, interest of, in Palestine, 50
Entente, 52; Triple, 62
Enver Pasha, 263
Eretz HaPrat, 218
Eritrea, deportation to, 192
Ethiopia, invasion of, 176
Ethnic groups, Turko-Arab, 56
Ezra, and Judaism, 5

Faris, Dr. Nimr, 66
Farouk, King, quarrels with Abdullah, 287; symbol of corruption, 301
Fatimids, 20
al-Fazari, on Jerusalem, 27
Feisal, King (Emir), 64-70; accepts Mandate, 69-70; Arab Congress repudiates, 69; on Arab nationalism, 168; and French intervention in Levant, 67; concern for Levant, 66-68; in Syria, 69
Fertile Crescent, 316; struggle for, 8
Feudalism, 48, 234
First Crusade, and siege of Jerusalem, 23
First World War. *See* World War I
Fitzgerald, Sir William, on Omar's conquest, 16
Foreign aid, 350, 353
Foreign debt, 350-351
Fourth Zionist Congress, 159
France, and Arab nationalism, 168; and battle of Acre, 34-35; and Bludan conference, 279; captures Damascus, 70; and Crusades, 42; in Lebanon, 39; in Middle East, 137-138, 142; and Ottoman Empire, 42; Sykes-Picot Agreement, 60-61; and Syria, control over, 92, 168
Francis I, 42
Franciscans, control Holy Sepulcher, 42
Frankfurter, Felix, on Arab nationalism, 168
Frederick II, 26
Freemasonry, 260
French revolution, and Jewish rights, 136

Galilee, and Assyrian conquest, 5
Ganem, Chekri, on Arab nationalism, 168-169
Gass, Oscar, on Negev, 317
Gawler, Colonel George, and resettlement, 136
Gaza, raid on, 15; refugees in, 295, 337-338
General strike (1935), 275; (1936), 276
Genoa, and trade with Levant, 31
Germany, anti-Semitism in, 176; and Arab propaganda, 281; and Arabs in World War I, 263-264; and Arabs in World War II, 270; seeks Jewish support, 63; pre-war interest in, 51-52. *See also* Nazi Germany
Ghali Pasha, Wasif Boutros, 279
Gibran, Khalil, 265
Ginsburg, Asher, 147
Gladstone, Prime Minister, on Turkish atrocities, 138-139
Goitein, S. D., on cultures, 201

Goldman, Dr. Nahum, 213
Goldschmid, Colonel, 149-150
Gomel, massacre in, 141
Gordon, David, 141
Grant, Elihu, and Christian communities, 242
Great Britain, armed forces in Palestine, 276; armed forces withdrawn after World War II, 284; arms Arab nations, 194; and battle of Acre, 34-35; finished in Palestine, 193; and force, use of, 94; guaranteed Turkey's Asian possessions, 138; and Hussein-McMahon correspondence, 58-59; influences of, 210-214; Italy embarrasses, 99; in Lebanon, 39; and Mehmet Ali, 40; in Middle East, France obstacle to, 137-138; interns Jewish leaders, 191; and Mandate, unworkable, 277; and military installations in Suez, 122; policy, vacillating, 65, 271, 174-175; reaction to, 185-187; Sykes-Picot Agreement, 60-61; on territorial limits, 165-166; and Trans-Jordan, 83; turns Palestine problem over to United Nations, 115; and Zionism, opposition to, 164; Zionist support in, 61-62. *See also* Balfour Declaration; Mandate; White Paper
Greek empire, influence of, 5
Grey, Sir Edward, 58; on British annexation of Palestine, 160
Gromyko, Andrei, 120-122
Guerrilla warfare, 276, 291-292. *See also* Terrorism
Guizot, on Jerusalem, 42

Ha'am, Ahad, 147, 152
Hadith, 27
Hadrian, and Judaic scholars, 6
Haganah, 108; Attlee on, 191; anti-British acts, 183; captures Acre, 130; and concessions from British, 191; and *Patria* affair, 180; terrorism of, 112, 129-130
Haifa, battle in (1948), 292; a British port, 60
al-Hakim, 21
Hapsburgs, 42
Hardships, of immigrants, 202
HaShomer, 183
Haskalah, 141
Health, standards of, 201
Health facilities, growth in, 82
Hebrew, established as language, 157
Hebron, holy place, 246
Hellenism, influence of, 5-6
Henriques, H. S., and anti-Semitism, 163
Heraclius, Jerusalem recaptured by (634), 8
Herzen, Alexander, 153
Herzl, Theodore, 136, 148; on Holy Land settlements, 155
Hijra (622), 12
Hibat Zion, 147
Hirsch Foundation, 150
Histadrut, 170-171
Hitler, Adolf, 176
Hoffman, Christophe, and Christian settlement, 51-52
Holy Land, Christian pilgrimages to, 18
Holy Places, in Jerusalem, 84
Holy Sepulcher, demolished, 21; controlled by Franciscans, 42
Holy War (634), 14
Home State, 133-139; Arabic concept of, 251-252. *See also* National Home
Homs, battle of, 38
Hope-Simpson, Sir John, 86; on land, 239
Hope-Simpson Report, 87, 271
Housing, standards of, 201
Hoveve Zion, 144, 147, 150
Huseini, Abd el-Qadir, 129
Hussein, King (Sherif), on British policy, 57-59, 64-65
Hussein-McMahon Correspondence, 58-59; and Trans-Jordan partition, 79
al-Husseini, Hajj Amin, 98; appointed Mufti, 174. *See also* Mufti
Husseini-Nashashibi feud, 269-270; and pan-Arabism, 277
Hutcheson, Judge Joseph, on Haganah, 191
Hydroelectric power, 318

Ibrahim Pasha, 38
Ignatiev, on pogroms, 140
Ikha'l-Arabi, 261
Immigration, 86, 109-110, 344; Arab protests, 185; artificial restrictions on, 165; hardships of, 203; illegal, 104-108, 111; and land, 324-329; after Mandate, 70; under Mandate, 75; and National Home, 324; and OETA, 76; post World War I, 170-172; post World War II, 185; underground movement, 111-112; U.S. resolutions on, 185; UNSCOP on, 118; of 1920's, 175; of 1925, 83; of 1930's, 176; of 1948-51, 343; of 1948-54 (table), 198-199
Imports, 345
Industrial development, 346
Industry, 322-323; postwar, 188
Inflation, 348
Intellectuals, and pogroms, 142
Intermarriage, 7
Internationalization, 60-61
Investments, 346
Iraq, feeling towards Arabs, 275; mandate established, 69; migration from, 124; pan-Arabism, 276; pro-German, 282
Irgun, massacre by, 130; terrorism, 192-193
Irgun Zvai Leumi, 183
Irrigation, 316-317, 359
Islam, Byzantine attack on, 15; and Christianity, 10; and Crusades, 26; "dark history," 36; history of, 8-22; Jerusalem one-time center, 14-15; and Judaism, 10; and religious tolerance, 12, 16-17; social ethic of, 13; spread of, 13-14; and toleration, 13
Israel, Arab invasion, 287; economy of, 342-352; financial contributions to, 208-209; politics in, 205-218; religion in, 219-221; under Solomon, 3; spread of Islam in, 14; state of, established, 130, 194-197
Israelites, arrive from Egypt, 3
I.T.O., 155
Italy, attack on Libya, 55; embarrasses Great Britain, 99; Jewish settlers in, 7
Ivan III, 44

Jabia, treaty of, 15
Jabotinsky, Vladimir, 159; on Royal Commission, 97
Jaffa, mobs in (1936), 92; to remain Arab, 124
Jazzar, 33, 48
Jerusalem, Christians expelled (1099), 23; conquered by Israelites, 3; fall of (586 B.C.), 5; Holy Places in, 84; Islamic center, 14; Jews in (1163), 24; Muslim pilgrimage to, 17; Persian capture of (614), 7; pilgrimages to, 19, 27; place of, in Islamic administration, 15; renaissance of, 17; sack of (1070), 21; (1244), 26; siege of (1099), 23; surrender of, 15
Jesus, and Messianic yearnings, 6
Jewish Agency, and terrorism, 291-292
Jewish National Fund, 76, 158; establishment, 171-172; land holdings, 331
Jewish rights, and French revolution, 136
Jewish Shadow Cabinet, 184
Jewish Territorial Organization, 155
Jews, and Advisory Council (1922), 80-82; and Arab persecution, 28-29; attacks on, prior to First Crusade, 23; and British protection, 41; eastern-western transition, 7; expulsion from Spain (1492), 29; expulsion from Yathrib, 13; and First Crusade, 23; and Holy Places in Jerusalem, 84; and homeland, longing for, 133-139; and Islamic version of Old Testament, 12; in Jerusalem (1163), 24; mass murders of, 109; Mohammed disappointed by, 12; in Nazi Germany, 106
Jidah, 22
John the Baptist, 6
Johnston, Eric, on Jordan River, 358-363
Jones, Creech, 193

Jordan, spread of Islam in, 14
Jordan River, use of, 358
Jordan Valley Authority, 188
Jordan Valley Development, 361
Joshua, subdues Palestine, 3
Judah, alliance with Egypt, 5
Judaism, a cultural community, 5; and intermarriage, 7; and Islamic religious heritage, 10; outlawed in Spain (1492), 29; reform, 146-147

Kaaba, Muslim religious center, 8
Karlowitz, treaty of (1699), 44
Kenya, deportation to, 192
Khwarizmi Turks, sack Jerusalem (1244), 26
Kibbutz, 172
King David Hotel, blown up, 192
King-Crane Commission, 74; on Zionist aims, 266
Kishinev, massacre in, 141; pogrom of, 142
Kitchener, Lord, 263-264
Knesset, election of, 205
Koran, on Mohammed, 9; on toleration, 13
Krochmal, on emigration, 141
Kupat Holim, 171
Kvutzot/Kibbutzim, 172
Kuchuk Kainardji, treaty of (1774), 45

Labour Party, favors Zionism, 189
Land, 312-323; and capital, 329-336; concept of, 231; government control of, 76; and immigration, 324-329; Jews banned from purchasing, 79-80; modernization, 82; ownership concept, 235; production from, 312
Land holdings, 326-330
Land Transfer Ordinance (1920), 76, 237
Land Transfer Regulation (1940), 240
Lansdowne, Lord, on Cyprus settlement, 154
Latrun, internment at, 191
Lawrence, T. E., on territorial limits, 166
Lausanne, Treaty of, 76
League of Arab States, 283
League of British Jews, 162
League of Nations, and Balfour Declaration, 64; and Royal Commission, 96
League of Nations Permanent Mandate Committee, on Holy Places, 85-86
League Refugee Settlement Committee, 86
Lebanon, British and French interests in, 39; Druze-Christian War, 138; independence of, 284; spread of Islam in, 14
Levant, Egyptian interest in, 257; Feisal's concern for, 66-68; trade in, 28; and West, 31
Levant Company, 39
Libya, Italian attack on, 55
Literature, Arabic, 258
Lloyd George, David, on British annexation of Palestine, 160; on "National Home," 73-75, 164-165
Louis Napoleon, and Bethlehem, 46
Lowdermilk, Dr. W. Clay, on Jordan Valley Authority, 188
Lyall, Sir Charles, on Arabs, 249-250

Ma'abara, 202
Maccabean state, collapse of, 5
MacDonald, Ramsay, on National Home, 87; "Black Letter" of, 88, 175-176, 271-272
McMahon, Sir Henry, 57-58, 65
McMahon-Hussein Correspondence, 264; and territorial limits, 166
MacMichael, Sir Harold, attempted assassination, 184
Madinah. *See* Yathrib
Madinah, Constitution of, 12, 251
Magnus, Sir Philip, and anti-Semitism, 163
Main, Charles T., on Jordan Valley, 361
al-Malik, Abd, and Jerusalem, renaissance of (685), 17
Mamluks, 26; independence of, 32
Mandate, 70-82; and Balfour Declaration, 64; chaos after establishment, 69-70; division of, 79; and economics, 309-311; end of, 126-

130, 194; immigration under, 75; post World War I, 309; and Royal Commission (1936), 94-95; termination recommended by UNSCOP, 118; and terrorism, 126-130; unworkable, 277
Manzikert, battle of, 21
Maronite Christians, 55; and Druzes, 39
Mass murders, 109
Massacres, Russian, 141
Maundrell, Henry, on Levant, 31
May Day riots (1921), 174
Mecca, pilgrimages to, 17, 19; religion and culture in, 9
Mehmet Ali Pasha, 37, 45, 256; and Britain, 40; Egyptian power, 38
Melchett, Lord, 87
Melkite Orthodoxy, 14
Mendelsohn, Moses, on emigration, 141
Midhat Pasha, 47, 49
Middle East, great powers in, 34-37; France and Britain in, 137-138; Russia's interest in, 43-44
Migration, 139-148; from Eastern Europe, 143-144; to U.S., 144
Millet, 12, 29; under foreign control, 242
Mineral resources, 317-318
Minorities, Zionists as, 25
Miri, 233
Mob demonstrations (1936), 92
Mocatta, Frederick, 149
Mohammed, as a man, 9; birth of, 8; death of, 13; divinity of, 10; familiarity with religions, 9; Hijra of (622), 12; hostility to, in Mecca, 11; interprets Word of God, 11; and Judaism and Christianity, 10; Jews disappoint, 12; Jews expelled from Yathrib, 13; in Taif, 11
Mongols, 26
Monophysitism, 14
Montagu, Sir Samuel, 149; on Hirsch foundation, 150
Montefiore, Claude, 149
Montefiore, Sir Moses, on schools, 50
Morgan, General, on immigration, 111
Morrison, Herbert, 178
Morrison Plan, 192
Moseley, Sir Oswald, 186
Moshavim, 172
Moyne, Lord, murdered, 108, 184, 284
Mufti, and Arab government (1948), 287; and Arab unity, 272; flees Palestine, 281; and terrorist attacks, 178
Mulk, 233
Mu'minun, 17
al-Muqaddasi, on Jerusalem, 19
al-Muqattam, 66
Muslims, and Christian conquests, 22; and Holy Places, 84; politically weak, 12; and religious interests, 27; social code, 12; and tolerance, 29. *See also* Arabs

Nablus group, 92
Nahhas, Premier, and League of Arab States, 283
Nahmanides, Moses, on Jerusalem (1267), 27
Naples, King of, 43
Napoleon, in Egypt, 34; and Jewish settlements, 136; in Middle East, 34
Nasi, Joseph, 30
Nathan, Robert, on Negev, 317
Nation, peasant concept of, 231
National economy, 342-353
National Home, 74-75; and Balfour Declaration, 162-163; clarification of, 77-79; effect of Europe on, 171; and immigration, 324; Weizman on, 164; Zionist ideology, 157
National income, 349
National resources, 316; limited, 32
National Syrian Congress, 73
Nationalism, 141-142; Arab, 254-265, 273-284; Balkan, 157. *See also* Arabism, Zionism
Naxos, Duke of the Isle of, 30
Nazi Germany, Jews in, 106; mass murders in, 109; persecution in, 180

Nazis, bestiality of, 110-111; rise of, and Zionist movement, 88-89
Negev, importance of, 188; land of plenty, 317
Nehru, and Bludan Conference, 278
Neo-crusades, 42
Nepotism, 207
Nestorian monks, and Biblical lore, 10
New Jerusalem, 28
New Order (1793), 254
Nicholas I, 45, 138; and British attack on Syria, 40; and Orthodox position, 46
Nicholas II, and anti-Semitism, 141
Nicholson, Harold, on Ganem, 169
Nikolaev, massacres in, 141
Nikon, 44
Nizam-i Jedid, 254
Nomads, 48-49
Non-Jewish communities, 225-240
Nordau, Dr. Max, 152, 154
Nuri, Premier, and League of Arab States, 283

O'Ballance, Major, on Arab-Israeli War, 293-294
October (1905) Revolution, and Aliyah, 156
Odessa, pogroms in, 140
OETA, 70; and immigration, 76
Oil pipelines, 355
Oliphant, Sir Laurence, on resettlement, 137; and Sursuk family land, 236-237
Omar, and religious tolerance, 16; and spread of Islam, 14; and surrender of Jerusalem, 16
Omayyad, social revolution (750), 19; ruling power of, 17
Ormsby-Gore, Major, 167
Orthodox Christianity, 17
Orthodox Judaism, 17
Orthodoxy, 149
Ottoman army, 56-57
Ottoman Empire, 29-33; and Bedouin tribes, 47-48; and Christians, 42; decline of, 32; France's relations with, 42; and taxation, 232-233; and Russia, 40; and West, 31
Ottoman Turks, win Syria, 29
"Ottomanism," 52-54

Pale of Settlement, 140
Palestine, Anglo-American relations, 185-187; Arab government (1948), 287; Arab revolt in (1011), 21; Arab state, proposed, 73; between World Wars, 106-110; Christian state, proposed, 43; early beginnings, 3; division of (1922), 79; economic plans, 189-193; English Jews' interest in, 50; established as Jewish Commonwealth, 181; history of, 3-8; internal conflicts, 170-179; Mandate established, 69; material growth, 82-94; Muslim interest, 27; postwar plans, 189-193; proposed U.S. mandate, 73; rule of, after fall of Jerusalem, 17; under Ottoman Turks, 29
Palestine Arab Congress, 83
Palestine Jewish Colonization Association, 331
Palestine Land Development Co., 76
Palestine Liberation Army, 194
Palestine Partition Commission, 98; on land, 237-238; recommendations of, 100-103
Palmach, 183; terrorism of, 113
Palmerston, Lord, and British protectorate, 41; and resettlement, 136-137
Pan-Arabism, 273-286
Paris, Treaty of (1856), 138
Partition, 97-98; plans for, 100
Passfield White Paper, 86-88, 90-92, 175
Passive resistance, 92-93
Patria, 107, 180
Peace Conference (1919), 64
Peasants, concept of political bodies, 231-233
Permanent Mandate Commission, 105-106
Persecution, in Germany, 180; in Russia, 140-141
Persia, captures Babylon, 5; invades

Palestine, 7; Jewish settlements in, 7
Pestel, Colonel Pavel, 45
Peter the Great, 44
Peter the Hermit, 23
Petroleum, 318
Phosphates, 317-318
Philistines, settle Palestine, 3
Phoenicians, trade with, 3
PICA, land holdings, 331
Picot, Georges, 64
Pilgrimages, 244; and dark ages, 18; Islamic, 17; to Jerusalem, 27
Pinsker, Leo, 136; on anti-Semitism, 144
"Pious Foundation Committee," 98
Pogroms, foster Zionism, 142; in Russia, 51, 139-140, 142-143, 169; in Ukraine, 169
Poland, fall of, 178-179; Jews in, 169
Polish currency, collapse of, 83
Political Zionism, 133; birth of, 148-159
Politics, in Israel, 205-218
Pompey's invasion, 6
Pope Pius IX, on Jerusalem, 43
Pope Urban II, on First Crusades, 22
Population, 312-323; agricultural, 318-319; Arab, 337; balance of, 97; increase, 310; Israel, 343; movement of, 336; problems of, 117-118. *See also* Immigration
Protectorate, plans for, 139
Public works, growth of, 82

al-Qahtaniya, 261
Qassam, Shaikh Izzu'd-Din, 275
el-Qawuqchi, Fawzi, 130, 276, 286

al-Rashid, Harun, 19
Rabbinowicz, 152
Rappoport, 141
Reform Judaism, 146-147
Refugees, 286-304; admission of, 112; Arab, 295, 337; bitterness of, 299; economics of, 336-341; problem of, 289, 300
Religion, 213-214; in Israel, 219-221; a party issue, 221
Resettlement, 133-139; not possible, 296-297
Richmond, E. T., 174
Riots (1936), 92
Rishon le Zion, 145
Roman Empire, Jews in, 6
Romans, and Christianity, conversion to, 7; destroy Second Temple, 5; and Bar-Cochba rebellion, 6; and Hellenism, 6; Muslim raid on (846), 22
Roosevelt, Franklin Delano, on Zionism, 185
Rothschild, Baron Edmond de, 51, 87, 150
Rothschild, Lord Nathaniel Mayer, on resettlement, 154
Rothschild family, 50
Royal Commission (1936), 94-95
Runciman, Stephen, on motives for Crusades, 23
Ruppin, Dr., on Royal Commission, 97
Russell, Sir Alison, on partition, 104
Russia, anti-Semitism in, 141; bans Zionist meetings, 155; cooperates with Dahir, 33; fear of, 40; Jews in, 169; Jews' positions in revolution, 62; and Middle East, interest in, 43-44; and Ottoman Empire, 40; pogroms in, 51, 139-140, 142-143, 169; revolution in, 62; Sykes-Picot Agreement, 60; Zionism in, 164. *See also* Soviet

Sabra, 204, 214
Said, Nuri, 66; as mediator, 276
Saida, 32
St. Peter's Basilica, sack of (846), 22
Saladin, 26
Salonika, Jews in, 30
Samaria, Assyrian conquest, 3
Samuel, Sir Herbert, 75, 159; and Advisory Council, 80; High Commissioner, 173-174; and immigration, 76-77; on National Home, 77; a Zionist, 80-82
San Remo Conference, 64, 69
Sassanian Empire, and Fertile Crescent, 8

Sassanian-Persian Empire, and Byzantine war, 14
Saudi Arabia, 276
Schools, English support of, 50-51
Scott, C. P., 61
Second Jewish Commonwealth, 5
Second Temple, destroyed, 5
Second World War. *See* World War II
Selim, Crown Prince, 30
Selim "the Grim," 29
Selim II, 30
Seljuq Turks, conquer Byzantium, 21
Sephardim, 200
Settlements, proposed, 154-155; types of, 172
Sèves, Colonel, 38
Sèvres, Treaty of, 75
Shaftesbury, Earl of, and resettlement, 136-137
Shaw, Sir Walter, on immigration, 324
Shaw Commission, and Arab subordination, 270; and Holy Places, 84-85; and immigration, 91
Shawqat, Sami, 281
Shemitta, 220
Shi'ite Muslim dynasty, 20
Shuna Agreement, 298
Sidebotham, Herbert, 61
Sidon, 32
Simon, Leon, 163
Sinai scheme, 154
Skilled workers, effect of, on economy, 325
Smolenskin, Perez, 141
Social ethic, Islamic, 13
Social system, development of, 204
Sokolow, Nahum, and immigration, 149
Solomon, consolidates empire, 3
Sophronius, on Omar, 16
Soviet, expansion plans, a threat, 190
Spain, expels Jews (1492), 29; Jewish settlement in, 7
State religions, 14
Stern, Alexander, 106, 107
Stern gang, 106-107, 183; murders Lord Moyne, 108, 284; terrorism of, 112
Stoic system, 5
Strike (1935), 275; (1936), 276
Struma affair, 181
Suez, British military in, 122
Suez Canal, boycott, 356; purchase of, 138
Sulaiman the Magnificent, 42
Sulaiman Pasha, 37
Sunna, 12
Supreme Arab Committee, 272
Sursuk family, 50; land ownership, 236
Sykes, Sir Mark, 61, 64, 161
Sykes-Picot Agreement, 60-61, 161; British views on, 67; territorial limits, 166; and Trans-Jordan partition, 79
Syria, and Bludan Conference, 279; civil rights curtailed in, 158; conquered by Fatimids, 20; conquered by Ottoman Turks, 29; and decline of Ottoman Empire, 32; defeated by French, 34; and Egypt (1832), 38; Feisal named king, 69; French control over, 168; French mandate over, 92; and Holy War (634), 14; independence of, 284; mandate established, 69; Mehmet Ali's attack on, 40; spread of Islam in, 13-14; tribes in, 19; Zionism in, 157
Syrkin, Marie, on Oriental Jews, 203
Syrkin, Nachman, 155

Taif, Mohammed in, 11
Talmudic colleges, 135
Tax collecting, 48-50
Taxation, under Ottoman Empire, 232-233
Tel el-Amarna tablets, 3
Tel Aviv, bombed by Egypt, 197; demonstrations in (1936), 92
Temple society, 51
Tenth Zionist Congress, 157
Territorial limits, 165-169
Terrorism, 108, 112, 191-192; Irgun, 192-193; and end of mandate,

126-130; of Jewish Agency, 291-292. *See also* Haganah
Theophanes, and Byzantine-Sassanian war, 14
Tiberias, Arabs evacuated from (1948), 292; battle of, 21; rebuilt, 30
Toleration, Islamic philosophy of, 12-13; in Jerusalem, after fall, 16-17; of Jews (1492), 29; religious, Omar on, 16; Koran on, 13
Tolstoi, Count Leo, on pogroms, 142
Torah state, 221
Tours, battle of (732), 22
Trade, and culture, 9; in Levant, 28
Traditions, rejection of, 215
Trans-Jordan, divided from Palestine, 79; government established, 83; independence, 284; and pan-Arabism, 276
Tribal affiliation, 248-249
Triple Entente. *See* Entente
Tristram, H. B., quoted, 48
Truman, Harry S., on displaced Jews, 189, 191; on refugees, 109, 112
Trumpeldor, Joseph, 158-159
Trusteeship (1947), proposed, 114
Turkey, dismemberment of, 45; enters World War I, 158; Great Britain guarantees Asian possessions, 138; nationalism, 54-55, 157; revolution, 52; Sick Man of Europe, 47-55; and Treaty of Lausanne, 76
Turkophobia, 138
Turks, conquer Byzantium, 21; rise of, 21; sack Jerusalem (1070), 21; (1244), 26. *See also* Ottoman Turks
Twelfth Point, 73
Twentieth Zionist Congress (1937), 88, 97, 177
Twenty-fourth Zionist Congress, 213

Uganda project, 154
Ukraine, pogroms in, 169
Underground movement, 111-112
Unemployment, 333
Uniate Christians, 43
United Nations, creates state of Israel, 194-197; Palestine problem turned over to, 115-116, 192
United Nations Commission of Inquiry, 192
UNRPR, 295
UNRWA, 296-297; budget and services, 338
UNSCOP, 116-122; on displaced Jews, 189; establishment of Palestine, 194; recommendations, 124
UN Truce Supervision Organization, 298
United States, economic aid from, 350; and immigration, resolutions on, 185; influence of, 210-214; migration to, 144; reaction to, 185-187; Zionist support, 108, 115
Unkiar Skelessi, Treaty of, 40

Vatican, and Balfour Declaration, 64
Vengeance, Arab trait, 249-250
Venice, and trade with Levant, 31
Village, concept of, 231
Volney, on Turkish politics, 32-33

Wagner, Senator Robert, 185
Wailing Wall, 84, 175; incident at (1929), 270
Waqf Committee, 98
Webster, Sir Charles, 40
Weizmann, Dr. Chaim, 64-70; and Arab contacts, 66; influences British policy, 160; on National Home, 79, 164; resigns from Jewish Agency, 87; rift with Ben-Gurion, 189; as Zionist leader, 61
West, and Ottoman Empire, 31; standards adopted, 201
White Paper (1939), 178-180, 186, 187; and land holdings, 330; and land transfers, 239. *See also* Passfield White Paper
Wilhelm, Kaiser, 51
Willkie, Wendell, 107
Wilson, Woodrow, on Balfour Declaration, 64; Twelfth Point, 73
Wise, Dr. Stephen, 87; on Balfour Declaration, 162

Woodhead Commission, 98; on land, 237-238
Woolf, Lucien, on anti-Semitism, 163
Work, zeal for, 202
World War I, 55-64; Arab entry, 263-264; Hussein-McMahon correspondence, 58-59; Jewish troops in, 159; in Middle East, 56-57; setback to Zionism, 158
World War II, and Biltmore Program, 179-185; and economy, 334; and German support, 270; start of, 106; and Zionist aims, 179

Yarmuk, battle of, 15
Yarmuk Project, 361
Yathrib, Jews expelled from, 13; Mohammed in, 11
al-Yaziji, Nasif, and Arabic literature, 258
ben Yehudah, Eliezer, 141-142
Yemen, Jewish conversions in, 7; migration from, 124
Yishuv, 201
Young Turk movement, 52, 54
Young Turks, revolt of (1908), 157
Youth, attitude of, 214-217

Zangwill, Israel, 155
Zion Mule Corps, 159
Zionism, American support, 108; and anti-Semitism, 163; Catholic hostility to, 278; controversy in, 147; English support of, 61-62; European background, 139-148; hostility to, 77; Jewish opposition to, 268; legal triumph of, 169; modern, and Crusades, 25; and National Home, 157; opposition to, 146, 156; and Passfield White Paper, 87-89; and pogroms, 142; political features of, 145; reaction to, 265-272; supporters of, 136; in Syria, 158; U.S. support, 115. *See also* Political Zionism
Zionist Organization, controversy in, 172-173
Zionist Organization and Actions Committee, 153
Zionist Program, established, 153
Zionists, illegal in Russia, 155; Israel presents problems to, 197-198; minority group, 25